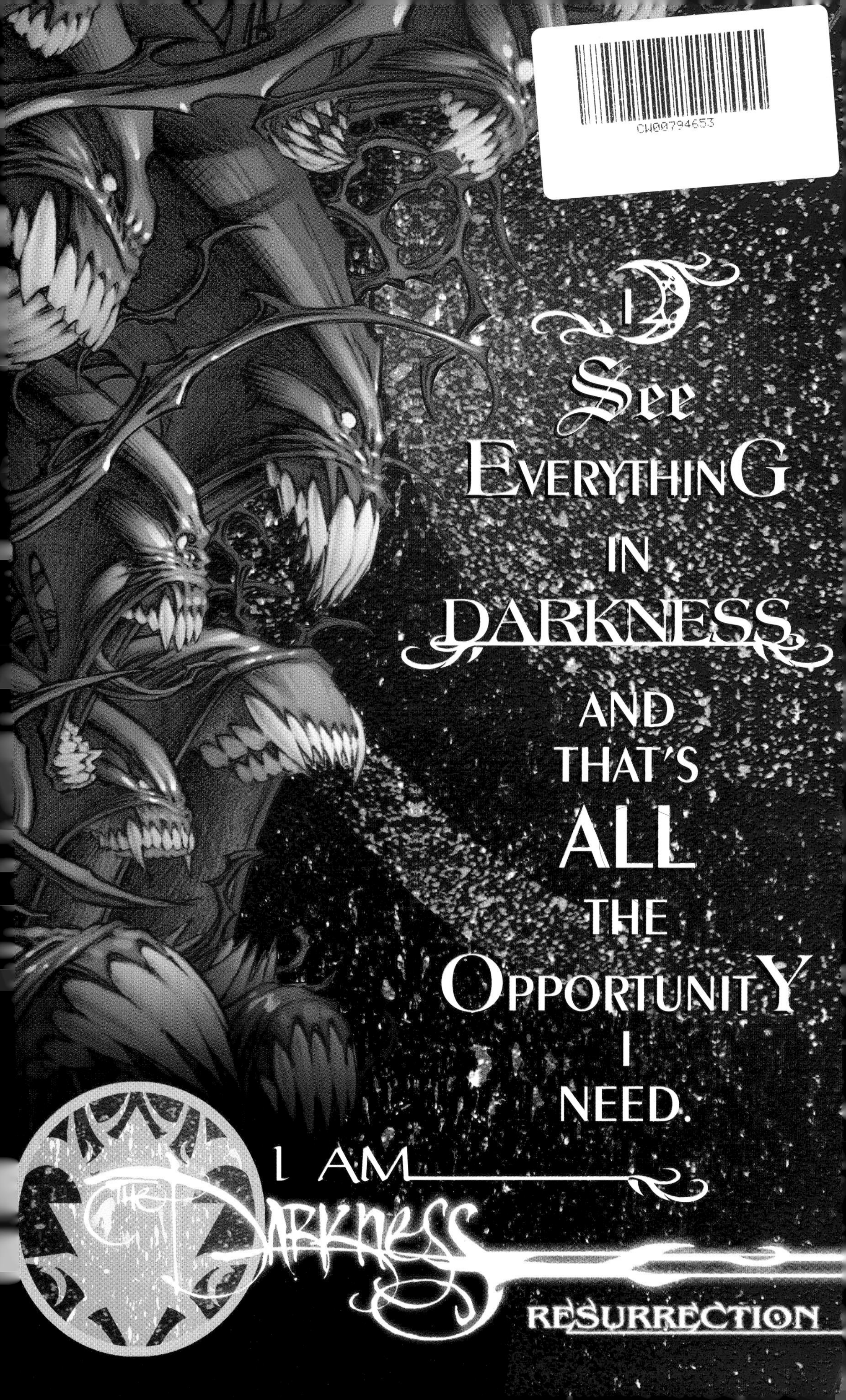
I See Everything in Darkness and that's all the opportunity I need.
I am The Darkness
Resurrection

PAUL JENKINS
DALE KEOWN
KEU CHA   CHRIS EVENHUIS
MATT MILLA
DREAMER DESIGN

ISBN: 1-58240-349-x

Published by Image Comics®
THE DARKNESS: RESURRECTION, FEBRUARY 2004. FIRST PRINTING.
Office of Publication: 1071 North Batavia Street Suite A Orange, California 92867.
Originally published as The DARKNESS Vol. 1 issue 40 and The DARKNESS Vol. 2 issues
1-6. The DARKNESS®, its logos, all related characters and their likenesses are ®,™ & ©
2004 Top Cow Productions Inc. ALL RIGHTS RESERVED. The entire contents of this book
are © 2004 Top Cow Productions Inc. Any similarities to persons living or dead is purely
coincidental. With the exception of artwork used for review purposes, none of the contents of
this book may be reprinted in any form without the express written consent of Marc Silvestri
or Top Cow Productions Inc.

To order by telephone call 1-888-TOPCOW1 (1-888-867-2691)
or go to a comics shop near you.

To find the comics shop nearest you call:
1-888-COMICBOOK (1-888-266-4226)

What did you think of this book? We love to hear from our readers.
Please email us at: darkness@topcow.com

or write to us at:
The Darkness c/o Top Cow Productions Inc.
10350 Santa Monica Blvd. Suite 100
Los Angeles, CA. 90025

for this edition
Book Design and Layout—Stephanie Lesniak
Cover art by—Dale Keown
Collected Editions Assistant Editor—Peter Lam, Phil Smith, and Sina Grace
Associate Editor—Scott Tucker
Managing Editor—Renae Geerlings
Editor In Chief—Jim McLauchlin
Production—Alvin Coats and Chaz Riggs

for Top Cow Productions Inc.
Marc Silvestri—chief executive officer
Matt Hawkins—president / chief operating officer
Jim McLauchlin–editor-in-chief
Renae Geerlings—vp of publishing / managing editor
Chris Carlisle—vp of creative affairs
David Wohl—consulting editor
Joel Elad—director of sales and marketing
Alvin Coats—production manager
Stephanie Lesniak–graphic designer
Scott Tucker–associate editor
Chaz Riggs–production

for Image Comics
Jim Valentino—publisher
Brent Braun—director of production

visit us on the web at
www.topcow.com

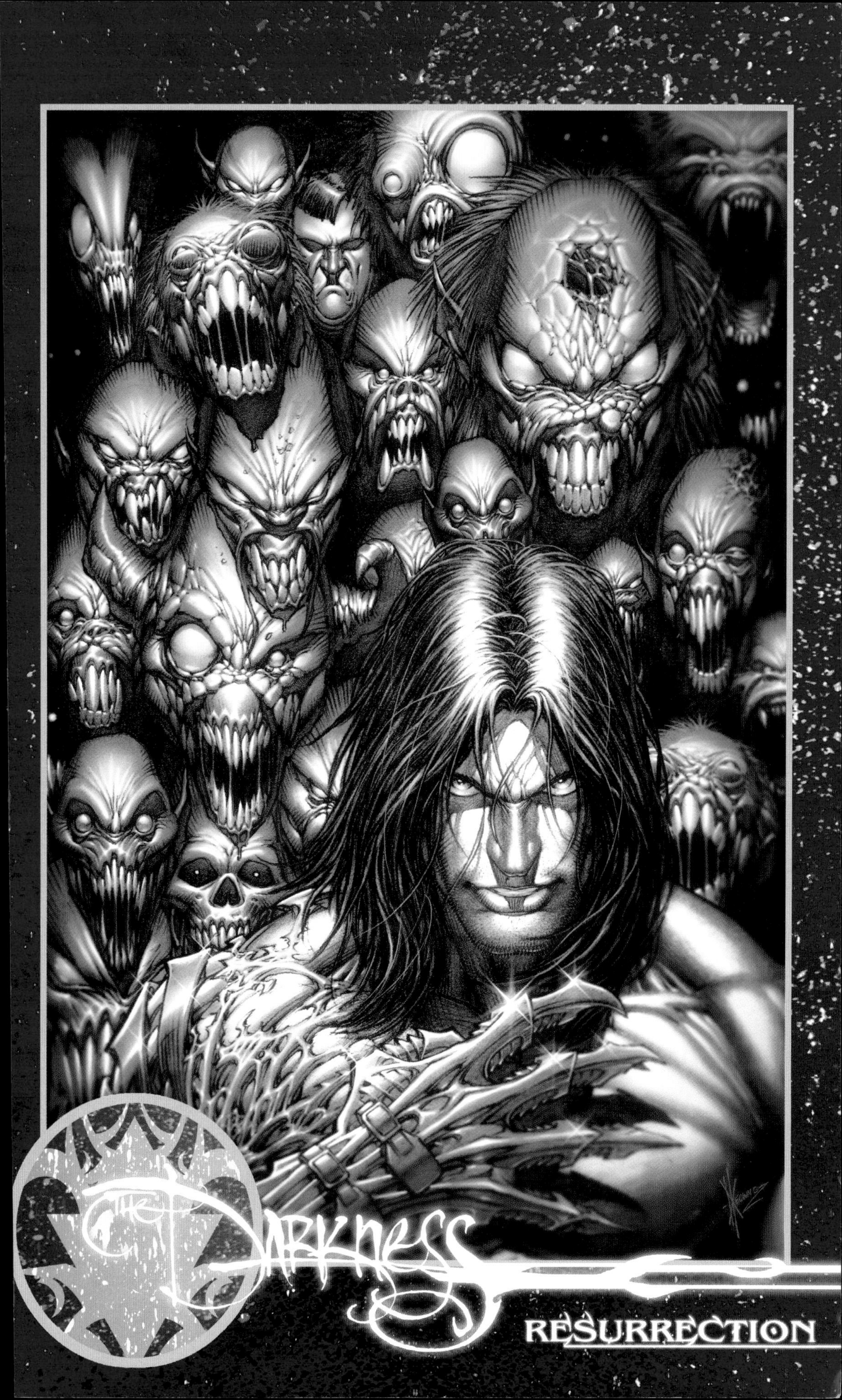
THE DARKNESS
RESURRECTION

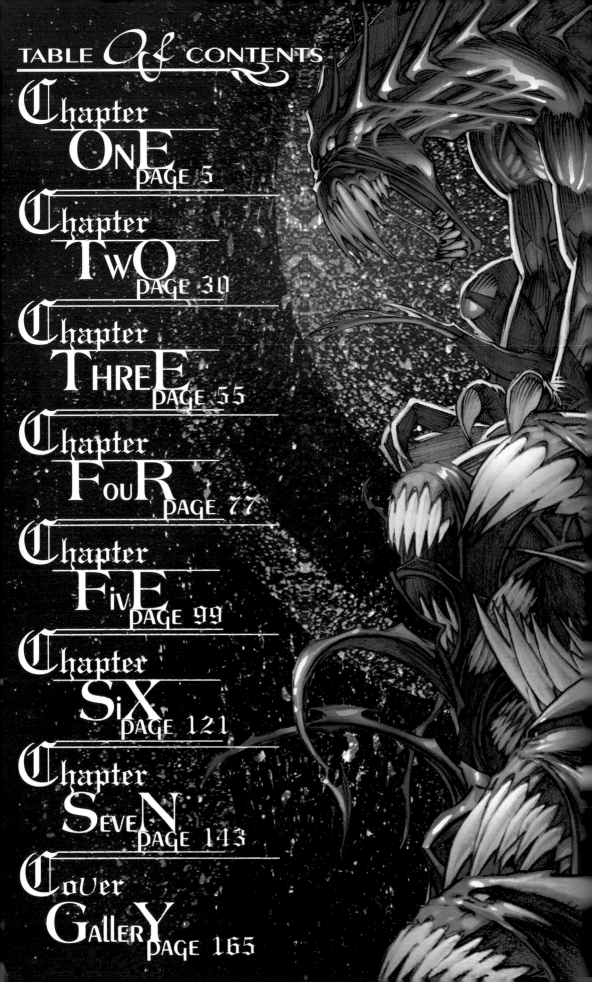

TABLE OF CONTENTS

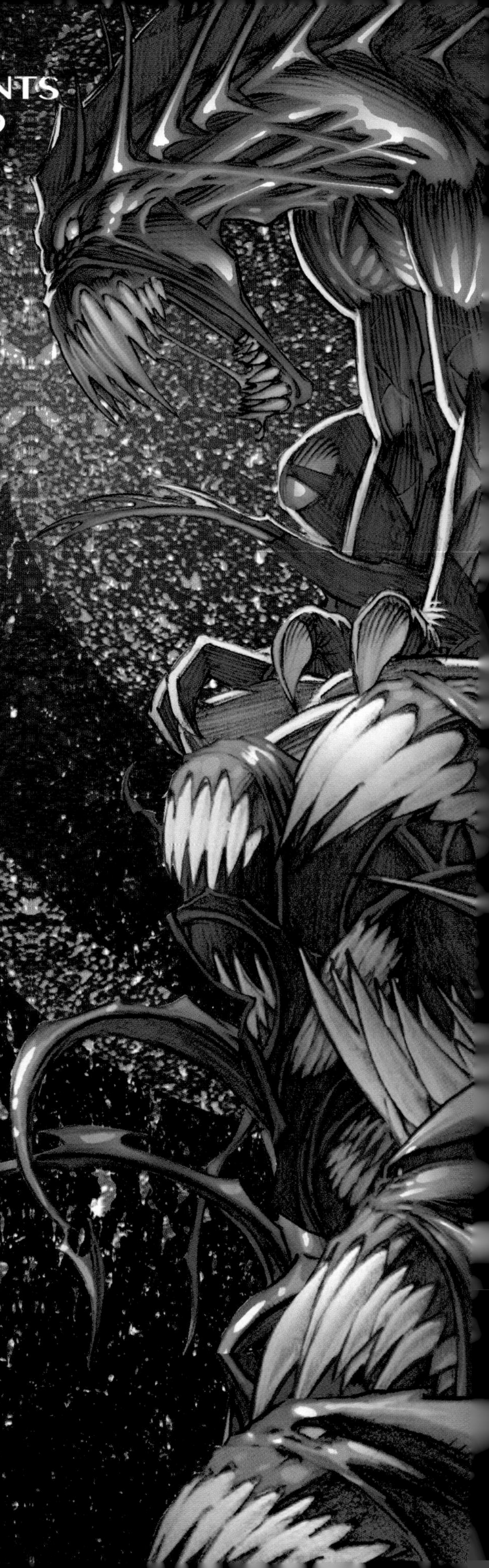

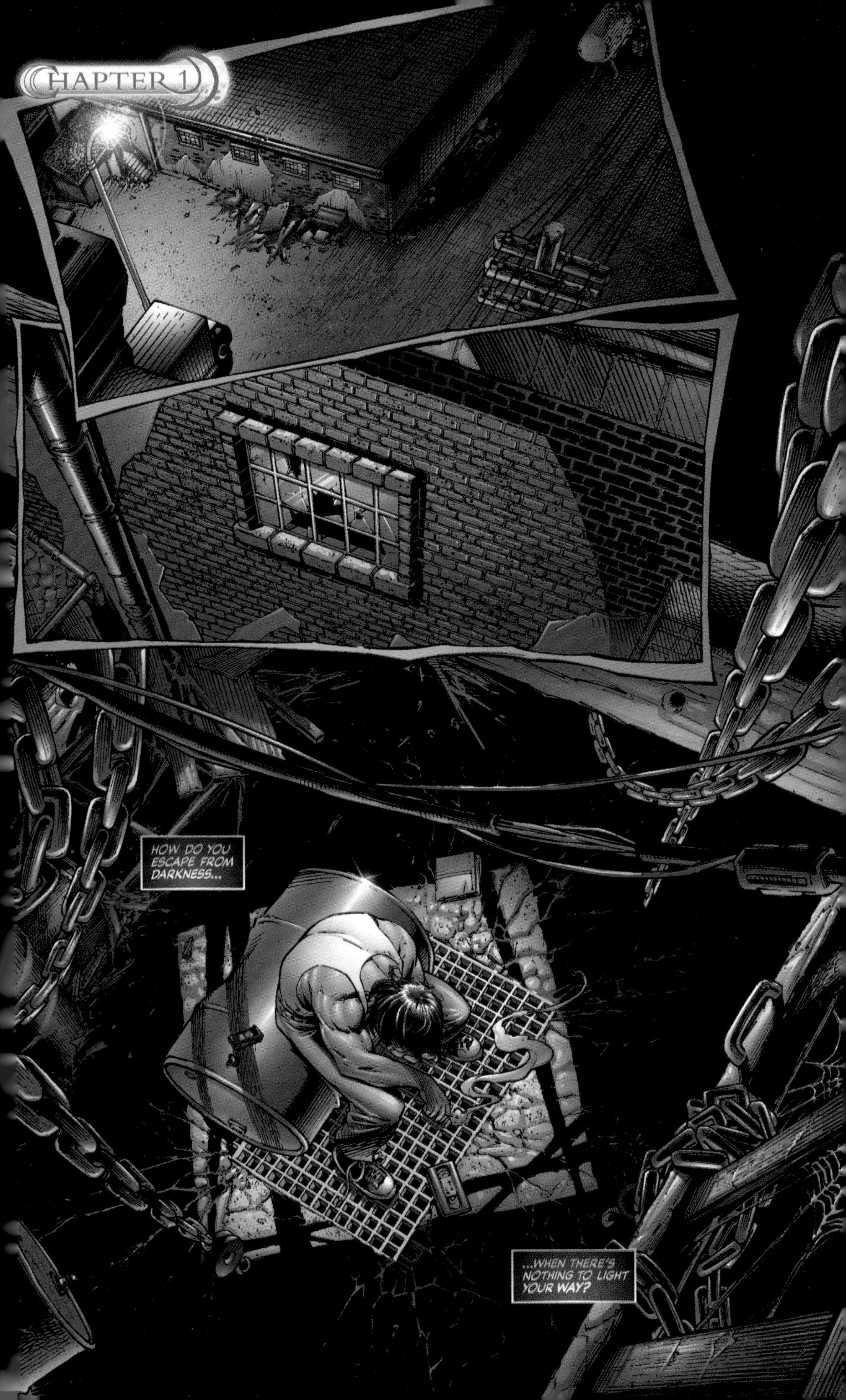
CHAPTER 1
HOW DO YOU ESCAPE FROM DARKNESS...
...WHEN THERE'S NOTHING TO LIGHT YOUR WAY?

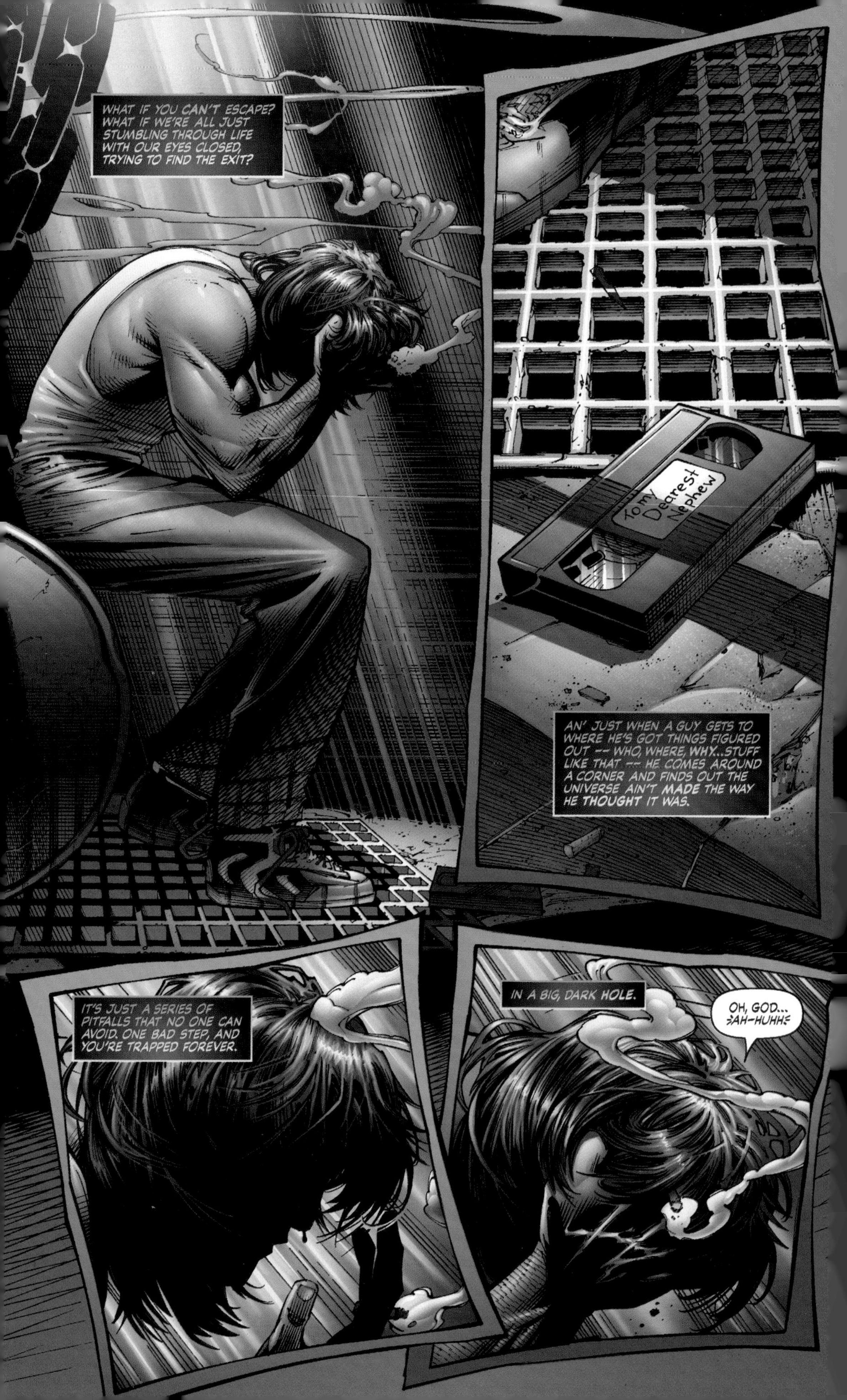
WHAT IF YOU CAN'T ESCAPE? WHAT IF WE'RE ALL JUST STUMBLING THROUGH LIFE WITH OUR EYES CLOSED, TRYING TO FIND THE EXIT?
To my Dearest Nephew
AN' JUST WHEN A GUY GETS TO WHERE HE'S GOT THINGS FIGURED OUT -- WHO, WHERE, WHY...STUFF LIKE THAT -- HE COMES AROUND A CORNER AND FINDS OUT THE UNIVERSE AIN'T MADE THE WAY HE THOUGHT IT WAS.
IT'S JUST A SERIES OF PITFALLS THAT NO ONE CAN AVOID. ONE BAD STEP, AND YOU'RE TRAPPED FOREVER.
IN A BIG, DARK HOLE.
OH, GOD... AH-HUHH

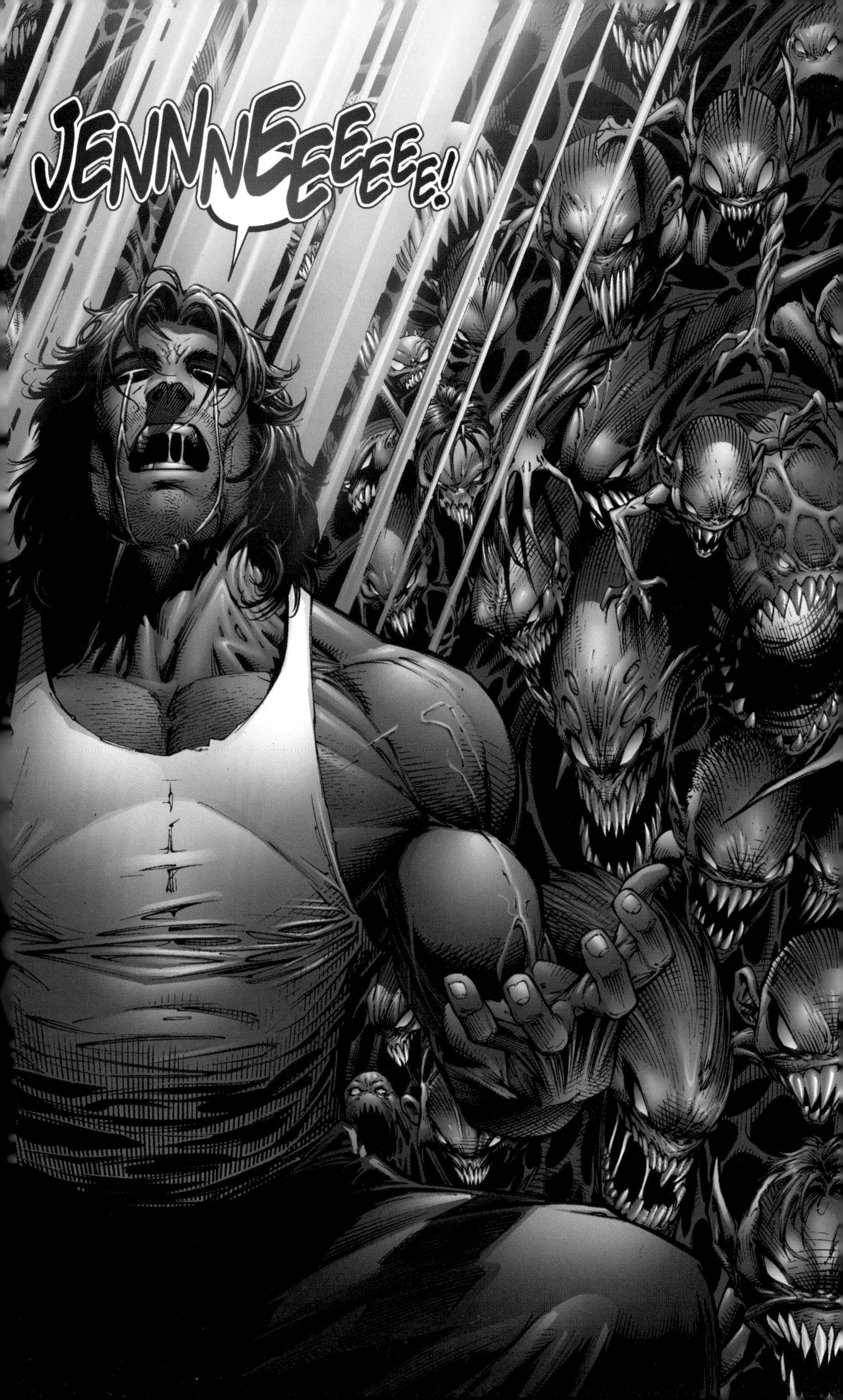
JENNNEEEEEE!

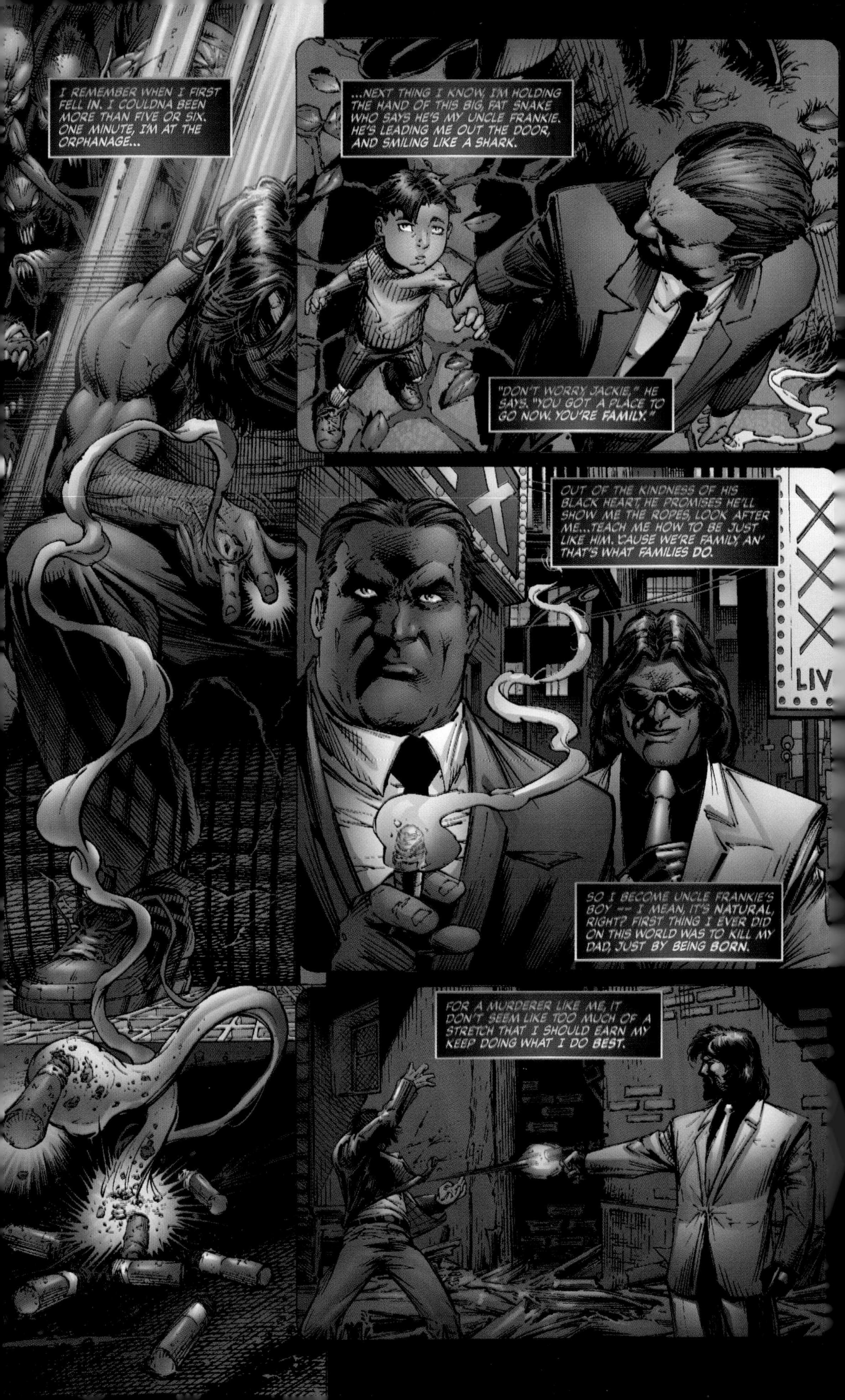
I REMEMBER WHEN I FIRST FELL IN. I COULDNA BEEN MORE THAN FIVE OR SIX. ONE MINUTE, I'M AT THE ORPHANAGE...
...NEXT THING I KNOW, I'M HOLDING THE HAND OF THIS BIG, FAT SNAKE WHO SAYS HE'S MY UNCLE FRANKIE. HE'S LEADING ME OUT THE DOOR, AND SMILING LIKE A SHARK.
"DON'T WORRY, JACKIE," HE SAYS. "YOU GOT A PLACE TO GO NOW. YOU'RE FAMILY."
OUT OF THE KINDNESS OF HIS BLACK HEART, HE PROMISES HE'LL SHOW ME THE ROPES, LOOK AFTER ME...TEACH ME HOW TO BE JUST LIKE HIM. 'CAUSE WE'RE FAMILY, AN' THAT'S WHAT FAMILIES DO.
XXX
LIV
SO I BECOME UNCLE FRANKIE'S BOY -- I MEAN, IT'S NATURAL, RIGHT? FIRST THING I EVER DID ON THIS WORLD WAS TO KILL MY DAD, JUST BY BEING BORN.
FOR A MURDERER LIKE ME, IT DON'T SEEM LIKE TOO MUCH OF A STRETCH THAT I SHOULD EARN MY KEEP DOING WHAT I DO BEST.

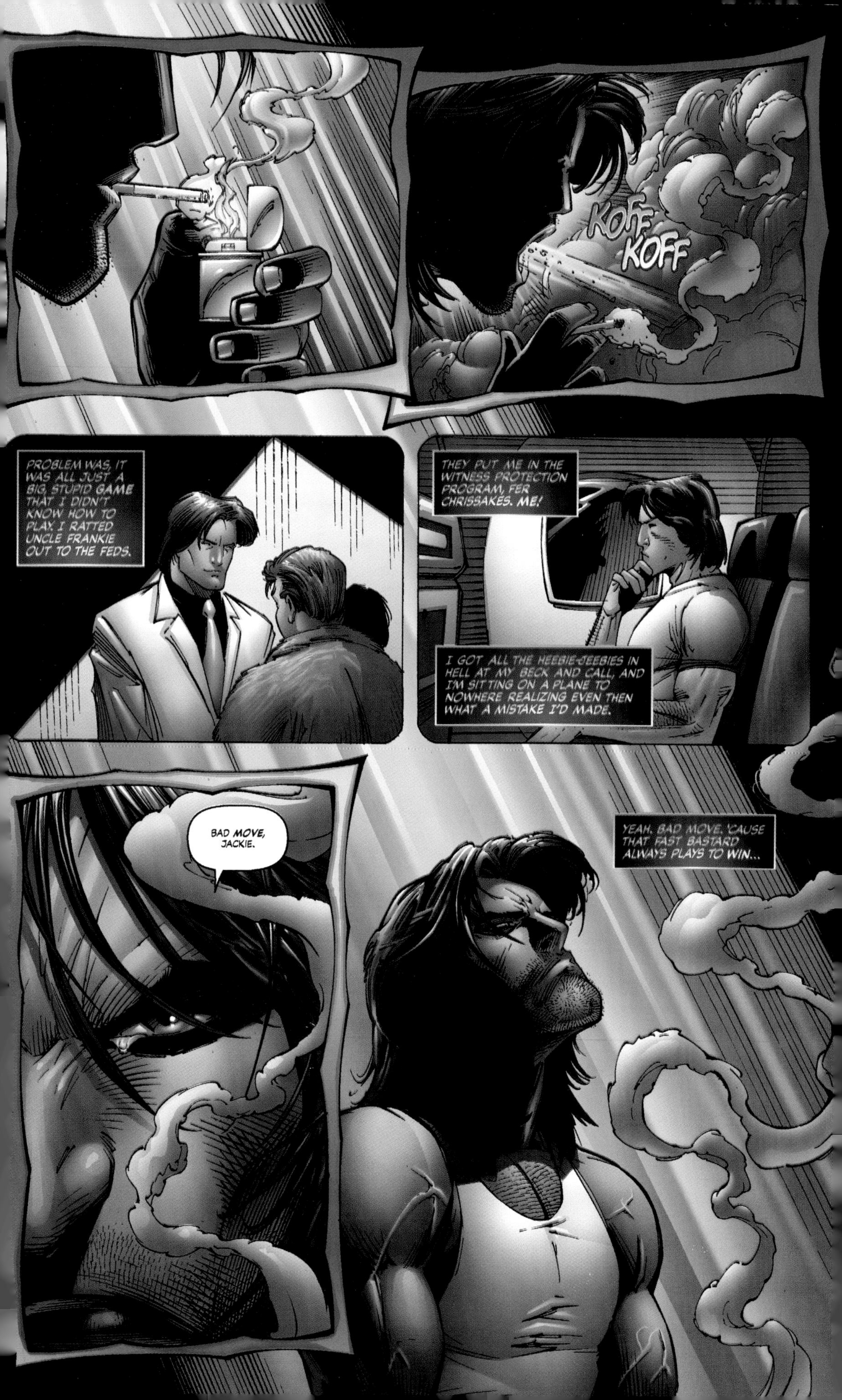
KOFF KOFF
PROBLEM WAS, IT WAS ALL JUST A BIG, STUPID GAME THAT I DIDN'T KNOW HOW TO PLAY. I RATTED UNCLE FRANKIE OUT TO THE FEDS.
THEY PUT ME IN THE WITNESS PROTECTION PROGRAM, FER CHRISSAKES. ME!
I GOT ALL THE HEEBIE-JEEBIES IN HELL AT MY BECK AND CALL, AND I'M SITTING ON A PLANE TO NOWHERE REALIZING EVEN THEN WHAT A MISTAKE I'D MADE.
BAD MOVE, JACKIE.
YEAH. BAD MOVE. 'CAUSE THAT FAST BASTARD ALWAYS PLAYS TO WIN...

OH, WHAT A BEE-YOOTIFUL MORR-NINN'...OH, WHAT A BEE-YOOTIFUL DAY..

KNOCK KNOCK

JACKIE, YOU IN THERE? IT'S ME! OPEN UP!

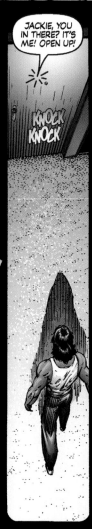

KNOCK KNOCK

YOU'RE FREAKIN' KIDDIN' ME...

HELLO, SON. YOU GOT A MINUTE OR TWO FOR AN OLD FRIEND?

BUTCHER, HOW THE HELL'D YOU FIND ME HERE? NO ONE'S SUPPOSED TO KNOW --

IT DOESN'T MATTER. I FOUND YOU, THAT'S ALL THE INFORMATION YOU NEED.

THIS AIN'T NO SOCIAL CALL, JACKIE. I CAME TO DELIVER A MESSAGE.

IT'S FROM YOUR UNCLE FRANKIE.

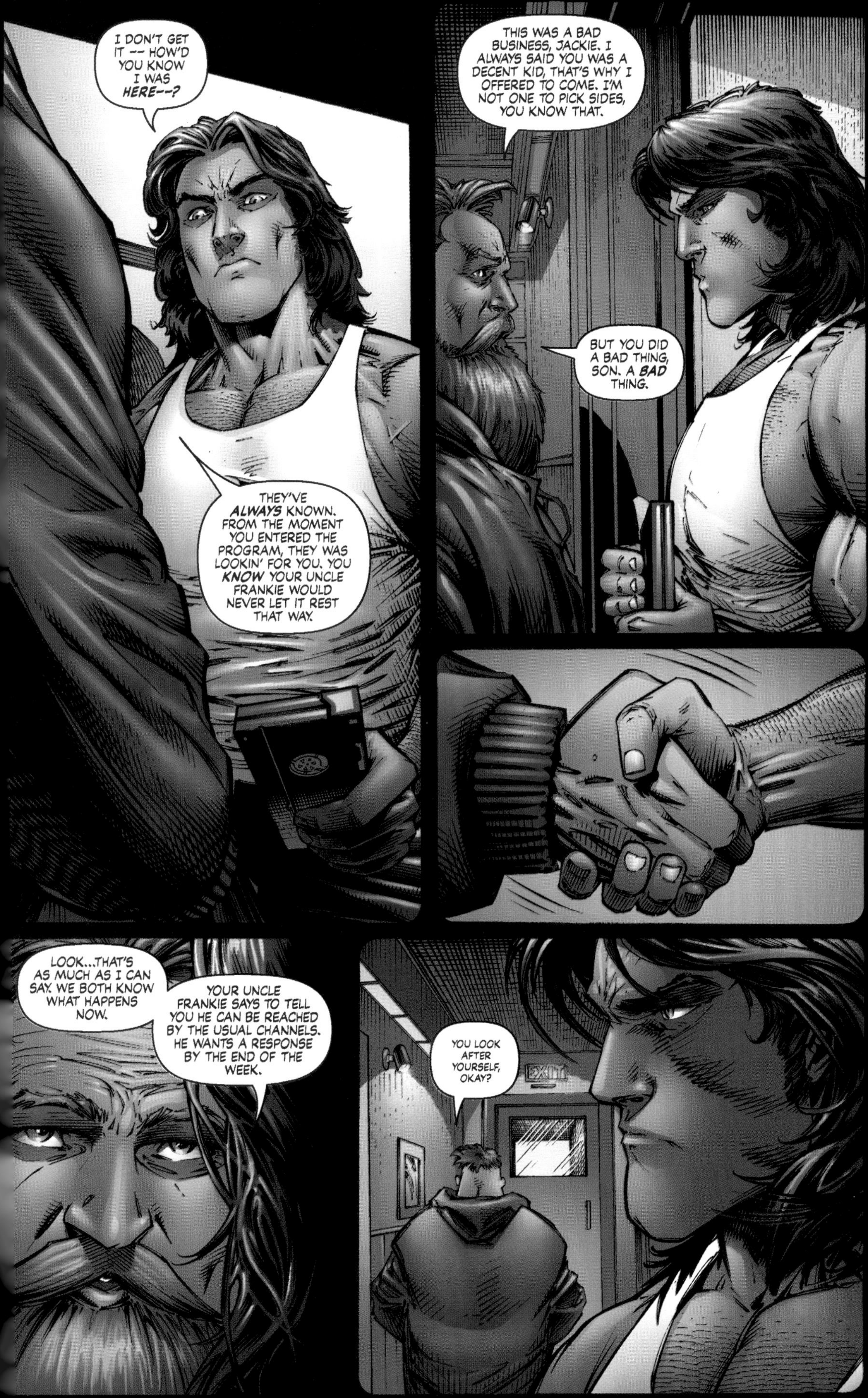
I DON'T GET IT -- HOW'D YOU KNOW I WAS *HERE--?*
THEY'VE *ALWAYS* KNOWN. FROM THE MOMENT YOU ENTERED THE PROGRAM, THEY WAS LOOKIN' FOR YOU. YOU *KNOW* YOUR UNCLE FRANKIE WOULD NEVER LET IT REST THAT WAY.
THIS WAS A BAD BUSINESS, JACKIE. I ALWAYS SAID YOU WAS A DECENT KID, THAT'S WHY I OFFERED TO COME. I'M NOT ONE TO PICK SIDES, YOU KNOW THAT.
BUT YOU DID A BAD THING, SON. A *BAD* THING.
LOOK...THAT'S AS MUCH AS I CAN SAY. WE BOTH KNOW WHAT HAPPENS NOW.
YOUR UNCLE FRANKIE SAYS TO TELL YOU HE CAN BE REACHED BY THE USUAL CHANNELS. HE WANTS A RESPONSE BY THE END OF THE WEEK.
YOU LOOK AFTER YOURSELF, OKAY?
EXIT

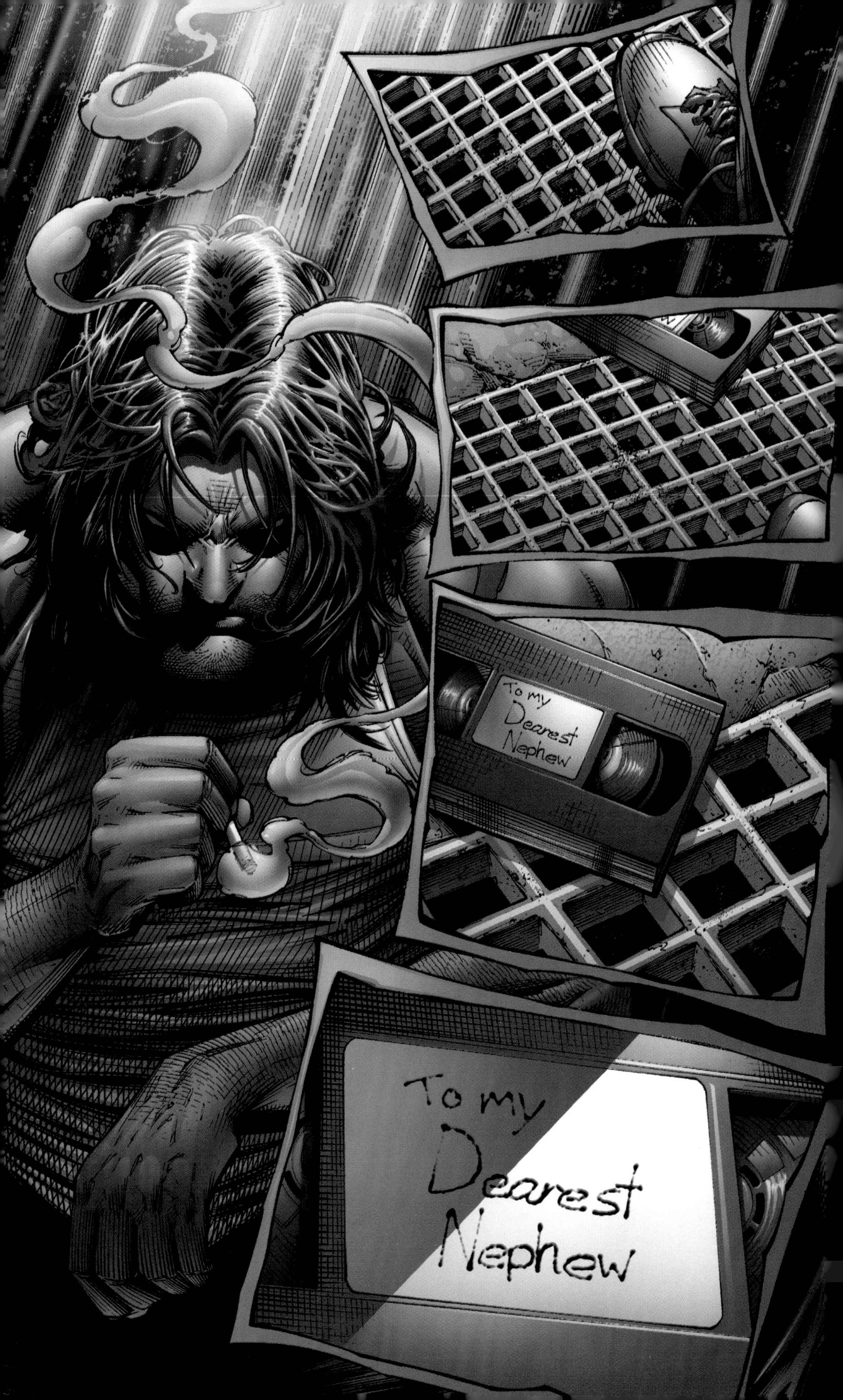
To my Dearest Nephew
To my Dearest Nephew

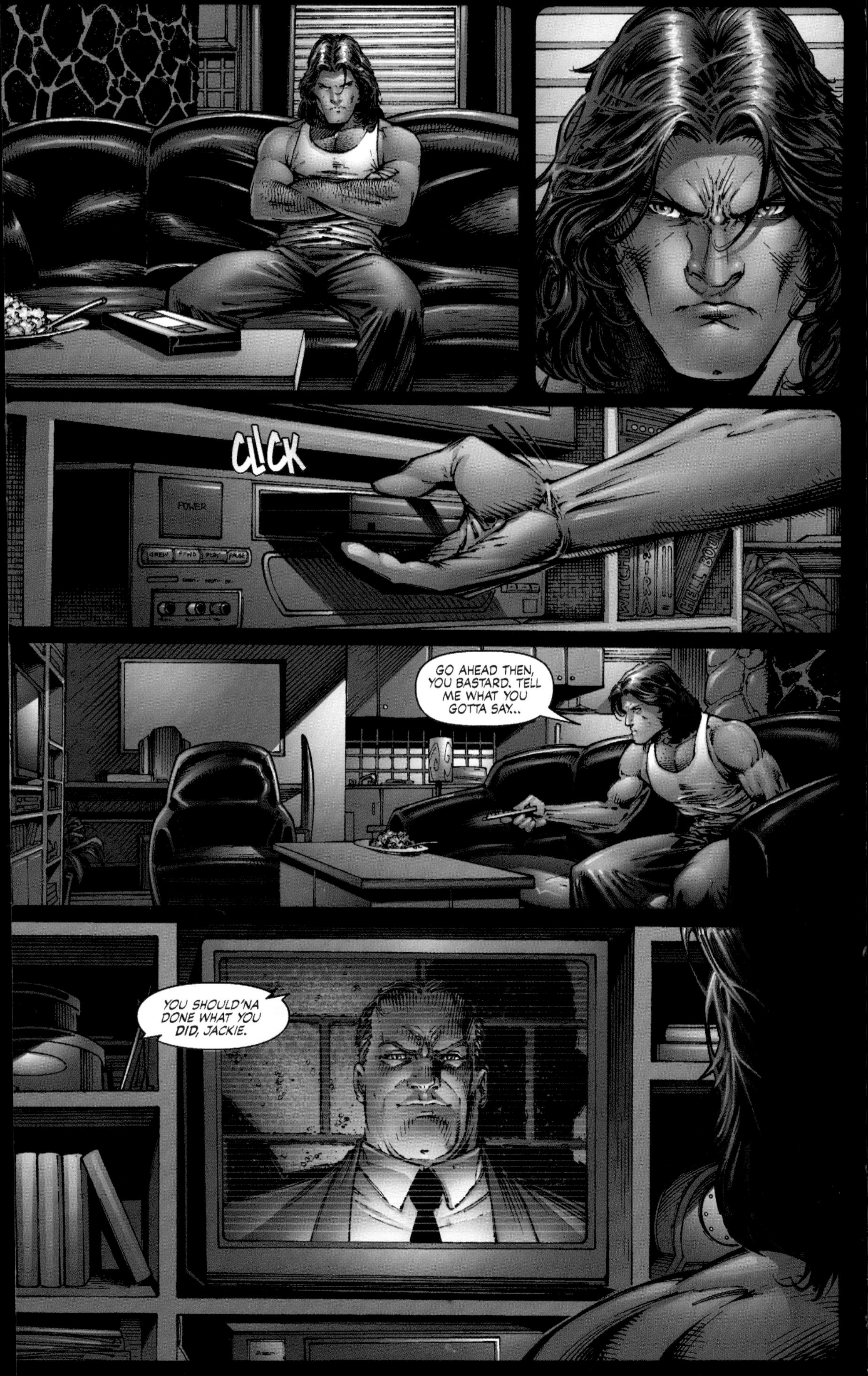
CLICK
POWER
GO AHEAD THEN, YOU BASTARD. TELL ME WHAT YOU GOTTA SAY...
YOU SHOULD'NA DONE WHAT YOU DID, JACKIE.

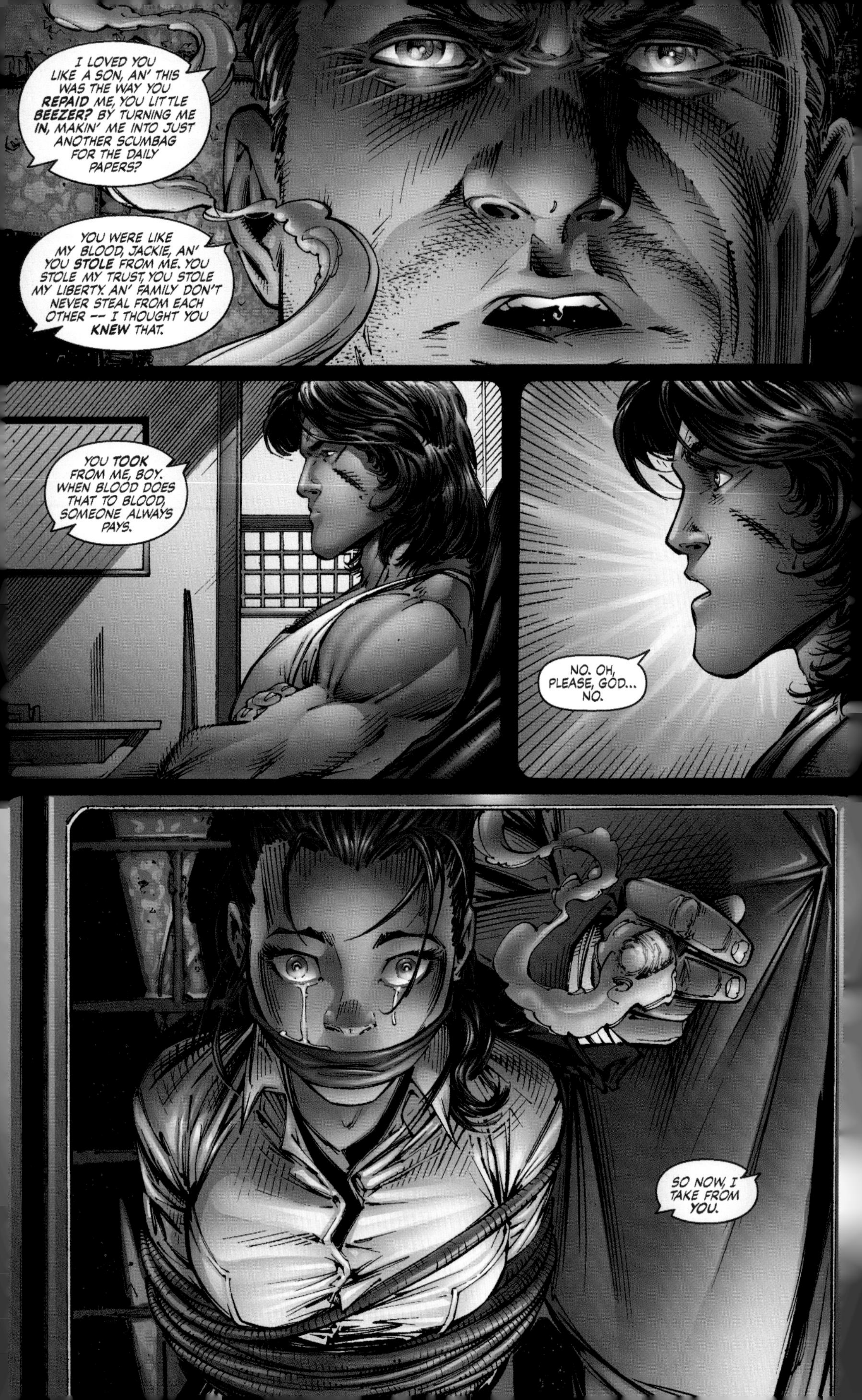
I LOVED YOU LIKE A SON, AN' THIS WAS THE WAY YOU **REPAID** ME, YOU LITTLE **BEEZER?** BY TURNING ME **IN**, MAKIN' ME INTO JUST ANOTHER SCUMBAG FOR THE DAILY PAPERS?
YOU WERE LIKE MY BLOOD, JACKIE, AN' YOU **STOLE** FROM ME. YOU STOLE MY TRUST, YOU STOLE MY LIBERTY. AN' FAMILY DON'T NEVER STEAL FROM EACH OTHER -- I THOUGHT YOU **KNEW** THAT.
YOU **TOOK** FROM ME, BOY. WHEN BLOOD DOES THAT TO BLOOD, SOMEONE ALWAYS PAYS.
NO. OH, PLEASE, GOD... NO.
SO NOW, I TAKE FROM YOU.

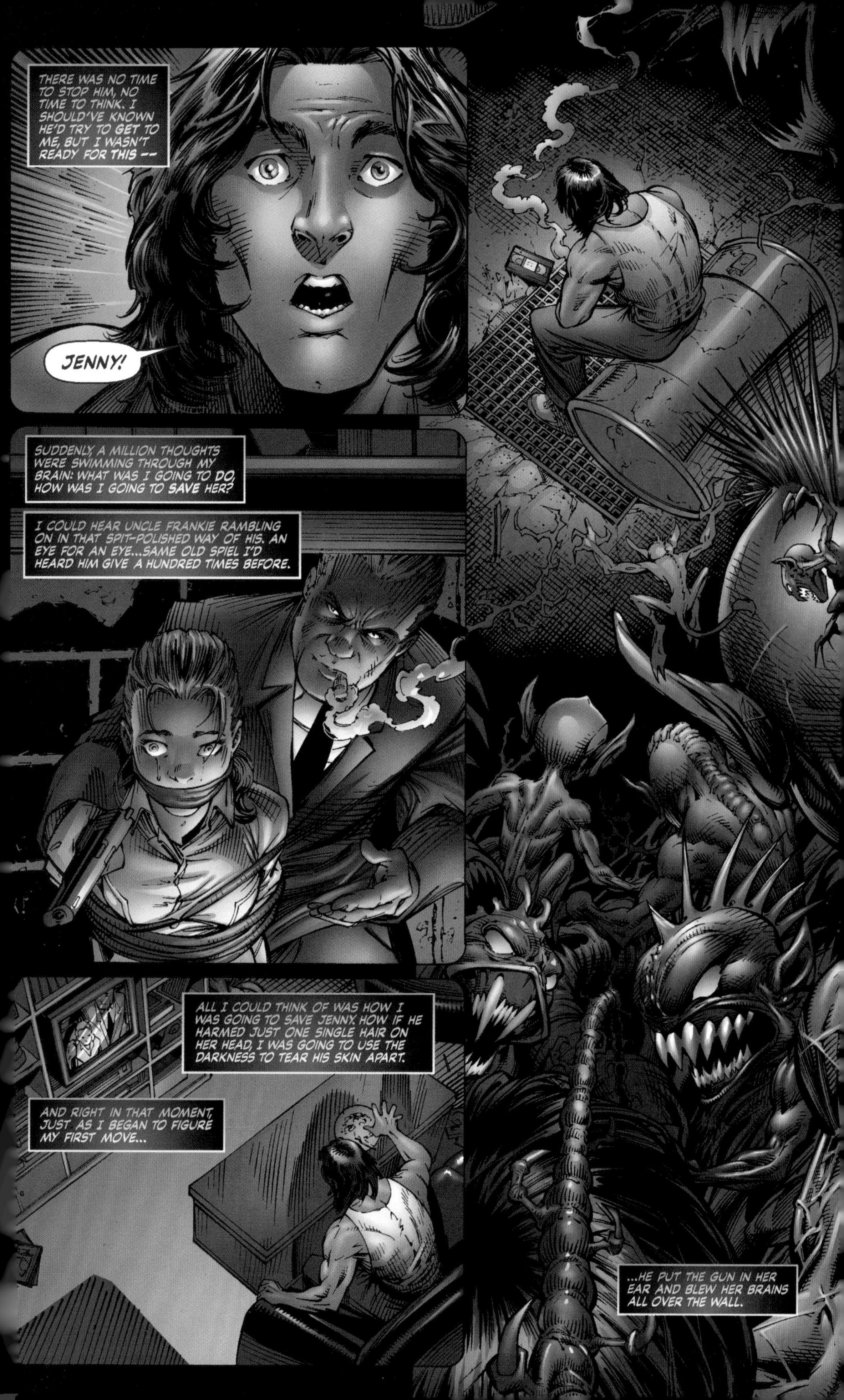
THERE WAS NO TIME TO STOP HIM, NO TIME TO THINK. I SHOULD'VE KNOWN HE'D TRY TO GET TO ME, BUT I WASN'T READY FOR THIS --
JENNY!
SUDDENLY, A MILLION THOUGHTS WERE SWIMMING THROUGH MY BRAIN: WHAT WAS I GOING TO DO, HOW WAS I GOING TO SAVE HER?
I COULD HEAR UNCLE FRANKIE RAMBLING ON IN THAT SPIT-POLISHED WAY OF HIS. AN EYE FOR AN EYE...SAME OLD SPIEL I'D HEARD HIM GIVE A HUNDRED TIMES BEFORE.
ALL I COULD THINK OF WAS HOW I WAS GOING TO SAVE JENNY. HOW IF HE HARMED JUST ONE SINGLE HAIR ON HER HEAD, I WAS GOING TO USE THE DARKNESS TO TEAR HIS SKIN APART.
AND RIGHT IN THAT MOMENT, JUST AS I BEGAN TO FIGURE MY FIRST MOVE...
...HE PUT THE GUN IN HER EAR AND BLEW HER BRAINS ALL OVER THE WALL.

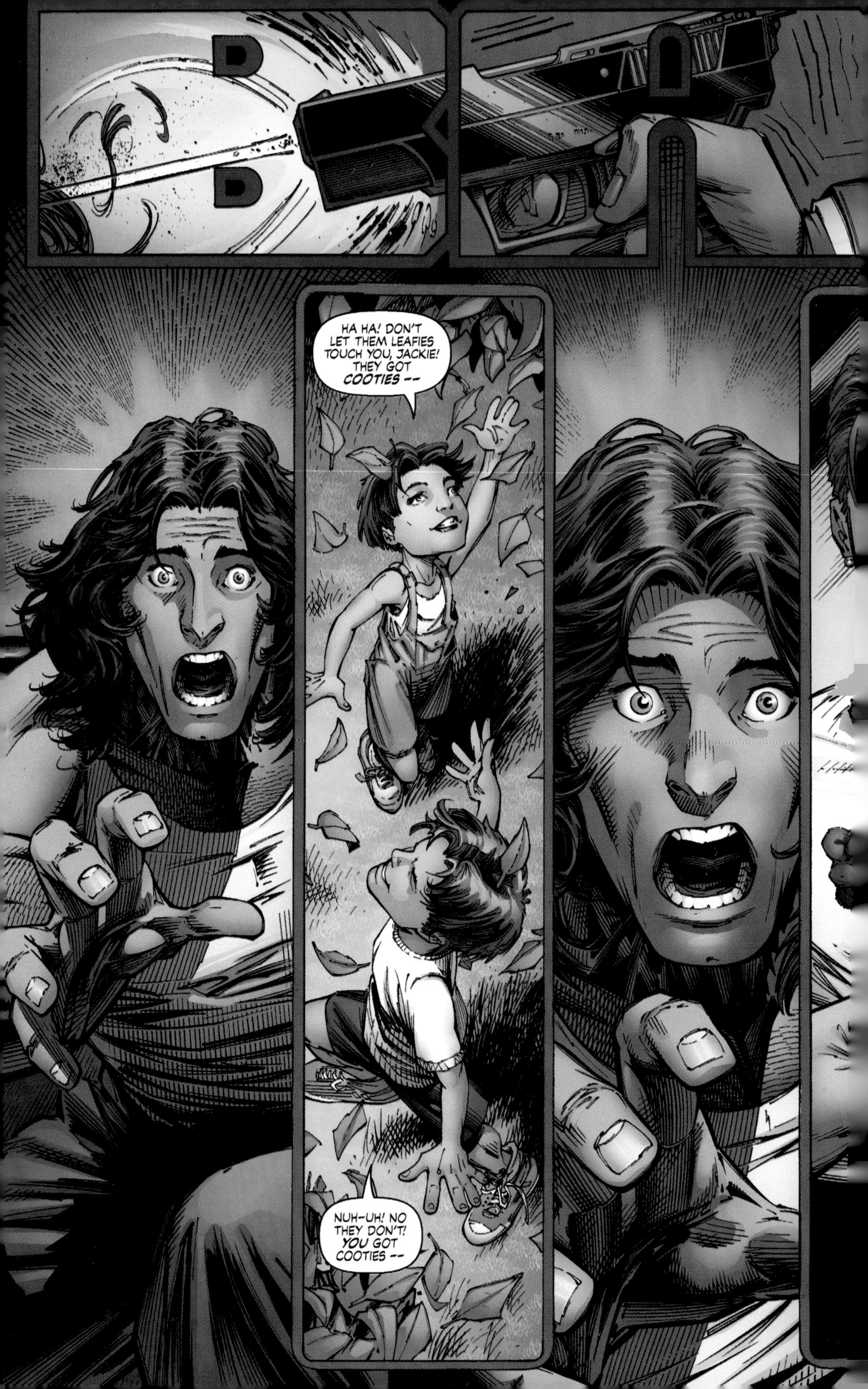
HA HA! DON'T LET THEM LEAFIES TOUCH YOU, JACKIE! THEY GOT COOTIES --
NUH-UH! NO THEY DON'T! YOU GOT COOTIES --

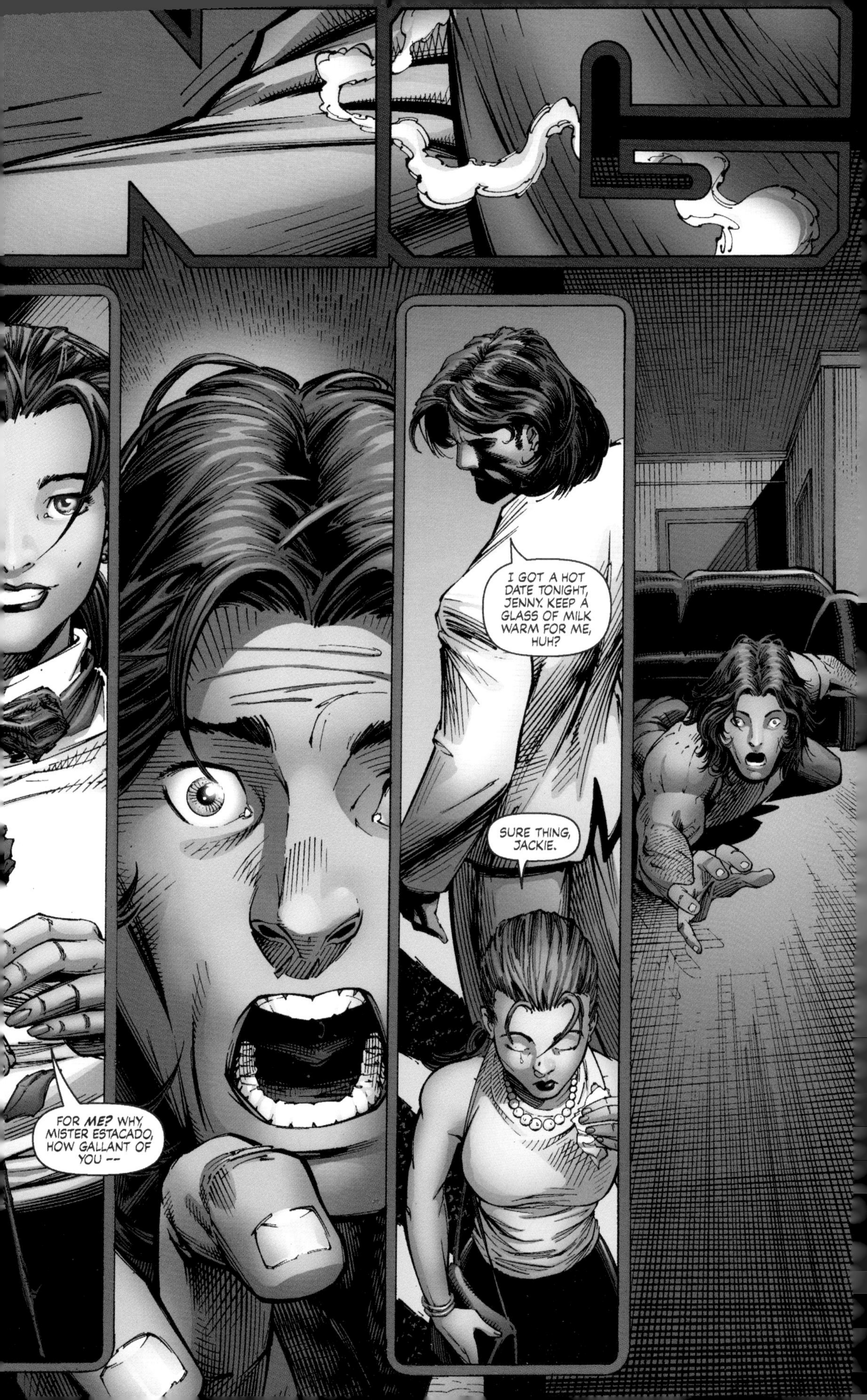
FOR ME? WHY, MISTER ESTACADO, HOW GALLANT OF YOU --
I GOT A HOT DATE TONIGHT, JENNY. KEEP A GLASS OF MILK WARM FOR ME, HUH?
SURE THING, JACKIE.

I DIDN'T EVEN HAVE A CHANCE. SHE WAS ALREADY GONE.
I NEVER HAD A CHANCE TO TELL HER.
CH-CLICK
HI, THIS IS ME. LEAVE A MESSAGE!
BEEP
JACKIE, THIS IS ROBERT! JACKIE, ARE YOU THERE? PICK UP THE PHONE, DAMMIT--
I NEVER TOLD HER BECAUSE I WAS TOO SCARED.
THAT GUN-TOTING LITTLE PLAYBOY IN WHITE, THAT WAS NEVER ME. I ONLY BECAME THAT OUT OF FEAR. FEAR OF WHAT SHE'D DO IF I EVEN TOLD HER.
THAT I LOVED HER FROM THE MOMENT I FIRST SAW HER.

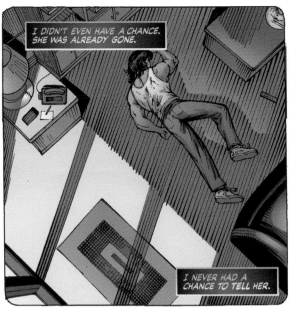

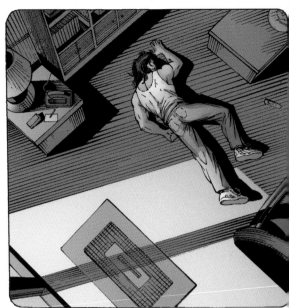

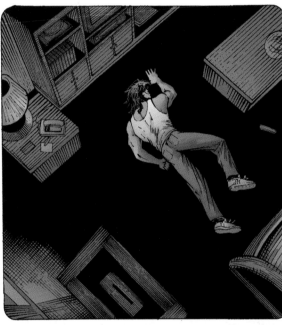

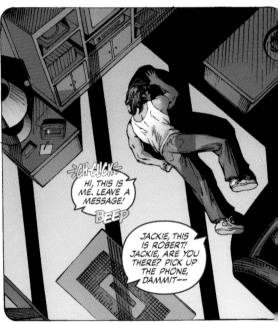

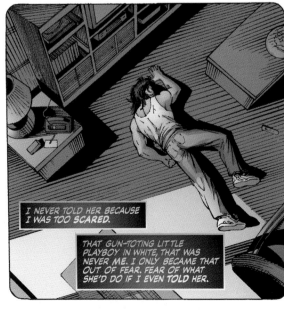

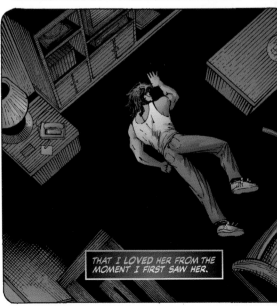

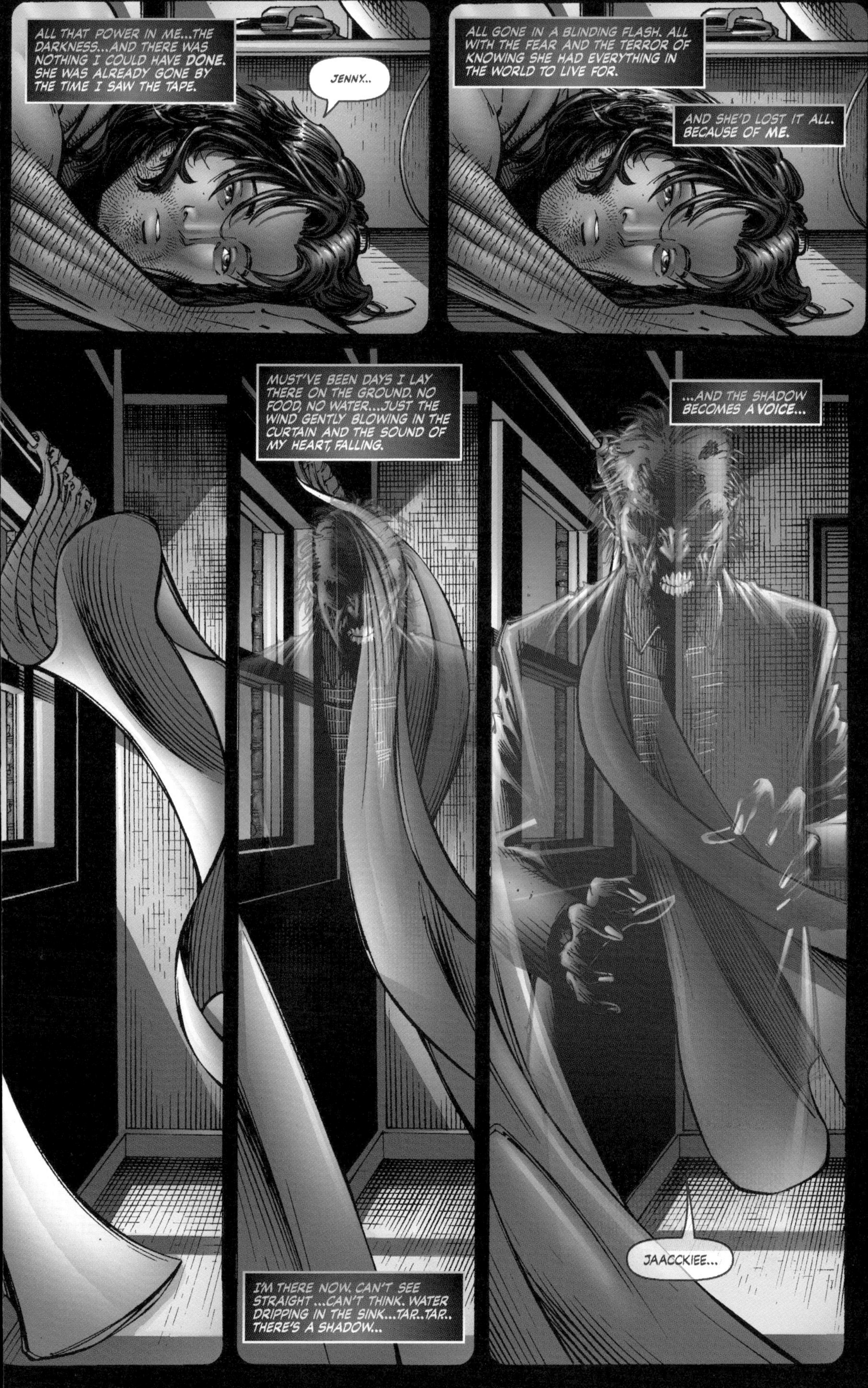
ALL THAT POWER IN ME...THE DARKNESS...AND THERE WAS NOTHING I COULD HAVE DONE. SHE WAS ALREADY GONE BY THE TIME I SAW THE TAPE.
JENNY..
ALL GONE IN A BLINDING FLASH. ALL WITH THE FEAR AND THE TERROR OF KNOWING SHE HAD EVERYTHING IN THE WORLD TO LIVE FOR.
AND SHE'D LOST IT ALL. BECAUSE OF ME.
MUST'VE BEEN DAYS I LAY THERE ON THE GROUND. NO FOOD, NO WATER...JUST THE WIND GENTLY BLOWING IN THE CURTAIN AND THE SOUND OF MY HEART, FALLING.
I'M THERE NOW. CAN'T SEE STRAIGHT...CAN'T THINK. WATER DRIPPING IN THE SINK...TAR..TAR.. THERE'S A SHADOW..
...AND THE SHADOW BECOMES A VOICE...
JAACCKIEE...

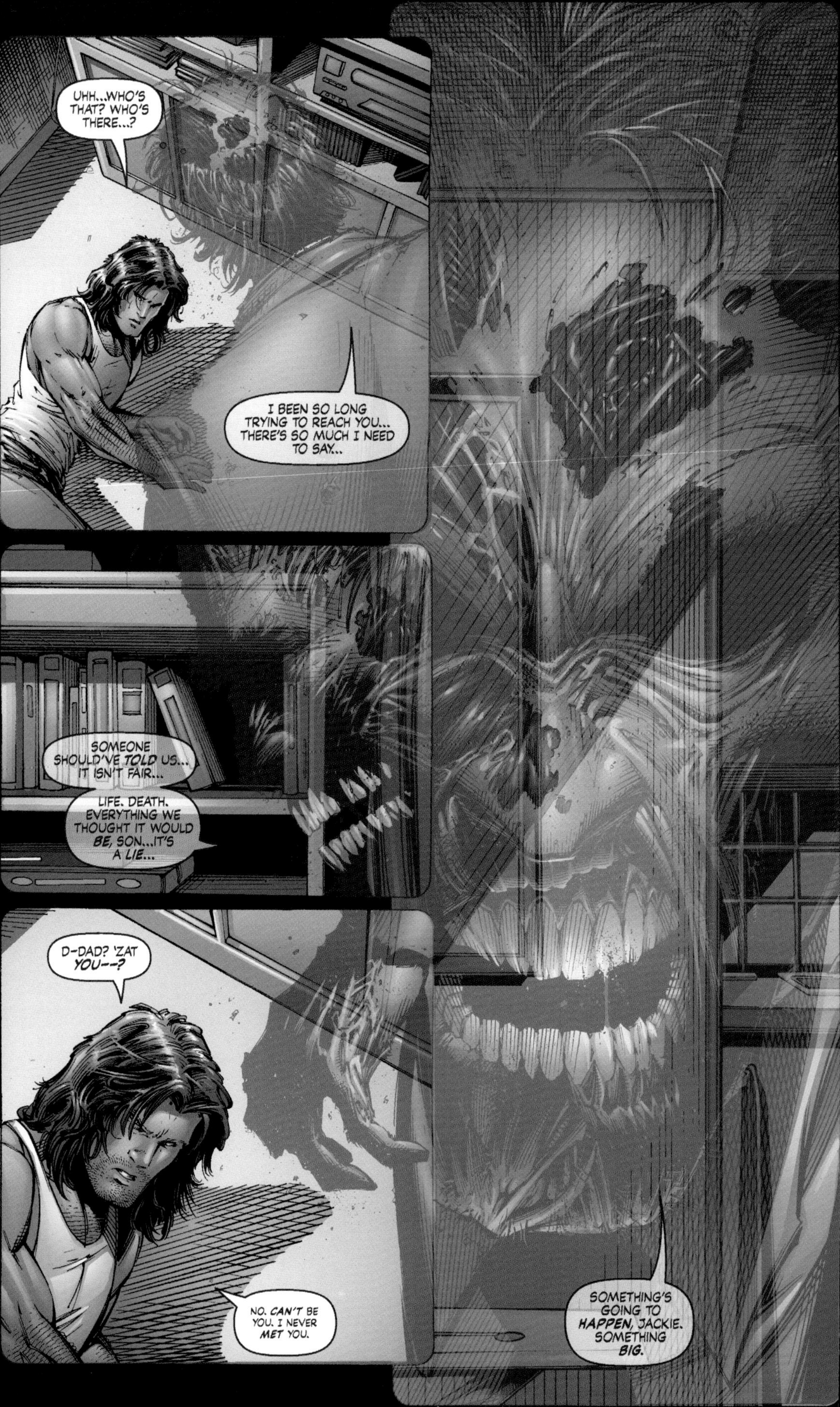
UHH...WHO'S THAT? WHO'S THERE...?
I BEEN SO LONG TRYING TO REACH YOU... THERE'S SO MUCH I NEED TO SAY...
SOMEONE SHOULD'VE *TOLD* US... IT ISN'T FAIR...
LIFE. DEATH. EVERYTHING WE THOUGHT IT WOULD *BE*, SON...IT'S A *LIE*...
D-DAD? 'ZAT *YOU*--?
NO. *CAN'T* BE YOU. I NEVER *MET* YOU.
SOMETHING'S GOING TO *HAPPEN*, JACKIE. SOMETHING *BIG*.

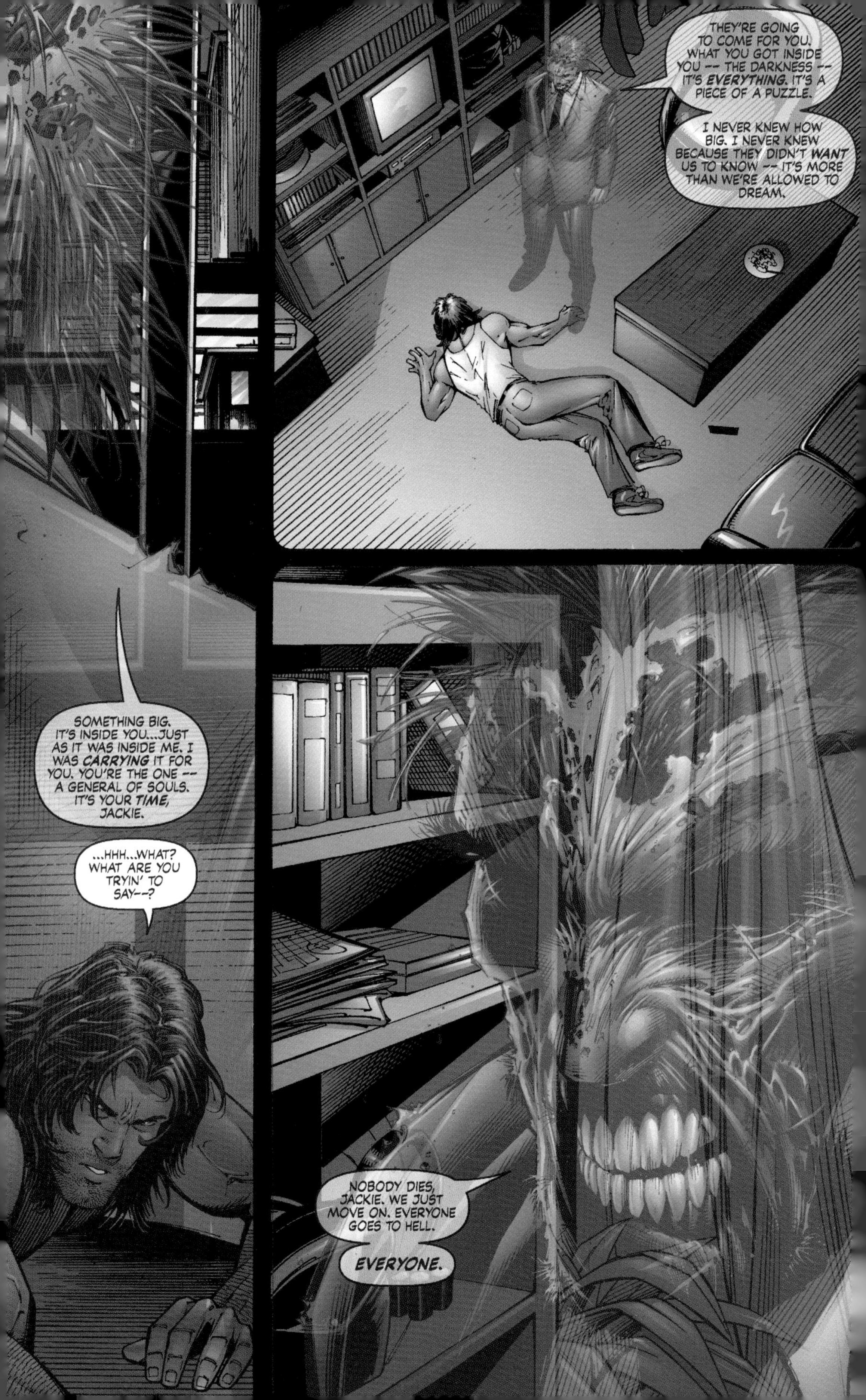
THEY'RE GOING TO COME FOR YOU. WHAT YOU GOT INSIDE YOU -- THE DARKNESS -- IT'S EVERYTHING. IT'S A PIECE OF A PUZZLE.
I NEVER KNEW HOW BIG. I NEVER KNEW BECAUSE THEY DIDN'T WANT US TO KNOW -- IT'S MORE THAN WE'RE ALLOWED TO DREAM.
SOMETHING BIG. IT'S INSIDE YOU...JUST AS IT WAS INSIDE ME. I WAS CARRYING IT FOR YOU. YOU'RE THE ONE -- A GENERAL OF SOULS. IT'S YOUR TIME, JACKIE.
...HHH...WHAT? WHAT ARE YOU TRYIN' TO SAY--?
NOBODY DIES, JACKIE. WE JUST MOVE ON. EVERYONE GOES TO HELL.
EVERYONE.

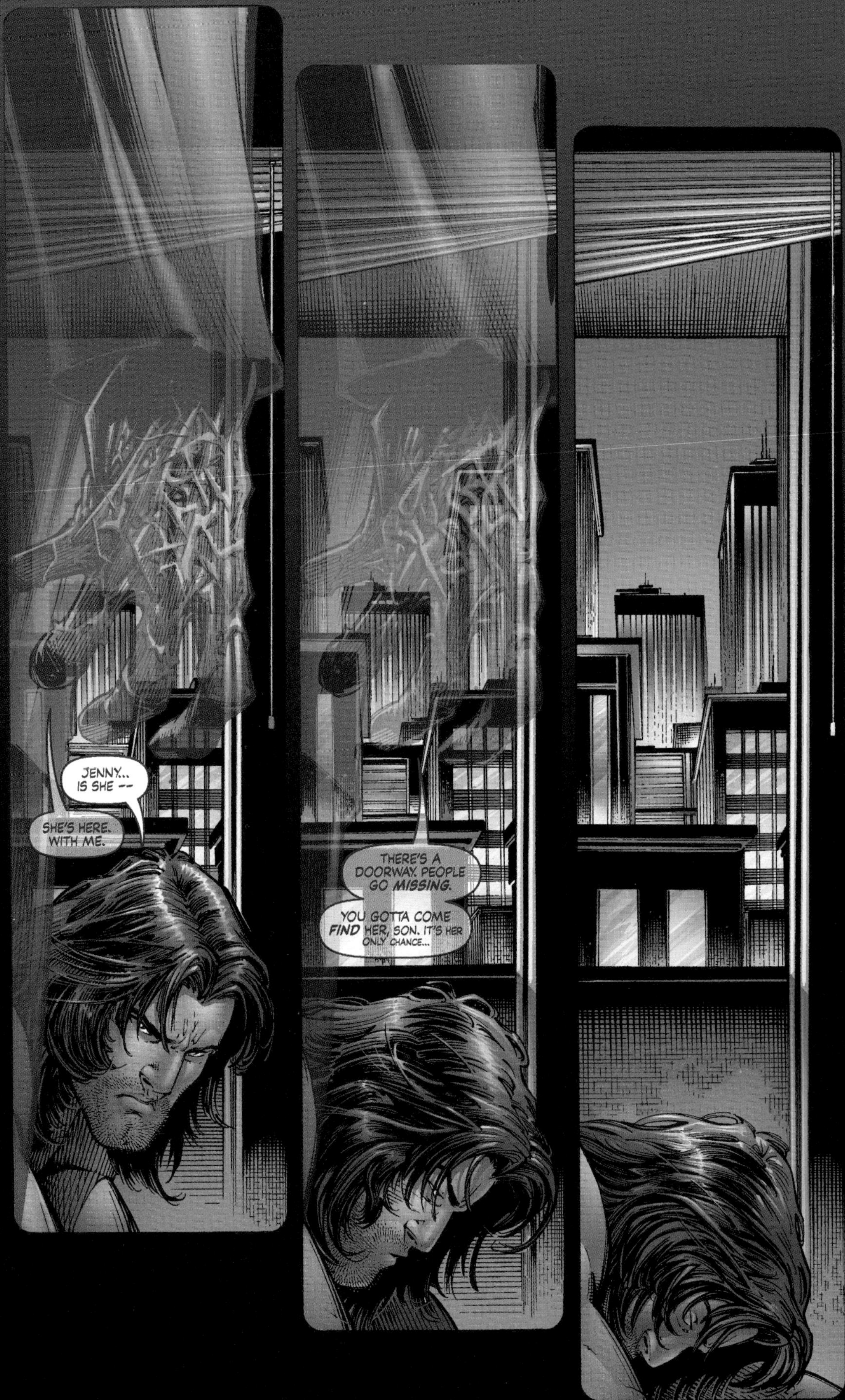
JENNY... IS SHE --
SHE'S HERE. WITH ME.
THERE'S A DOORWAY. PEOPLE GO MISSING.
YOU GOTTA COME FIND HER, SON. IT'S HER ONLY CHANCE...

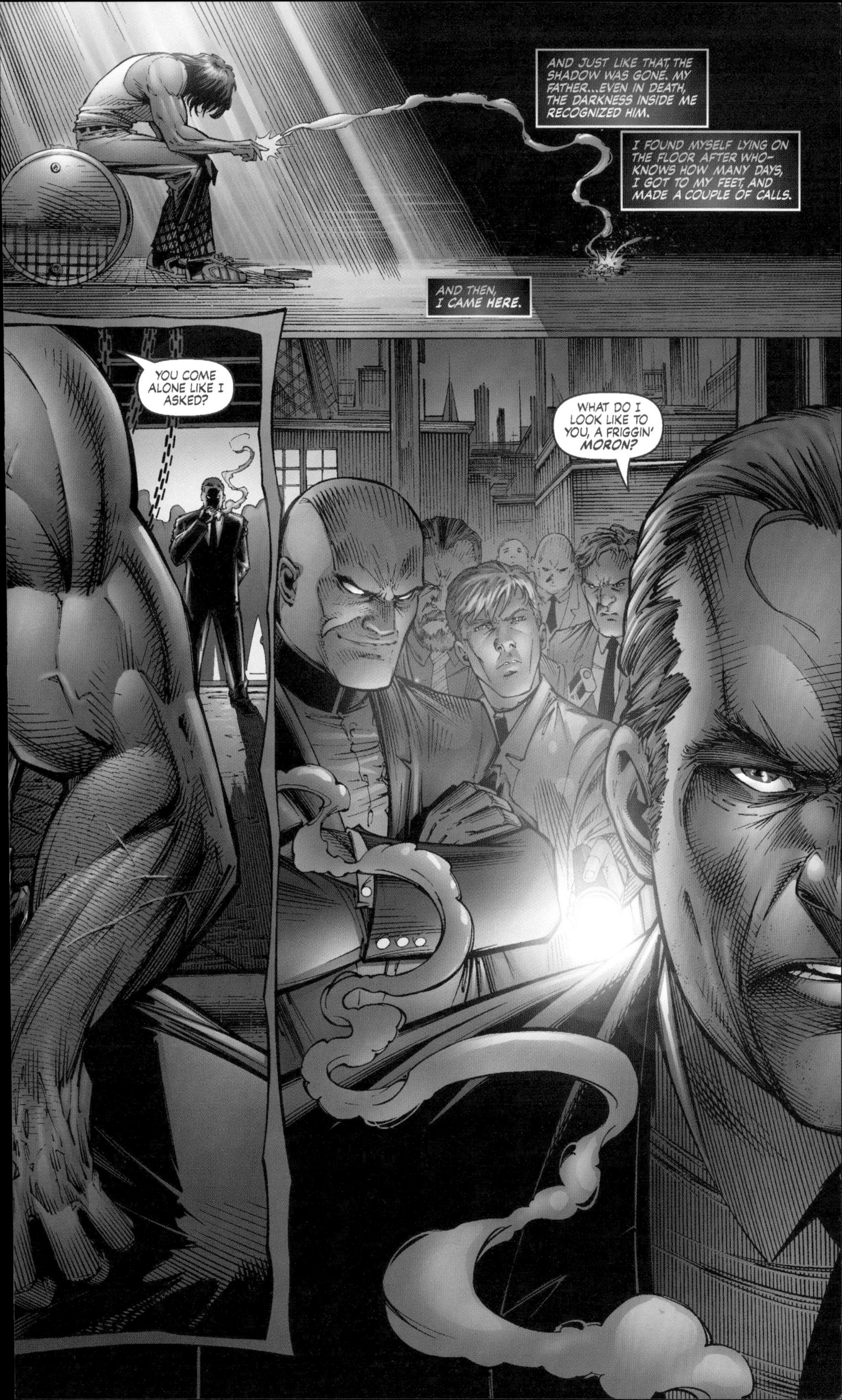
AND JUST LIKE THAT, THE SHADOW WAS GONE. MY FATHER...EVEN IN DEATH, THE DARKNESS INSIDE ME RECOGNIZED HIM.
I FOUND MYSELF LYING ON THE FLOOR AFTER WHO-KNOWS HOW MANY DAYS, I GOT TO MY FEET, AND MADE A COUPLE OF CALLS.
AND THEN, I CAME HERE.
YOU COME ALONE LIKE I ASKED?
WHAT DO I LOOK LIKE TO YOU, A FRIGGIN' MORON?

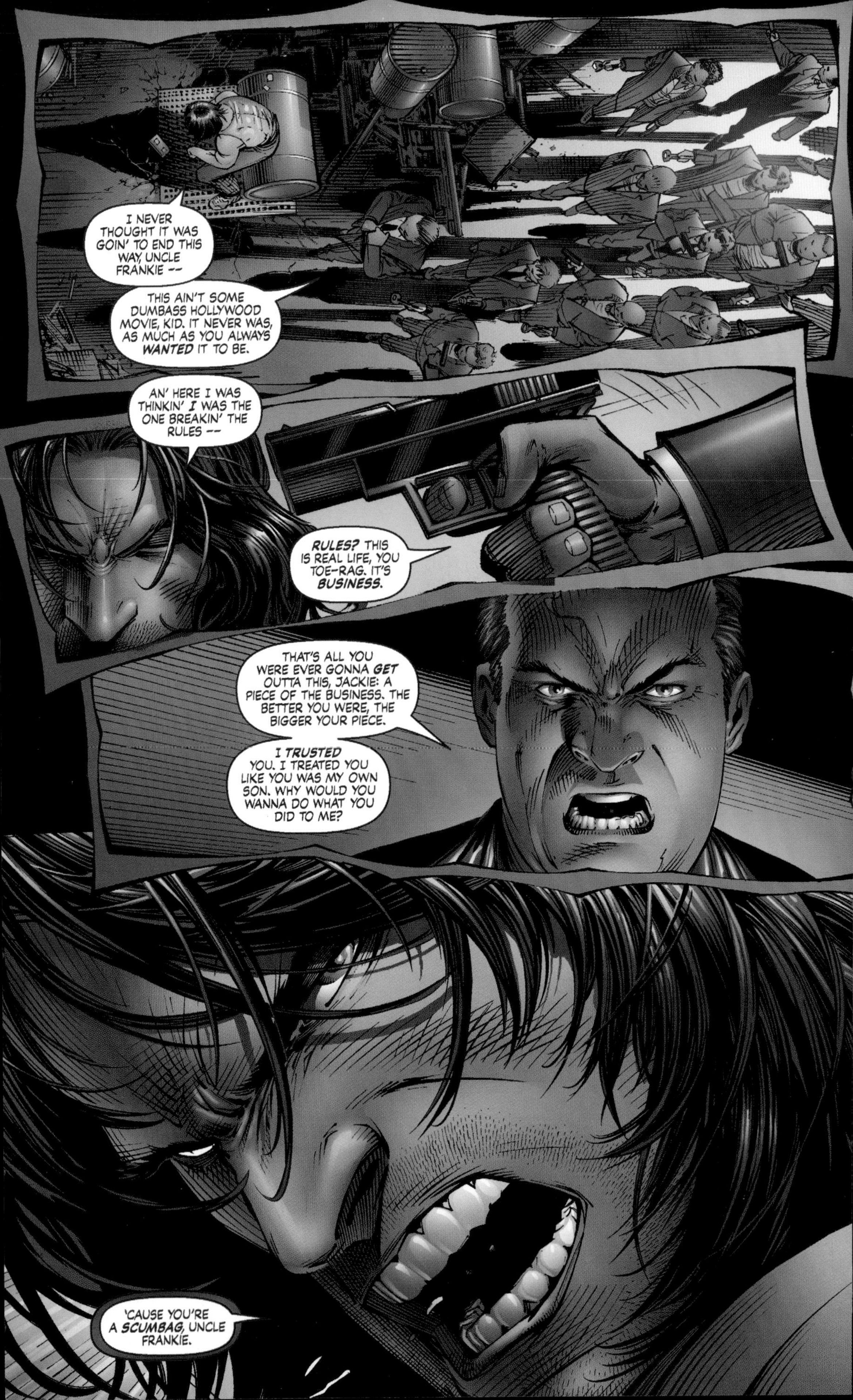
I NEVER THOUGHT IT WAS GOIN' TO END THIS WAY, UNCLE FRANKIE --
THIS AIN'T SOME DUMBASS HOLLYWOOD MOVIE, KID. IT NEVER WAS, AS MUCH AS YOU ALWAYS ***WANTED*** IT TO BE.
AN' HERE I WAS THINKIN' ***I*** WAS THE ONE BREAKIN' THE RULES --
RULES? THIS IS REAL LIFE, YOU TOE-RAG. IT'S ***BUSINESS.***
THAT'S ALL YOU WERE EVER GONNA ***GET*** OUTTA THIS, JACKIE: A PIECE OF THE BUSINESS. THE BETTER YOU WERE, THE BIGGER YOUR PIECE.
I TRUSTED YOU. I TREATED YOU LIKE YOU WAS MY OWN SON. WHY WOULD YOU WANNA DO WHAT YOU DID TO ME?
'CAUSE YOU'RE A ***SCUMBAG***, UNCLE FRANKIE.

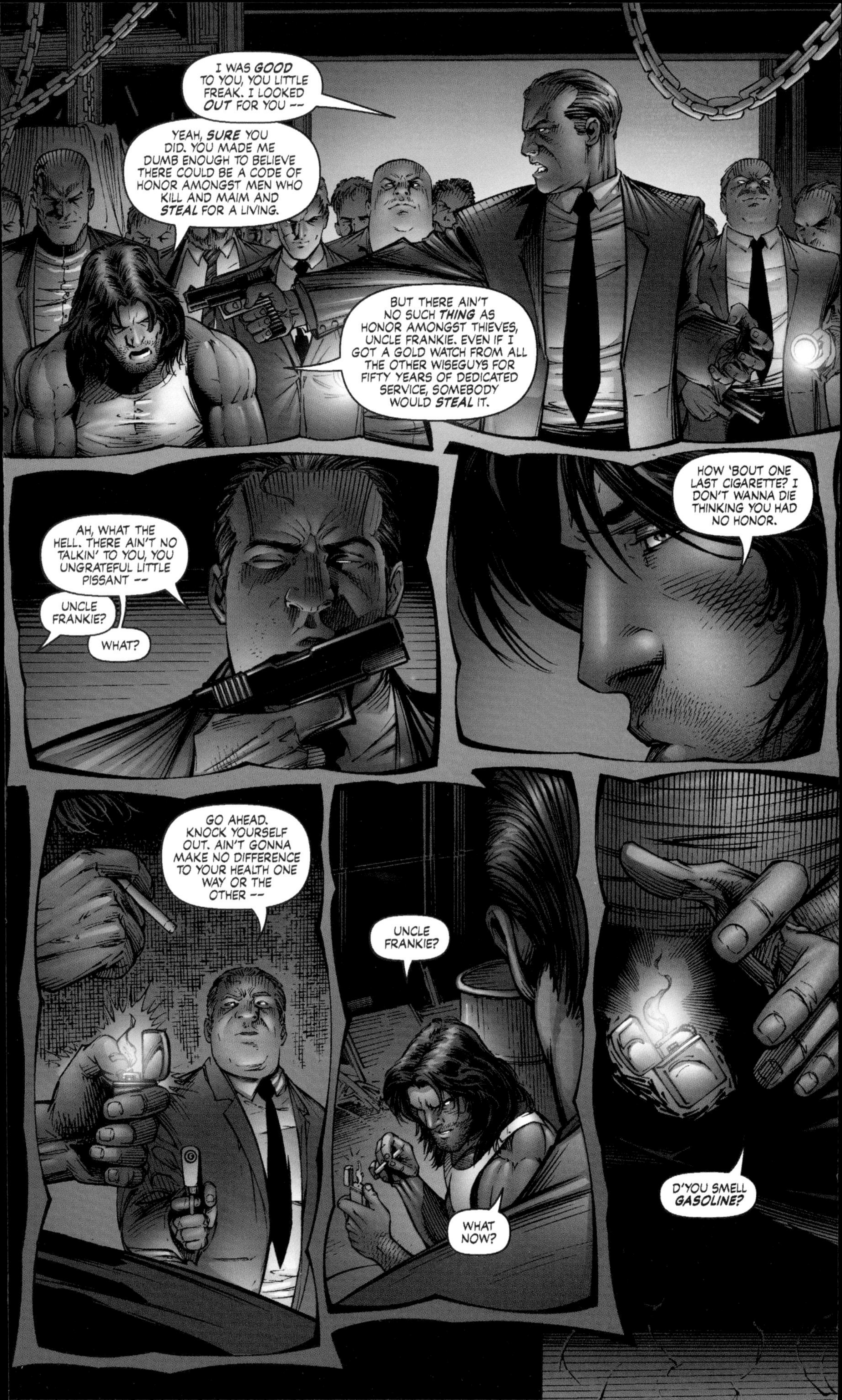
I WAS GOOD TO YOU, YOU LITTLE FREAK. I LOOKED OUT FOR YOU --
YEAH, SURE YOU DID. YOU MADE ME DUMB ENOUGH TO BELIEVE THERE COULD BE A CODE OF HONOR AMONGST MEN WHO KILL AND MAIM AND STEAL FOR A LIVING.
BUT THERE AIN'T NO SUCH THING AS HONOR AMONGST THIEVES, UNCLE FRANKIE. EVEN IF I GOT A GOLD WATCH FROM ALL THE OTHER WISEGUYS FOR FIFTY YEARS OF DEDICATED SERVICE, SOMEBODY WOULD STEAL IT.
AH, WHAT THE HELL. THERE AIN'T NO TALKIN' TO YOU, YOU UNGRATEFUL LITTLE PISSANT --
UNCLE FRANKIE?
WHAT?
HOW 'BOUT ONE LAST CIGARETTE? I DON'T WANNA DIE THINKING YOU HAD NO HONOR.
GO AHEAD. KNOCK YOURSELF OUT. AIN'T GONNA MAKE NO DIFFERENCE TO YOUR HEALTH ONE WAY OR THE OTHER --
UNCLE FRANKIE?
WHAT NOW?
D'YOU SMELL GASOLINE?

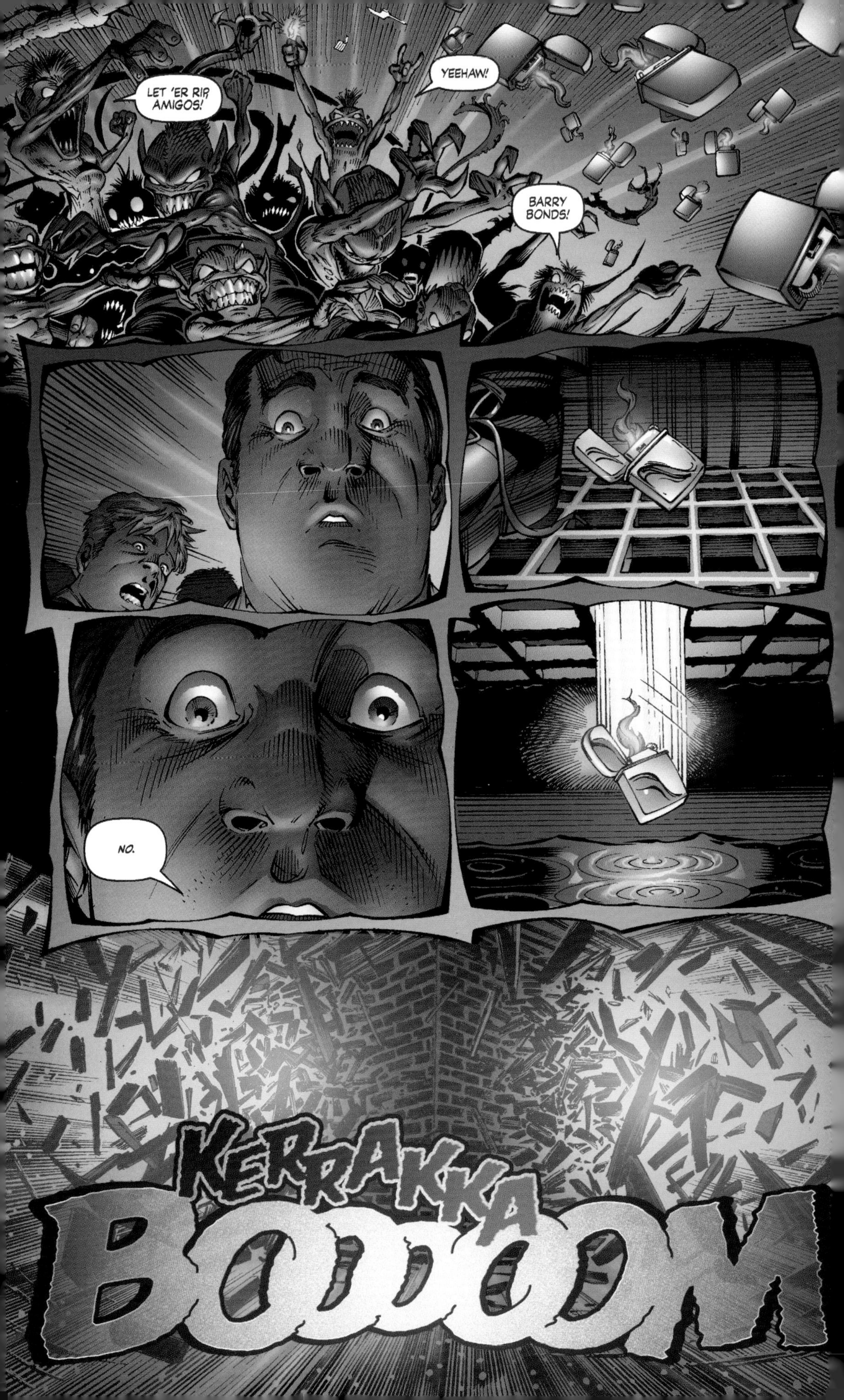
LET 'ER RIP AMIGOS!
YEEHAW!
BARRY BONDS!
NO.
KERRAKKA BOOOOM

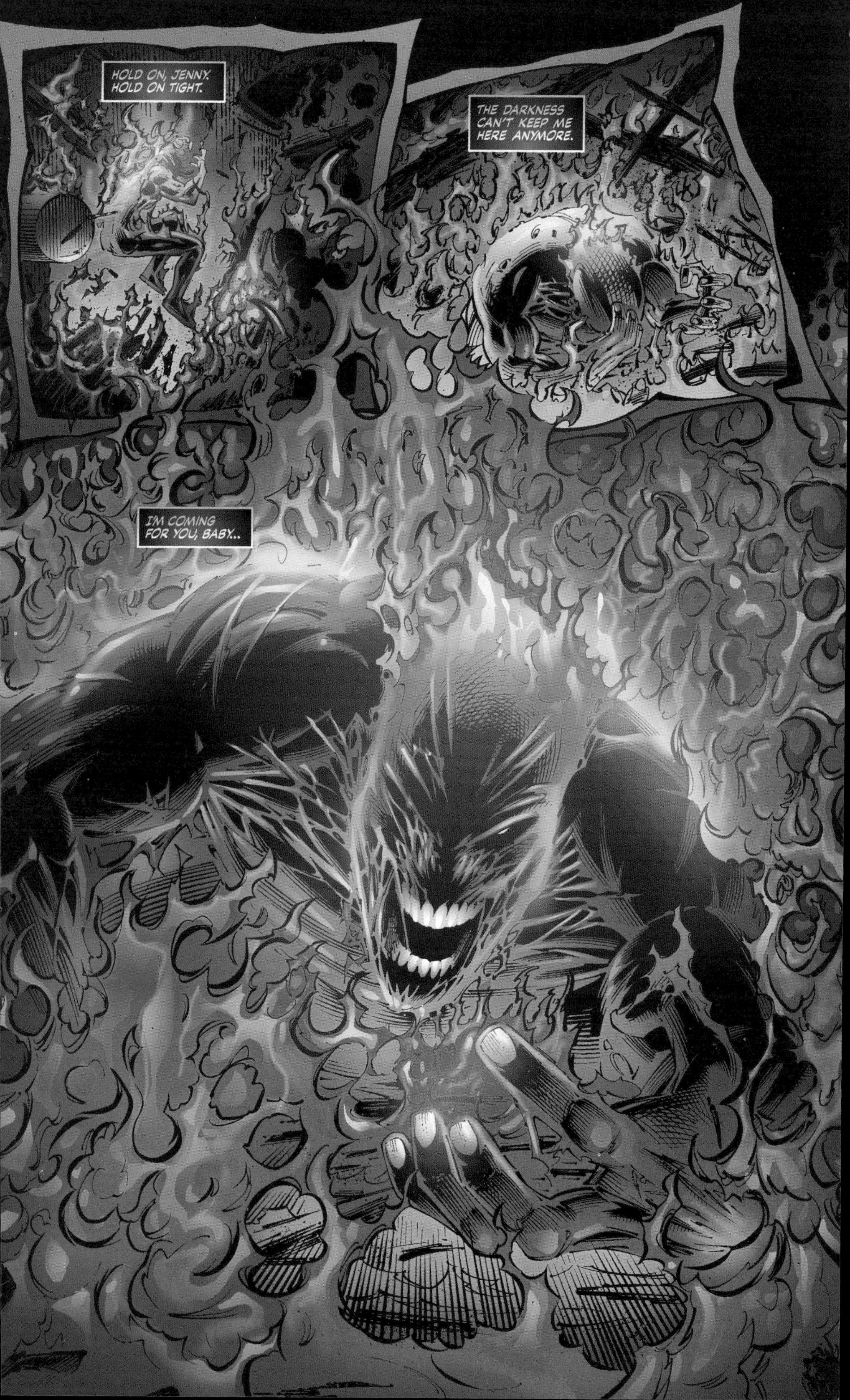
HOLD ON, JENNY. HOLD ON TIGHT.
THE DARKNESS CAN'T KEEP ME HERE ANYMORE.
I'M COMING FOR YOU, BABY..

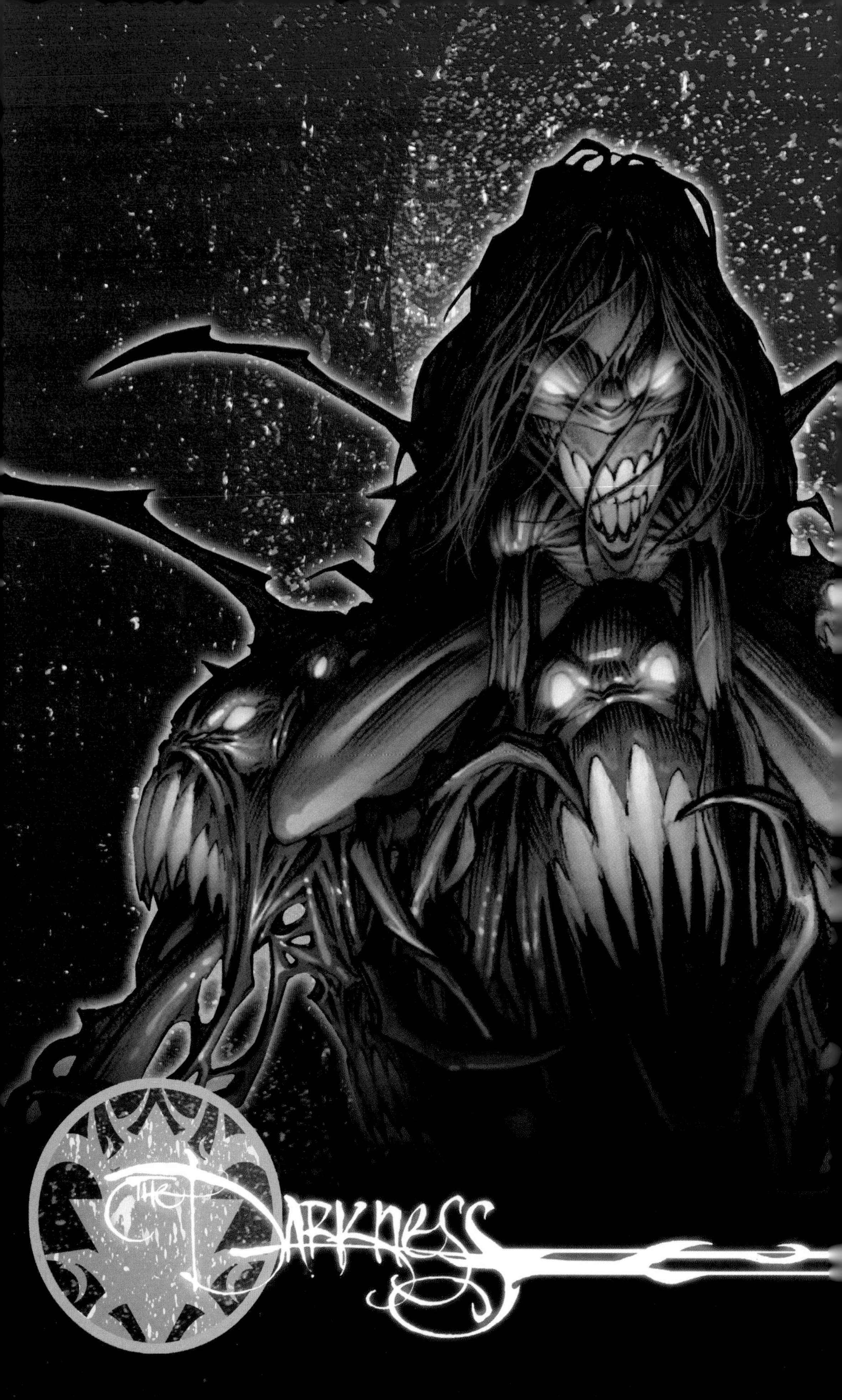
THE DARKNESS

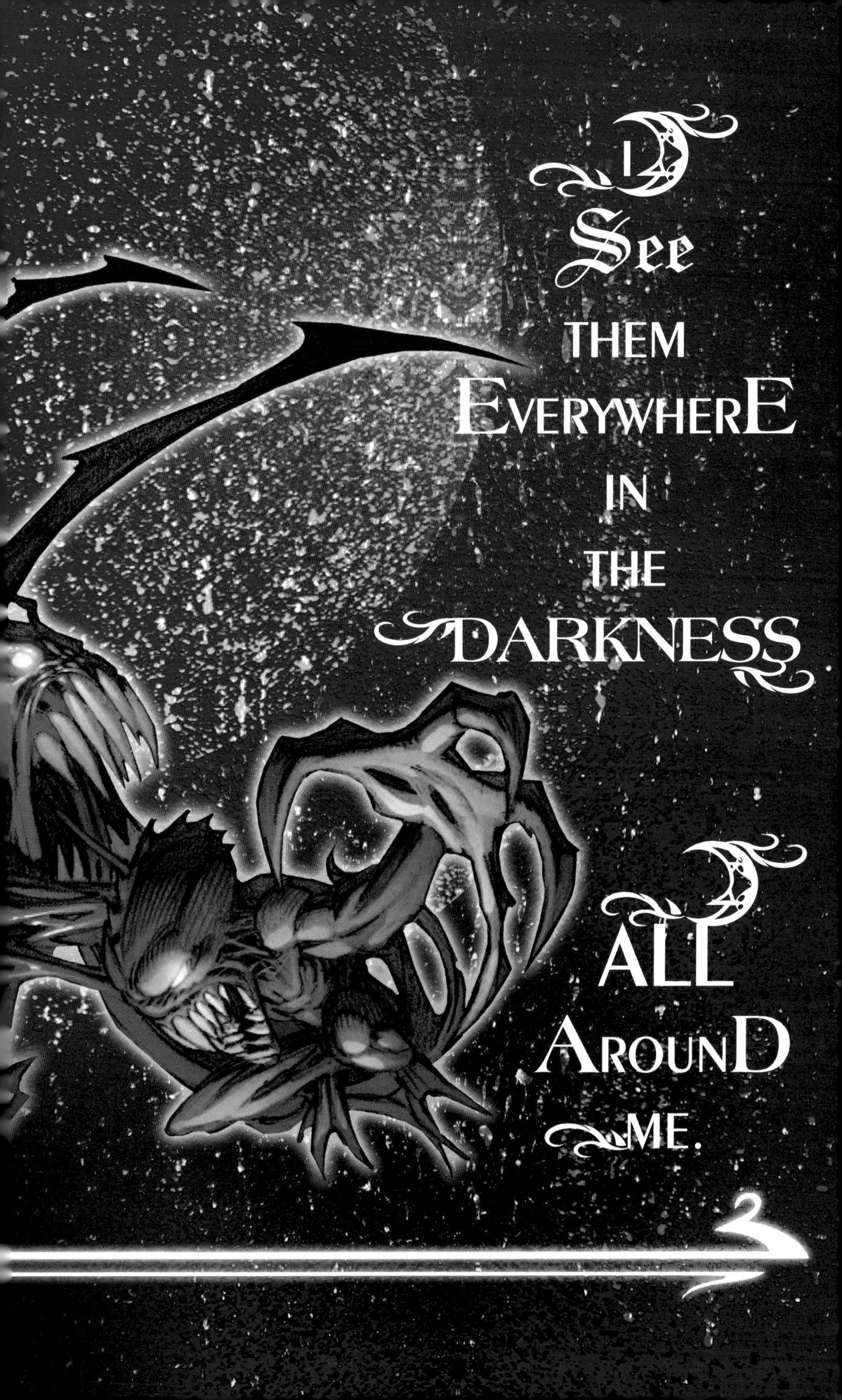
I
See
THEM
EVERYWHERE
IN
THE
DARKNESS
ALL
AROUND
ME.

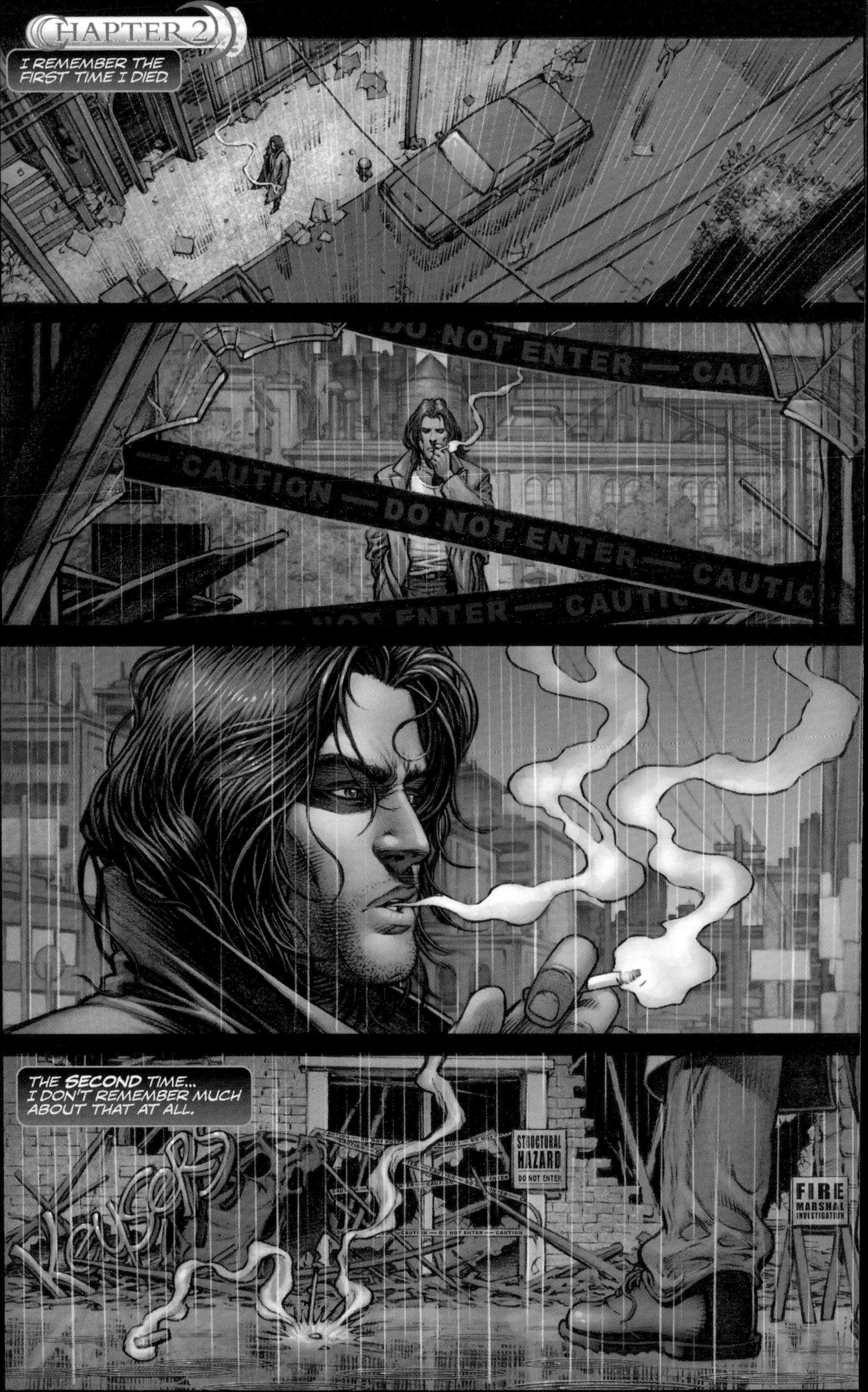
CHAPTER 2
I REMEMBER THE FIRST TIME I DIED.
DO NOT ENTER — CAU
— CAUTION — DO NOT ENTER — CAUTIC
NOT ENTER — CAUTIC
THE SECOND TIME... I DON'T REMEMBER MUCH ABOUT THAT AT ALL.
STRUCTURAL HAZARD
DO NOT ENTER
FIRE MARSHAL INVESTIGATION

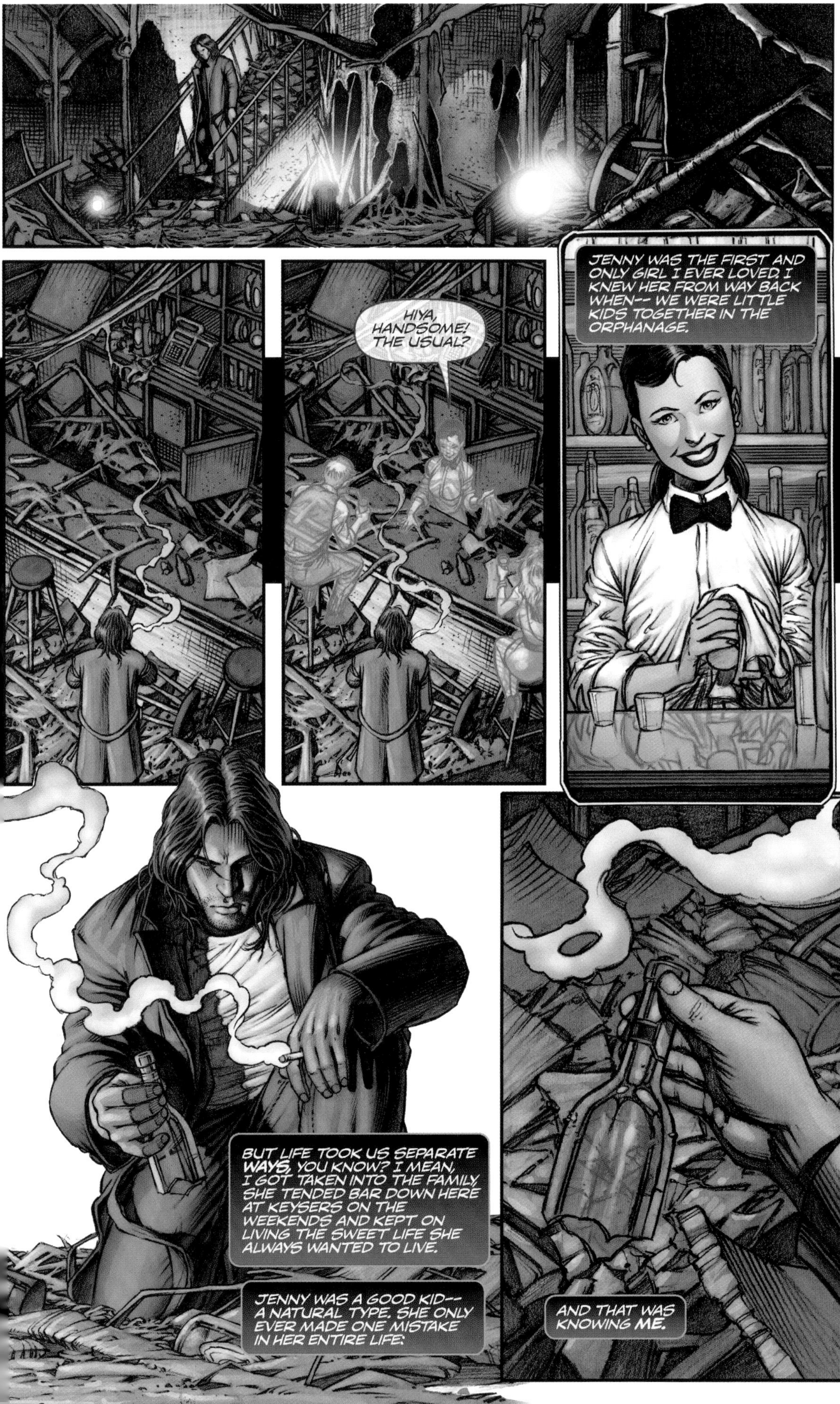
HIYA, HANDSOME! THE USUAL?
JENNY WAS THE FIRST AND ONLY GIRL I EVER LOVED. I KNEW HER FROM WAY BACK WHEN-- WE WERE LITTLE KIDS TOGETHER IN THE ORPHANAGE.
BUT LIFE TOOK US SEPARATE WAYS, YOU KNOW? I MEAN, I GOT TAKEN INTO THE FAMILY, SHE TENDED BAR DOWN HERE AT KEYSERS ON THE WEEKENDS AND KEPT ON LIVING THE SWEET LIFE SHE ALWAYS WANTED TO LIVE.
JENNY WAS A GOOD KID-- A NATURAL TYPE. SHE ONLY EVER MADE ONE MISTAKE IN HER ENTIRE LIFE:
AND THAT WAS KNOWING ME.

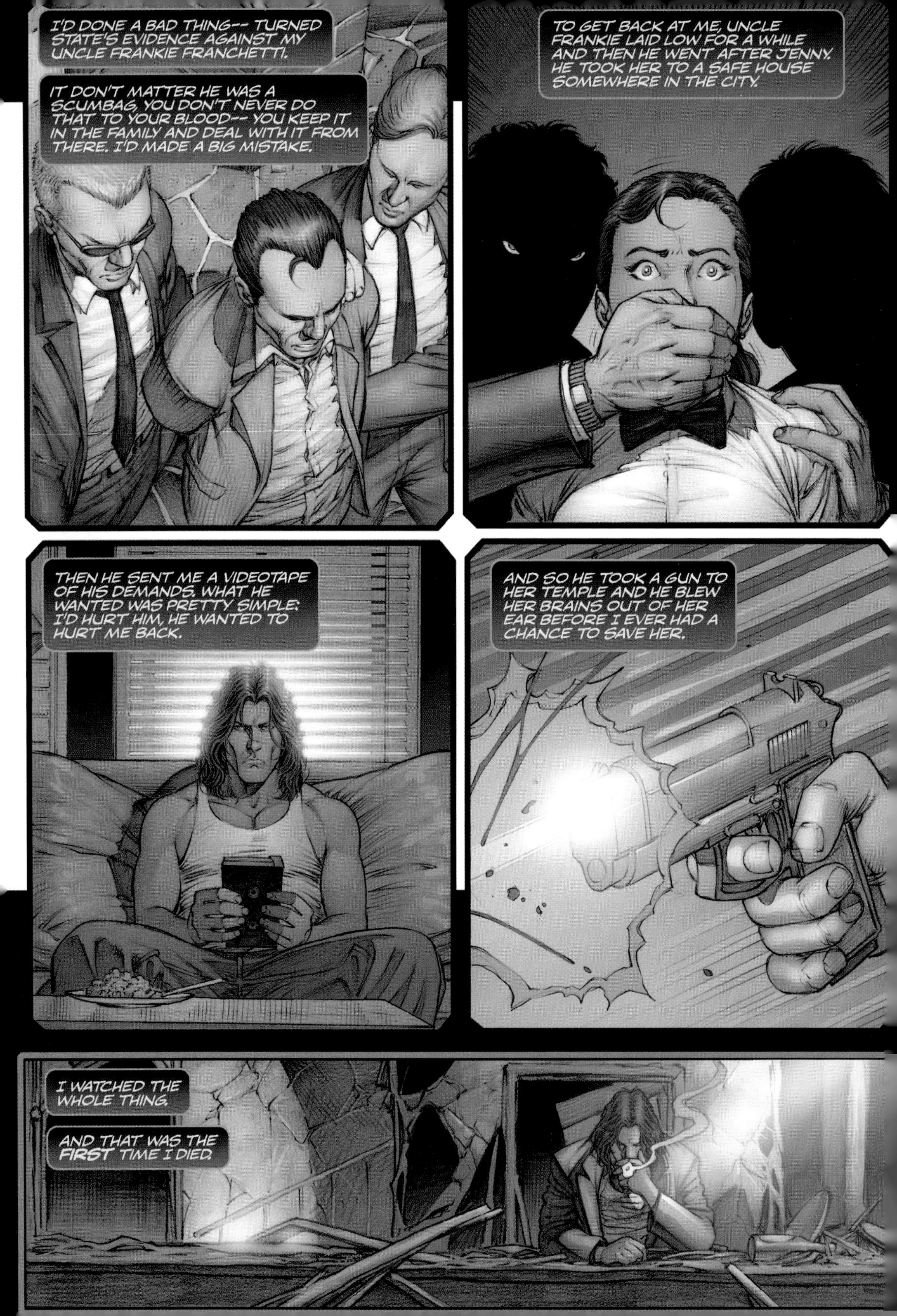
I'D DONE A BAD THING-- TURNED STATE'S EVIDENCE AGAINST MY UNCLE FRANKIE FRANCHETTI.
IT DON'T MATTER HE WAS A SCUMBAG, YOU DON'T NEVER DO THAT TO YOUR BLOOD-- YOU KEEP IT IN THE FAMILY AND DEAL WITH IT FROM THERE. I'D MADE A BIG MISTAKE.
TO GET BACK AT ME, UNCLE FRANKIE LAID LOW FOR A WHILE AND THEN HE WENT AFTER JENNY. HE TOOK HER TO A SAFE HOUSE SOMEWHERE IN THE CITY.
THEN HE SENT ME A VIDEOTAPE OF HIS DEMANDS. WHAT HE WANTED WAS PRETTY SIMPLE: I'D HURT HIM, HE WANTED TO HURT ME BACK.
AND SO HE TOOK A GUN TO HER TEMPLE AND HE BLEW HER BRAINS OUT OF HER EAR BEFORE I EVER HAD A CHANCE TO SAVE HER.
I WATCHED THE WHOLE THING.
AND THAT WAS THE FIRST TIME I DIED.

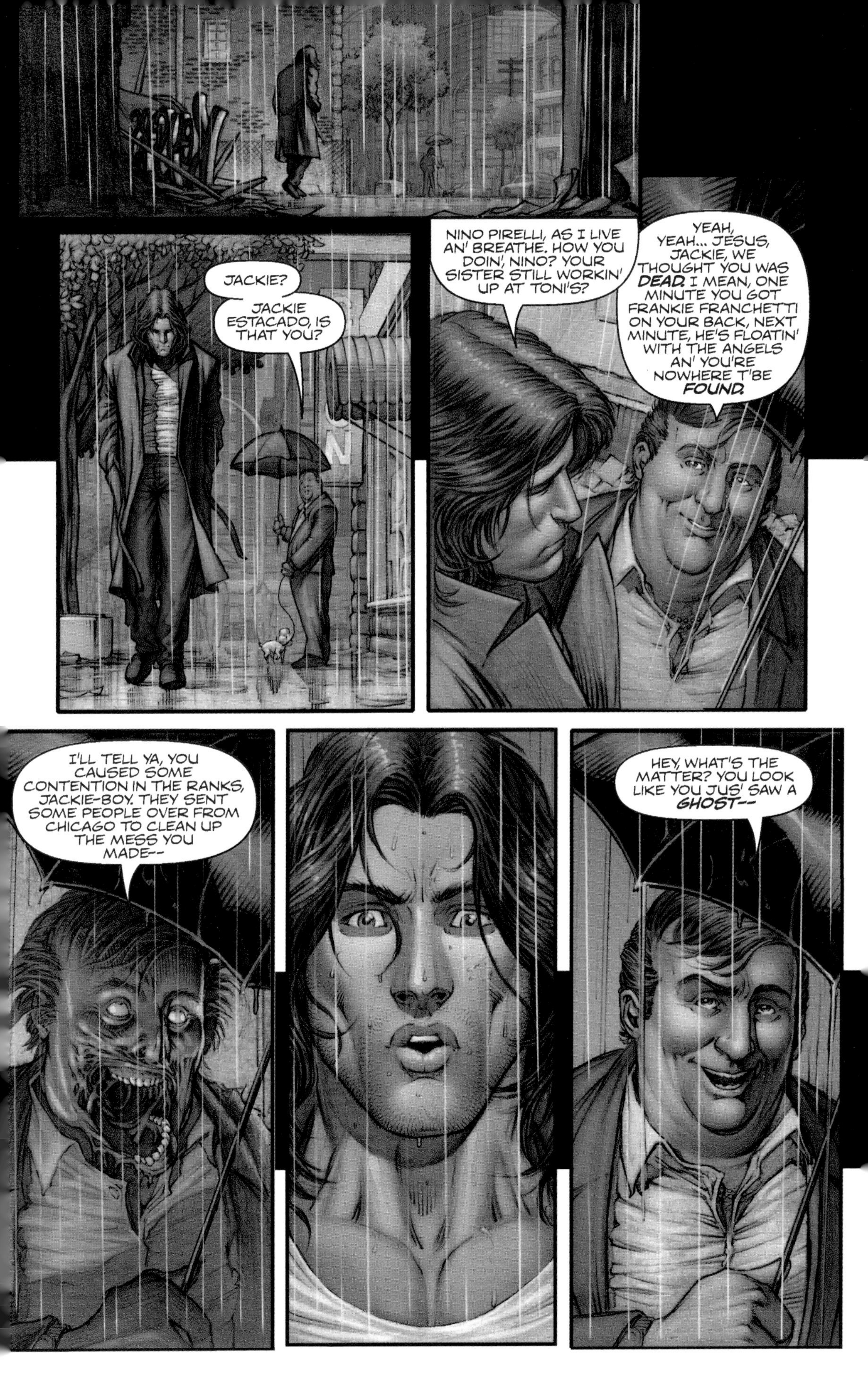
JACKIE?
JACKIE ESTACADO, IS THAT YOU?
NINO PIRELLI, AS I LIVE AN' BREATHE. HOW YOU DOIN', NINO? YOUR SISTER STILL WORKIN' UP AT TONI'S?
YEAH, YEAH... JESUS, JACKIE, WE THOUGHT YOU WAS **DEAD.** I MEAN, ONE MINUTE YOU GOT FRANKIE FRANCHETTI ON YOUR BACK, NEXT MINUTE, HE'S FLOATIN' WITH THE ANGELS AN' YOU'RE NOWHERE T'BE **FOUND.**
I'LL TELL YA, YOU CAUSED SOME CONTENTION IN THE RANKS, JACKIE-BOY. THEY SENT SOME PEOPLE OVER FROM CHICAGO TO CLEAN UP THE MESS YOU MADE--
HEY, WHAT'S THE MATTER? YOU LOOK LIKE YOU JUS' SAW A ***GHOST--***

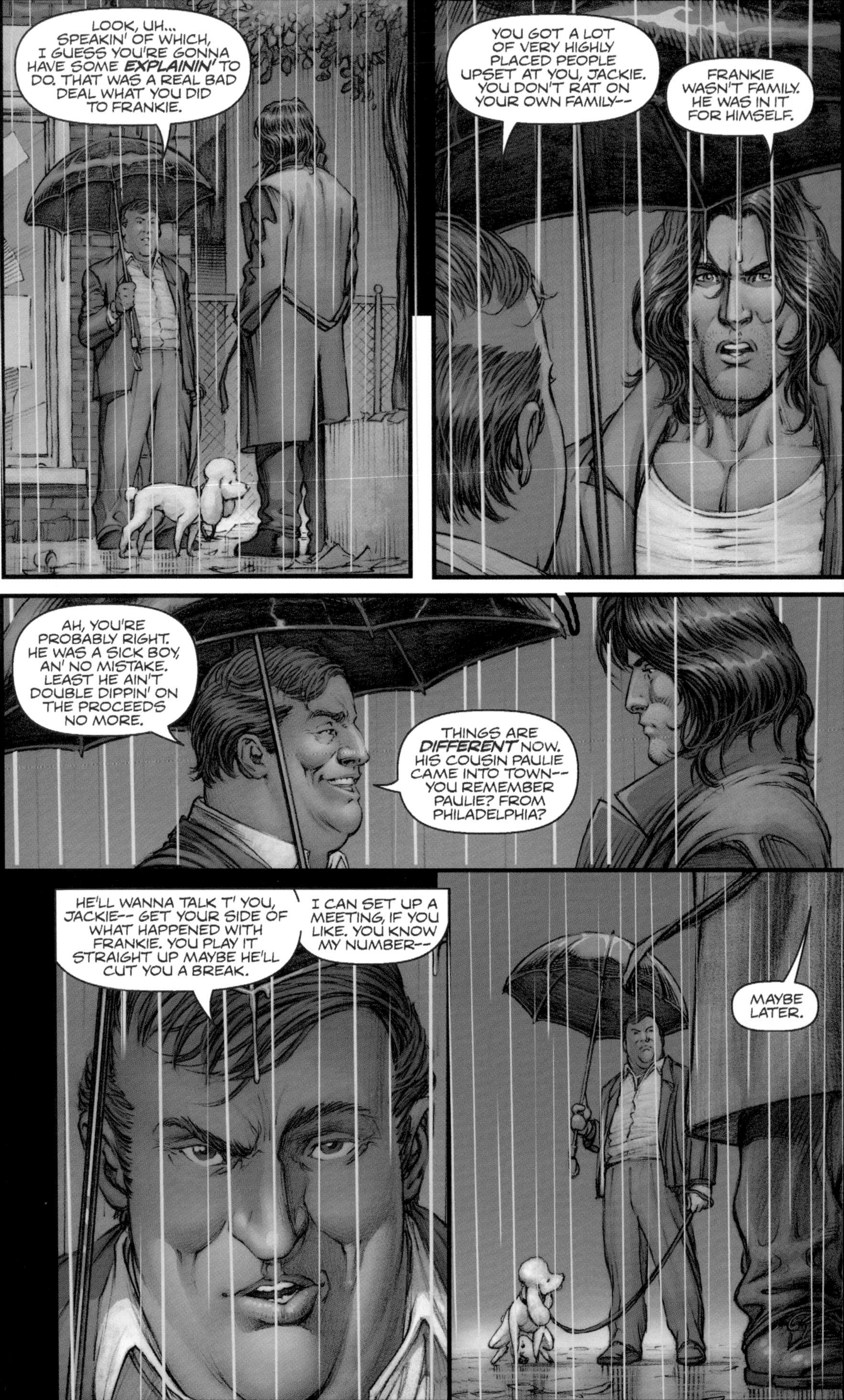
LOOK, UH... SPEAKIN' OF WHICH, I GUESS YOU'RE GONNA HAVE SOME EXPLAININ' TO DO. THAT WAS A REAL BAD DEAL WHAT YOU DID TO FRANKIE.
YOU GOT A LOT OF VERY HIGHLY PLACED PEOPLE UPSET AT YOU, JACKIE. YOU DON'T RAT ON YOUR OWN FAMILY--
FRANKIE WASN'T FAMILY. HE WAS IN IT FOR HIMSELF.
AH, YOU'RE PROBABLY RIGHT. HE WAS A SICK BOY, AN' NO MISTAKE. LEAST HE AIN'T DOUBLE DIPPIN' ON THE PROCEEDS NO MORE.
THINGS ARE DIFFERENT NOW. HIS COUSIN PAULIE CAME INTO TOWN-- YOU REMEMBER PAULIE? FROM PHILADELPHIA?
HE'LL WANNA TALK T' YOU, JACKIE-- GET YOUR SIDE OF WHAT HAPPENED WITH FRANKIE. YOU PLAY IT STRAIGHT UP MAYBE HE'LL CUT YOU A BREAK.
I CAN SET UP A MEETING, IF YOU LIKE. YOU KNOW MY NUMBER--
MAYBE LATER.

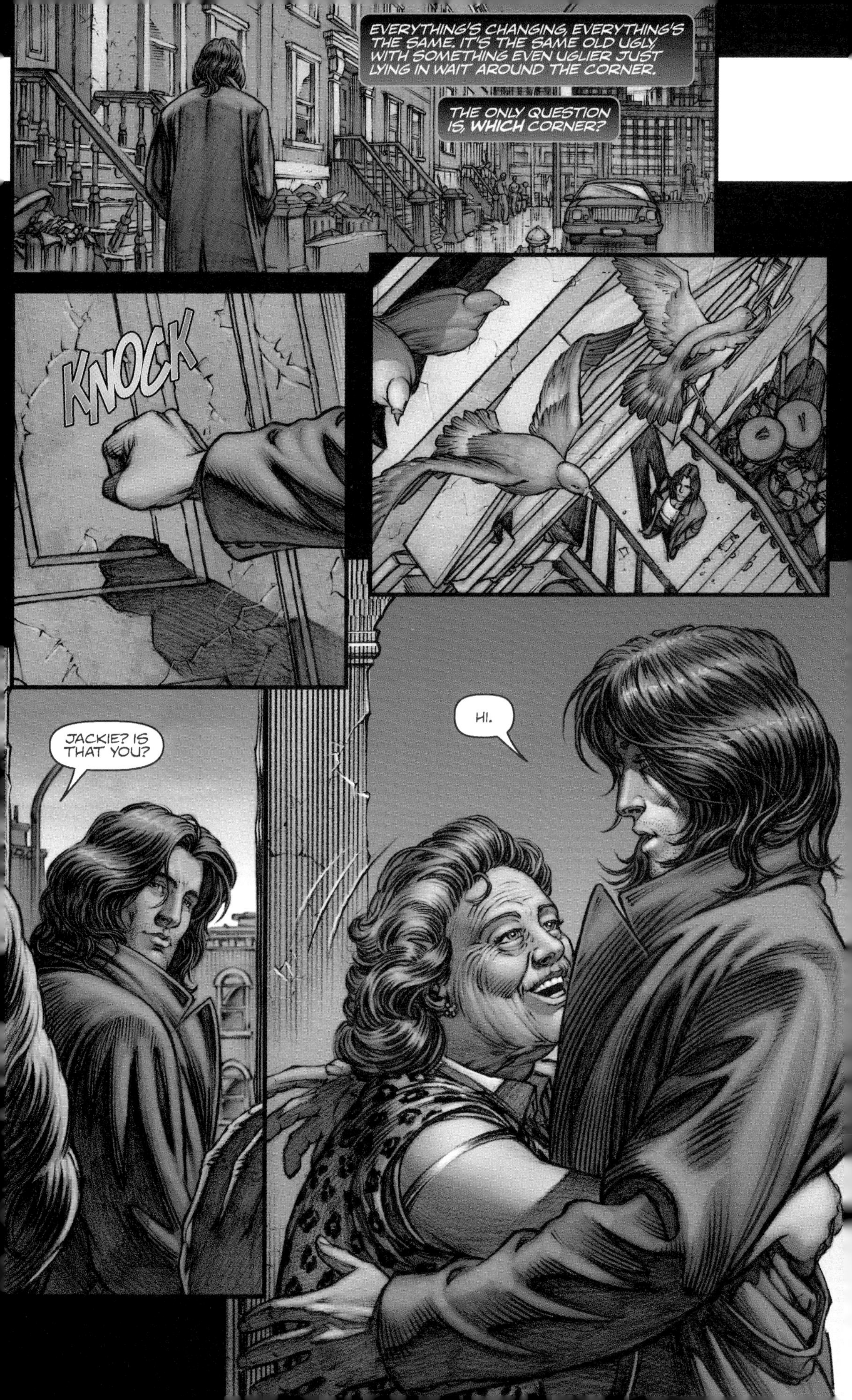
EVERYTHING'S CHANGING, EVERYTHING'S THE SAME. IT'S THE SAME OLD UGLY, WITH SOMETHING EVEN UGLIER JUST LYING IN WAIT AROUND THE CORNER.
THE ONLY QUESTION IS, WHICH CORNER?
KNOCK
JACKIE? IS THAT YOU?
HI.

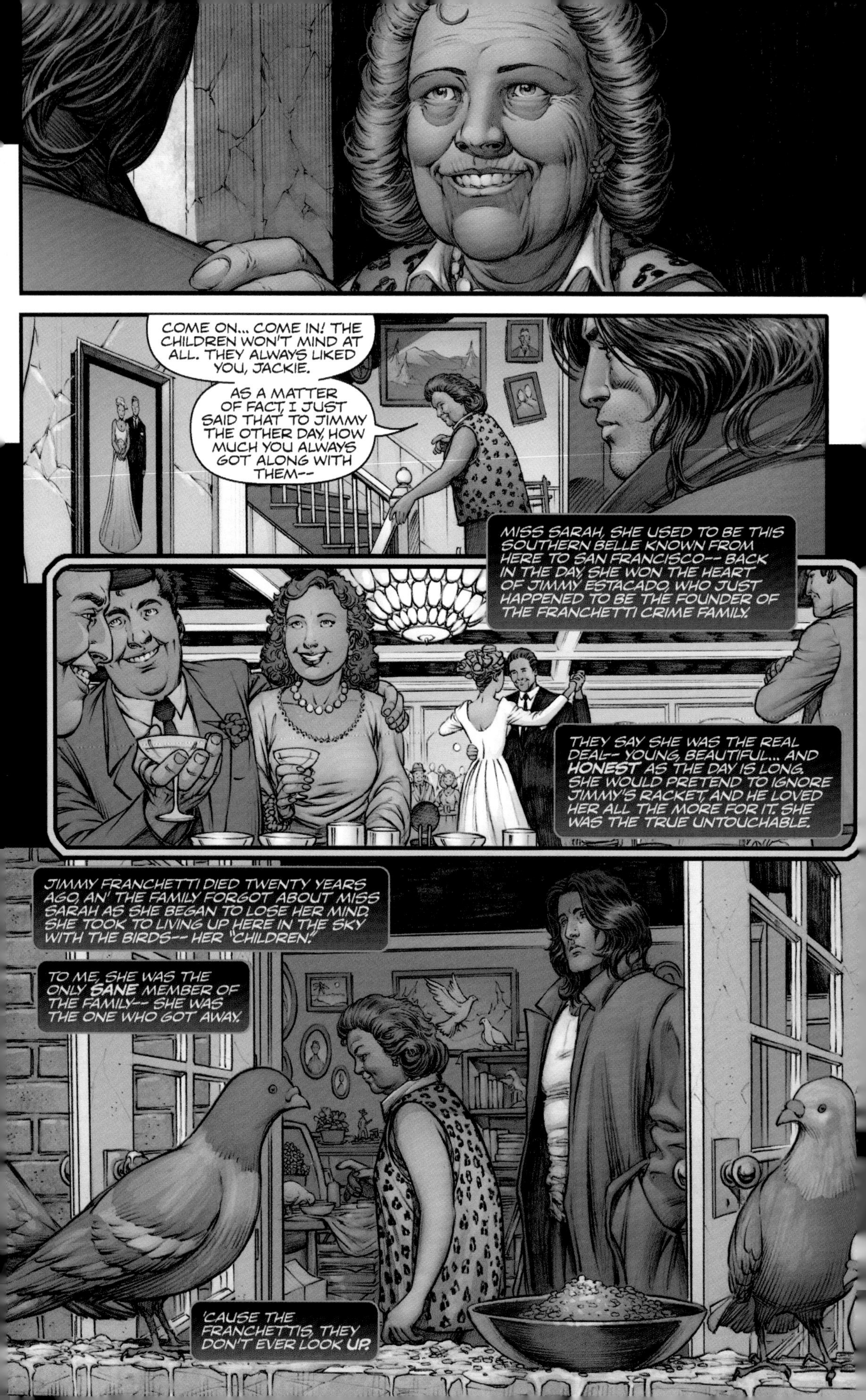
COME ON... COME IN! THE CHILDREN WON'T MIND AT ALL. THEY ALWAYS LIKED YOU, JACKIE.
AS A MATTER OF FACT, I JUST SAID THAT TO JIMMY THE OTHER DAY, HOW MUCH YOU ALWAYS GOT ALONG WITH THEM--
MISS SARAH, SHE USED TO BE THIS SOUTHERN BELLE KNOWN FROM HERE TO SAN FRANCISCO-- BACK IN THE DAY, SHE WON THE HEART OF JIMMY ESTACADO, WHO JUST HAPPENED TO BE THE FOUNDER OF THE FRANCHETTI CRIME FAMILY.
THEY SAY SHE WAS THE REAL DEAL-- YOUNG, BEAUTIFUL... AND HONEST AS THE DAY IS LONG. SHE WOULD PRETEND TO IGNORE JIMMY'S RACKET, AND HE LOVED HER ALL THE MORE FOR IT. SHE WAS THE TRUE UNTOUCHABLE.
JIMMY FRANCHETTI DIED TWENTY YEARS AGO, AN' THE FAMILY FORGOT ABOUT MISS SARAH AS SHE BEGAN TO LOSE HER MIND. SHE TOOK TO LIVING UP HERE IN THE SKY WITH THE BIRDS-- HER "CHILDREN."
TO ME, SHE WAS THE ONLY SANE MEMBER OF THE FAMILY-- SHE WAS THE ONE WHO GOT AWAY.
'CAUSE THE FRANCHETTIS, THEY DON'T EVER LOOK UP.

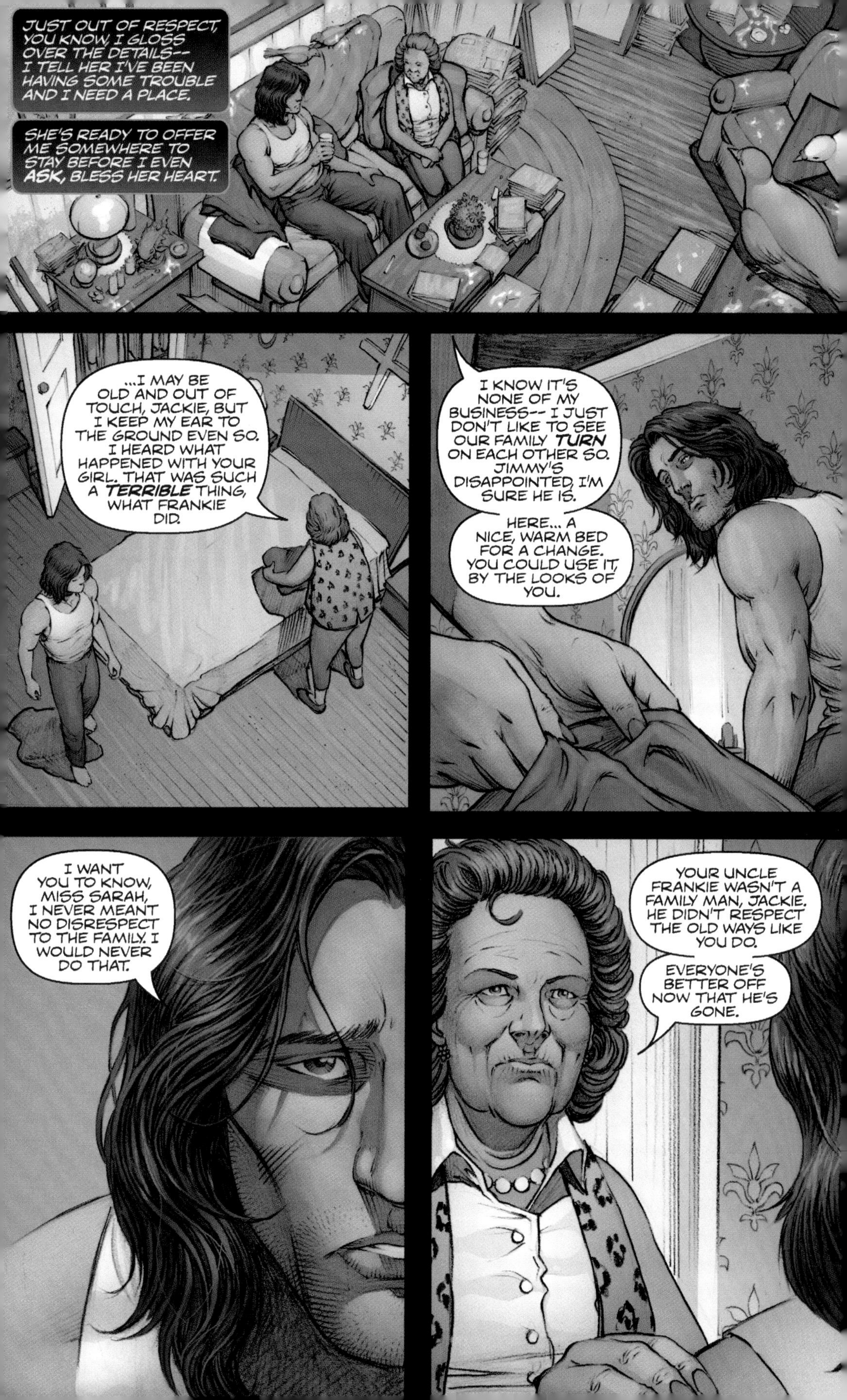
JUST OUT OF RESPECT, YOU KNOW, I GLOSS OVER THE DETAILS-- I TELL HER I'VE BEEN HAVING SOME TROUBLE AND I NEED A PLACE.
SHE'S READY TO OFFER ME SOMEWHERE TO STAY BEFORE I EVEN ASK, BLESS HER HEART.
...I MAY BE OLD AND OUT OF TOUCH, JACKIE, BUT I KEEP MY EAR TO THE GROUND EVEN SO. I HEARD WHAT HAPPENED WITH YOUR GIRL. THAT WAS SUCH A TERRIBLE THING, WHAT FRANKIE DID.
I KNOW IT'S NONE OF MY BUSINESS-- I JUST DON'T LIKE TO SEE OUR FAMILY TURN ON EACH OTHER SO. JIMMY'S DISAPPOINTED, I'M SURE HE IS.
HERE... A NICE, WARM BED FOR A CHANGE. YOU COULD USE IT, BY THE LOOKS OF YOU.
I WANT YOU TO KNOW, MISS SARAH, I NEVER MEANT NO DISRESPECT TO THE FAMILY. I WOULD NEVER DO THAT.
YOUR UNCLE FRANKIE WASN'T A FAMILY MAN, JACKIE. HE DIDN'T RESPECT THE OLD WAYS LIKE YOU DO.
EVERYONE'S BETTER OFF NOW THAT HE'S GONE.

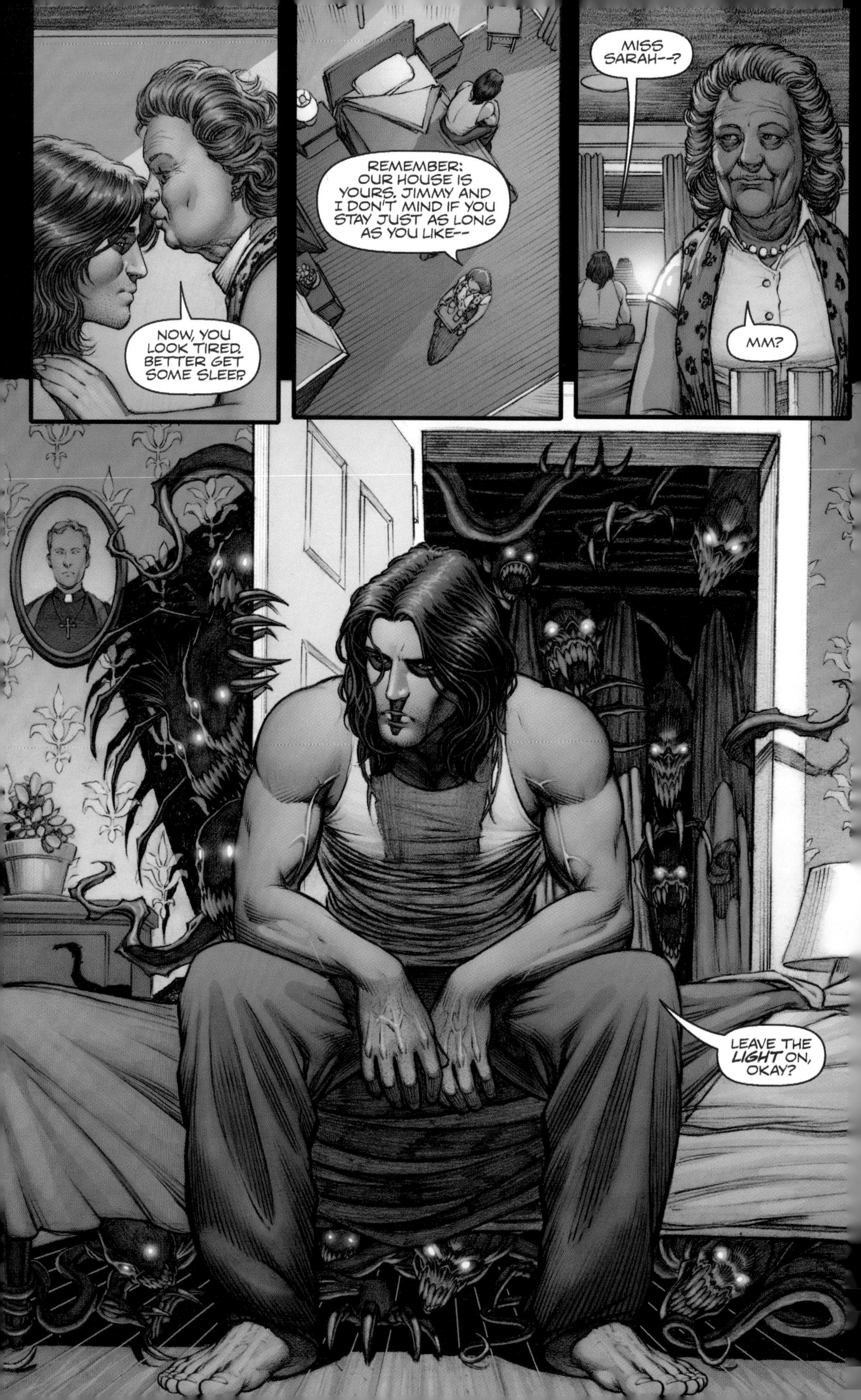
NOW, YOU LOOK TIRED. BETTER GET SOME SLEEP.
REMEMBER: OUR HOUSE IS YOURS. JIMMY AND I DON'T MIND IF YOU STAY JUST AS LONG AS YOU LIKE--
MISS SARAH--?
MM?
LEAVE THE LIGHT ON, OKAY?

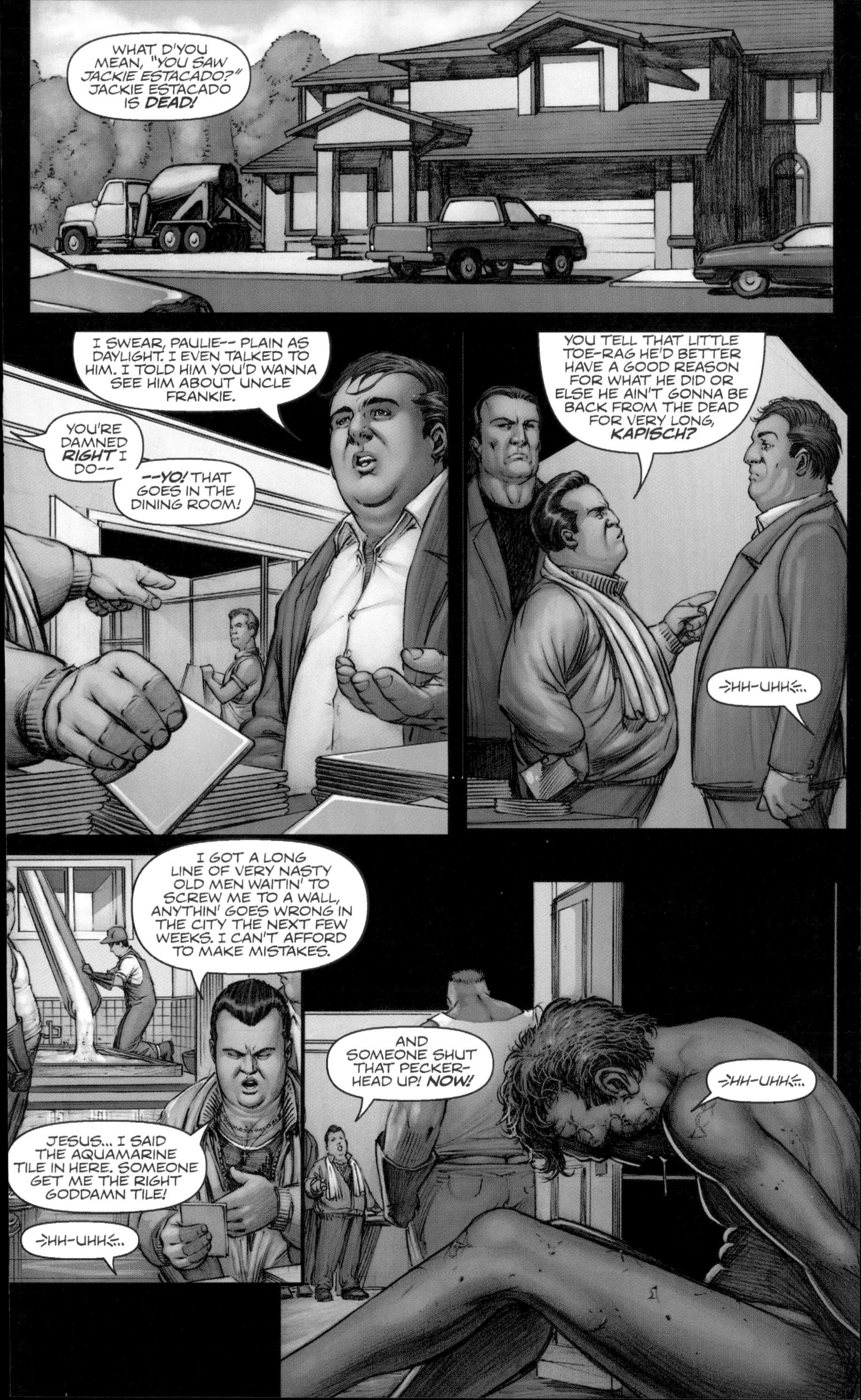
WHAT D'YOU MEAN, "YOU SAW JACKIE ESTACADO?" JACKIE ESTACADO IS DEAD!
I SWEAR, PAULIE-- PLAIN AS DAYLIGHT. I EVEN TALKED TO HIM. I TOLD HIM YOU'D WANNA SEE HIM ABOUT UNCLE FRANKIE.
YOU'RE DAMNED RIGHT I DO--
--YO! THAT GOES IN THE DINING ROOM!
YOU TELL THAT LITTLE TOE-RAG HE'D BETTER HAVE A GOOD REASON FOR WHAT HE DID OR ELSE HE AIN'T GONNA BE BACK FROM THE DEAD FOR VERY LONG, KAPISCH?
HH-UHH...
I GOT A LONG LINE OF VERY NASTY OLD MEN WAITIN' TO SCREW ME TO A WALL, ANYTHIN' GOES WRONG IN THE CITY THE NEXT FEW WEEKS. I CAN'T AFFORD TO MAKE MISTAKES.
JESUS... I SAID THE AQUAMARINE TILE IN HERE. SOMEONE GET ME THE RIGHT GODDAMN TILE!
HH-UHH...
AND SOMEONE SHUT THAT PECKER-HEAD UP! NOW!
HH-UHH...

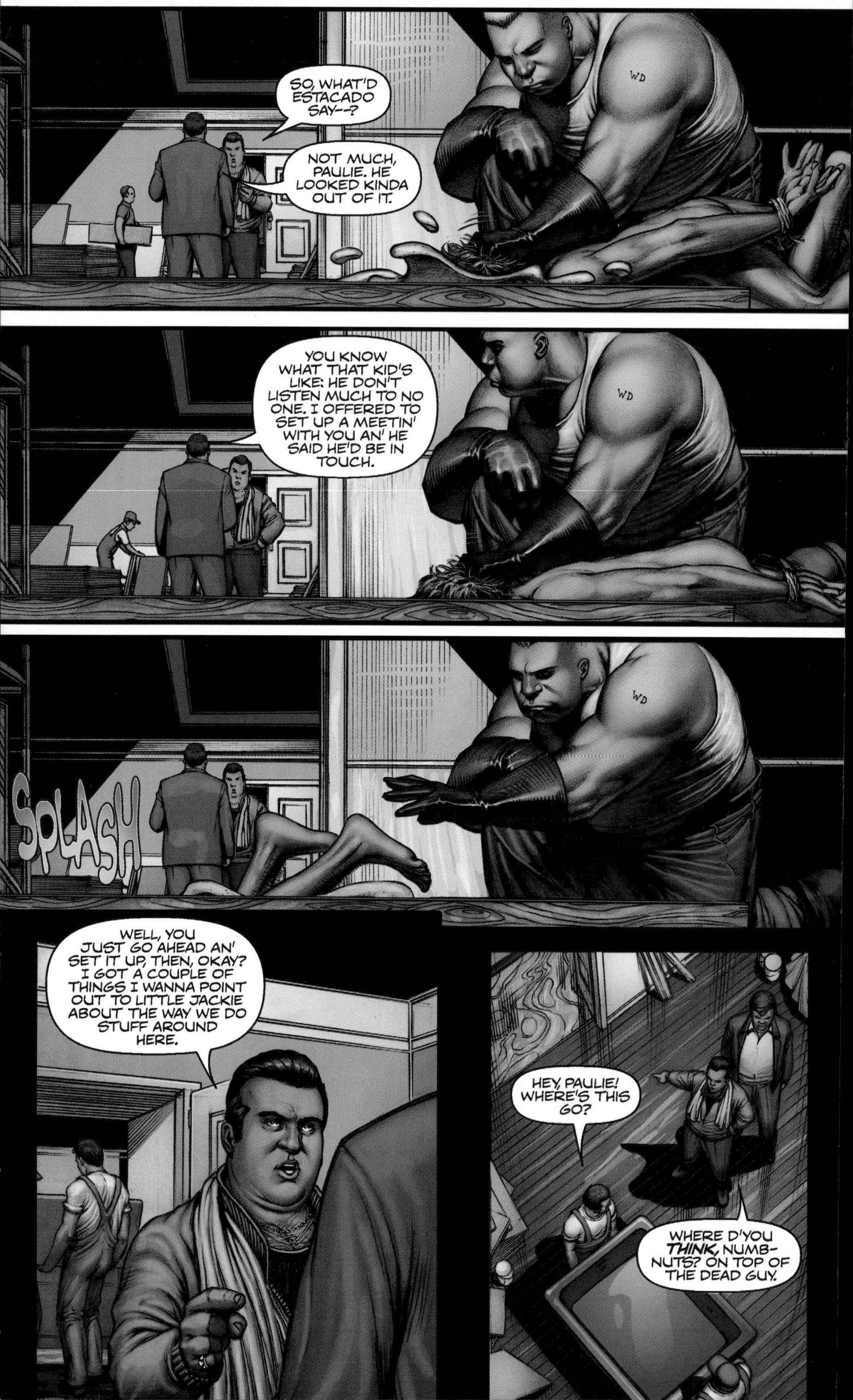
SO, WHAT'D ESTACADO SAY--?
WD
NOT MUCH, PAULIE. HE LOOKED KINDA OUT OF IT.
YOU KNOW WHAT THAT KID'S LIKE: HE DON'T LISTEN MUCH TO NO ONE. I OFFERED TO SET UP A MEETIN' WITH YOU AN' HE SAID HE'D BE IN TOUCH.
WD
SPLASH
WD
WELL, YOU JUST GO AHEAD AN' SET IT UP, THEN, OKAY? I GOT A COUPLE OF THINGS I WANNA POINT OUT TO LITTLE JACKIE ABOUT THE WAY WE DO STUFF AROUND HERE.
HEY, PAULIE! WHERE'S THIS GO?
WHERE D'YOU *THINK,* NUMB-NUTS? ON TOP OF THE DEAD GUY.

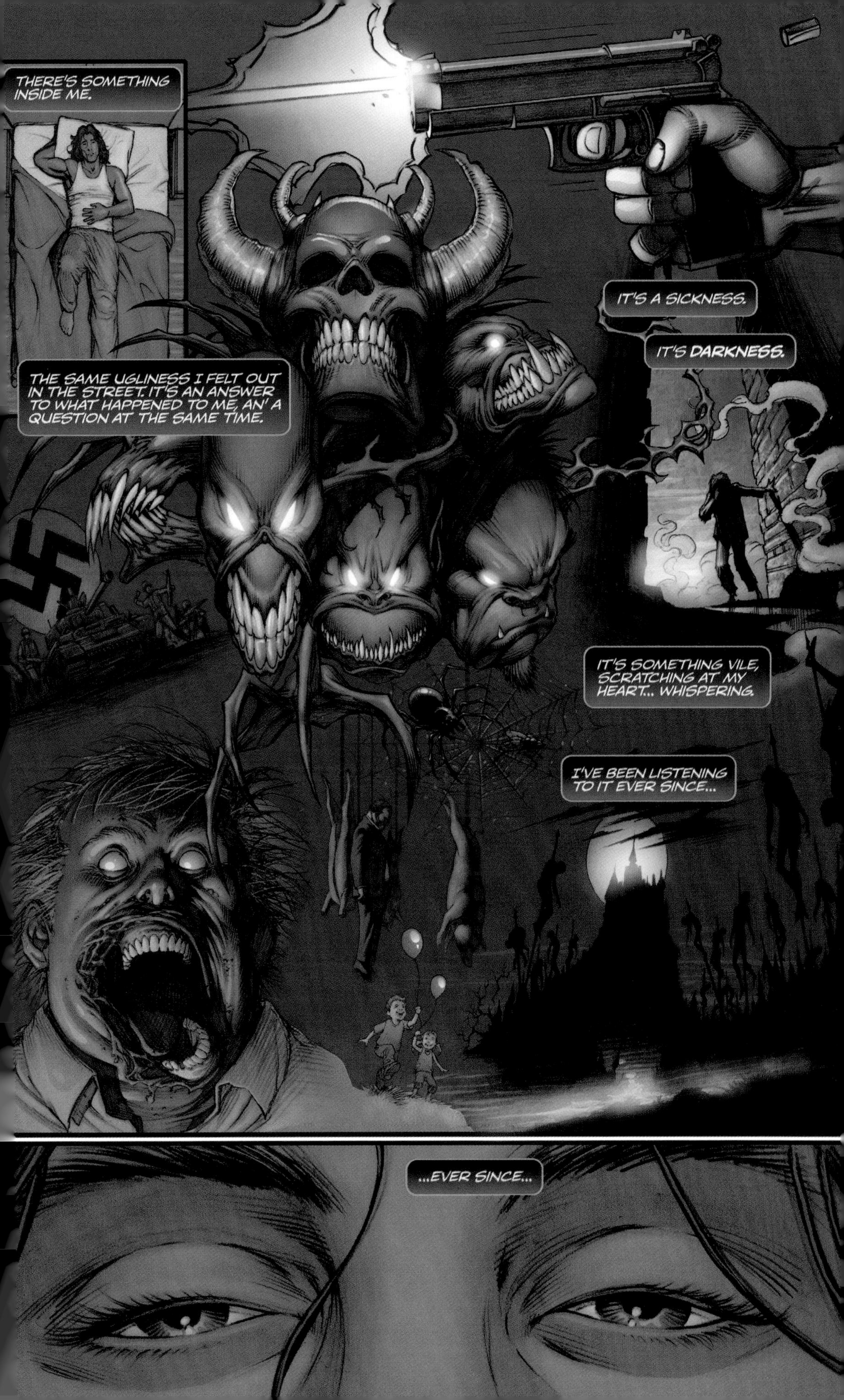
THERE'S SOMETHING INSIDE ME.
THE SAME UGLINESS I FELT OUT IN THE STREET. IT'S AN ANSWER TO WHAT HAPPENED TO ME, AN' A QUESTION AT THE SAME TIME.
IT'S A SICKNESS.
IT'S DARKNESS.
IT'S SOMETHING VILE, SCRATCHING AT MY HEART... WHISPERING.
I'VE BEEN LISTENING TO IT EVER SINCE...
...EVER SINCE...

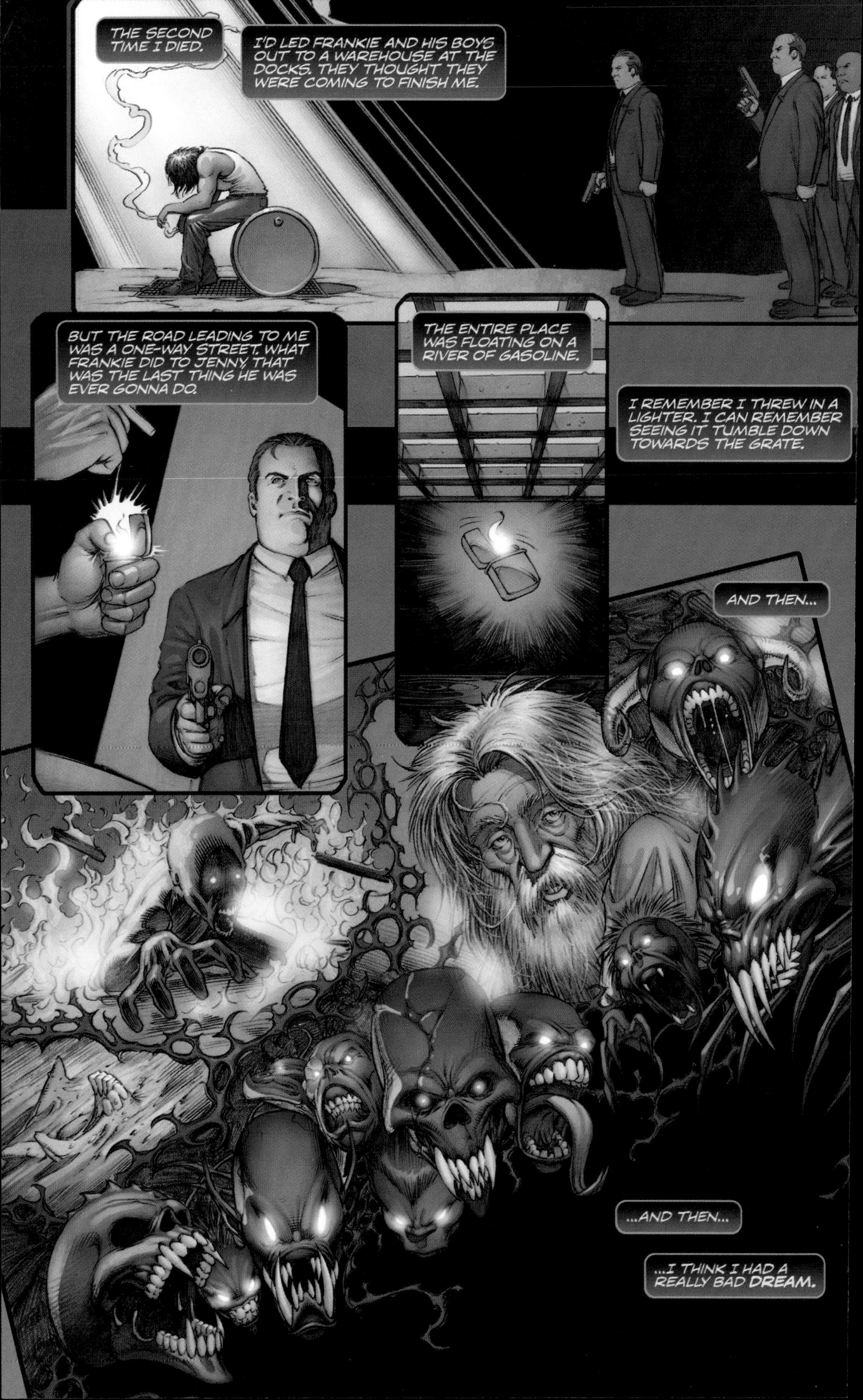

THE SECOND TIME I DIED.
I'D LED FRANKIE AND HIS BOYS OUT TO A WAREHOUSE AT THE DOCKS. THEY THOUGHT THEY WERE COMING TO FINISH ME.
BUT THE ROAD LEADING TO ME WAS A ONE-WAY STREET. WHAT FRANKIE DID TO JENNY, THAT WAS THE LAST THING HE WAS EVER GONNA DO.
THE ENTIRE PLACE WAS FLOATING ON A RIVER OF GASOLINE.
I REMEMBER I THREW IN A LIGHTER. I CAN REMEMBER SEEING IT TUMBLE DOWN TOWARDS THE GRATE.
AND THEN...
...AND THEN...
...I THINK I HAD A REALLY BAD DREAM.

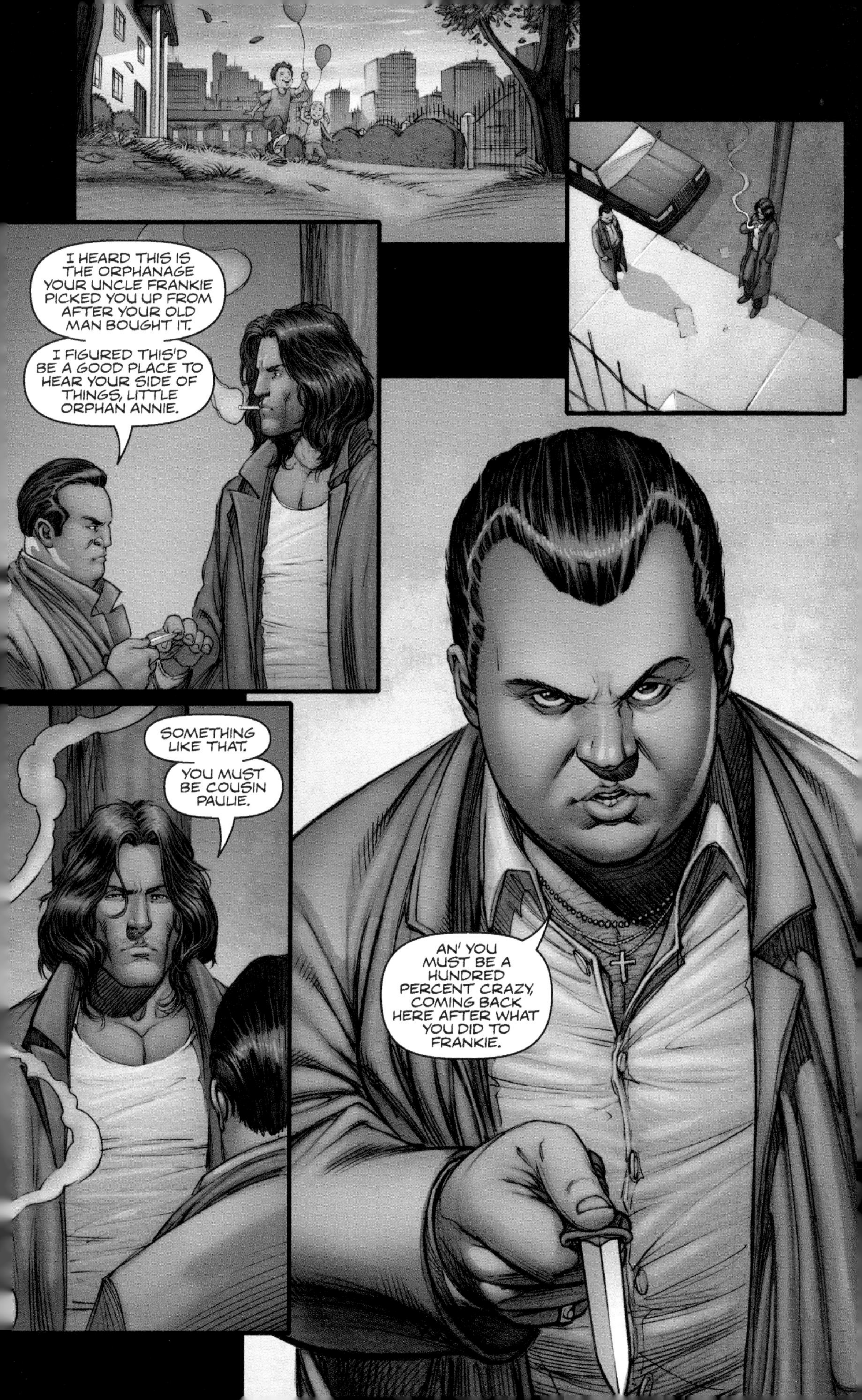
I HEARD THIS IS THE ORPHANAGE YOUR UNCLE FRANKIE PICKED YOU UP FROM AFTER YOUR OLD MAN BOUGHT IT.
I FIGURED THIS'D BE A GOOD PLACE TO HEAR YOUR SIDE OF THINGS, LITTLE ORPHAN ANNIE.
SOMETHING LIKE THAT.
YOU MUST BE COUSIN PAULIE.
AN' YOU MUST BE A HUNDRED PERCENT CRAZY, COMING BACK HERE AFTER WHAT YOU DID TO FRANKIE.

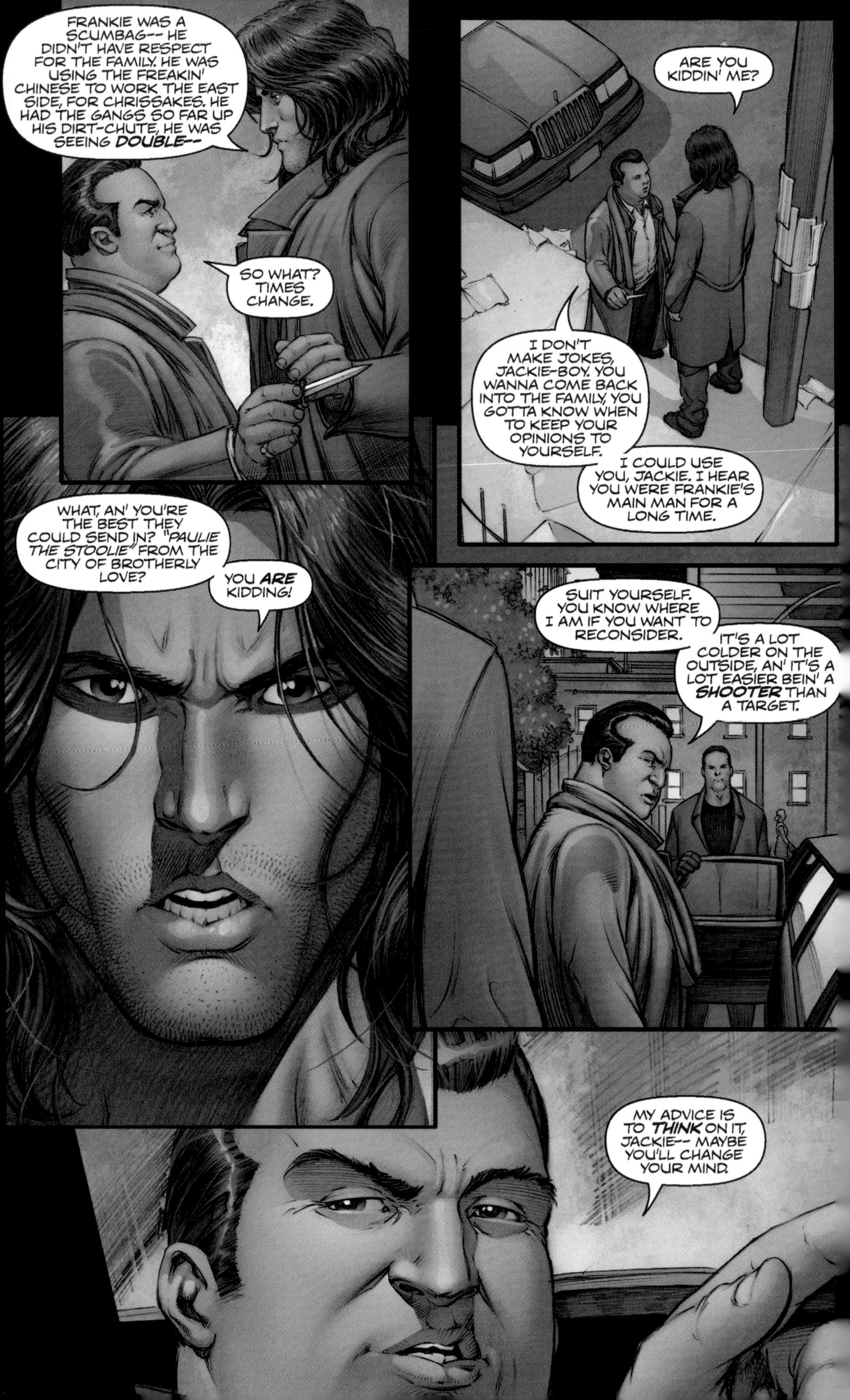
FRANKIE WAS A SCUMBAG-- HE DIDN'T HAVE RESPECT FOR THE FAMILY. HE WAS USING THE FREAKIN' CHINESE TO WORK THE EAST SIDE, FOR CHRISSAKES. HE HAD THE GANGS SO FAR UP HIS DIRT-CHUTE, HE WAS SEEING DOUBLE--
SO WHAT? TIMES CHANGE.
ARE YOU KIDDIN' ME?
I DON'T MAKE JOKES, JACKIE-BOY. YOU WANNA COME BACK INTO THE FAMILY, YOU GOTTA KNOW WHEN TO KEEP YOUR OPINIONS TO YOURSELF.
I COULD USE YOU, JACKIE. I HEAR YOU WERE FRANKIE'S MAIN MAN FOR A LONG TIME.
WHAT, AN' YOU'RE THE BEST THEY COULD SEND IN? "PAULIE THE STOOLIE" FROM THE CITY OF BROTHERLY LOVE?
YOU ARE KIDDING!
SUIT YOURSELF. YOU KNOW WHERE I AM IF YOU WANT TO RECONSIDER.
IT'S A LOT COLDER ON THE OUTSIDE, AN' IT'S A LOT EASIER BEIN' A SHOOTER THAN A TARGET.
MY ADVICE IS TO THINK ON IT, JACKIE-- MAYBE YOU'LL CHANGE YOUR MIND.

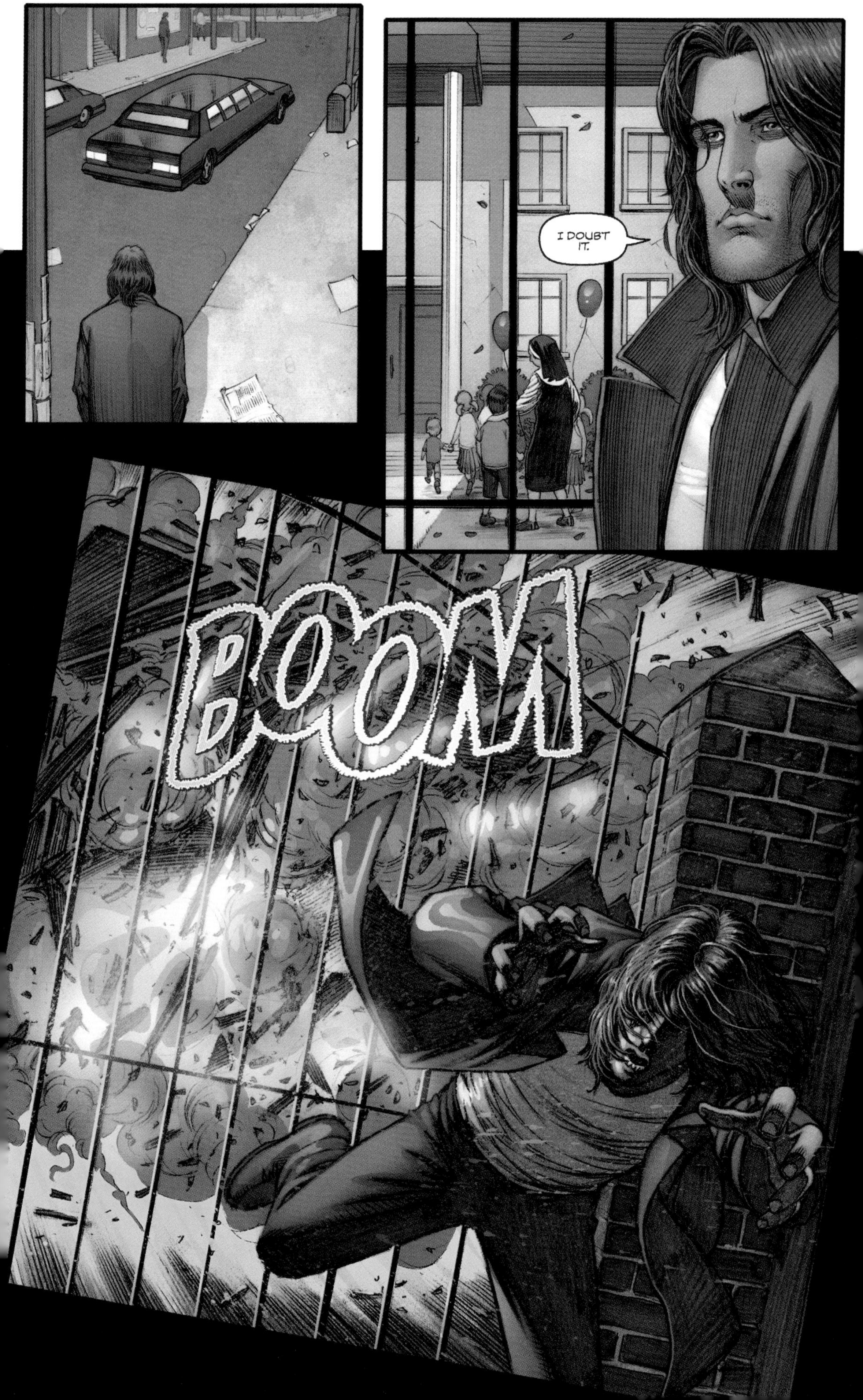
I DOUBT IT.
BOOM

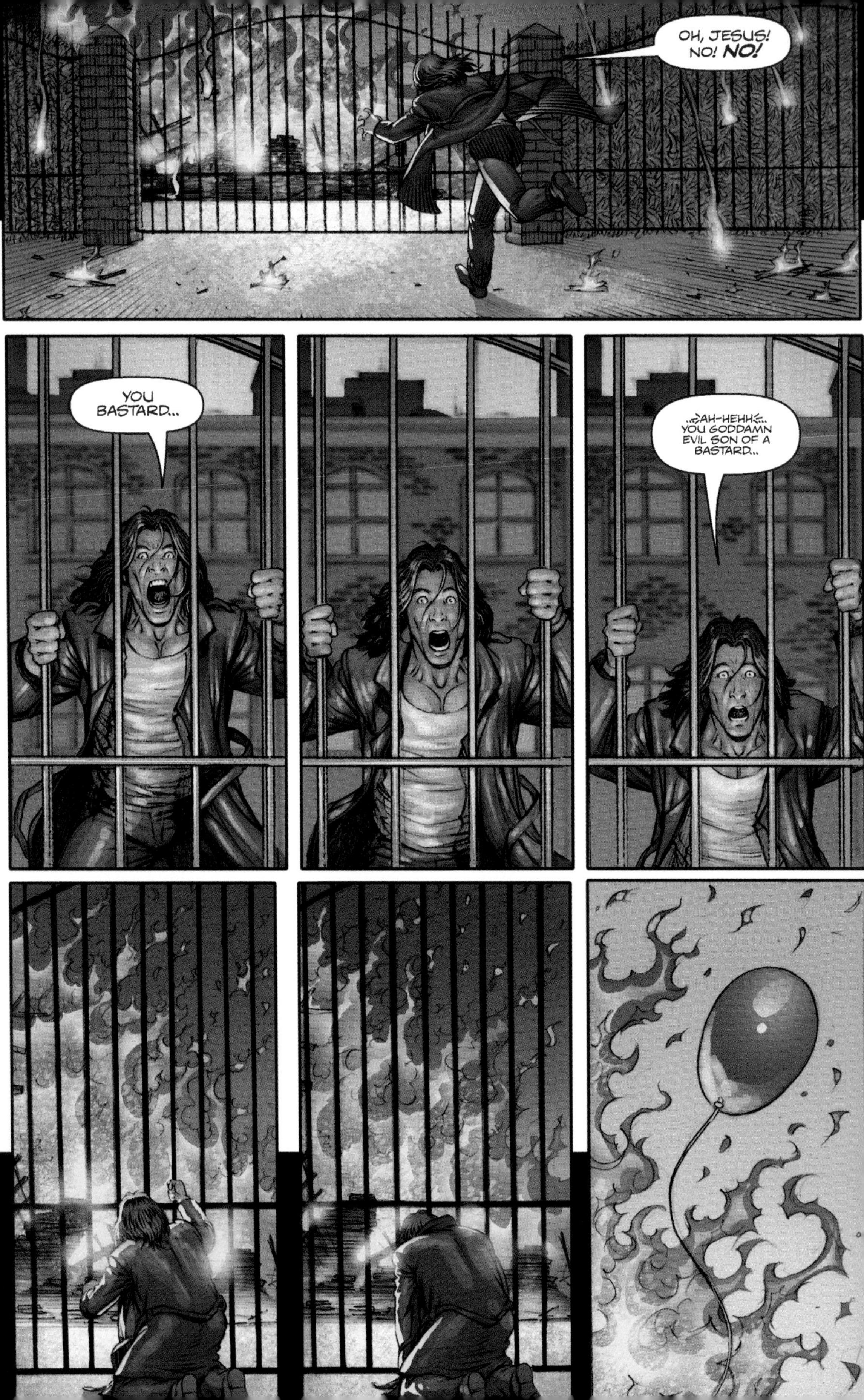
OH, JESUS! NO! **NO!**
YOU BASTARD...
...AH-HEHH... YOU GODDAMN EVIL SON OF A BASTARD...

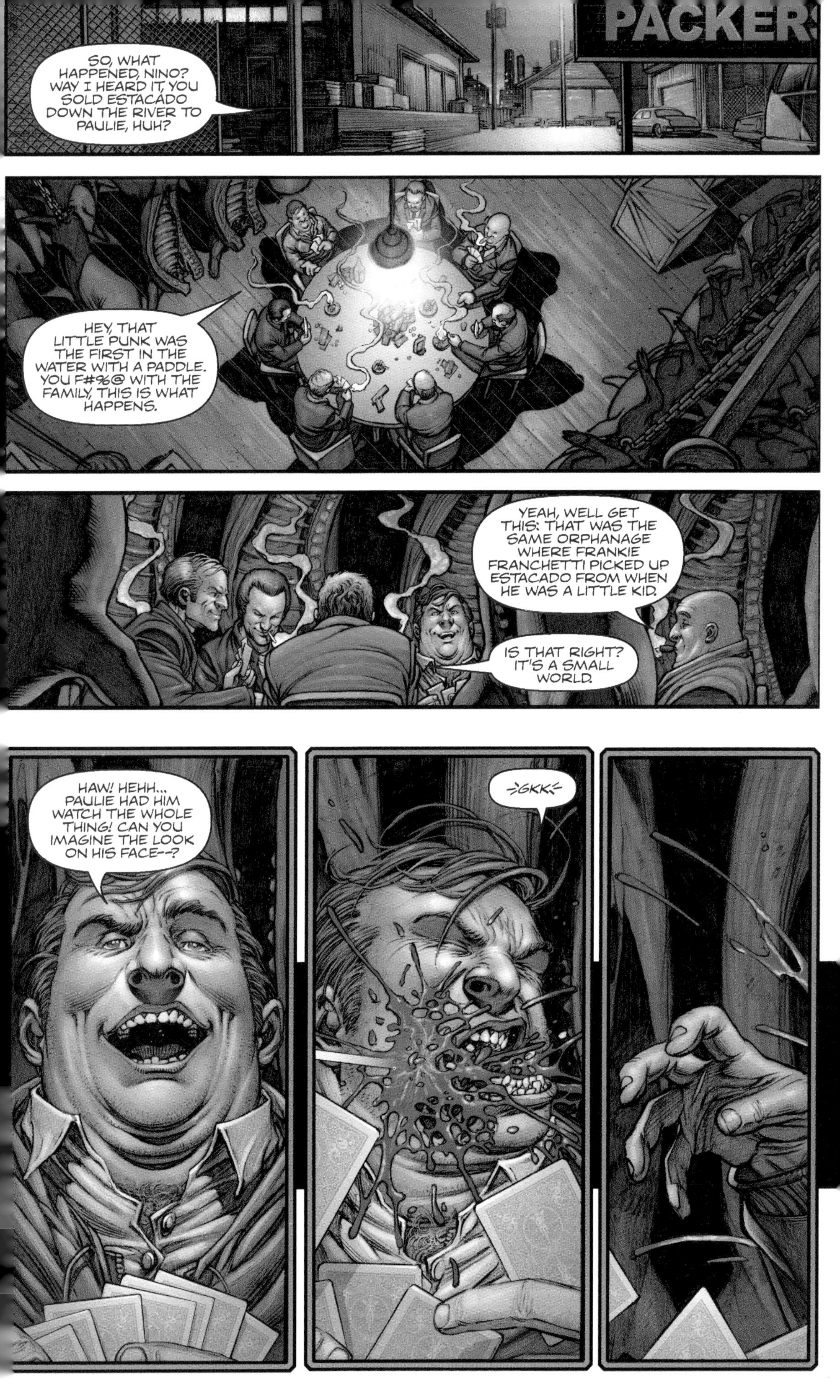
PACKERS
SO, WHAT HAPPENED, NINO? WAY I HEARD IT, YOU SOLD ESTACADO DOWN THE RIVER TO PAULIE, HUH?
HEY, THAT LITTLE PUNK WAS THE FIRST IN THE WATER WITH A PADDLE. YOU F#%@ WITH THE FAMILY, THIS IS WHAT HAPPENS.
YEAH, WELL GET THIS: THAT WAS THE SAME ORPHANAGE WHERE FRANKIE FRANCHETTI PICKED UP ESTACADO FROM WHEN HE WAS A LITTLE KID.
IS THAT RIGHT? IT'S A SMALL WORLD.
HAW! HEHH... PAULIE HAD HIM WATCH THE WHOLE THING! CAN YOU IMAGINE THE LOOK ON HIS FACE--?
GKK

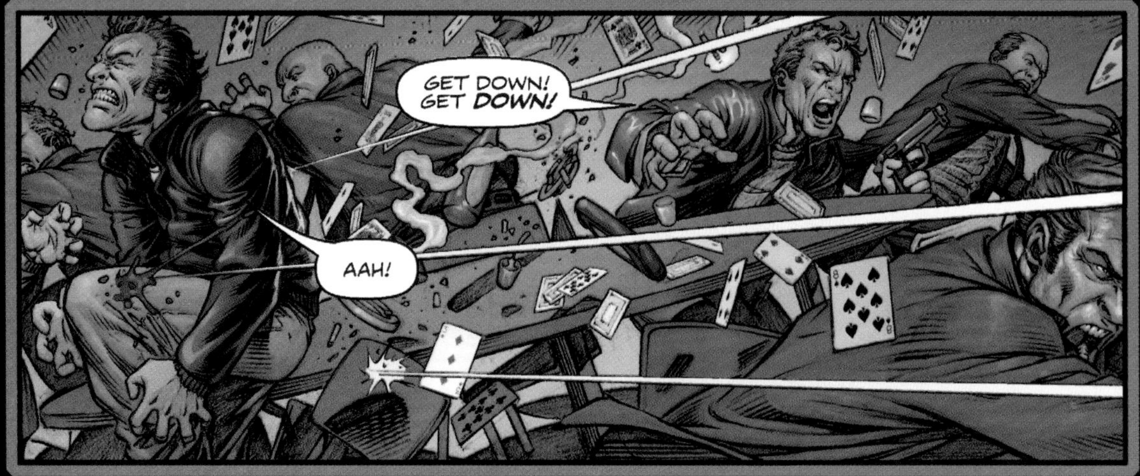
GET DOWN! GET DOWN!
AAH!

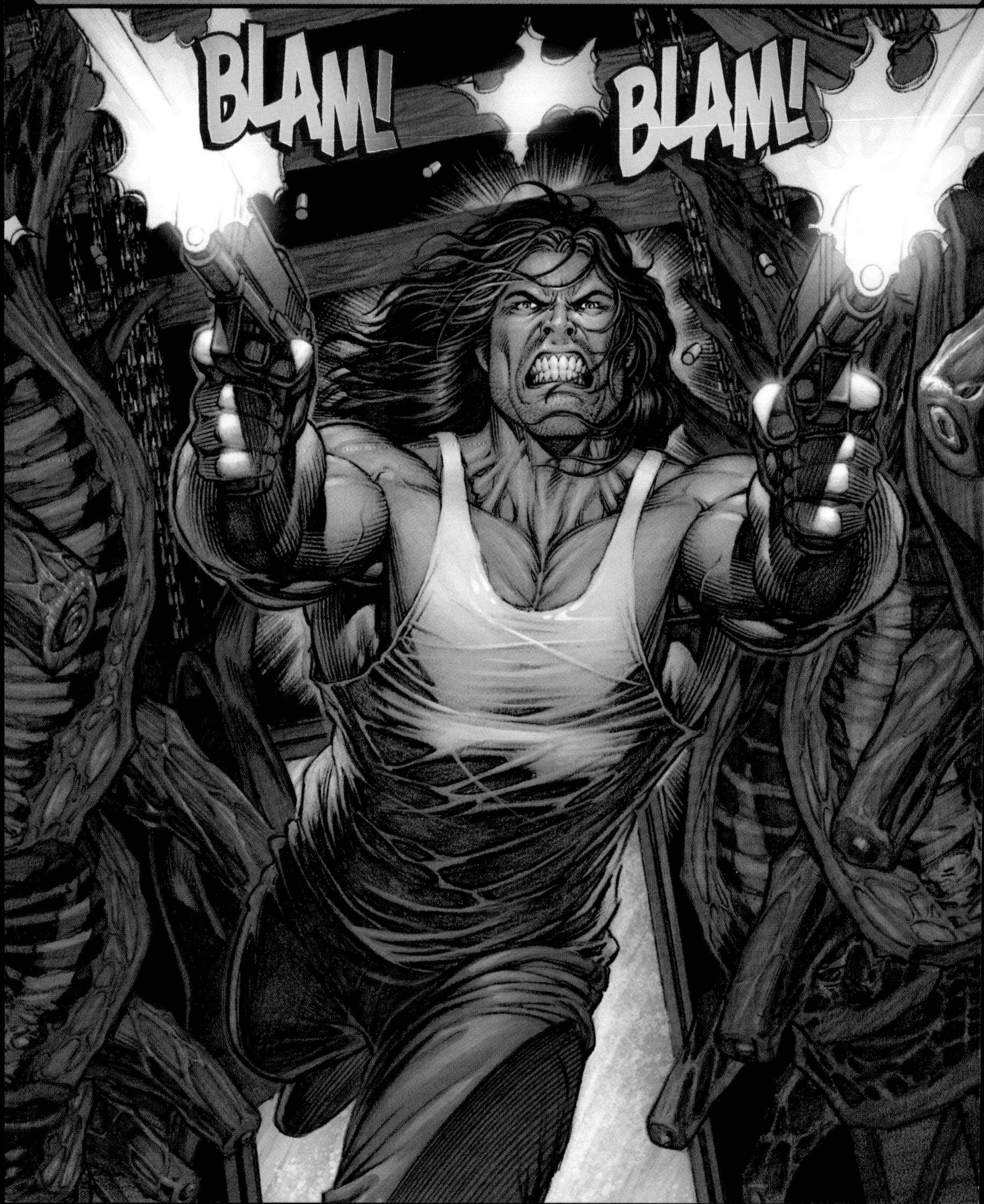
BLAM!
BLAM!

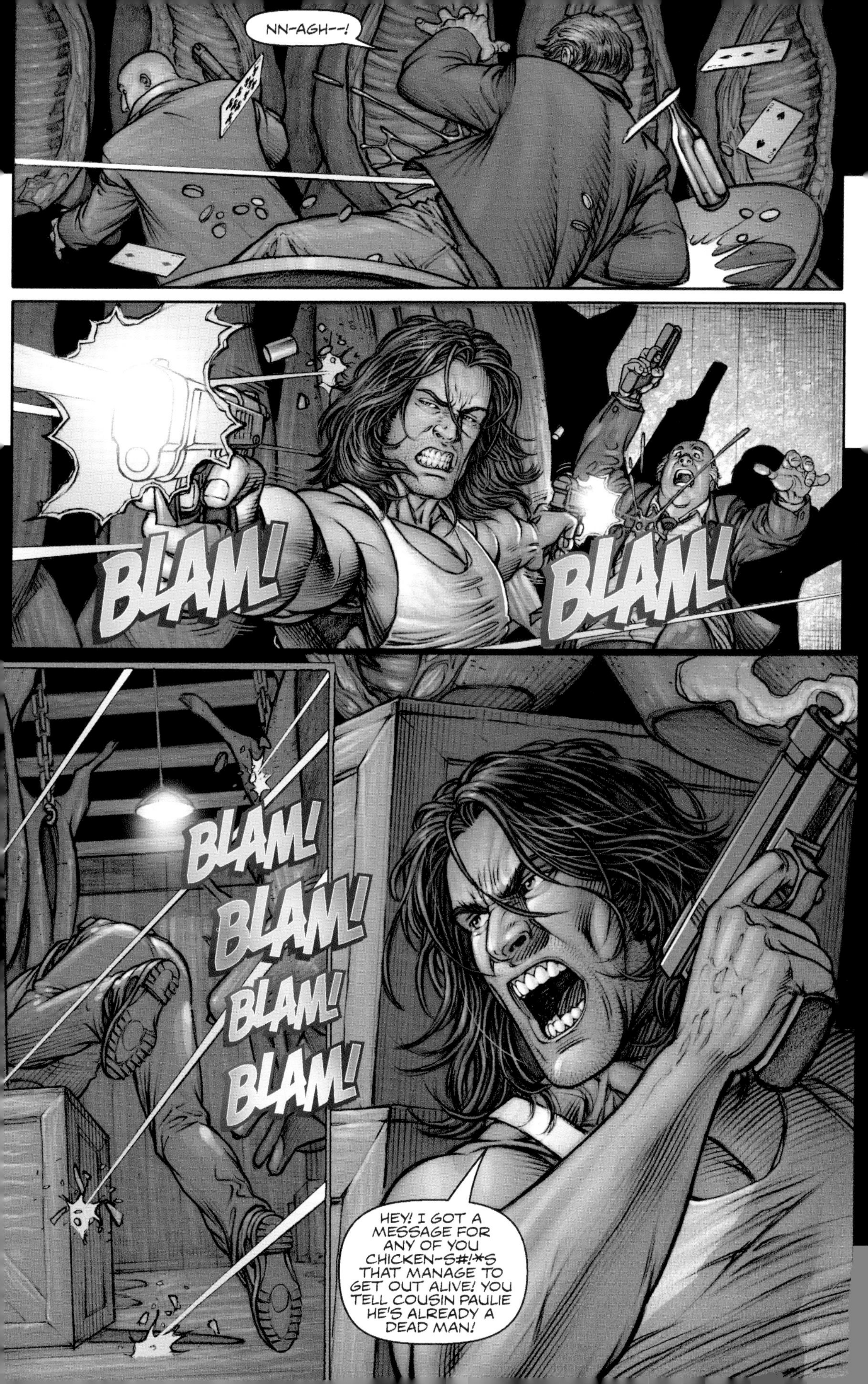
NN-AGH--!
BLAM!
BLAM!
BLAM!
BLAM!
BLAM!
BLAM!
HEY! I GOT A MESSAGE FOR ANY OF YOU CHICKEN-S#!*S THAT MANAGE TO GET OUT ALIVE! YOU TELL COUSIN PAULIE HE'S ALREADY A DEAD MAN!

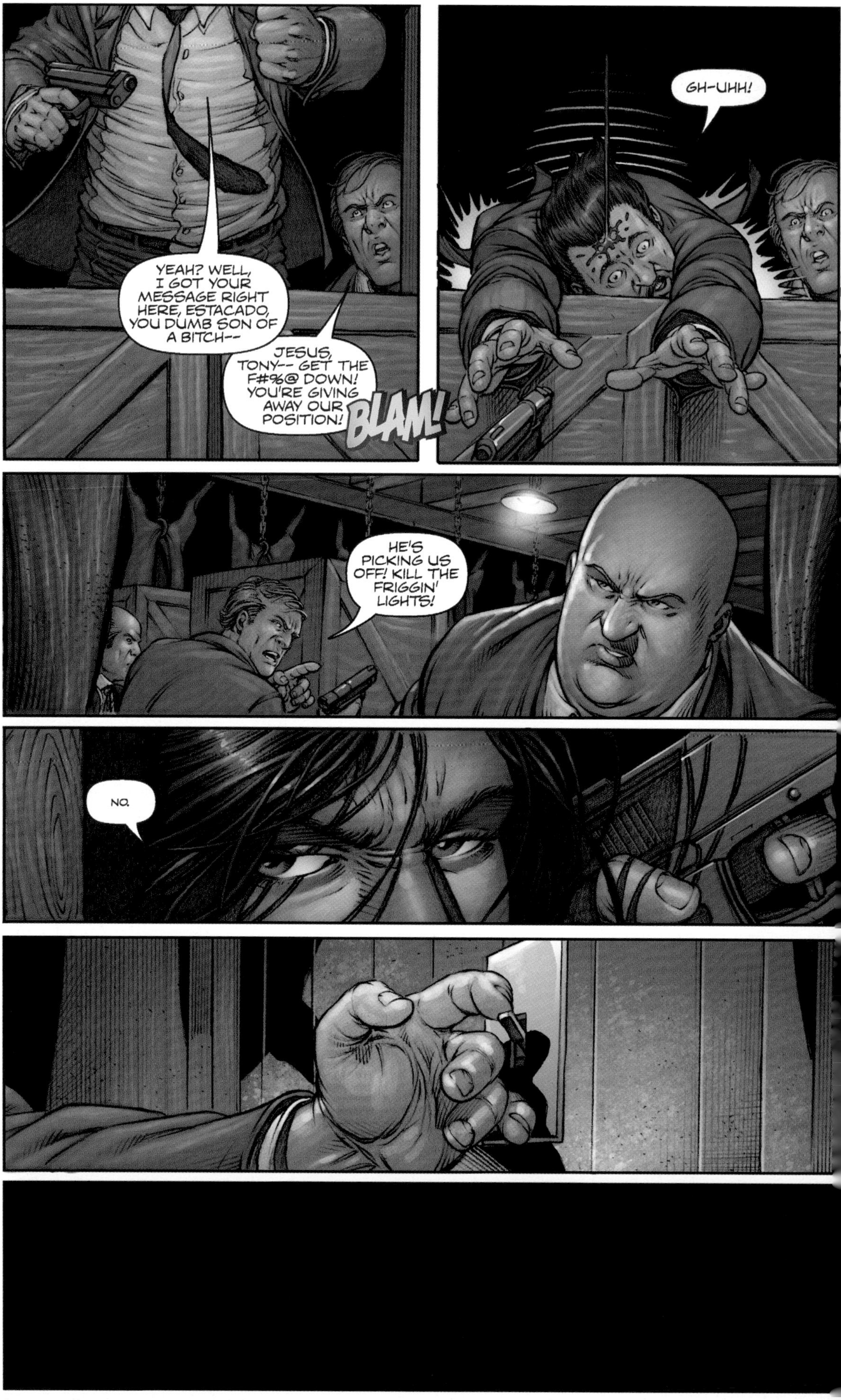
YEAH? WELL, I GOT YOUR MESSAGE RIGHT HERE, ESTACADO, YOU DUMB SON OF A BITCH--
JESUS, TONY-- GET THE F#%@ DOWN! YOU'RE GIVING AWAY OUR POSITION!
BLAM!
GH-UHH!
HE'S PICKING US OFF! KILL THE FRIGGIN' LIGHTS!
NO.

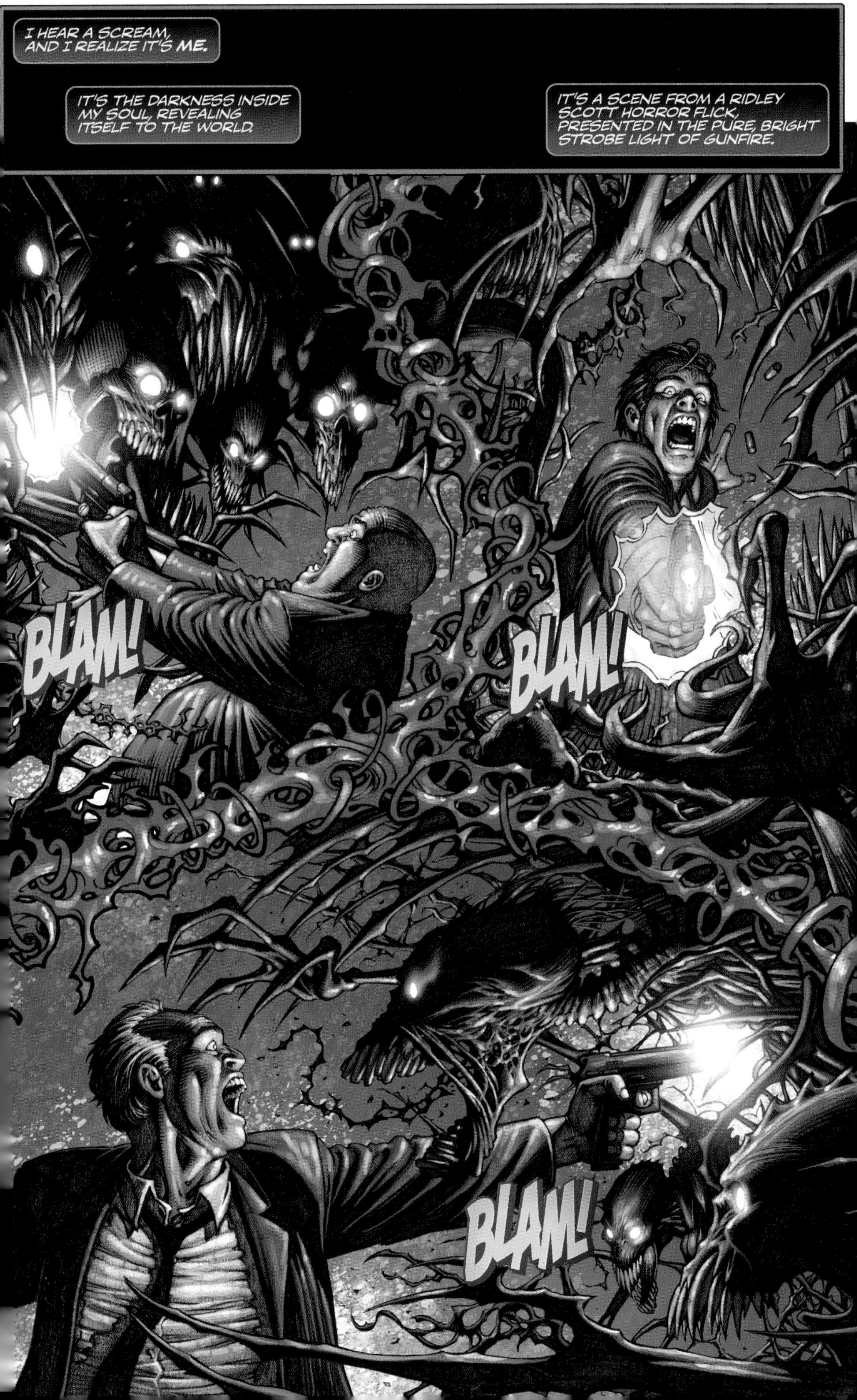
I HEAR A SCREAM, AND I REALIZE IT'S ME.
IT'S THE DARKNESS INSIDE MY SOUL, REVEALING ITSELF TO THE WORLD.
IT'S A SCENE FROM A RIDLEY SCOTT HORROR FLICK, PRESENTED IN THE PURE, BRIGHT STROBE LIGHT OF GUNFIRE.
BLAM!
BLAM!
BLAM!

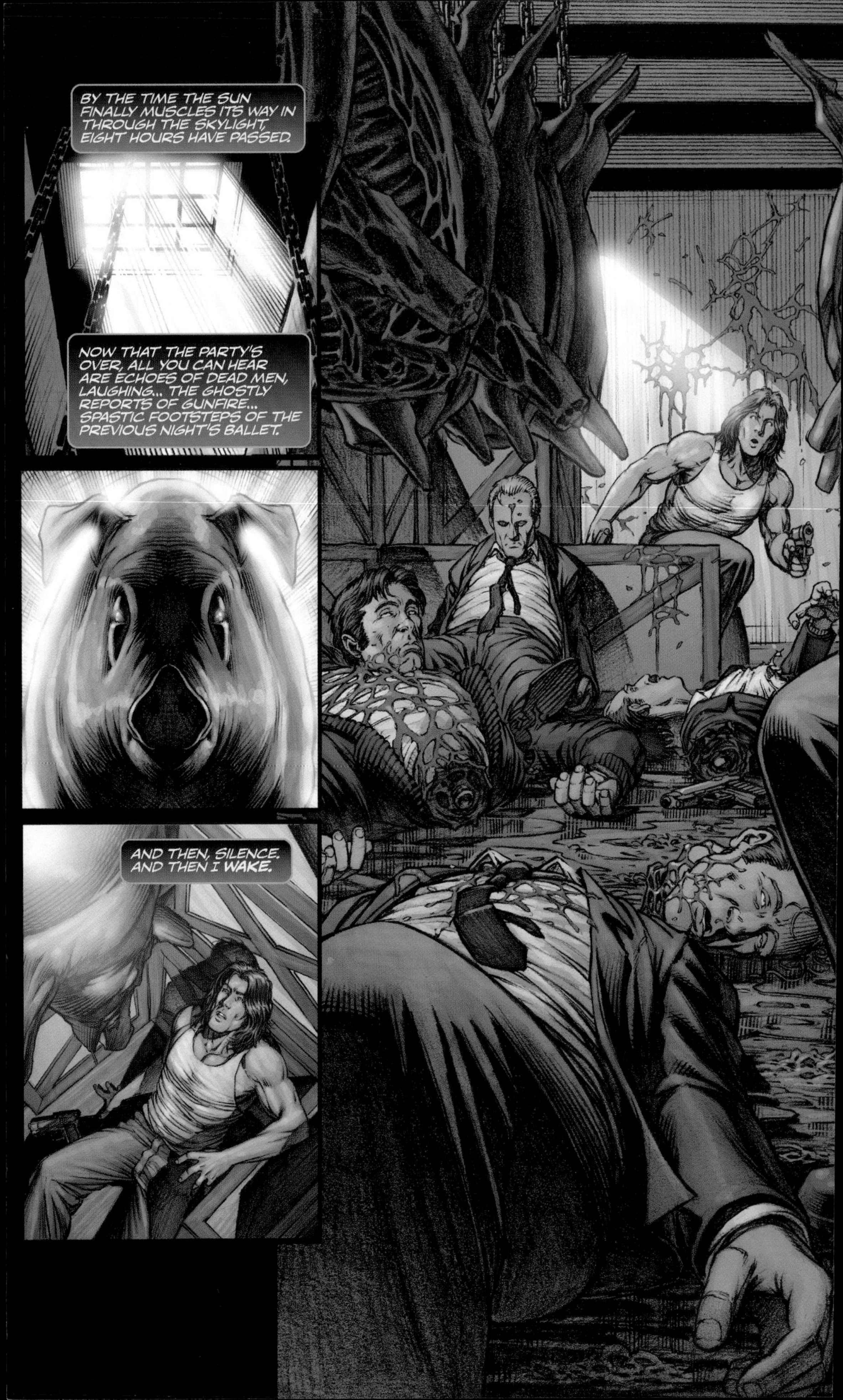
BY THE TIME THE SUN FINALLY MUSCLES ITS WAY IN THROUGH THE SKYLIGHT, EIGHT HOURS HAVE PASSED.
NOW THAT THE PARTY'S OVER, ALL YOU CAN HEAR ARE ECHOES OF DEAD MEN, LAUGHING... THE GHOSTLY REPORTS OF GUNFIRE... SPASTIC FOOTSTEPS OF THE PREVIOUS NIGHT'S BALLET.
AND THEN, SILENCE. AND THEN I WAKE.

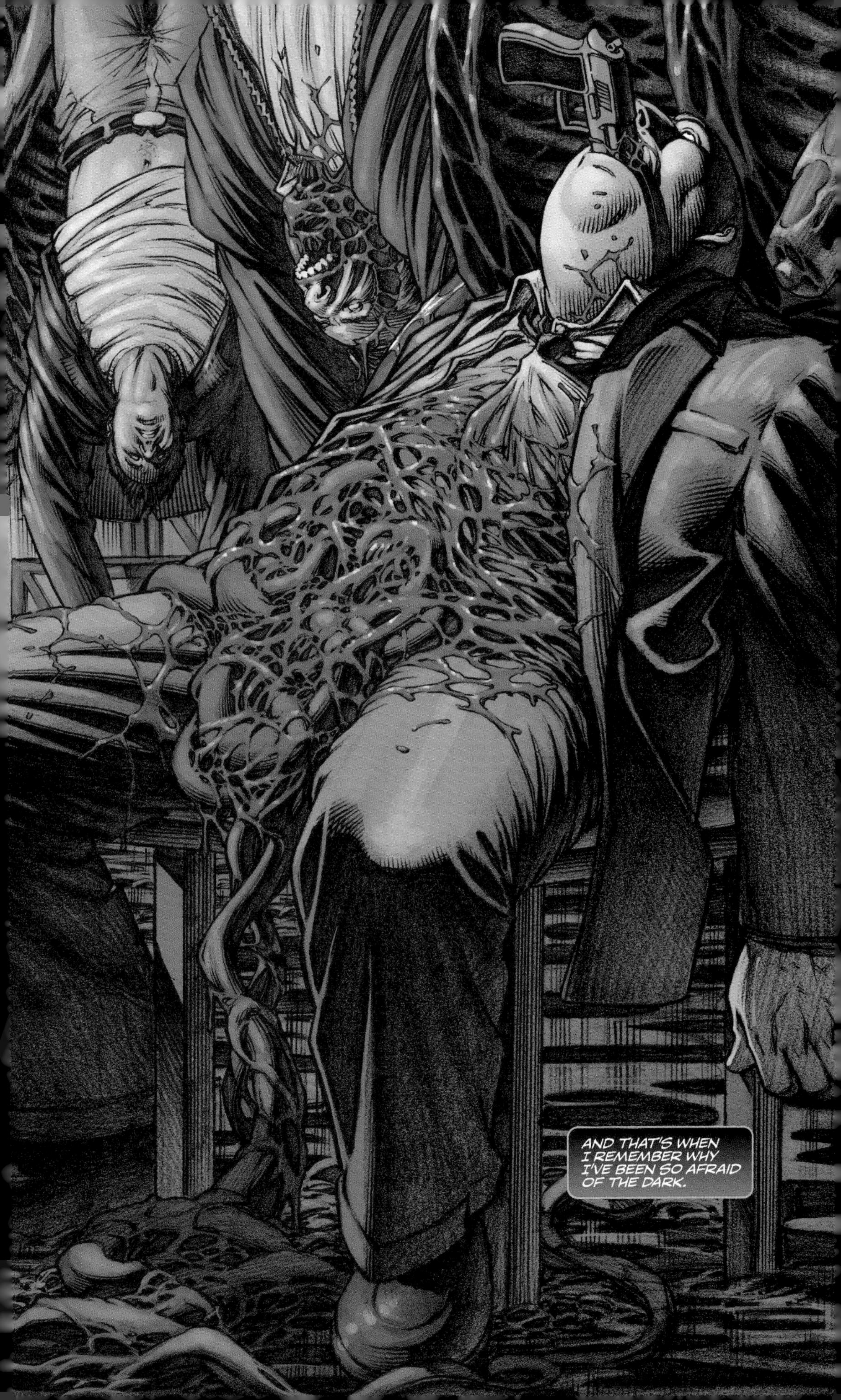
AND THAT'S WHEN I REMEMBER WHY I'VE BEEN SO AFRAID OF THE DARK.

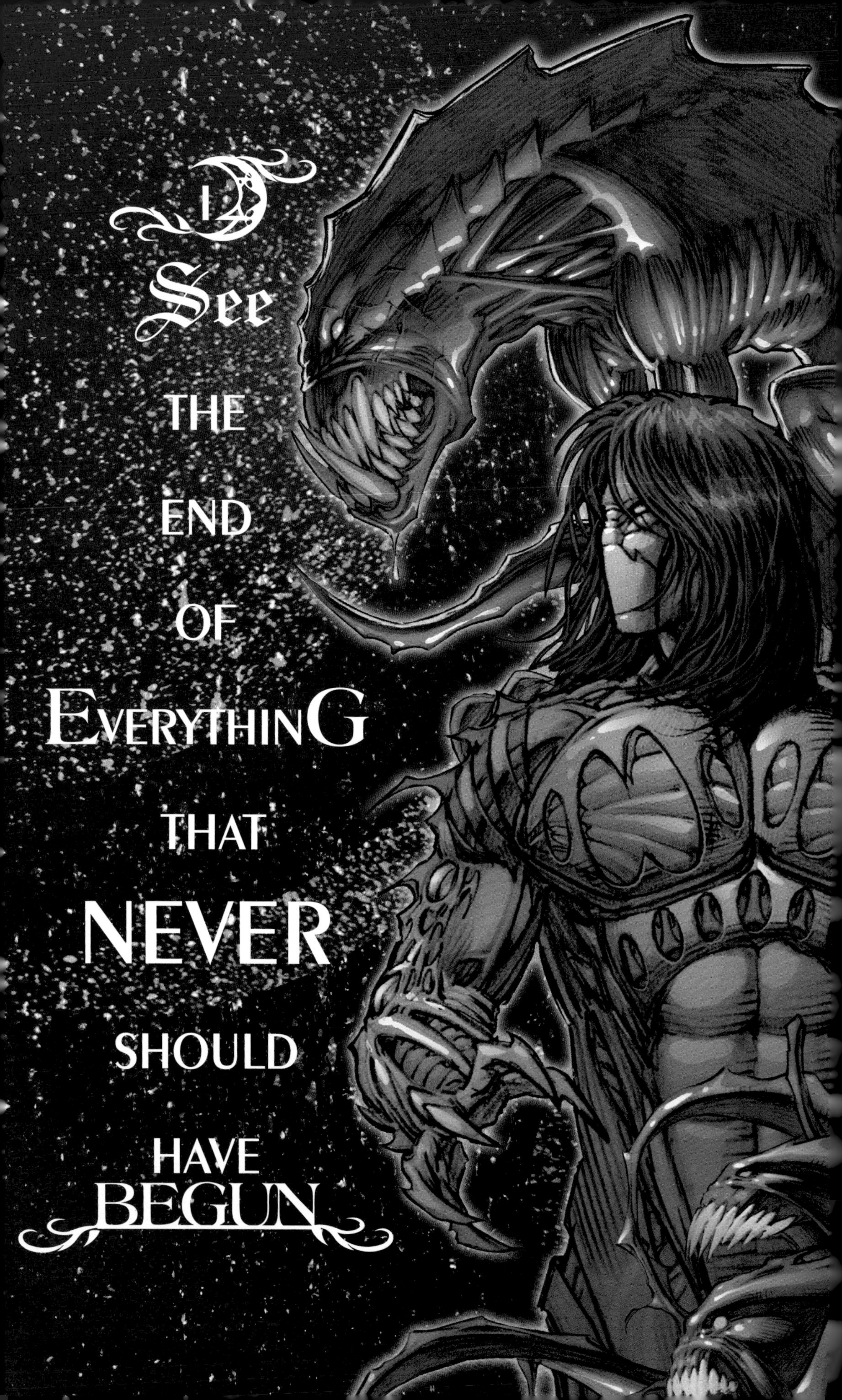
I See
THE
END
OF
EVERYTHING
THAT
NEVER
SHOULD
HAVE
BEGUN

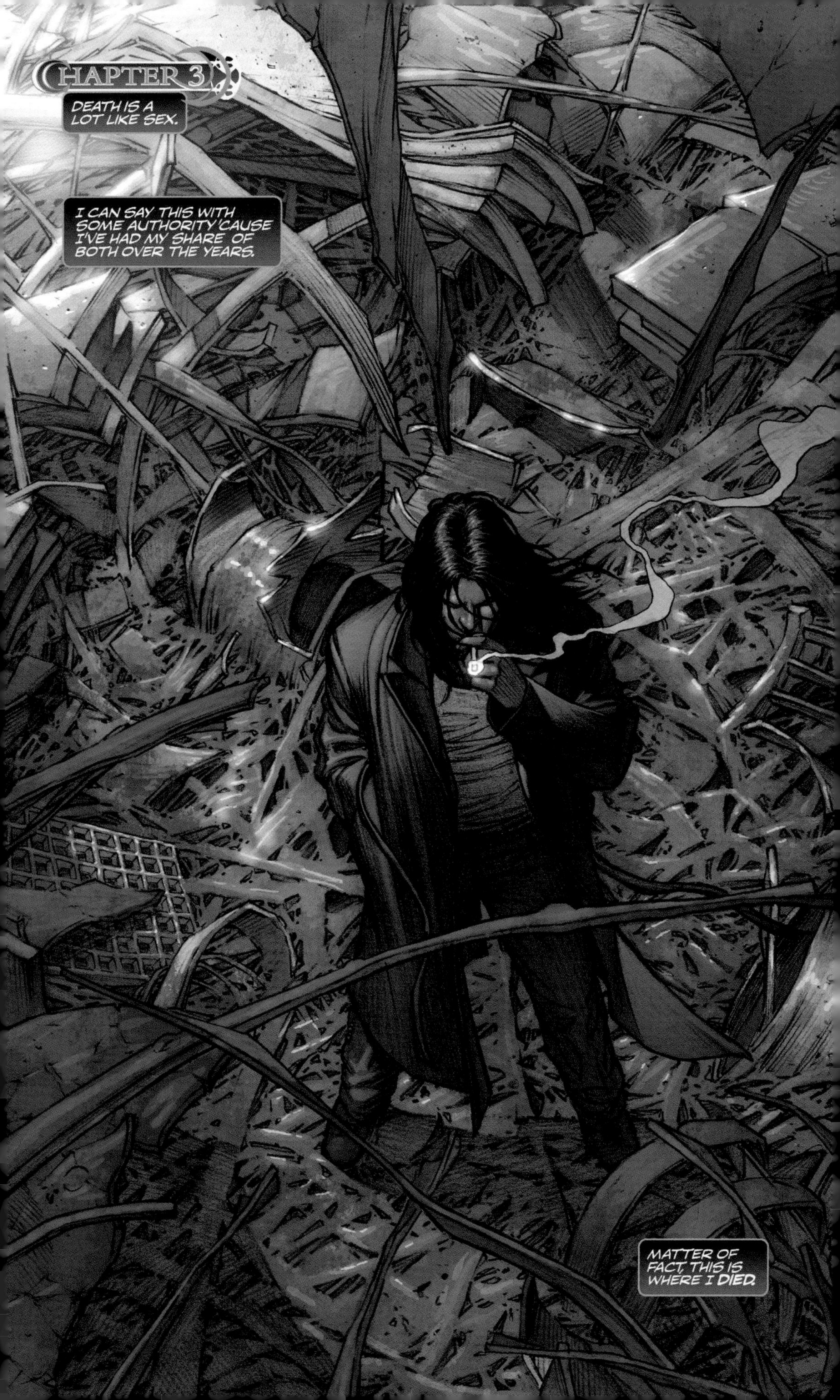
CHAPTER 3
DEATH IS A LOT LIKE SEX.
I CAN SAY THIS WITH SOME AUTHORITY 'CAUSE I'VE HAD MY SHARE OF BOTH OVER THE YEARS.
MATTER OF FACT, THIS IS WHERE I DIED.

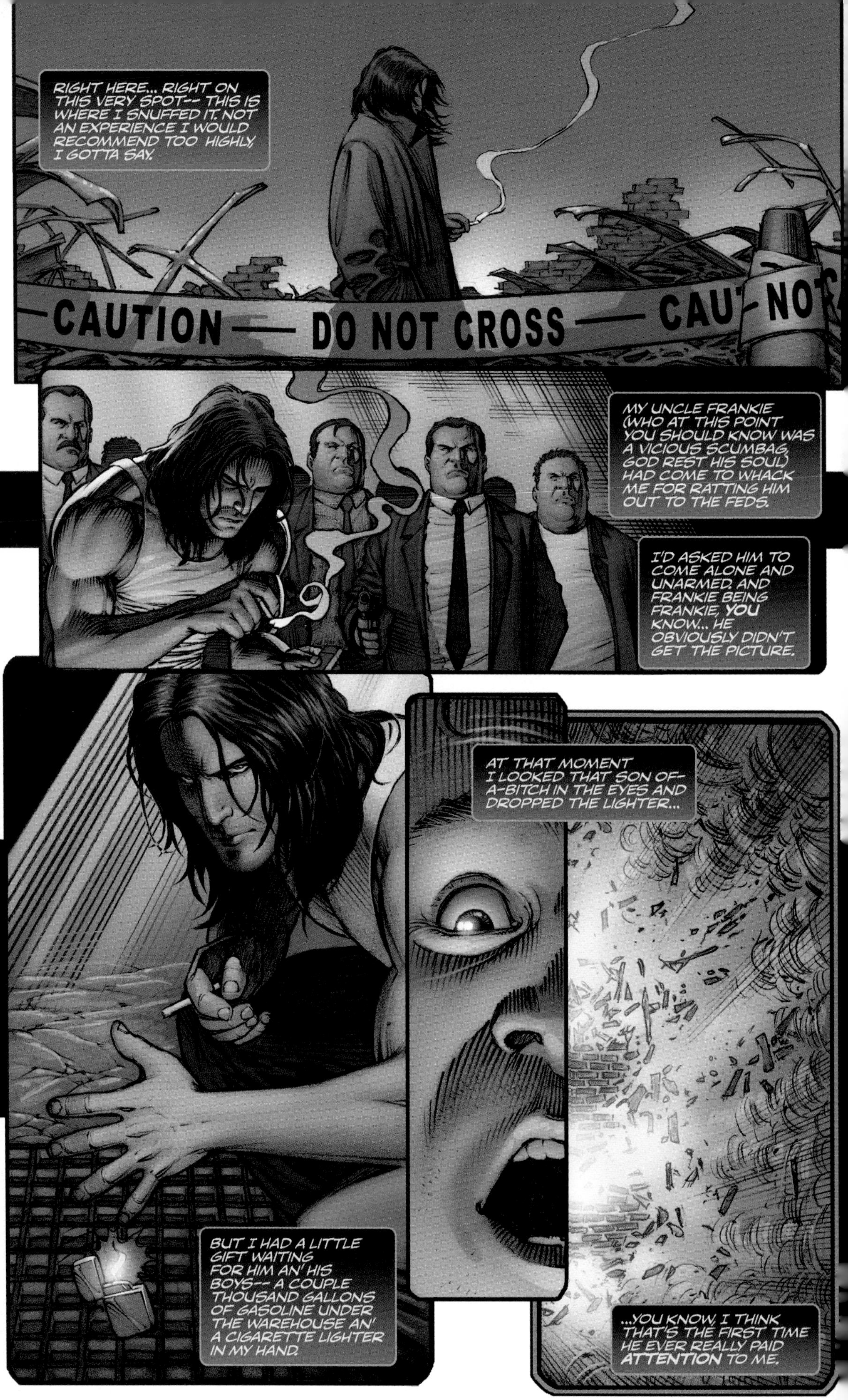

RIGHT HERE... RIGHT ON THIS VERY SPOT-- THIS IS WHERE I SNUFFED IT. NOT AN EXPERIENCE I WOULD RECOMMEND TOO HIGHLY, I GOTTA SAY.
CAUTION — DO NOT CROSS — CAUT- NOT
MY UNCLE FRANKIE (WHO AT THIS POINT YOU SHOULD KNOW WAS A VICIOUS SCUMBAG, GOD REST HIS SOUL) HAD COME TO WHACK ME FOR RATTING HIM OUT TO THE FEDS.
I'D ASKED HIM TO COME ALONE AND UNARMED. AND FRANKIE BEING FRANKIE, YOU KNOW... HE OBVIOUSLY DIDN'T GET THE PICTURE.
AT THAT MOMENT I LOOKED THAT SON OF-A-BITCH IN THE EYES AND DROPPED THE LIGHTER...
BUT I HAD A LITTLE GIFT WAITING FOR HIM AN' HIS BOYS-- A COUPLE THOUSAND GALLONS OF GASOLINE UNDER THE WAREHOUSE AN' A CIGARETTE LIGHTER IN MY HAND.
...YOU KNOW, I THINK THAT'S THE FIRST TIME HE EVER REALLY PAID ATTENTION TO ME.

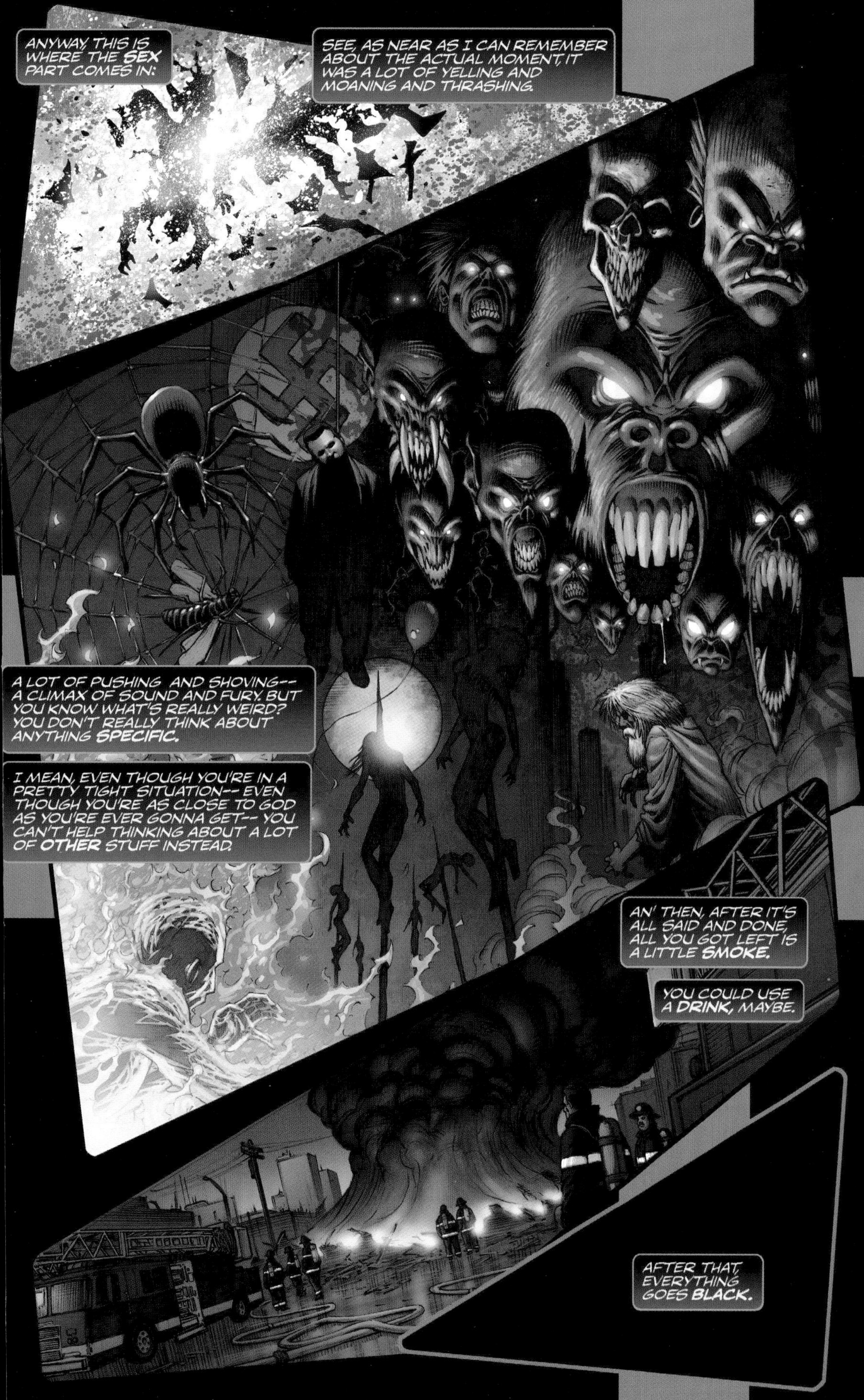
ANYWAY, THIS IS WHERE THE SEX PART COMES IN:
SEE, AS NEAR AS I CAN REMEMBER ABOUT THE ACTUAL MOMENT, IT WAS A LOT OF YELLING AND MOANING AND THRASHING.
A LOT OF PUSHING AND SHOVING-- A CLIMAX OF SOUND AND FURY. BUT YOU KNOW WHAT'S REALLY WEIRD? YOU DON'T REALLY THINK ABOUT ANYTHING SPECIFIC.
I MEAN, EVEN THOUGH YOU'RE IN A PRETTY TIGHT SITUATION-- EVEN THOUGH YOU'RE AS CLOSE TO GOD AS YOU'RE EVER GONNA GET-- YOU CAN'T HELP THINKING ABOUT A LOT OF OTHER STUFF INSTEAD.
AN' THEN, AFTER IT'S ALL SAID AND DONE, ALL YOU GOT LEFT IS A LITTLE SMOKE.
YOU COULD USE A DRINK, MAYBE.
AFTER THAT, EVERYTHING GOES BLACK.

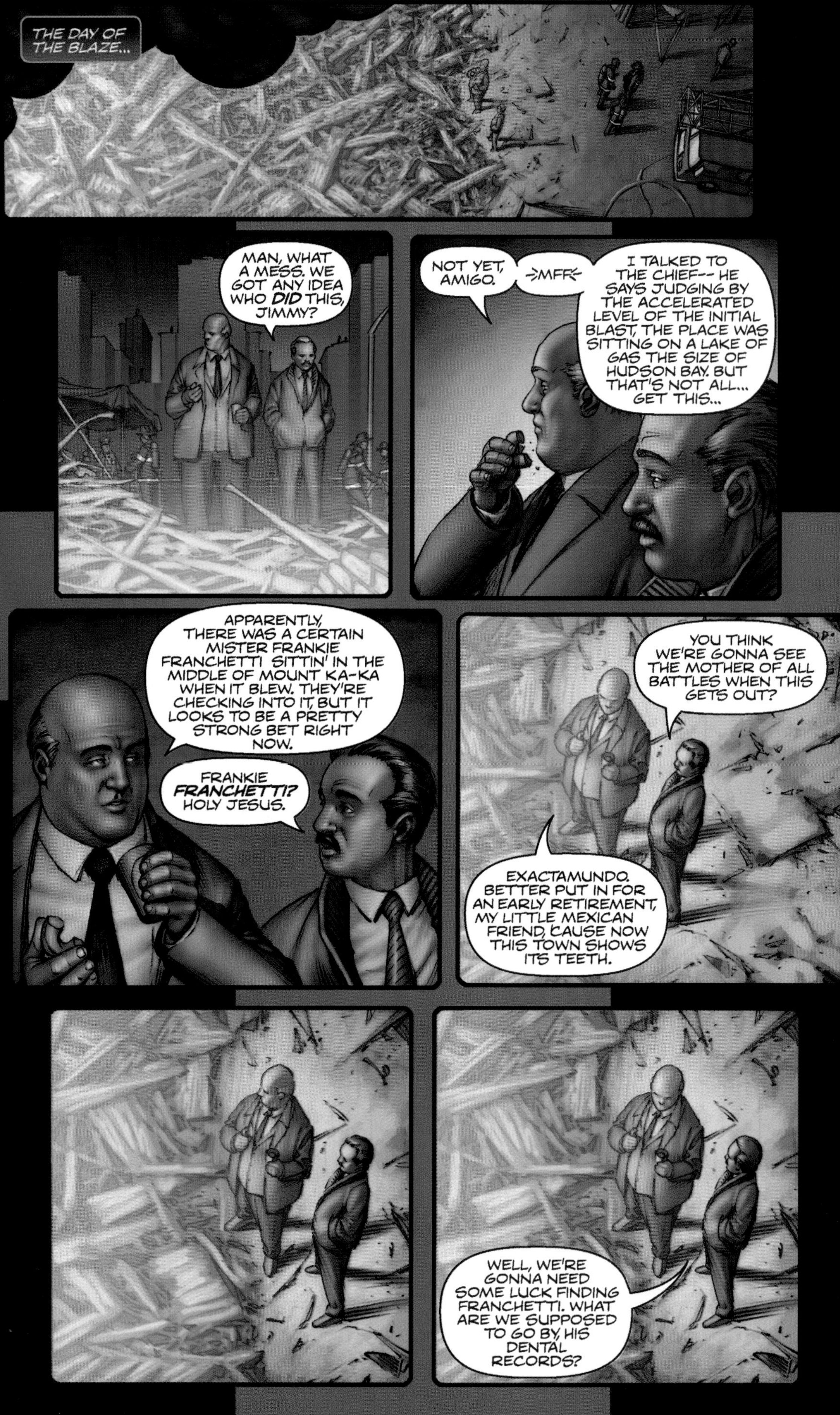
THE DAY OF THE BLAZE...
MAN, WHAT A MESS. WE GOT ANY IDEA WHO *DID* THIS, JIMMY?
NOT YET, AMIGO.
MFF
I TALKED TO THE CHIEF-- HE SAYS JUDGING BY THE ACCELERATED LEVEL OF THE INITIAL BLAST, THE PLACE WAS SITTING ON A LAKE OF GAS THE SIZE OF HUDSON BAY. BUT THAT'S NOT ALL... GET THIS...
APPARENTLY, THERE WAS A CERTAIN MISTER FRANKIE FRANCHETTI SITTIN' IN THE MIDDLE OF MOUNT KA-KA WHEN IT BLEW. THEY'RE CHECKING INTO IT, BUT IT LOOKS TO BE A PRETTY STRONG BET RIGHT NOW.
FRANKIE ***FRANCHETTI?*** HOLY JESUS.
YOU THINK WE'RE GONNA SEE THE MOTHER OF ALL BATTLES WHEN THIS GETS OUT?
EXACTAMUNDO. BETTER PUT IN FOR AN EARLY RETIREMENT, MY LITTLE MEXICAN FRIEND, 'CAUSE NOW THIS TOWN SHOWS ITS TEETH.
WELL, WE'RE GONNA NEED SOME LUCK FINDING FRANCHETTI. WHAT ARE WE SUPPOSED TO GO BY, HIS DENTAL RECORDS?

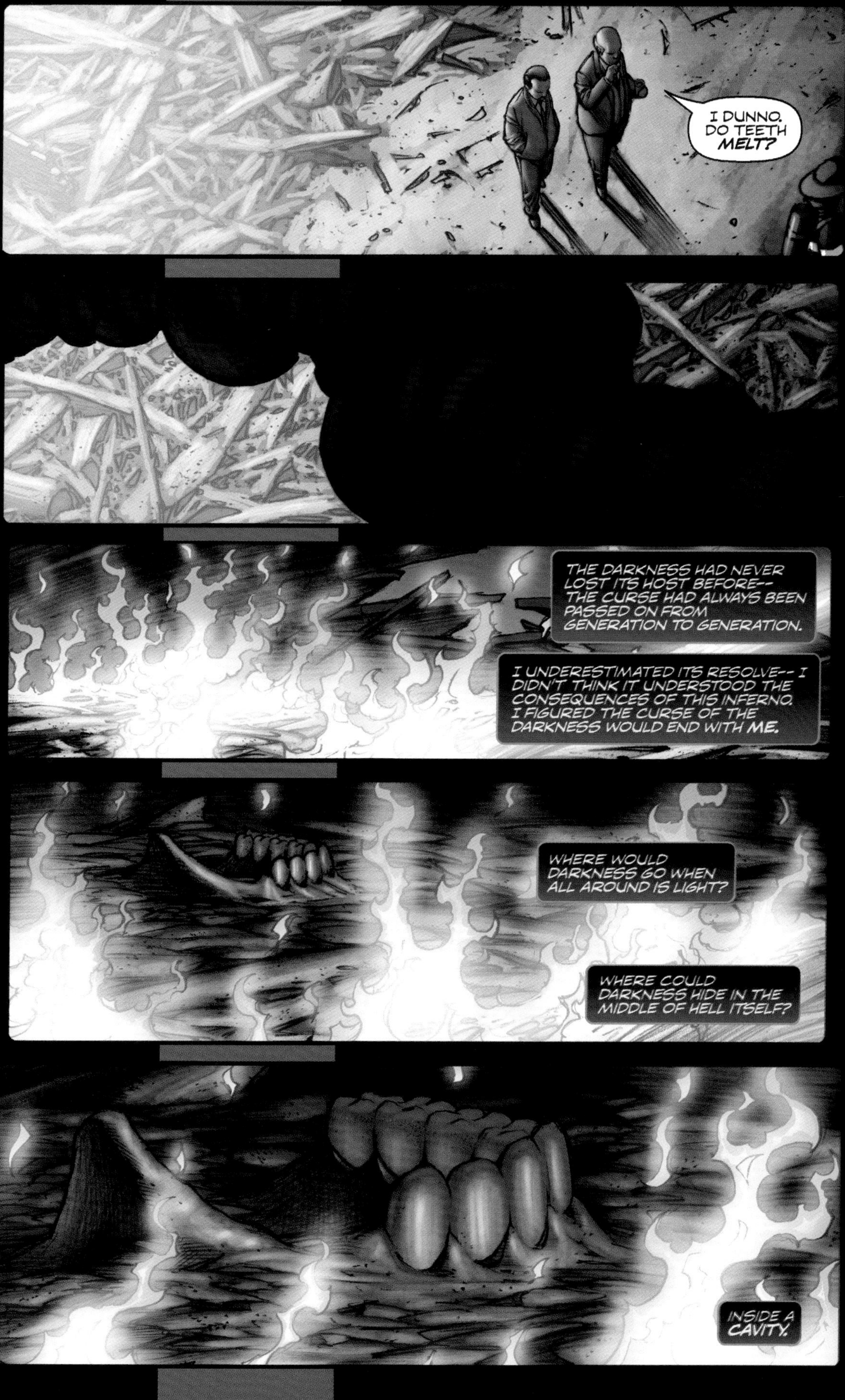

I DUNNO. DO TEETH MELT?
THE DARKNESS HAD NEVER LOST ITS HOST BEFORE-- THE CURSE HAD ALWAYS BEEN PASSED ON FROM GENERATION TO GENERATION.
I UNDERESTIMATED ITS RESOLVE-- I DIDN'T THINK IT UNDERSTOOD THE CONSEQUENCES OF THIS INFERNO. I FIGURED THE CURSE OF THE DARKNESS WOULD END WITH ME.
WHERE WOULD DARKNESS GO WHEN ALL AROUND IS LIGHT?
WHERE COULD DARKNESS HIDE IN THE MIDDLE OF HELL ITSELF?
INSIDE A CAVITY.

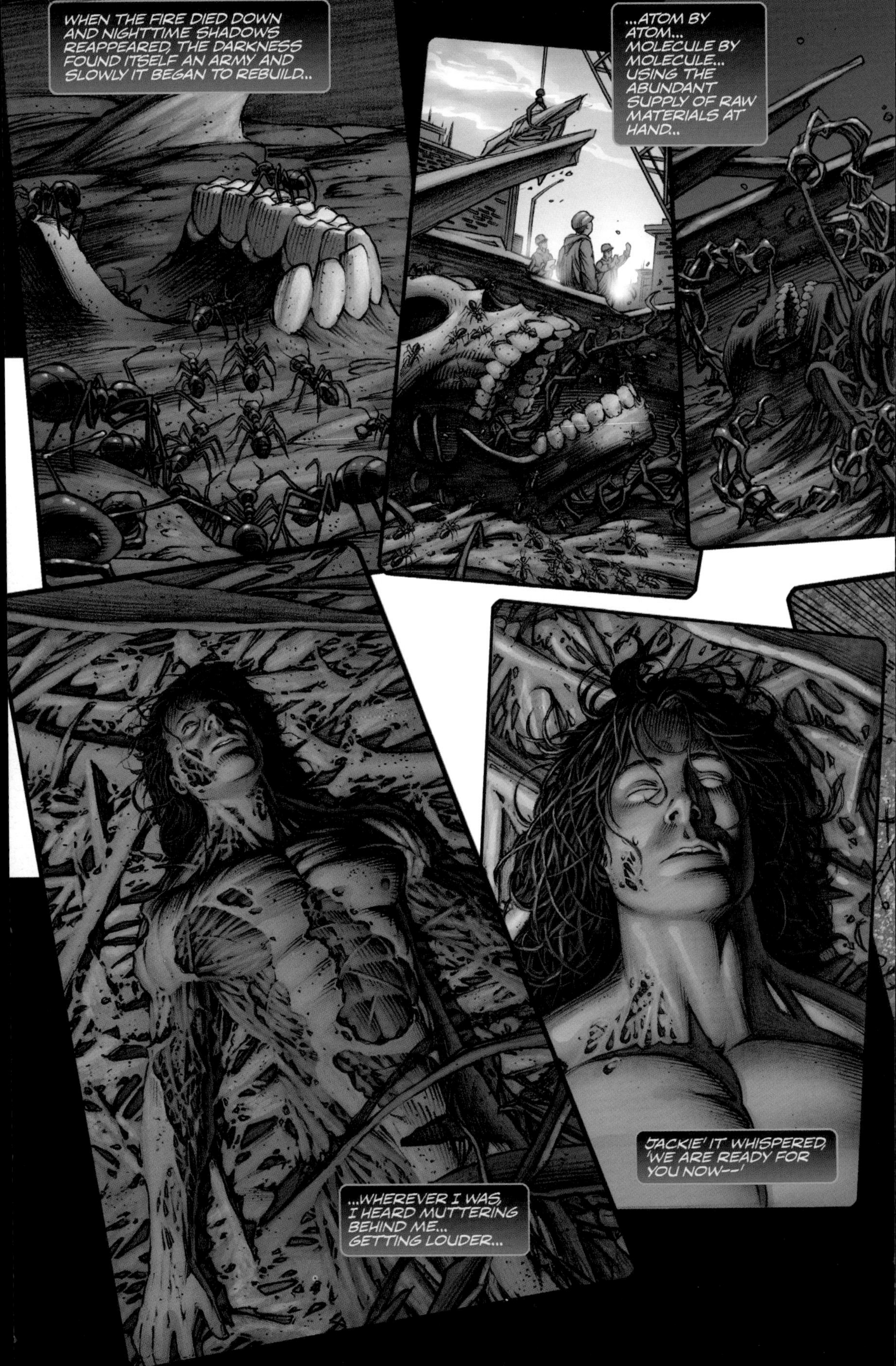
WHEN THE FIRE DIED DOWN AND NIGHTTIME SHADOWS REAPPEARED, THE DARKNESS FOUND ITSELF AN ARMY AND SLOWLY IT BEGAN TO REBUILD...
...ATOM BY ATOM... MOLECULE BY MOLECULE... USING THE ABUNDANT SUPPLY OF RAW MATERIALS AT HAND...
...WHEREVER I WAS, I HEARD MUTTERING BEHIND ME... GETTING LOUDER...
'JACKIE' IT WHISPERED, 'WE ARE READY FOR YOU NOW--'

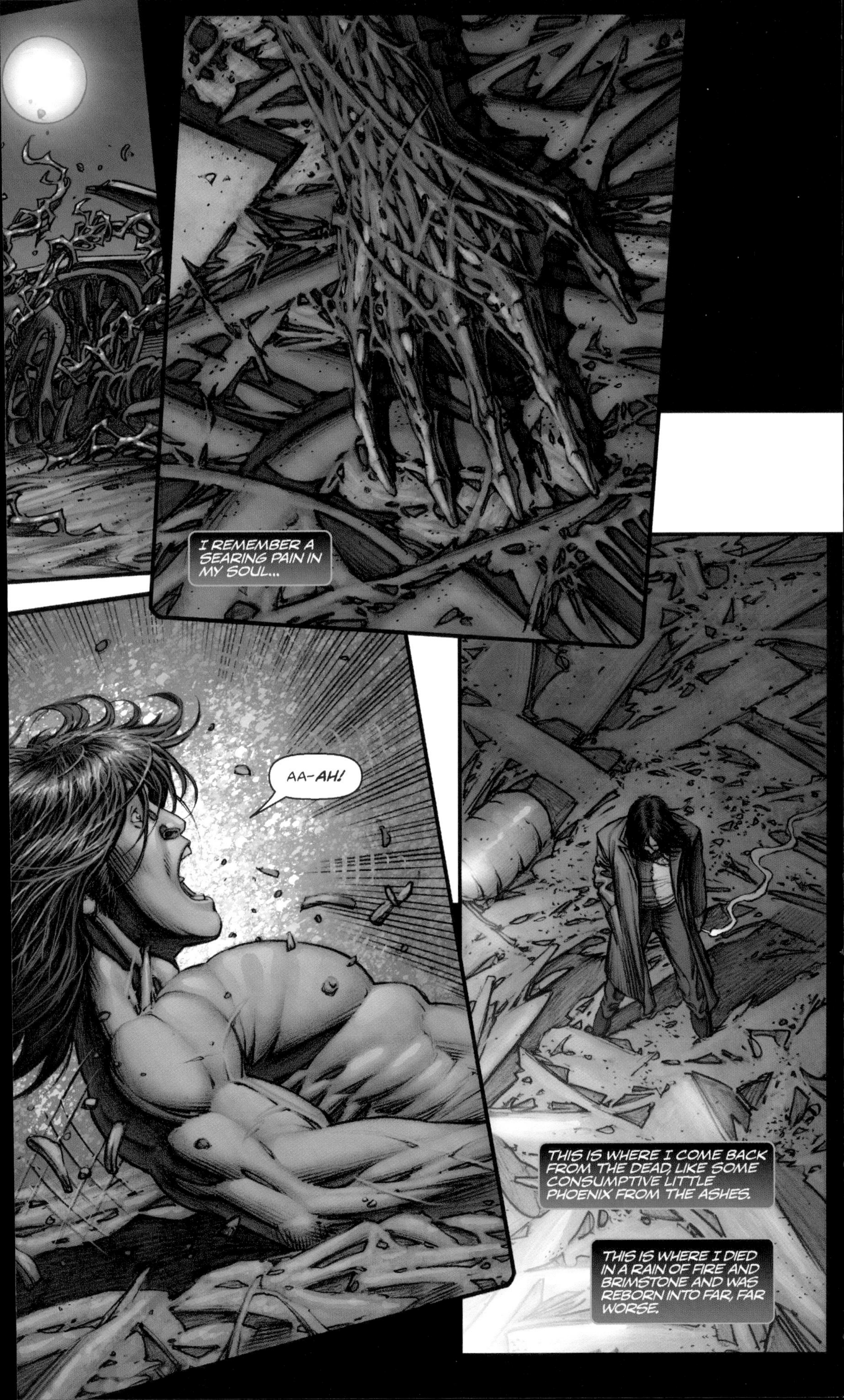
I REMEMBER A SEARING PAIN IN MY SOUL...
AA-AH!
THIS IS WHERE I COME BACK FROM THE DEAD, LIKE SOME CONSUMPTIVE LITTLE PHOENIX FROM THE ASHES.
THIS IS WHERE I DIED IN A RAIN OF FIRE AND BRIMSTONE AND WAS REBORN INTO FAR, FAR WORSE.

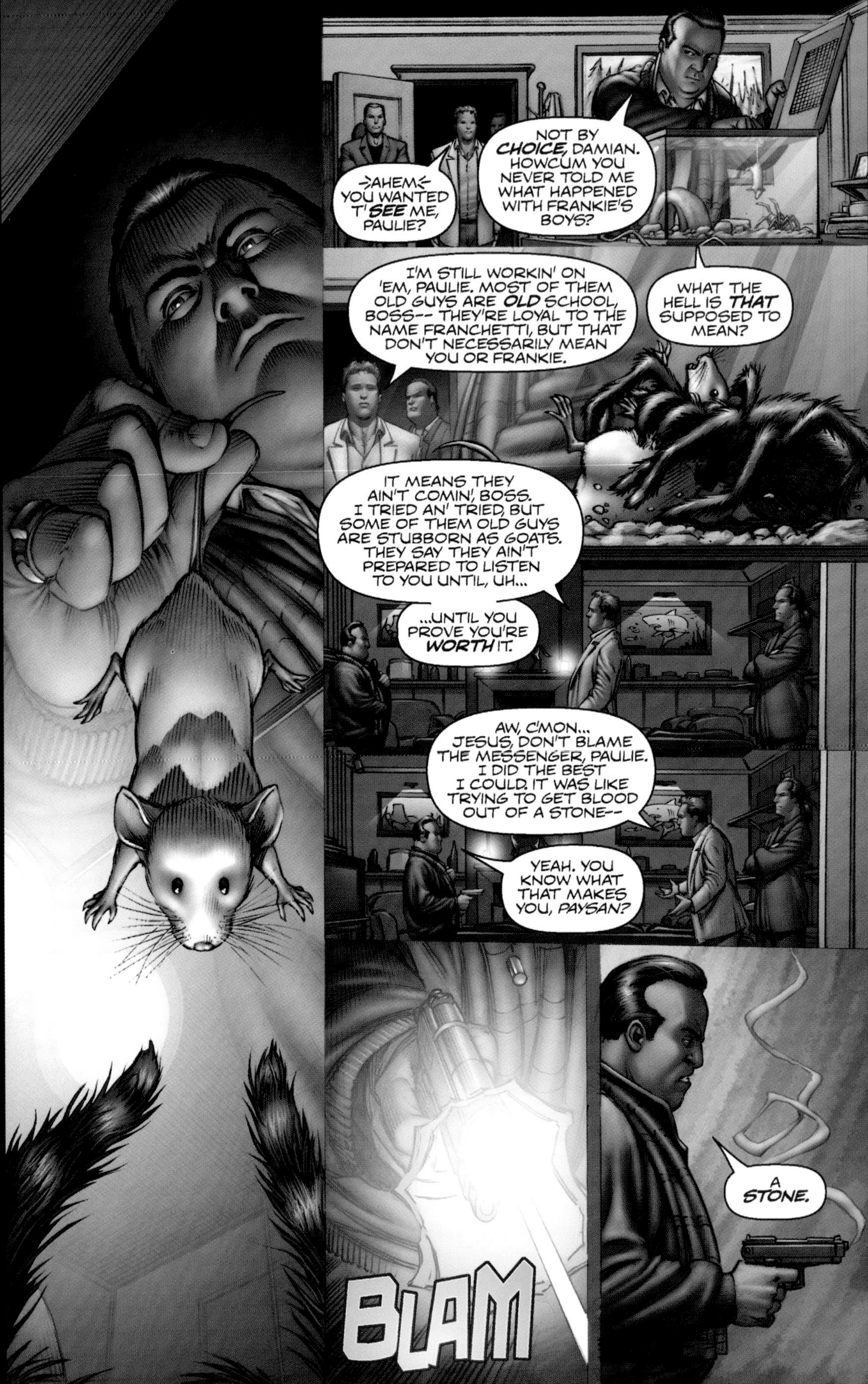

-AHEM- YOU WANTED T'SEE ME, PAULIE?
NOT BY CHOICE, DAMIAN. HOWCUM YOU NEVER TOLD ME WHAT HAPPENED WITH FRANKIE'S BOYS?
I'M STILL WORKIN' ON 'EM, PAULIE. MOST OF THEM OLD GUYS ARE OLD SCHOOL, BOSS-- THEY'RE LOYAL TO THE NAME FRANCHETTI, BUT THAT DON'T NECESSARILY MEAN YOU OR FRANKIE.
WHAT THE HELL IS THAT SUPPOSED TO MEAN?
IT MEANS THEY AIN'T COMIN', BOSS. I TRIED AN' TRIED, BUT SOME OF THEM OLD GUYS ARE STUBBORN AS GOATS. THEY SAY THEY AIN'T PREPARED TO LISTEN TO YOU UNTIL, UH...
...UNTIL YOU PROVE YOU'RE WORTH IT.
AW, C'MON... JESUS, DON'T BLAME THE MESSENGER, PAULIE. I DID THE BEST I COULD. IT WAS LIKE TRYING TO GET BLOOD OUT OF A STONE--
YEAH. YOU KNOW WHAT THAT MAKES YOU, PAYSAN?
BLAM
A STONE.

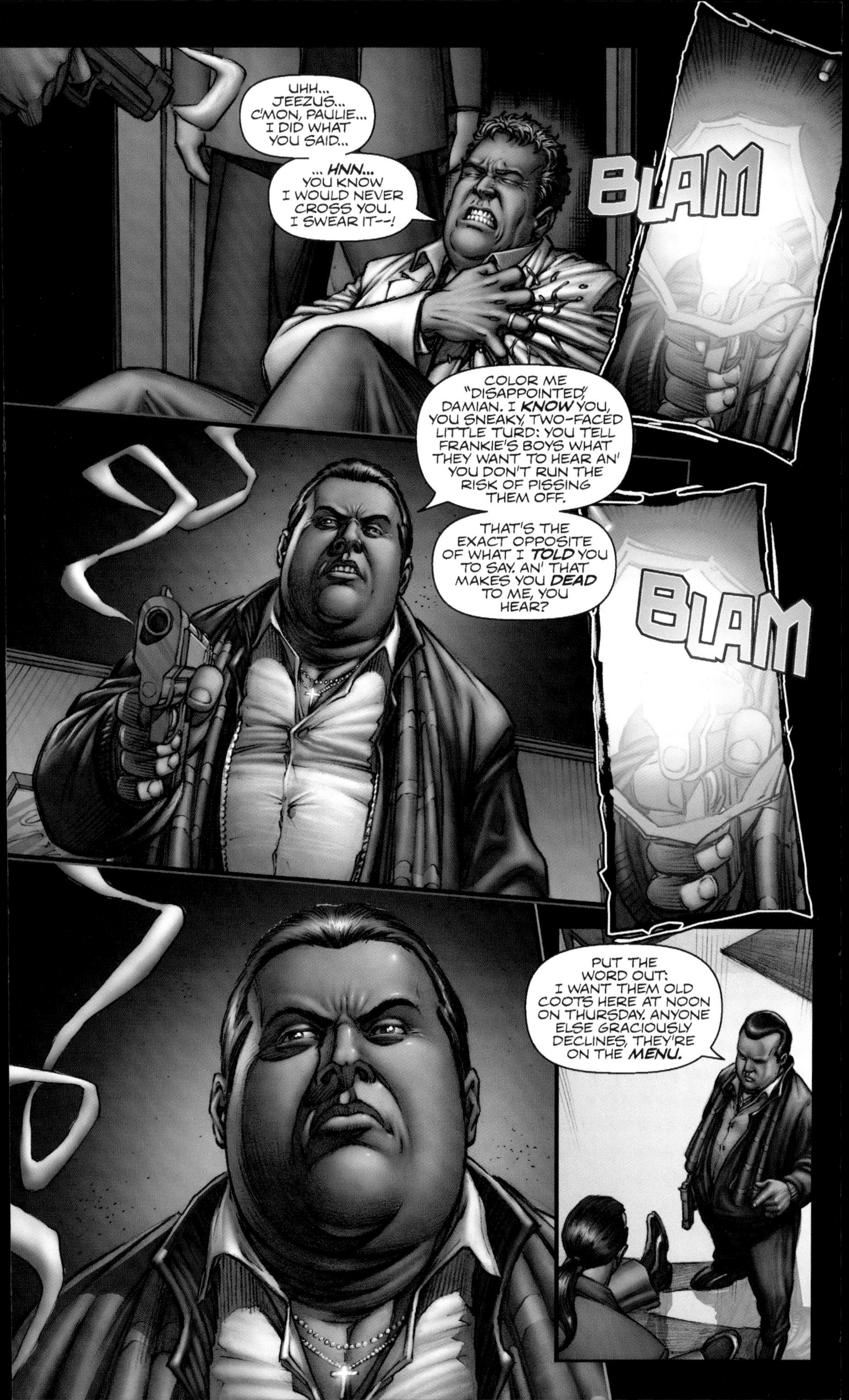

UHH... JEEZUS... C'MON, PAULIE... I DID WHAT YOU SAID...
... HNN... YOU KNOW I WOULD NEVER CROSS YOU. I SWEAR IT--!
BLAM
COLOR ME "DISAPPOINTED," DAMIAN. I KNOW YOU, YOU SNEAKY, TWO-FACED LITTLE TURD: YOU TELL FRANKIE'S BOYS WHAT THEY WANT TO HEAR AN' YOU DON'T RUN THE RISK OF PISSING THEM OFF.
THAT'S THE EXACT OPPOSITE OF WHAT I TOLD YOU TO SAY. AN' THAT MAKES YOU DEAD TO ME, YOU HEAR?
BLAM
PUT THE WORD OUT: I WANT THEM OLD COOTS HERE AT NOON ON THURSDAY. ANYONE ELSE GRACIOUSLY DECLINES, THEY'RE ON THE MENU.

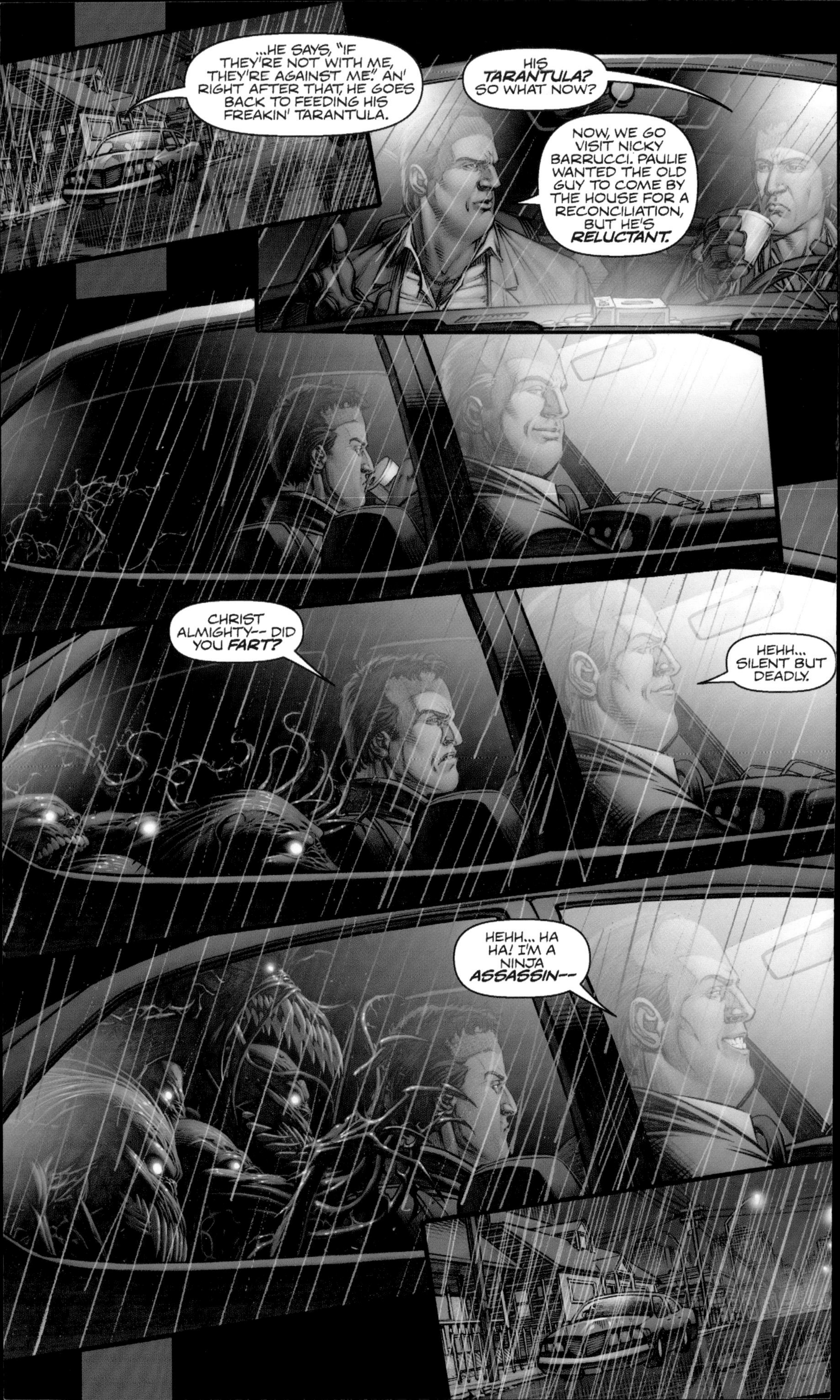
...HE SAYS, "IF THEY'RE NOT WITH ME, THEY'RE AGAINST ME." AN' RIGHT AFTER THAT, HE GOES BACK TO FEEDING HIS FREAKIN' TARANTULA.
HIS *TARANTULA?* SO WHAT NOW?
NOW, WE GO VISIT NICKY BARRUCCI. PAULIE WANTED THE OLD GUY TO COME BY THE HOUSE FOR A RECONCILIATION, BUT HE'S *RELUCTANT.*
CHRIST ALMIGHTY-- DID YOU *FART?*
HEHH... SILENT BUT DEADLY.
HEHH... HA HA! I'M A NINJA *ASSASSIN--*

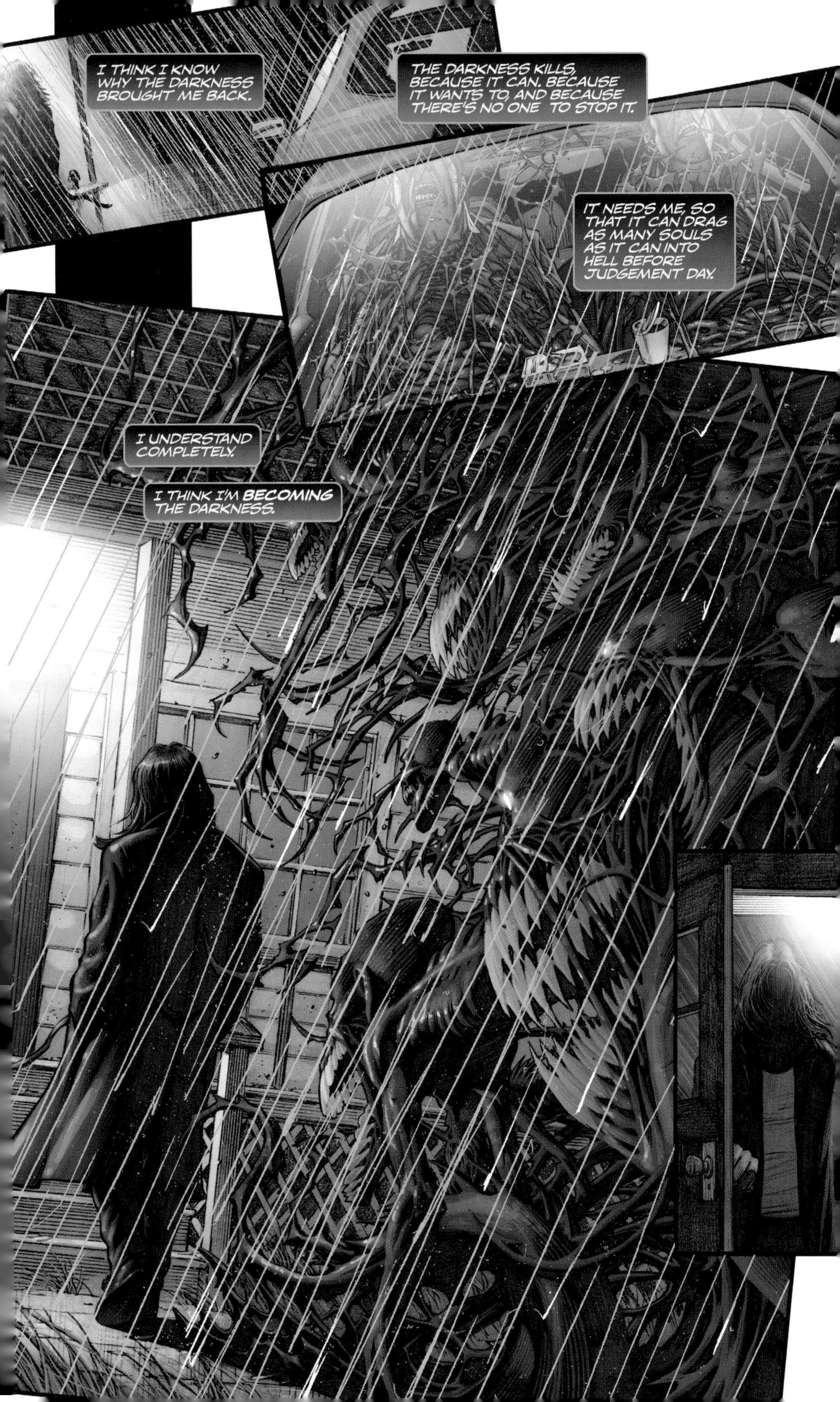
I THINK I KNOW WHY THE DARKNESS BROUGHT ME BACK.
THE DARKNESS KILLS, BECAUSE IT CAN. BECAUSE IT WANTS TO, AND BECAUSE THERE'S NO ONE TO STOP IT.
IT NEEDS ME, SO THAT IT CAN DRAG AS MANY SOULS AS IT CAN INTO HELL BEFORE JUDGEMENT DAY.
I UNDERSTAND COMPLETELY.
I THINK I'M BECOMING THE DARKNESS.

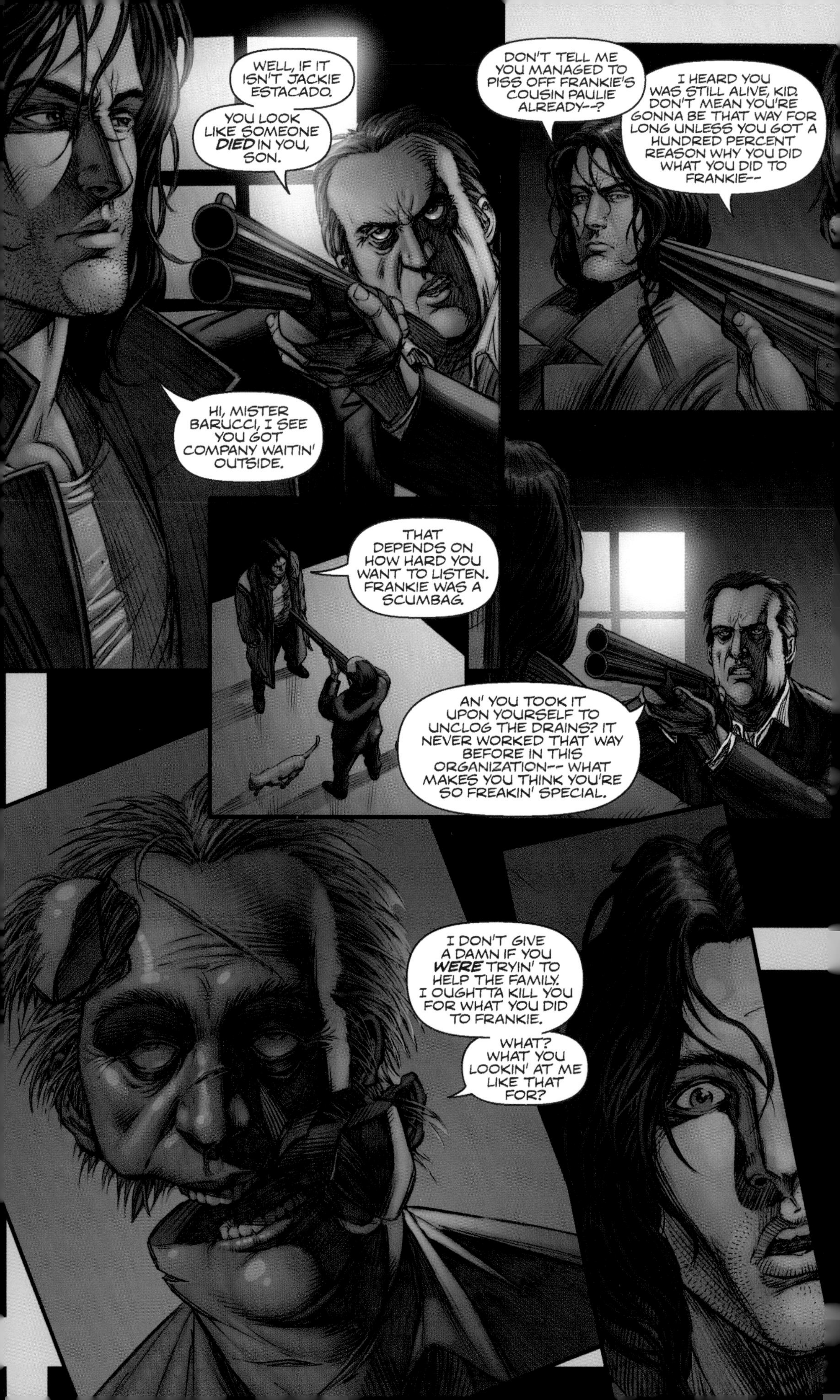
WELL, IF IT ISN'T JACKIE ESTACADO.
YOU LOOK LIKE SOMEONE DIED IN YOU, SON.
HI, MISTER BARUCCI, I SEE YOU GOT COMPANY WAITIN' OUTSIDE.
DON'T TELL ME YOU MANAGED TO PISS OFF FRANKIE'S COUSIN PAULIE ALREADY--?
I HEARD YOU WAS STILL ALIVE, KID. DON'T MEAN YOU'RE GONNA BE THAT WAY FOR LONG UNLESS YOU GOT A HUNDRED PERCENT REASON WHY YOU DID WHAT YOU DID TO FRANKIE--
THAT DEPENDS ON HOW HARD YOU WANT TO LISTEN. FRANKIE WAS A SCUMBAG.
AN' YOU TOOK IT UPON YOURSELF TO UNCLOG THE DRAINS? IT NEVER WORKED THAT WAY BEFORE IN THIS ORGANIZATION-- WHAT MAKES YOU THINK YOU'RE SO FREAKIN' SPECIAL.
I DON'T GIVE A DAMN IF YOU WERE TRYIN' TO HELP THE FAMILY. I OUGHTTA KILL YOU FOR WHAT YOU DID TO FRANKIE.
WHAT? WHAT YOU LOOKIN' AT ME LIKE THAT FOR?

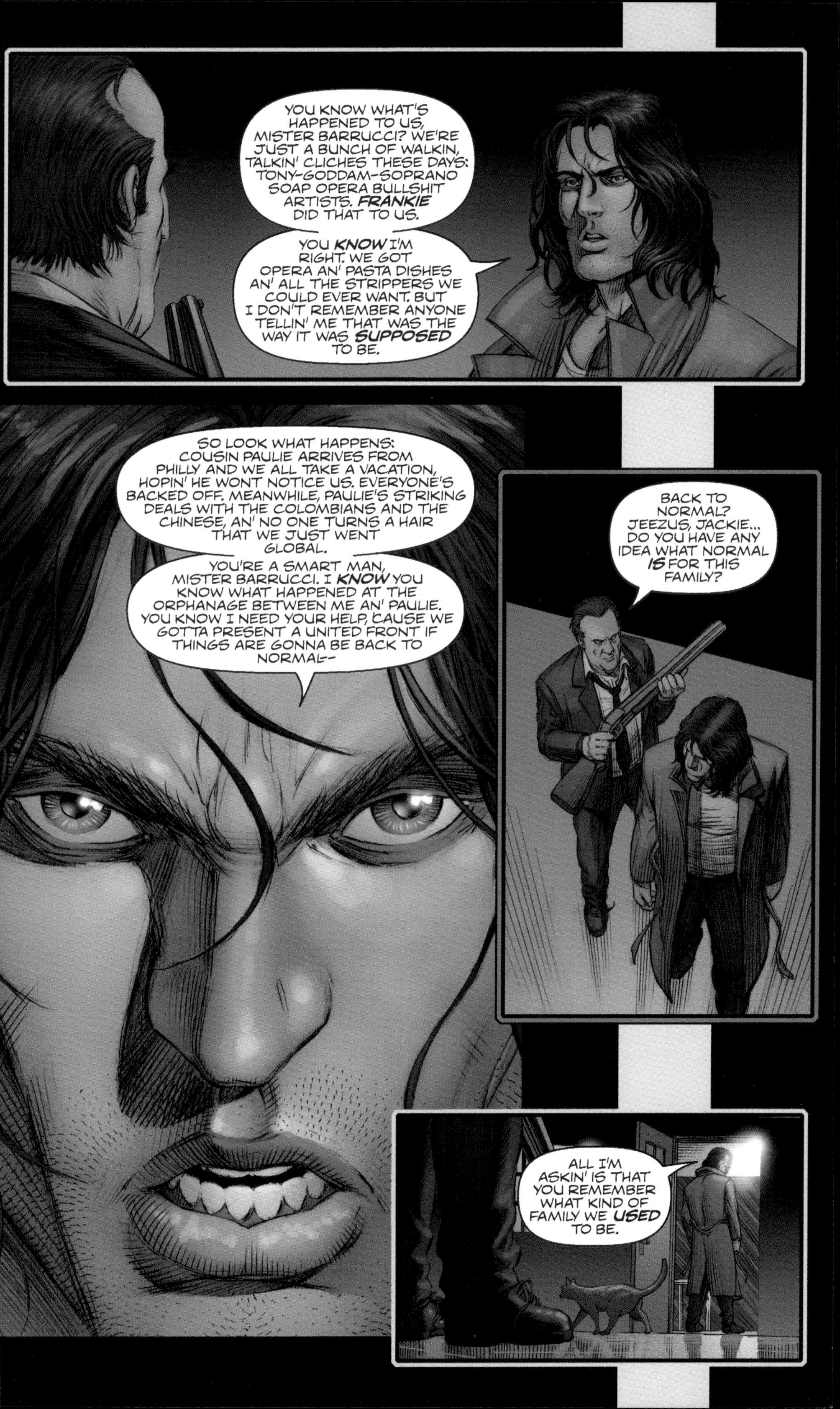
YOU KNOW WHAT'S HAPPENED TO US, MISTER BARRUCCI? WE'RE JUST A BUNCH OF WALKIN, TALKIN' CLICHES THESE DAYS: TONY-GODDAM-SOPRANO SOAP OPERA BULLSHIT ARTISTS. FRANKIE DID THAT TO US.
YOU KNOW I'M RIGHT. WE GOT OPERA AN' PASTA DISHES AN' ALL THE STRIPPERS WE COULD EVER WANT. BUT I DON'T REMEMBER ANYONE TELLIN' ME THAT WAS THE WAY IT WAS SUPPOSED TO BE.
SO LOOK WHAT HAPPENS: COUSIN PAULIE ARRIVES FROM PHILLY AND WE ALL TAKE A VACATION, HOPIN' HE WONT NOTICE US. EVERYONE'S BACKED OFF. MEANWHILE, PAULIE'S STRIKING DEALS WITH THE COLOMBIANS AND THE CHINESE, AN' NO ONE TURNS A HAIR THAT WE JUST WENT GLOBAL.
YOU'RE A SMART MAN, MISTER BARRUCCI. I KNOW YOU KNOW WHAT HAPPENED AT THE ORPHANAGE BETWEEN ME AN' PAULIE. YOU KNOW I NEED YOUR HELP, CAUSE WE GOTTA PRESENT A UNITED FRONT IF THINGS ARE GONNA BE BACK TO NORMAL--
BACK TO NORMAL? JEEZUS, JACKIE... DO YOU HAVE ANY IDEA WHAT NORMAL IS FOR THIS FAMILY?
ALL I'M ASKIN' IS THAT YOU REMEMBER WHAT KIND OF FAMILY WE USED TO BE.

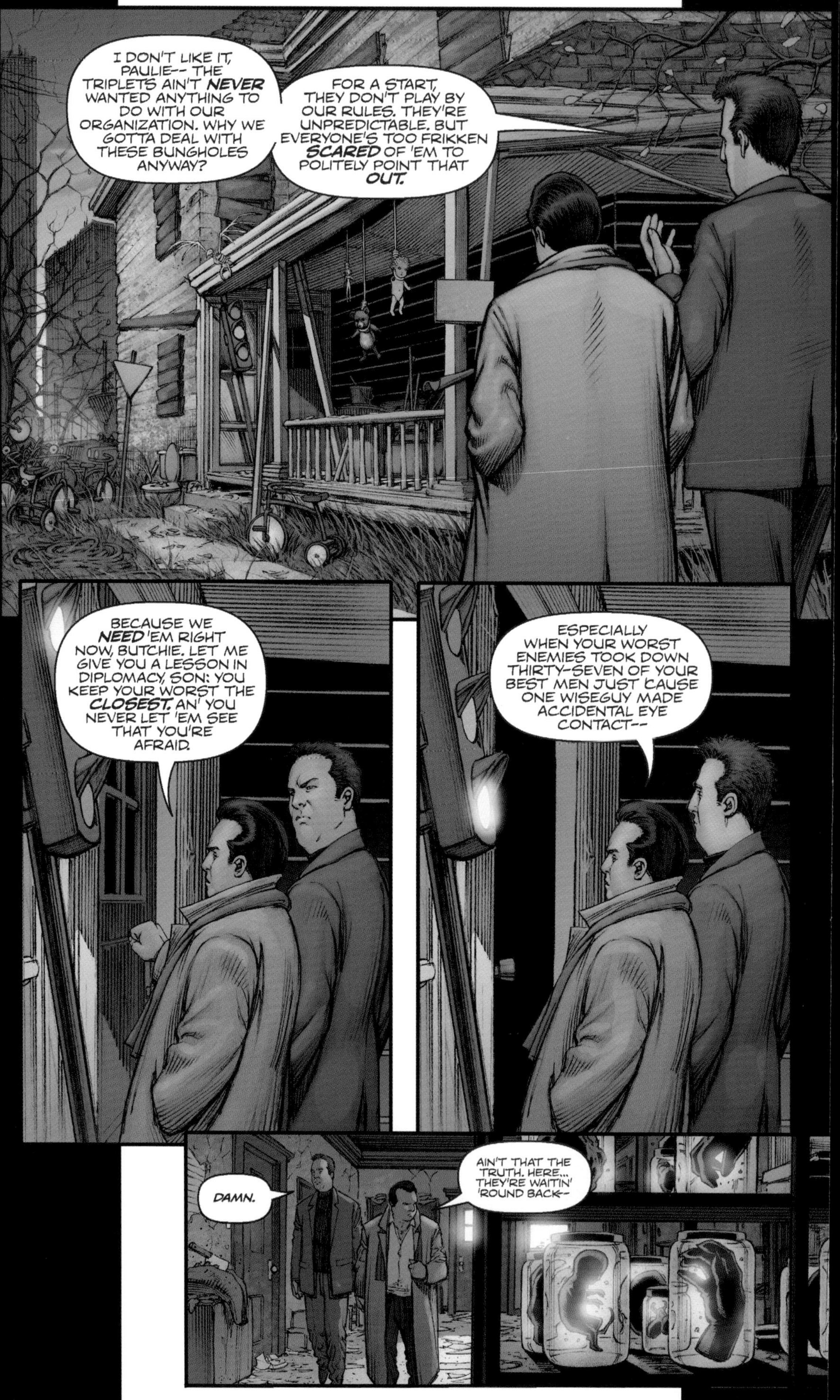
I DON'T LIKE IT, PAULIE-- THE TRIPLETS AIN'T NEVER WANTED ANYTHING TO DO WITH OUR ORGANIZATION. WHY WE GOTTA DEAL WITH THESE BUNGHOLES ANYWAY?
FOR A START, THEY DON'T PLAY BY OUR RULES. THEY'RE UNPREDICTABLE. BUT EVERYONE'S TOO FRIKKEN SCARED OF 'EM TO POLITELY POINT THAT OUT.
BECAUSE WE NEED 'EM RIGHT NOW, BUTCHIE. LET ME GIVE YOU A LESSON IN DIPLOMACY, SON: YOU KEEP YOUR WORST THE CLOSEST. AN' YOU NEVER LET 'EM SEE THAT YOU'RE AFRAID.
ESPECIALLY WHEN YOUR WORST ENEMIES TOOK DOWN THIRTY-SEVEN OF YOUR BEST MEN JUST 'CAUSE ONE WISEGUY MADE ACCIDENTAL EYE CONTACT--
DAMN.
AIN'T THAT THE TRUTH. HERE... THEY'RE WAITIN' 'ROUND BACK--

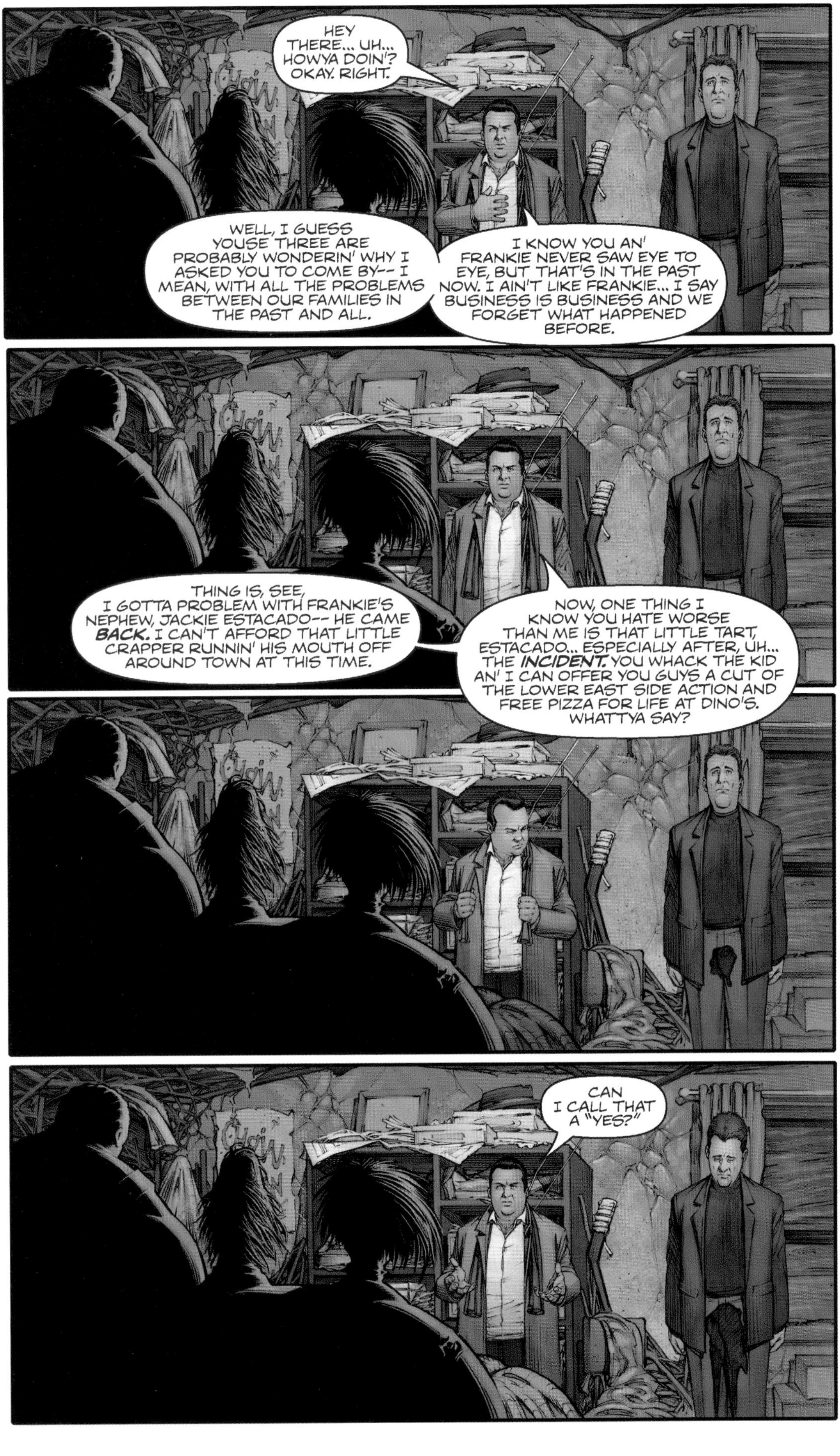

HEY THERE... UH... HOWYA DOIN'? OKAY. RIGHT.
WELL, I GUESS YOUSE THREE ARE PROBABLY WONDERIN' WHY I ASKED YOU TO COME BY-- I MEAN, WITH ALL THE PROBLEMS BETWEEN OUR FAMILIES IN THE PAST AND ALL.
I KNOW YOU AN' FRANKIE NEVER SAW EYE TO EYE, BUT THAT'S IN THE PAST NOW. I AIN'T LIKE FRANKIE... I SAY BUSINESS IS BUSINESS AND WE FORGET WHAT HAPPENED BEFORE.
THING IS, SEE, I GOTTA PROBLEM WITH FRANKIE'S NEPHEW, JACKIE ESTACADO-- HE CAME *BACK.* I CAN'T AFFORD THAT LITTLE CRAPPER RUNNIN' HIS MOUTH OFF AROUND TOWN AT THIS TIME.
NOW, ONE THING I KNOW YOU HATE WORSE THAN ME IS THAT LITTLE TART, ESTACADO... ESPECIALLY AFTER, UH... THE *INCIDENT.* YOU WHACK THE KID AN' I CAN OFFER YOU GUYS A CUT OF THE LOWER EAST SIDE ACTION AND FREE PIZZA FOR LIFE AT DINO'S. WHATTYA SAY?
CAN I CALL THAT A "YES?"

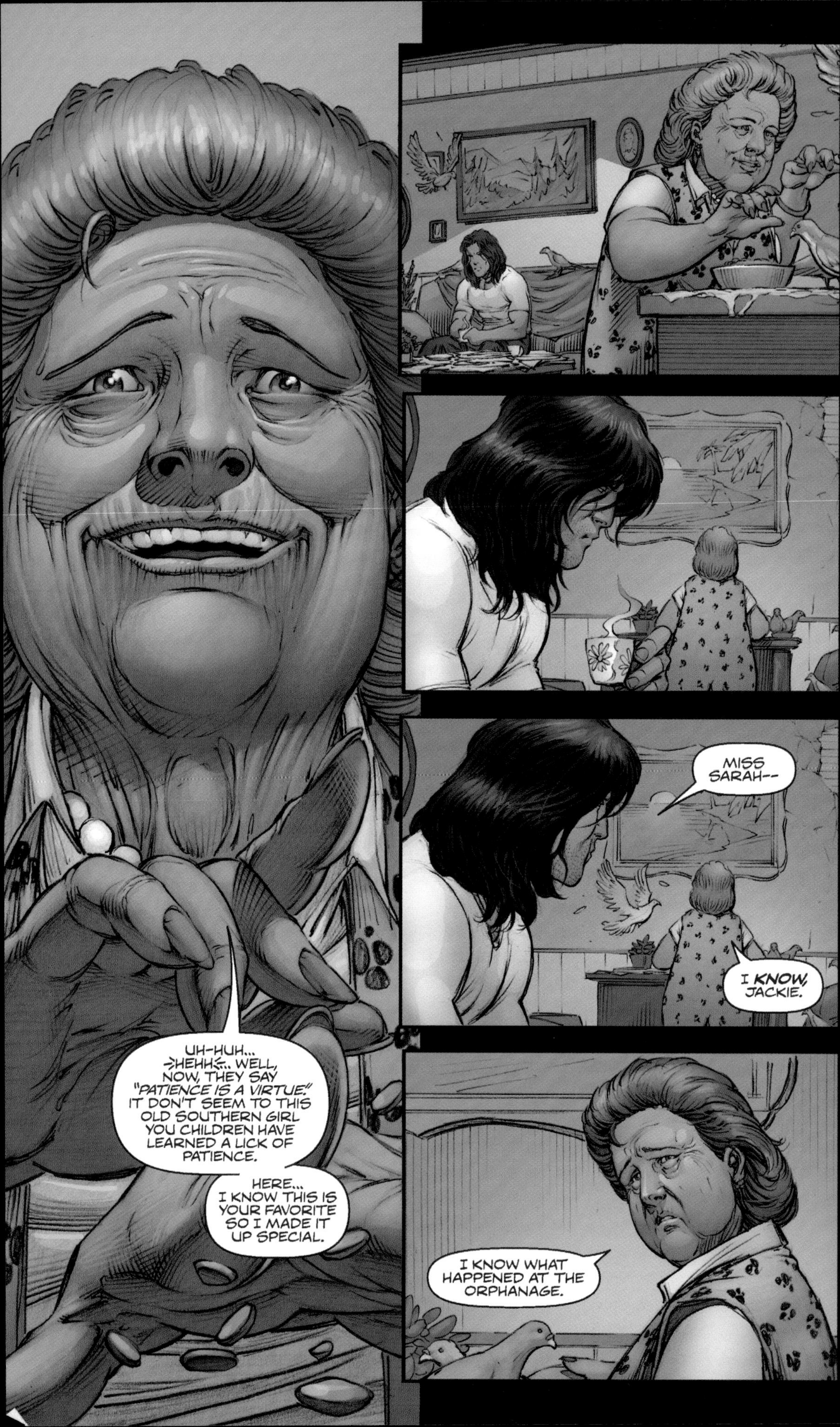
UH-HUH... >HEHH<... WELL, NOW, THEY SAY "PATIENCE IS A VIRTUE." IT DON'T SEEM TO THIS OLD SOUTHERN GIRL YOU CHILDREN HAVE LEARNED A LICK OF PATIENCE.
HERE... I KNOW THIS IS YOUR FAVORITE SO I MADE IT UP SPECIAL.
MISS SARAH--
I KNOW, JACKIE.
I KNOW WHAT HAPPENED AT THE ORPHANAGE.

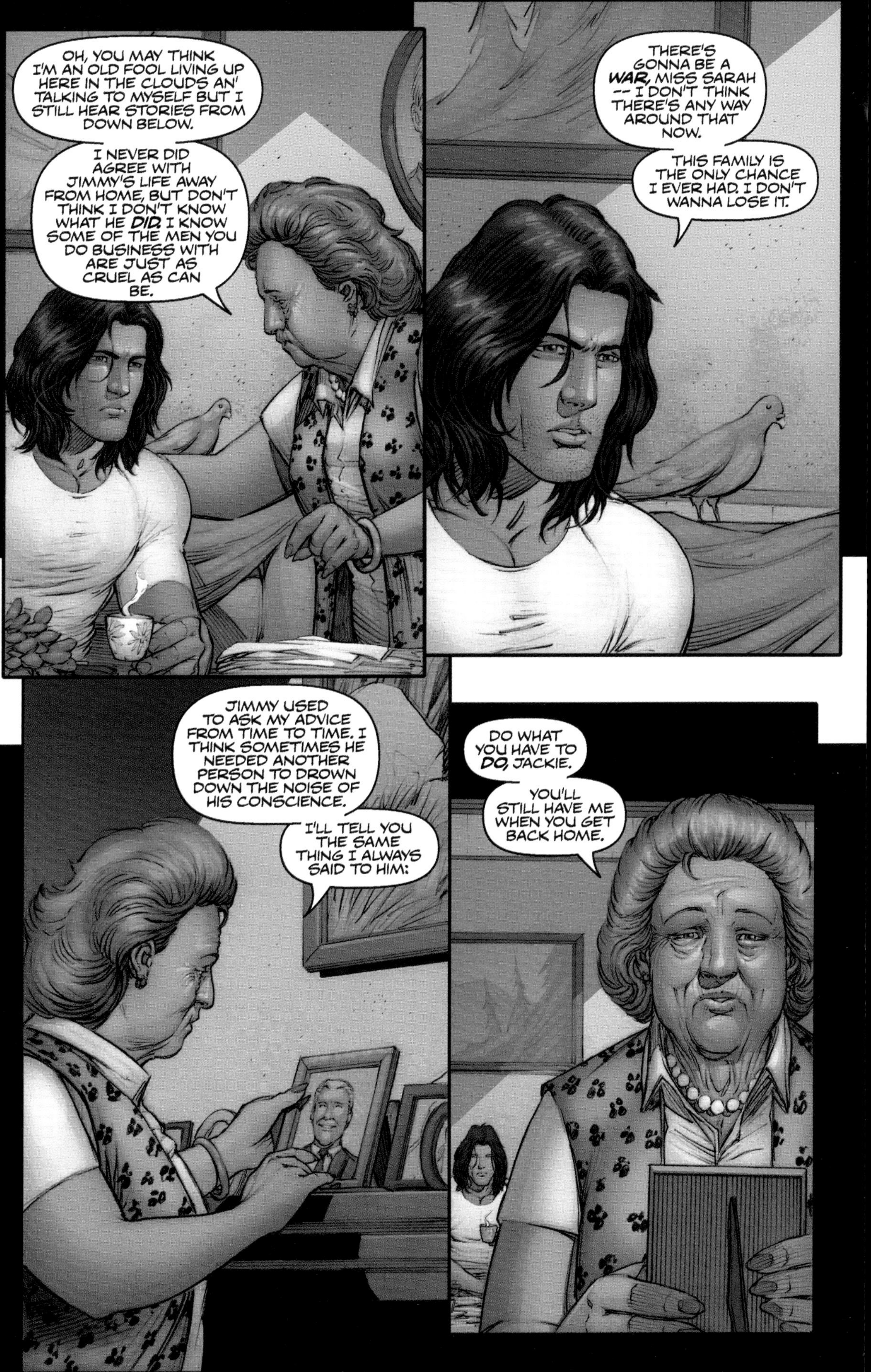
OH, YOU MAY THINK I'M AN OLD FOOL LIVING UP HERE IN THE CLOUDS AN' TALKING TO MYSELF BUT I STILL HEAR STORIES FROM DOWN BELOW.
I NEVER DID AGREE WITH JIMMY'S LIFE AWAY FROM HOME, BUT DON'T THINK I DON'T KNOW WHAT HE DID. I KNOW SOME OF THE MEN YOU DO BUSINESS WITH ARE JUST AS CRUEL AS CAN BE.
THERE'S GONNA BE A WAR, MISS SARAH -- I DON'T THINK THERE'S ANY WAY AROUND THAT NOW.
THIS FAMILY IS THE ONLY CHANCE I EVER HAD. I DON'T WANNA LOSE IT.
JIMMY USED TO ASK MY ADVICE FROM TIME TO TIME. I THINK SOMETIMES HE NEEDED ANOTHER PERSON TO DROWN DOWN THE NOISE OF HIS CONSCIENCE.
I'LL TELL YOU THE SAME THING I ALWAYS SAID TO HIM:
DO WHAT YOU HAVE TO DO, JACKIE.
YOU'LL STILL HAVE ME WHEN YOU GET BACK HOME.

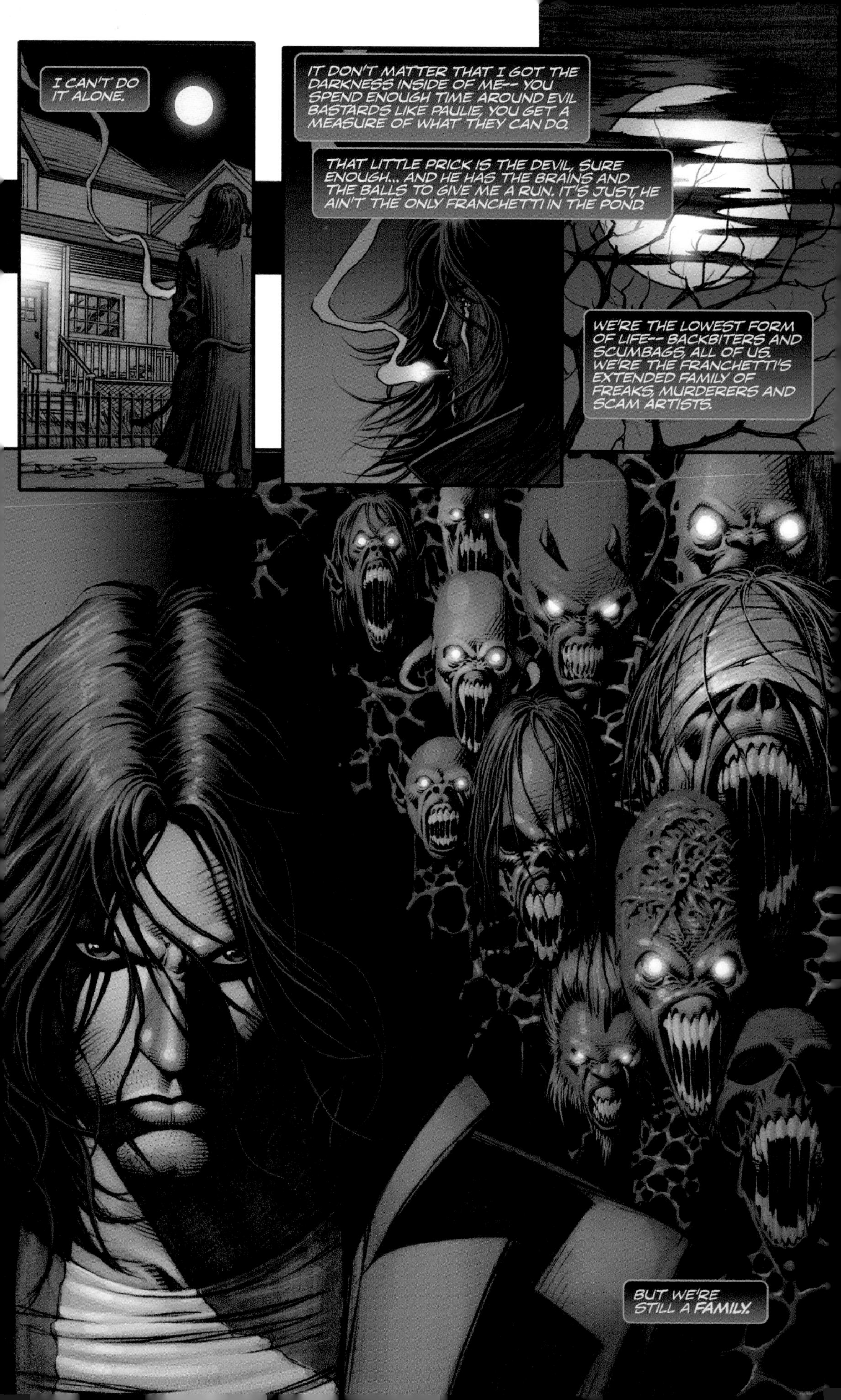
I CAN'T DO IT ALONE.
IT DON'T MATTER THAT I GOT THE DARKNESS INSIDE OF ME-- YOU SPEND ENOUGH TIME AROUND EVIL BASTARDS LIKE PAULIE, YOU GET A MEASURE OF WHAT THEY CAN DO.
THAT LITTLE PRICK IS THE DEVIL, SURE ENOUGH... AND HE HAS THE BRAINS AND THE BALLS TO GIVE ME A RUN. IT'S JUST, HE AIN'T THE ONLY FRANCHETTI IN THE POND.
WE'RE THE LOWEST FORM OF LIFE-- BACKBITERS AND SCUMBAGS, ALL OF US. WE'RE THE FRANCHETTI'S EXTENDED FAMILY OF FREAKS, MURDERERS AND SCAM ARTISTS.
BUT WE'RE STILL A FAMILY.

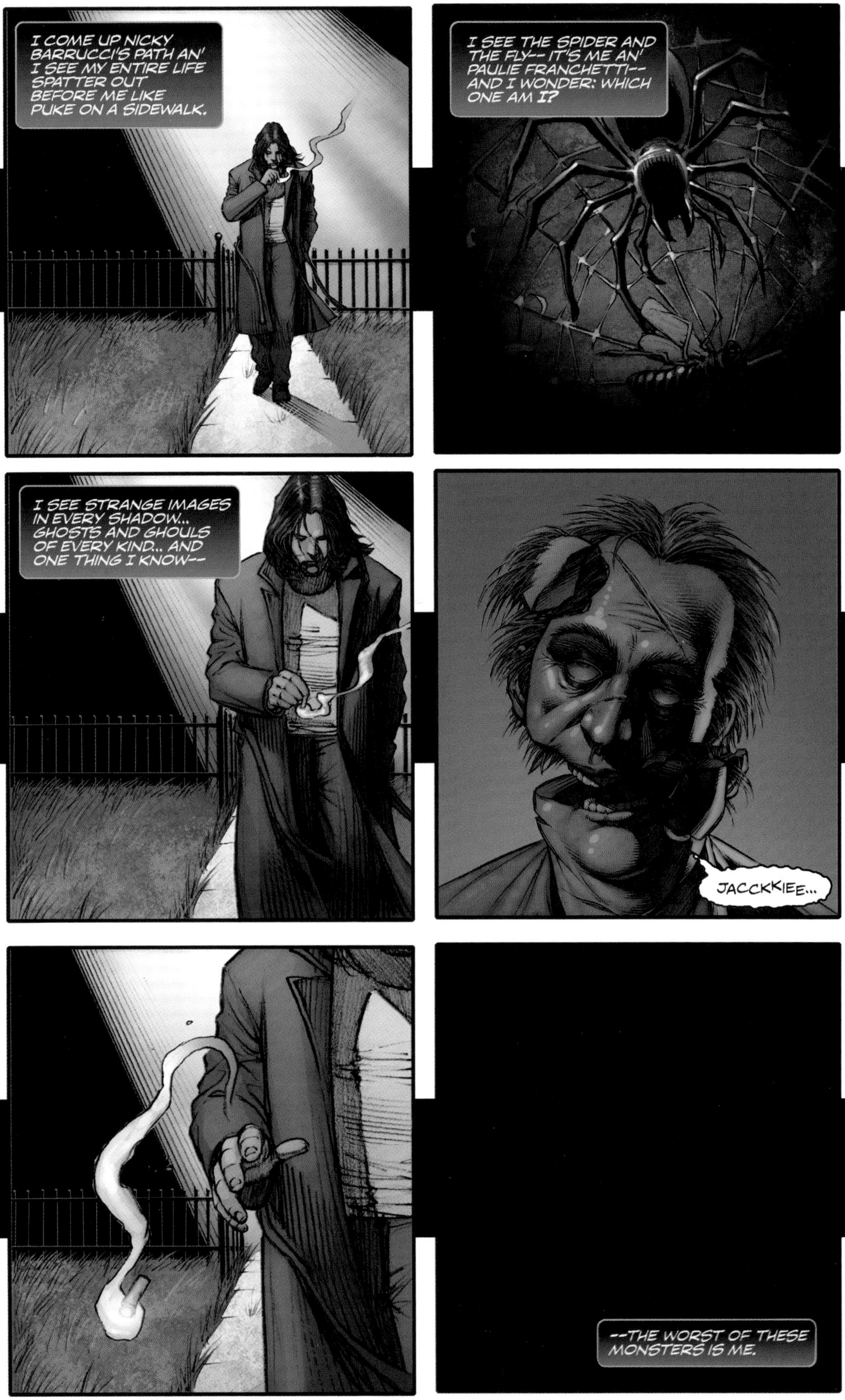
I COME UP NICKY BARRUCCI'S PATH AN' I SEE MY ENTIRE LIFE SPATTER OUT BEFORE ME LIKE PUKE ON A SIDEWALK.
I SEE THE SPIDER AND THE FLY-- IT'S ME AN' PAULIE FRANCHETTI-- AND I WONDER: WHICH ONE AM I?
I SEE STRANGE IMAGES IN EVERY SHADOW... GHOSTS AND GHOULS OF EVERY KIND... AND ONE THING I KNOW--
JACCKKIEE...
--THE WORST OF THESE MONSTERS IS ME.

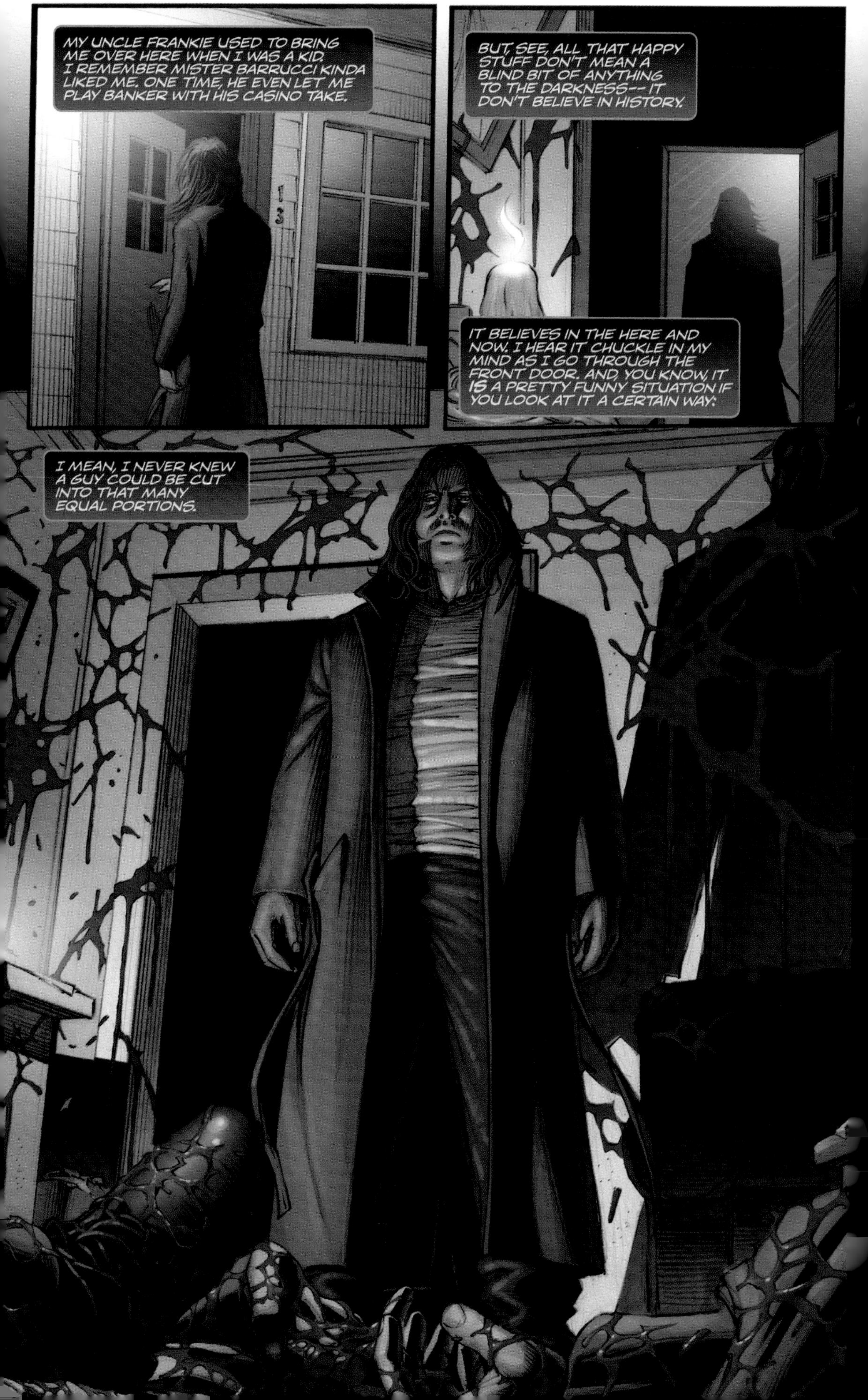
MY UNCLE FRANKIE USED TO BRING ME OVER HERE WHEN I WAS A KID. I REMEMBER MISTER BARRUCCI KINDA LIKED ME. ONE TIME, HE EVEN LET ME PLAY BANKER WITH HIS CASINO TAKE.
BUT, SEE, ALL THAT HAPPY STUFF DON'T MEAN A BLIND BIT OF ANYTHING TO THE DARKNESS-- IT DON'T BELIEVE IN HISTORY.
IT BELIEVES IN THE HERE AND NOW. I HEAR IT CHUCKLE IN MY MIND AS I GO THROUGH THE FRONT DOOR. AND, YOU KNOW, IT IS A PRETTY FUNNY SITUATION IF YOU LOOK AT IT A CERTAIN WAY:
I MEAN, I NEVER KNEW A GUY COULD BE CUT INTO THAT MANY EQUAL PORTIONS.

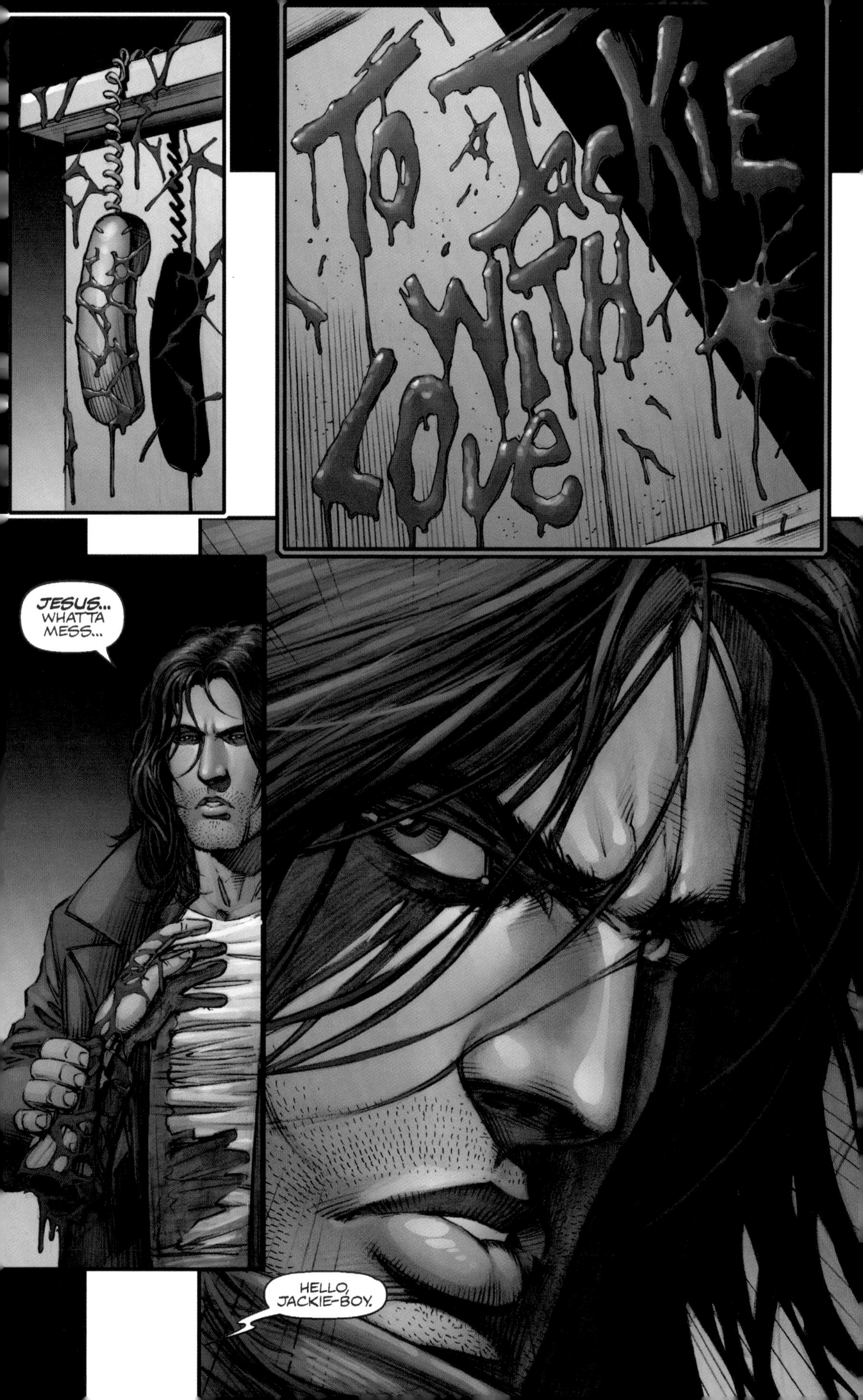
TO JACKIE WITH LOVE
JESUS... WHATTA MESS...
HELLO, JACKIE-BOY.

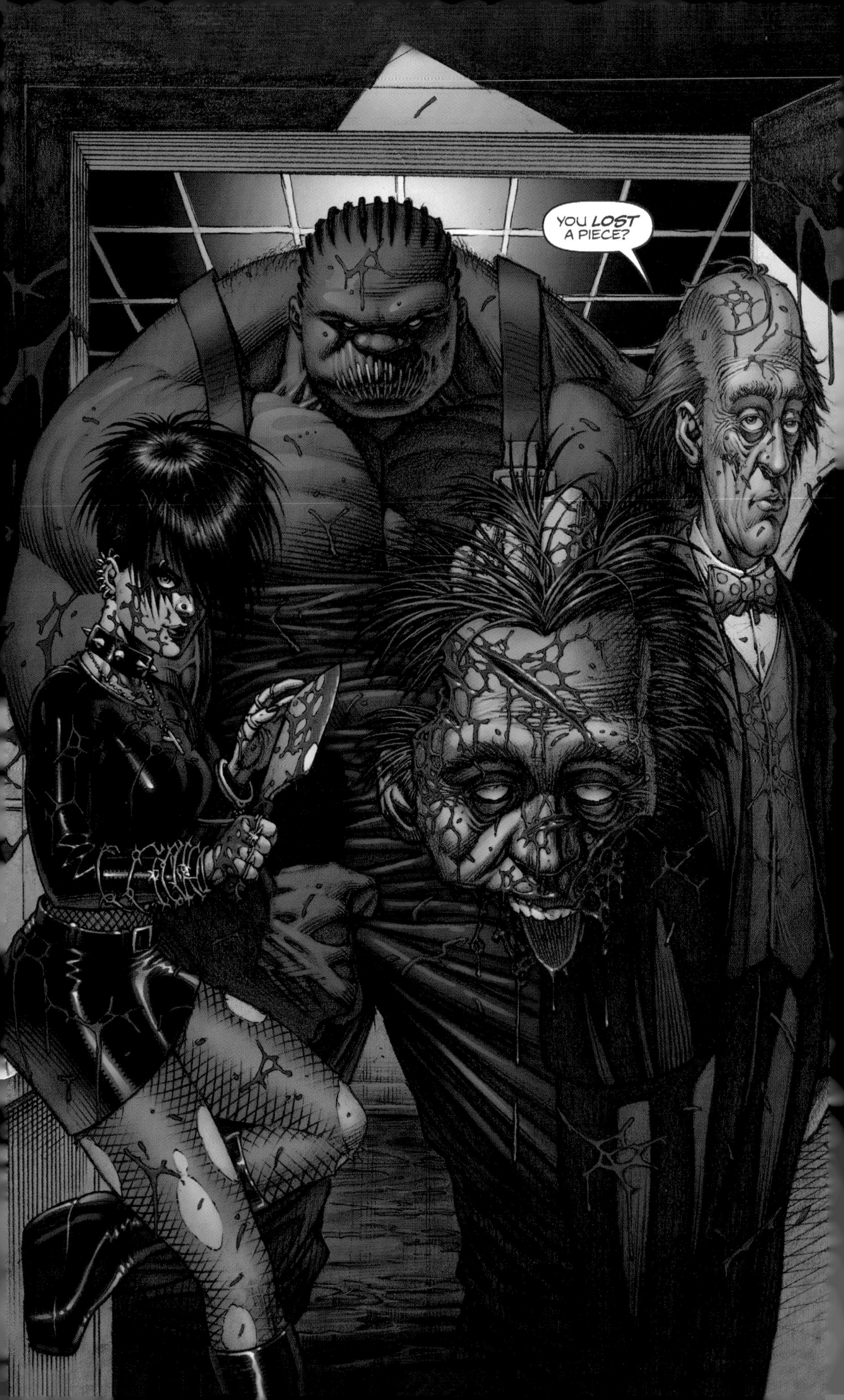
YOU LOST A PIECE?

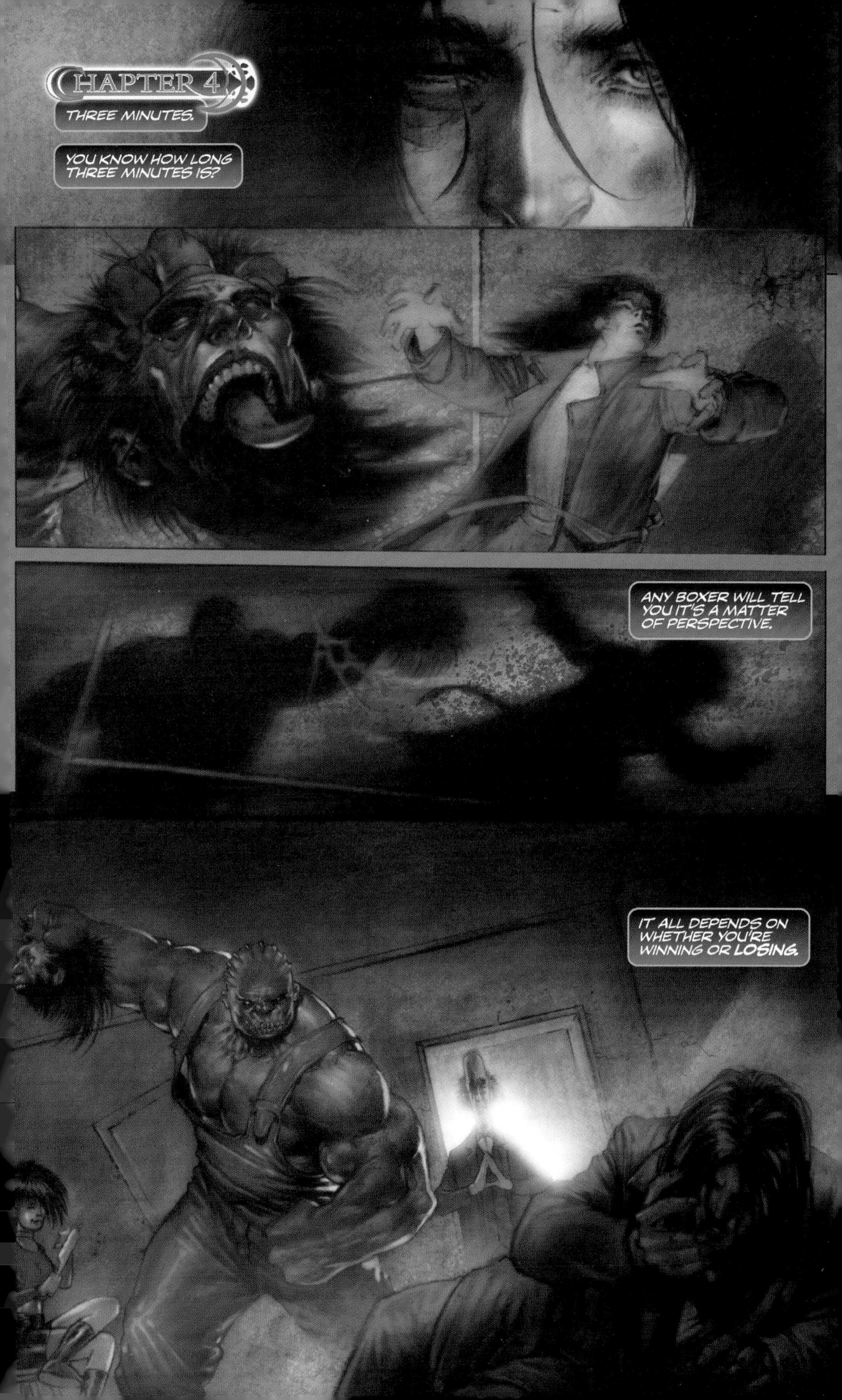
CHAPTER 4
THREE MINUTES.
YOU KNOW HOW LONG THREE MINUTES IS?
ANY BOXER WILL TELL YOU IT'S A MATTER OF PERSPECTIVE.
IT ALL DEPENDS ON WHETHER YOU'RE WINNING OR LOSING.

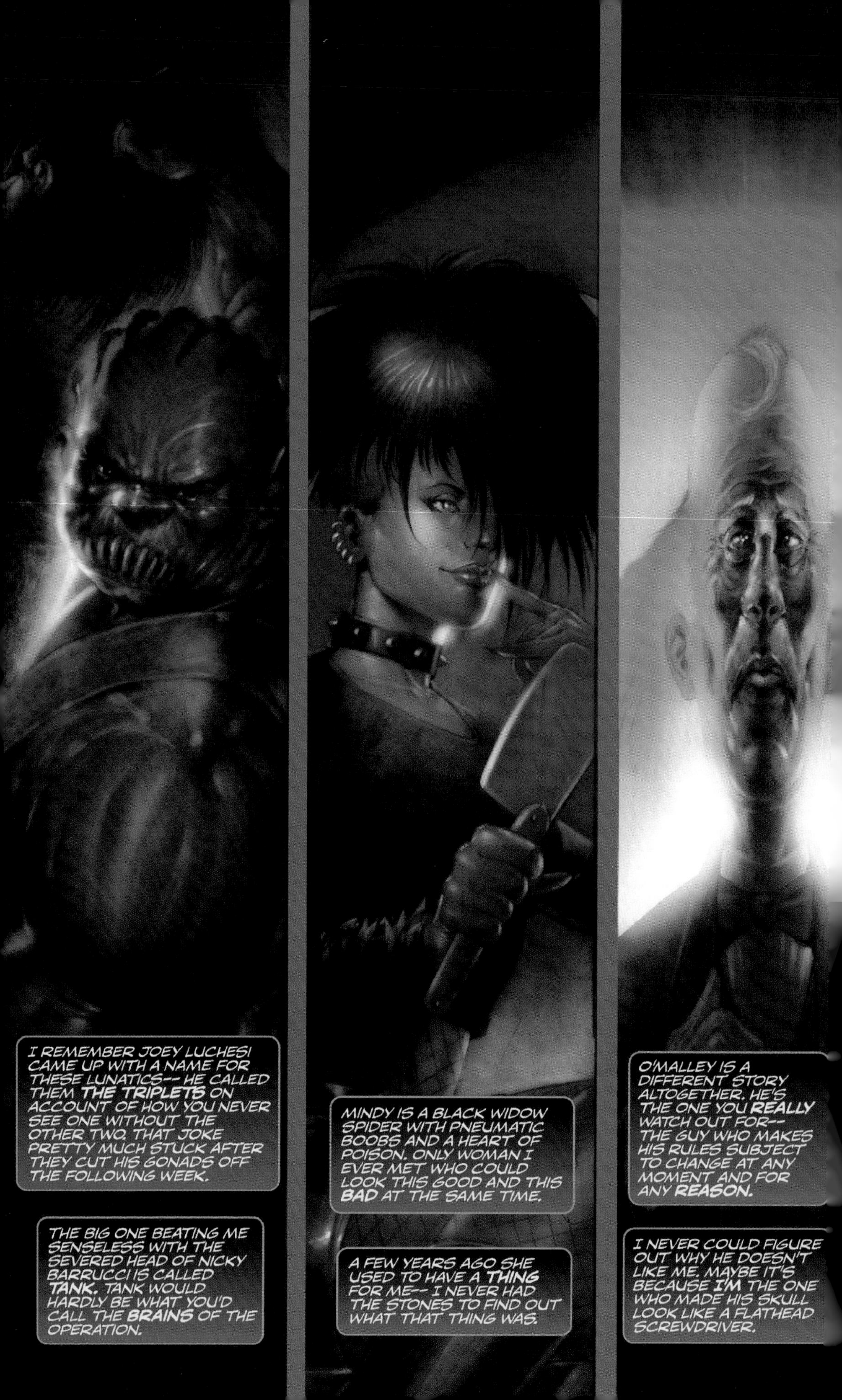
I REMEMBER JOEY LUCHESI CAME UP WITH A NAME FOR THESE LUNATICS-- HE CALLED THEM THE TRIPLETS ON ACCOUNT OF HOW YOU NEVER SEE ONE WITHOUT THE OTHER TWO. THAT JOKE PRETTY MUCH STUCK AFTER THEY CUT HIS GONADS OFF THE FOLLOWING WEEK.
THE BIG ONE BEATING ME SENSELESS WITH THE SEVERED HEAD OF NICKY BARRUCCI IS CALLED TANK. TANK WOULD HARDLY BE WHAT YOU'D CALL THE BRAINS OF THE OPERATION.
MINDY IS A BLACK WIDOW SPIDER WITH PNEUMATIC BOOBS AND A HEART OF POISON. ONLY WOMAN I EVER MET WHO COULD LOOK THIS GOOD AND THIS BAD AT THE SAME TIME.
A FEW YEARS AGO SHE USED TO HAVE A THING FOR ME-- I NEVER HAD THE STONES TO FIND OUT WHAT THAT THING WAS.
O'MALLEY IS A DIFFERENT STORY ALTOGETHER. HE'S THE ONE YOU REALLY WATCH OUT FOR-- THE GUY WHO MAKES HIS RULES SUBJECT TO CHANGE AT ANY MOMENT AND FOR ANY REASON.
I NEVER COULD FIGURE OUT WHY HE DOESN'T LIKE ME. MAYBE IT'S BECAUSE I'M THE ONE WHO MADE HIS SKULL LOOK LIKE A FLATHEAD SCREWDRIVER.

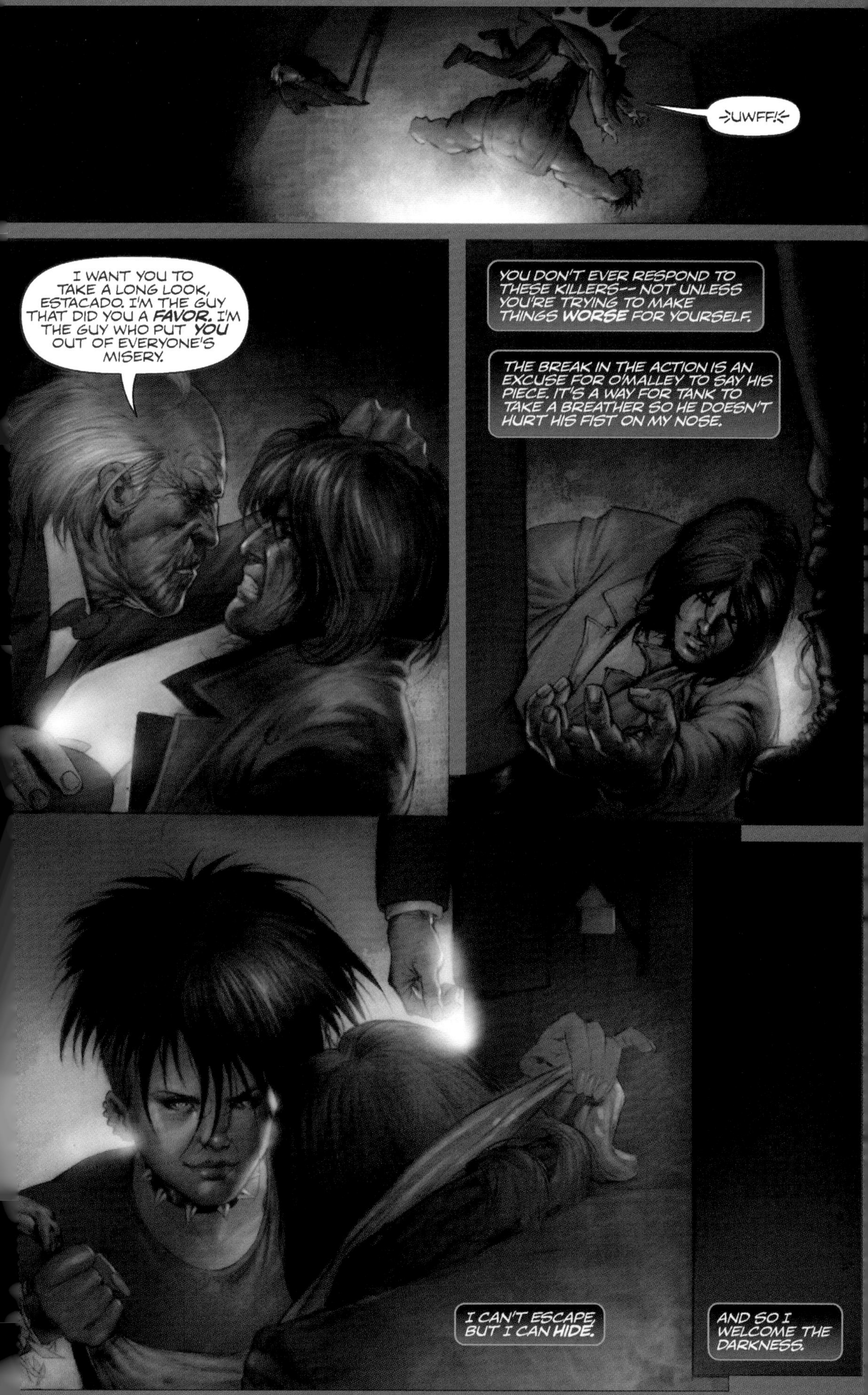
>UWFF!<
I WANT YOU TO TAKE A LONG LOOK, ESTACADO. I'M THE GUY THAT DID YOU A FAVOR. I'M THE GUY WHO PUT YOU OUT OF EVERYONE'S MISERY.
YOU DON'T EVER RESPOND TO THESE KILLERS-- NOT UNLESS YOU'RE TRYING TO MAKE THINGS WORSE FOR YOURSELF.
THE BREAK IN THE ACTION IS AN EXCUSE FOR O'MALLEY TO SAY HIS PIECE. IT'S A WAY FOR TANK TO TAKE A BREATHER SO HE DOESN'T HURT HIS FIST ON MY NOSE.
I CAN'T ESCAPE, BUT I CAN HIDE.
AND SO I WELCOME THE DARKNESS.

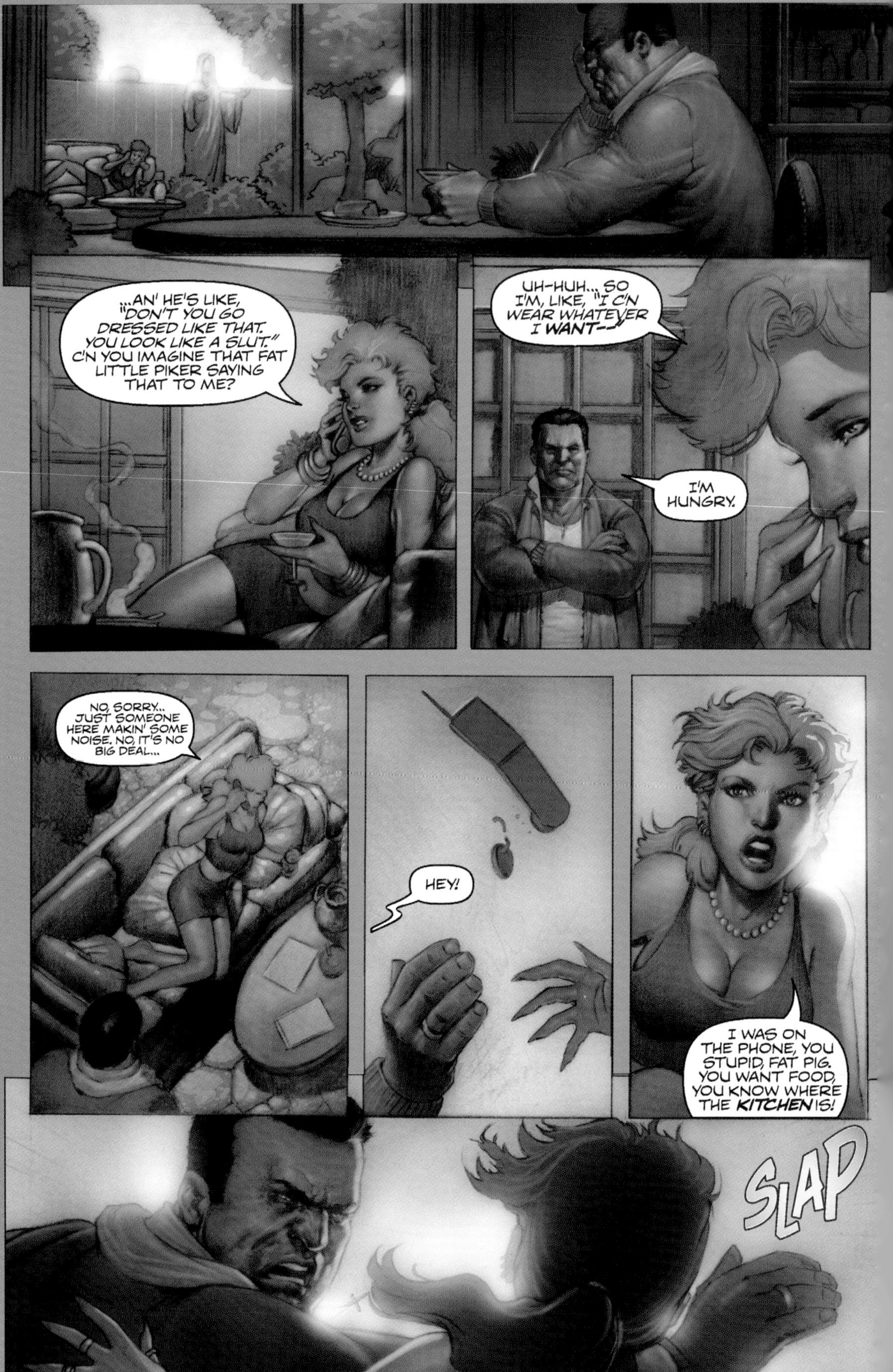
...AN' HE'S LIKE, "DON'T YOU GO DRESSED LIKE THAT. YOU LOOK LIKE A SLUT." C'N YOU IMAGINE THAT FAT LITTLE PIKER SAYING THAT TO ME?
UH-HUH... SO I'M, LIKE, "I C'N WEAR WHATEVER I WANT--"
I'M HUNGRY.
NO, SORRY... JUST SOMEONE HERE MAKIN' SOME NOISE. NO, IT'S NO BIG DEAL...
HEY!
I WAS ON THE PHONE, YOU STUPID, FAT PIG. YOU WANT FOOD, YOU KNOW WHERE THE KITCHEN IS!
SLAP

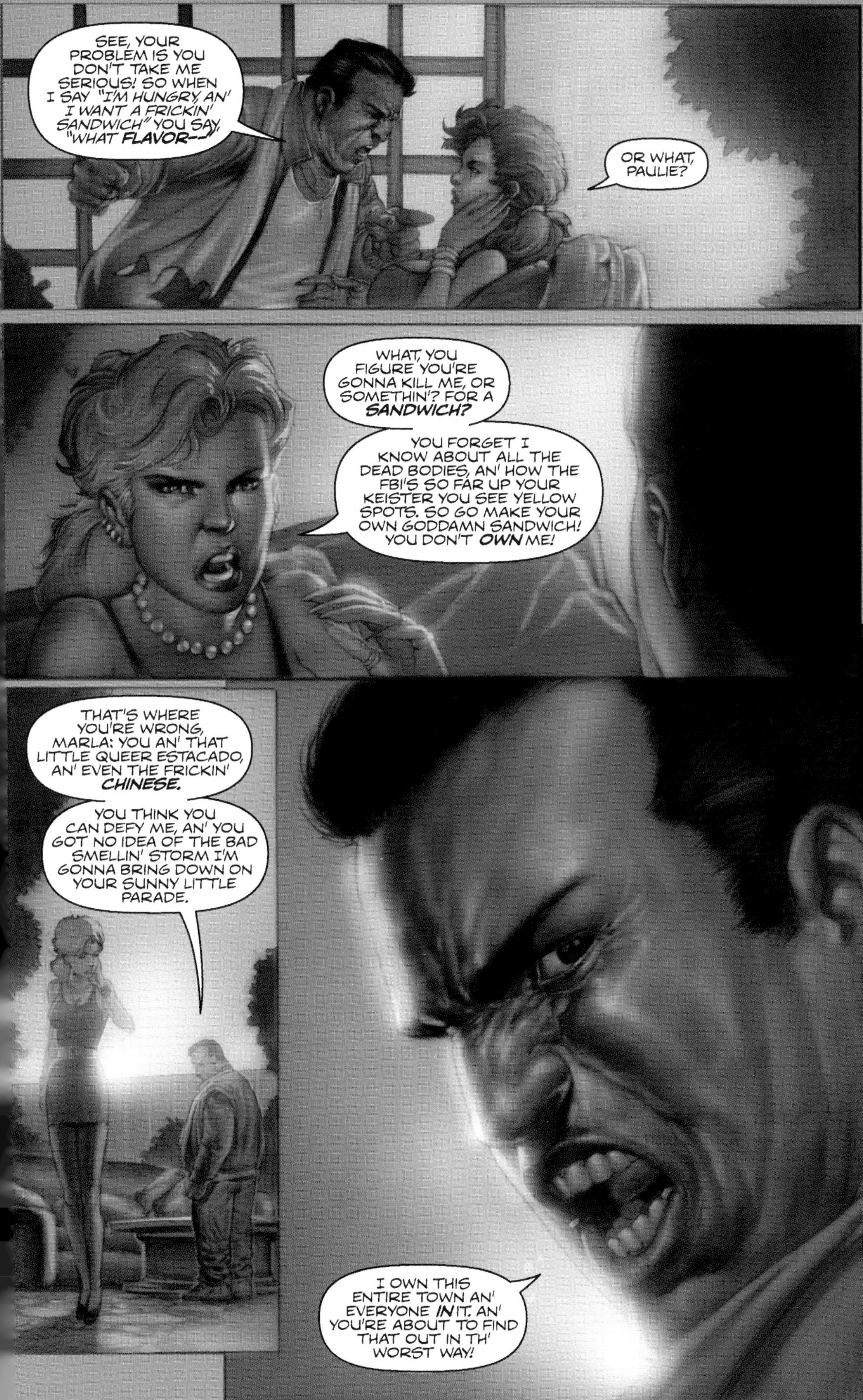
SEE, YOUR PROBLEM IS YOU DON'T TAKE ME SERIOUS! SO WHEN I SAY "I'M HUNGRY, AN' I WANT A FRICKIN' SANDWICH" YOU SAY, "WHAT FLAVOR--"
OR WHAT, PAULIE?
WHAT, YOU FIGURE YOU'RE GONNA KILL ME, OR SOMETHIN'? FOR A SANDWICH?
YOU FORGET I KNOW ABOUT ALL THE DEAD BODIES, AN' HOW THE FBI'S SO FAR UP YOUR KEISTER YOU SEE YELLOW SPOTS. SO GO MAKE YOUR OWN GODDAMN SANDWICH! YOU DON'T OWN ME!
THAT'S WHERE YOU'RE WRONG, MARLA: YOU AN' THAT LITTLE QUEER ESTACADO, AN' EVEN THE FRICKIN' CHINESE.
YOU THINK YOU CAN DEFY ME, AN' YOU GOT NO IDEA OF THE BAD SMELLIN' STORM I'M GONNA BRING DOWN ON YOUR SUNNY LITTLE PARADE.
I OWN THIS ENTIRE TOWN AN' EVERYONE IN IT. AN' YOU'RE ABOUT TO FIND THAT OUT IN TH' WORST WAY!

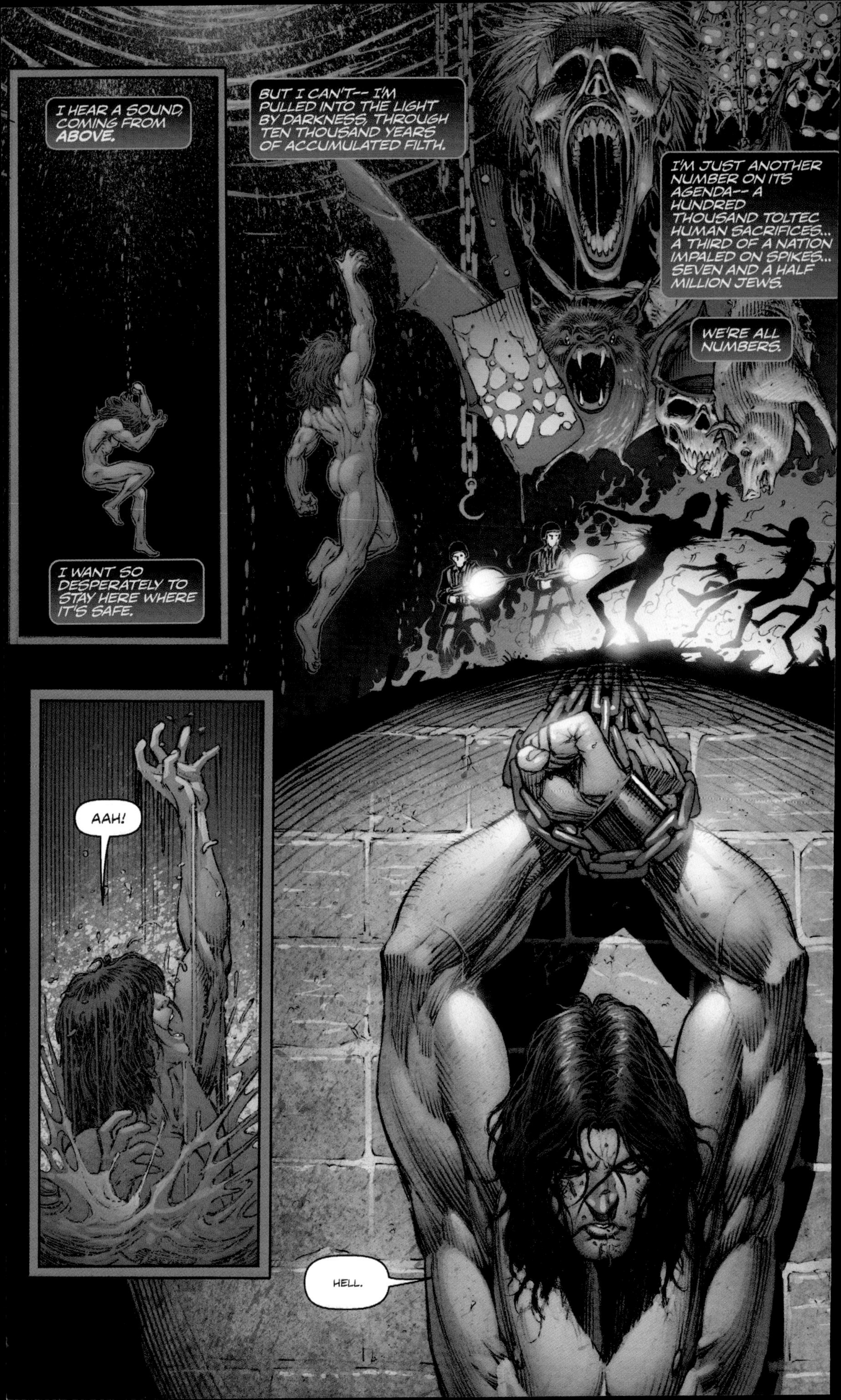
I HEAR A SOUND, COMING FROM ABOVE.
I WANT SO DESPERATELY TO STAY HERE WHERE IT'S SAFE.
BUT I CAN'T-- I'M PULLED INTO THE LIGHT BY DARKNESS, THROUGH TEN THOUSAND YEARS OF ACCUMULATED FILTH.
I'M JUST ANOTHER NUMBER ON ITS AGENDA-- A HUNDRED THOUSAND TOLTEC HUMAN SACRIFICES... A THIRD OF A NATION IMPALED ON SPIKES... SEVEN AND A HALF MILLION JEWS.
WE'RE ALL NUMBERS.
AAH!
HELL.

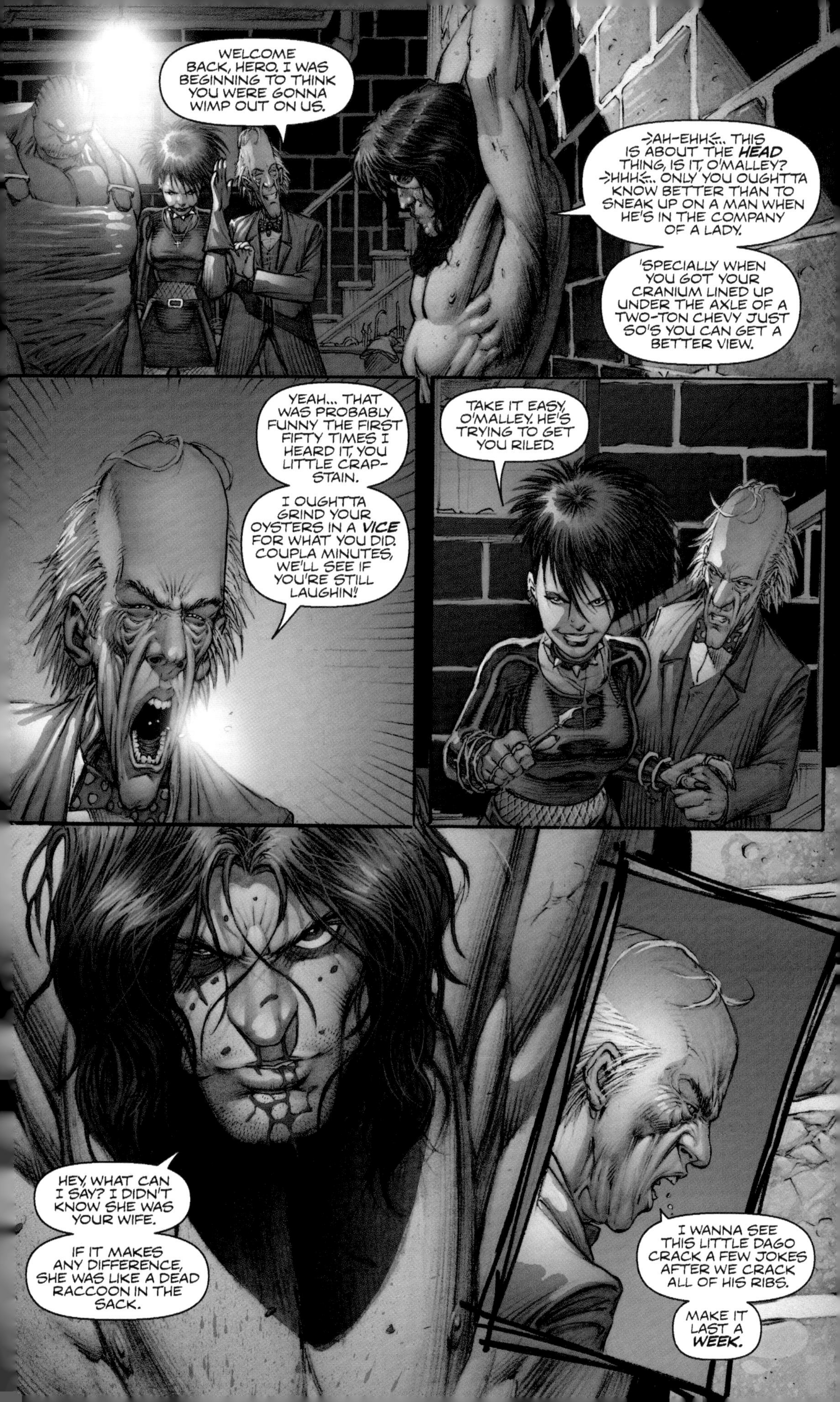
WELCOME BACK, HERO. I WAS BEGINNING TO THINK YOU WERE GONNA WIMP OUT ON US.
>AH-EHH<.. THIS IS ABOUT THE **HEAD** THING, IS IT, O'MALLEY? >HHH<.. ONLY YOU OUGHTTA KNOW BETTER THAN TO SNEAK UP ON A MAN WHEN HE'S IN THE COMPANY OF A LADY.
'SPECIALLY WHEN YOU GOT YOUR CRANIUM LINED UP UNDER THE AXLE OF A TWO-TON CHEVY JUST SO'S YOU CAN GET A BETTER VIEW.
YEAH... THAT WAS PROBABLY FUNNY THE FIRST FIFTY TIMES I HEARD IT, YOU LITTLE CRAP-STAIN.
I OUGHTTA GRIND YOUR OYSTERS IN A **VICE** FOR WHAT YOU DID. COUPLA MINUTES, WE'LL SEE IF YOU'RE STILL LAUGHIN'!
TAKE IT EASY, O'MALLEY. HE'S TRYING TO GET YOU RILED.
HEY, WHAT CAN I SAY? I DIDN'T KNOW SHE WAS YOUR WIFE.
IF IT MAKES ANY DIFFERENCE, SHE WAS LIKE A DEAD RACCOON IN THE SACK.
I WANNA SEE THIS LITTLE DAGO CRACK A FEW JOKES AFTER WE CRACK ALL OF HIS RIBS.
MAKE IT LAST A **WEEK.**

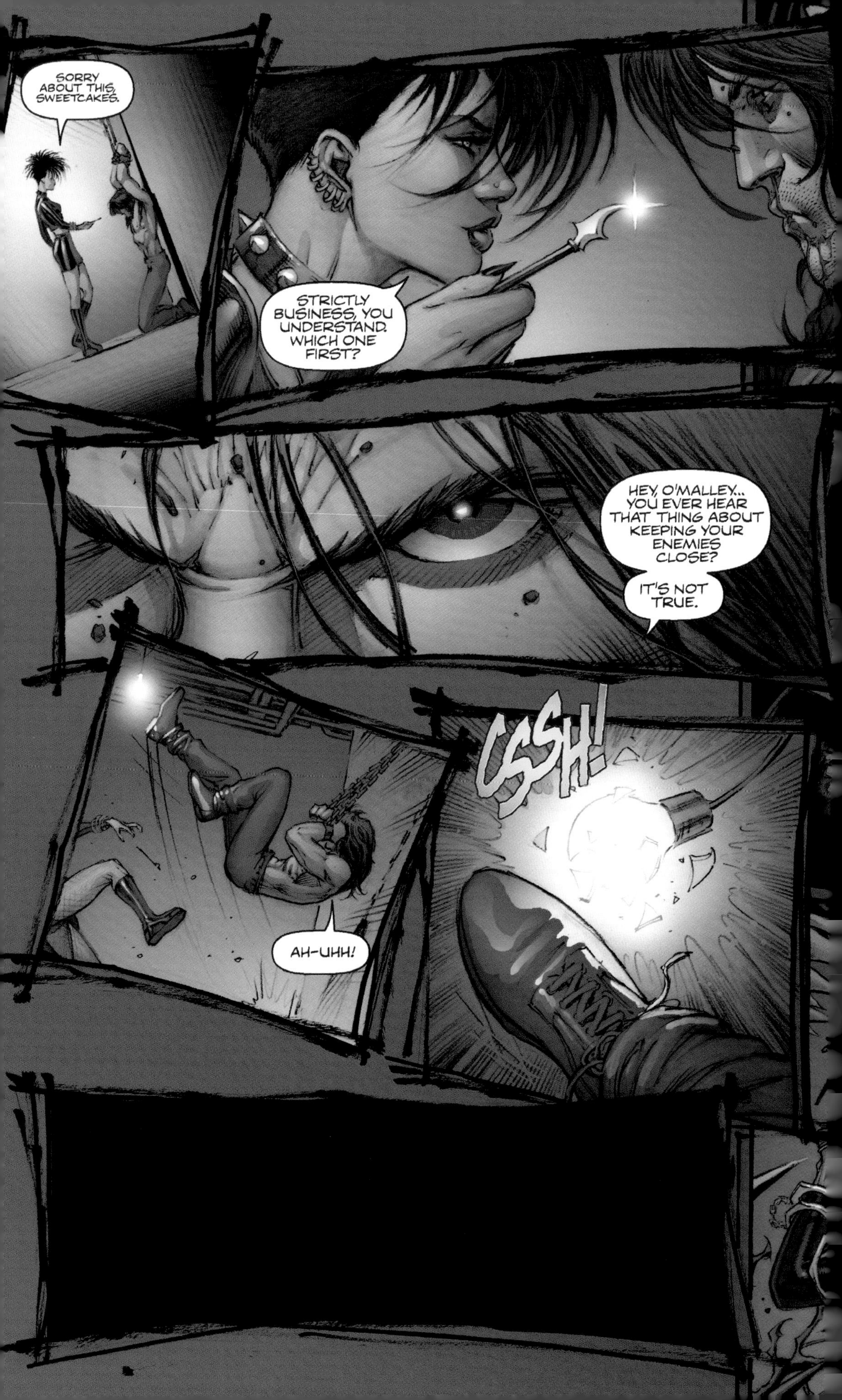
SORRY ABOUT THIS, SWEETCAKES.
STRICTLY BUSINESS, YOU UNDERSTAND. WHICH ONE FIRST?
HEY, O'MALLEY.. YOU EVER HEAR THAT THING ABOUT KEEPING YOUR ENEMIES CLOSE?
IT'S NOT TRUE.
AH-UHH!
CSSH!

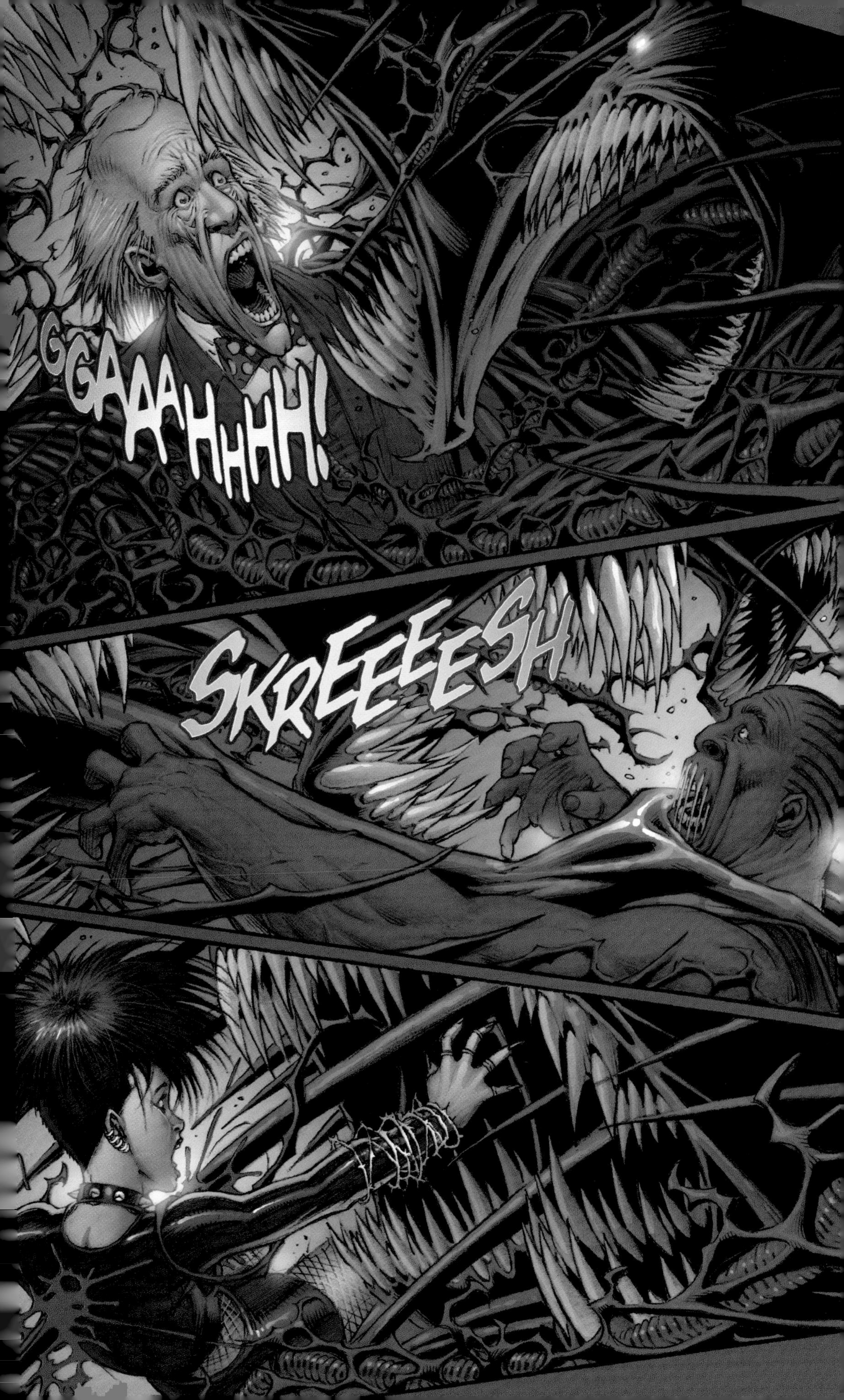
GGAAAHHHH!
SKREEEESH

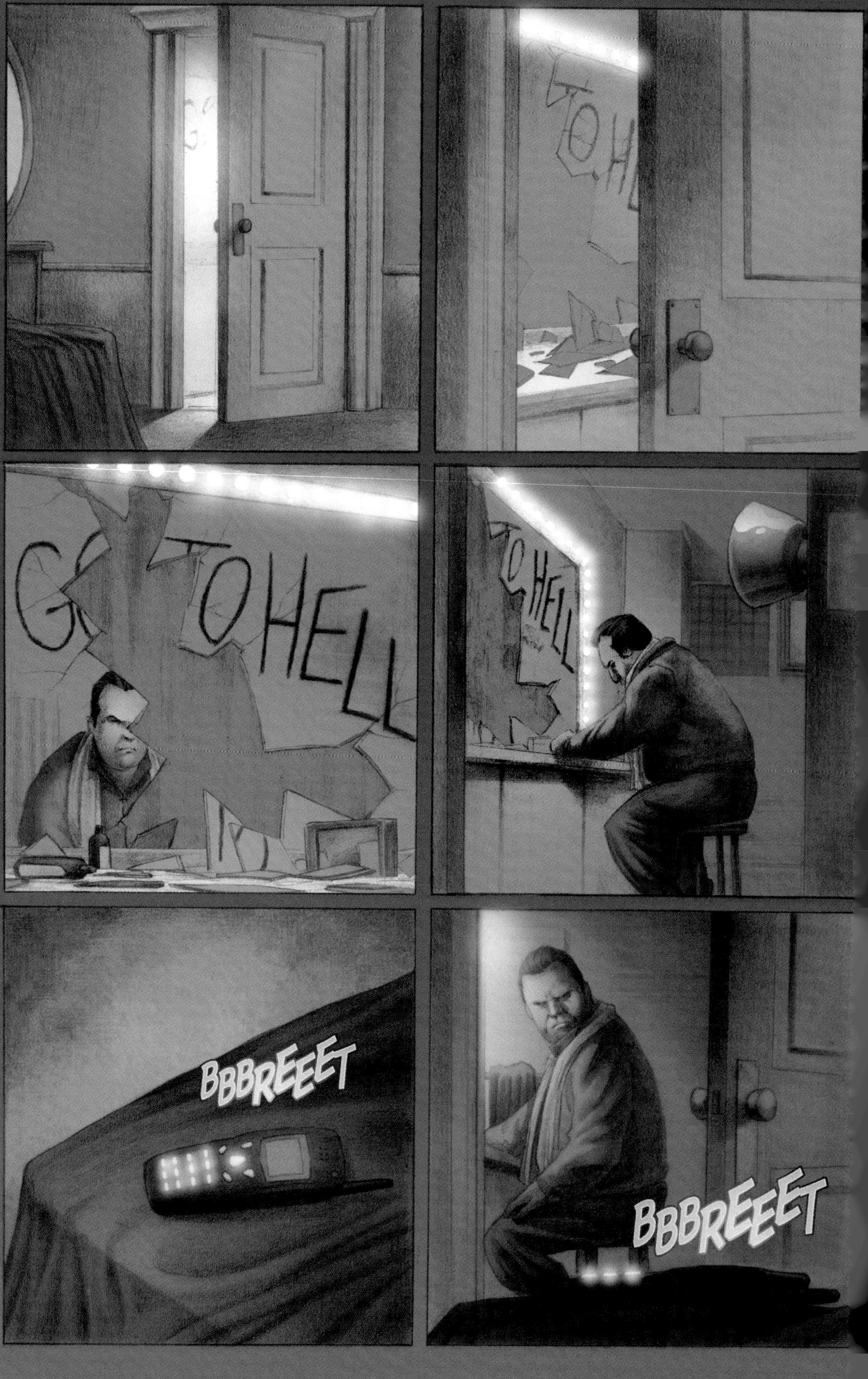

TO HELL
TO HELL
BBBREEET
BBBREEET

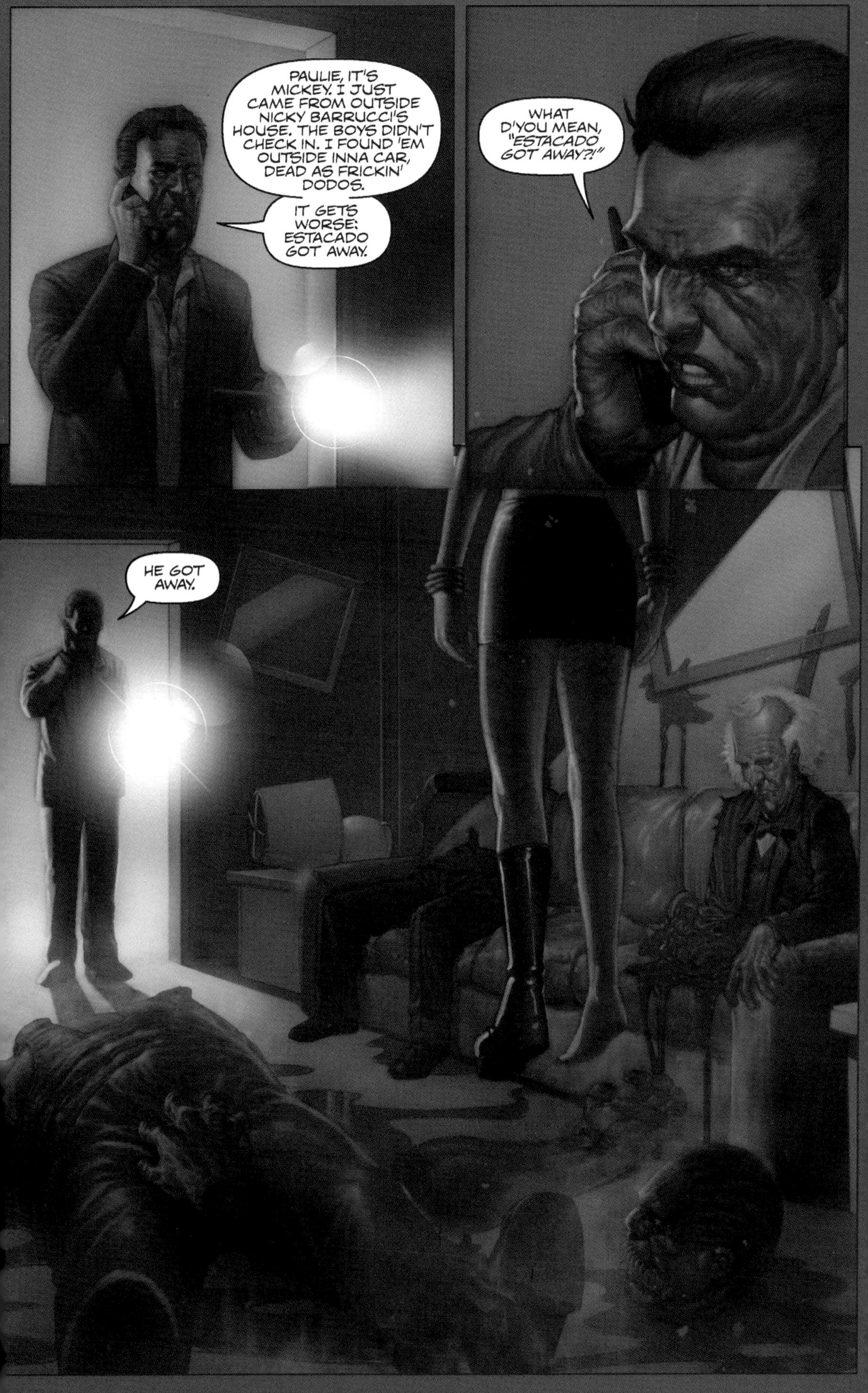
PAULIE, IT'S MICKEY. I JUST CAME FROM OUTSIDE NICKY BARRUCCI'S HOUSE. THE BOYS DIDN'T CHECK IN. I FOUND 'EM OUTSIDE INNA CAR, DEAD AS FRICKIN' DODOS.
IT GETS WORSE: ESTACADO GOT AWAY.
WHAT D'YOU MEAN, "ESTACADO GOT AWAY?!"
HE GOT AWAY.

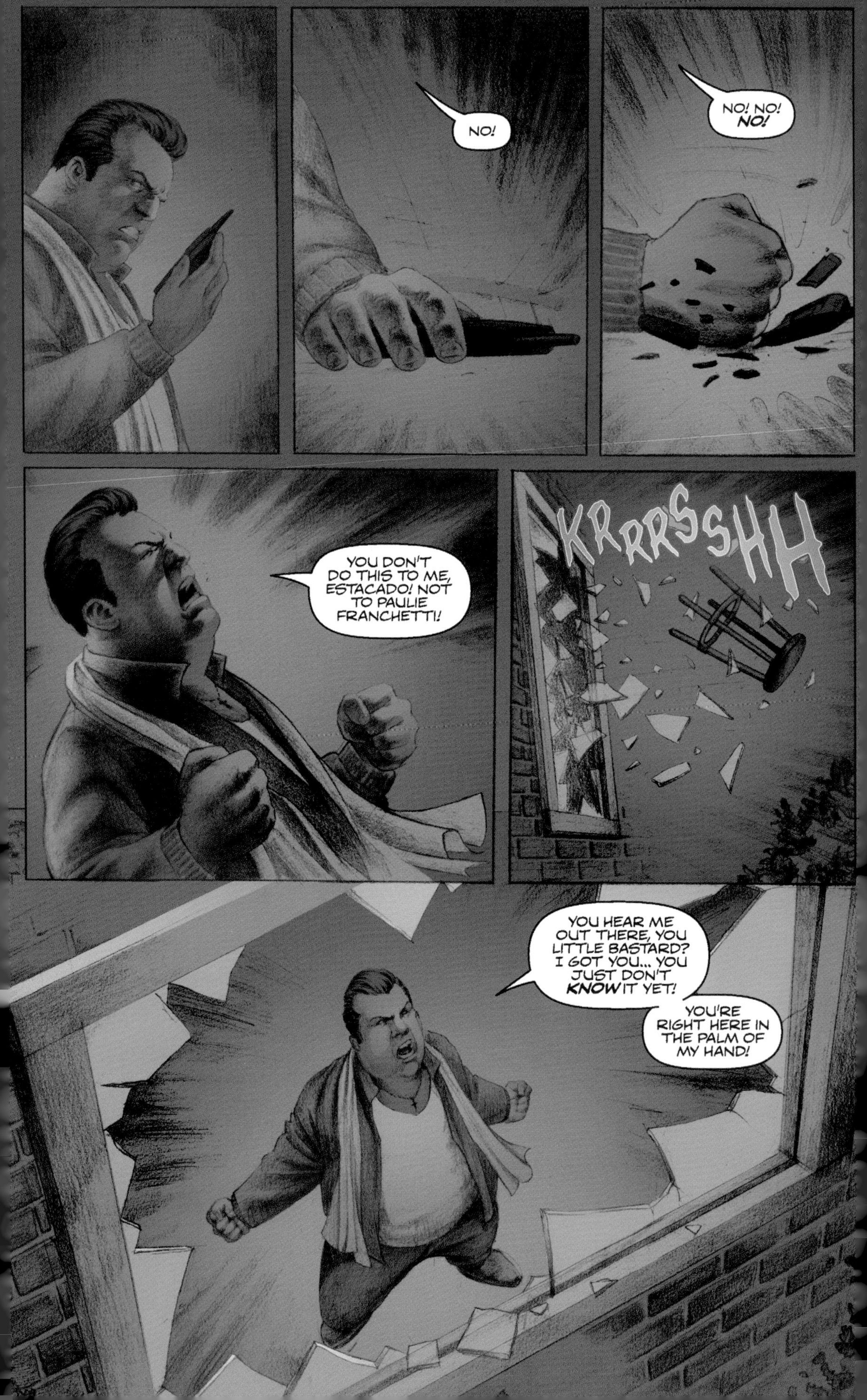
NO!
NO! NO! NO!
YOU DON'T DO THIS TO ME, ESTACADO! NOT TO PAULIE FRANCHETTI!
KRRRSSHH
YOU HEAR ME OUT THERE, YOU LITTLE BASTARD? I GOT YOU... YOU JUST DON'T KNOW IT YET!
YOU'RE RIGHT HERE IN THE PALM OF MY HAND!

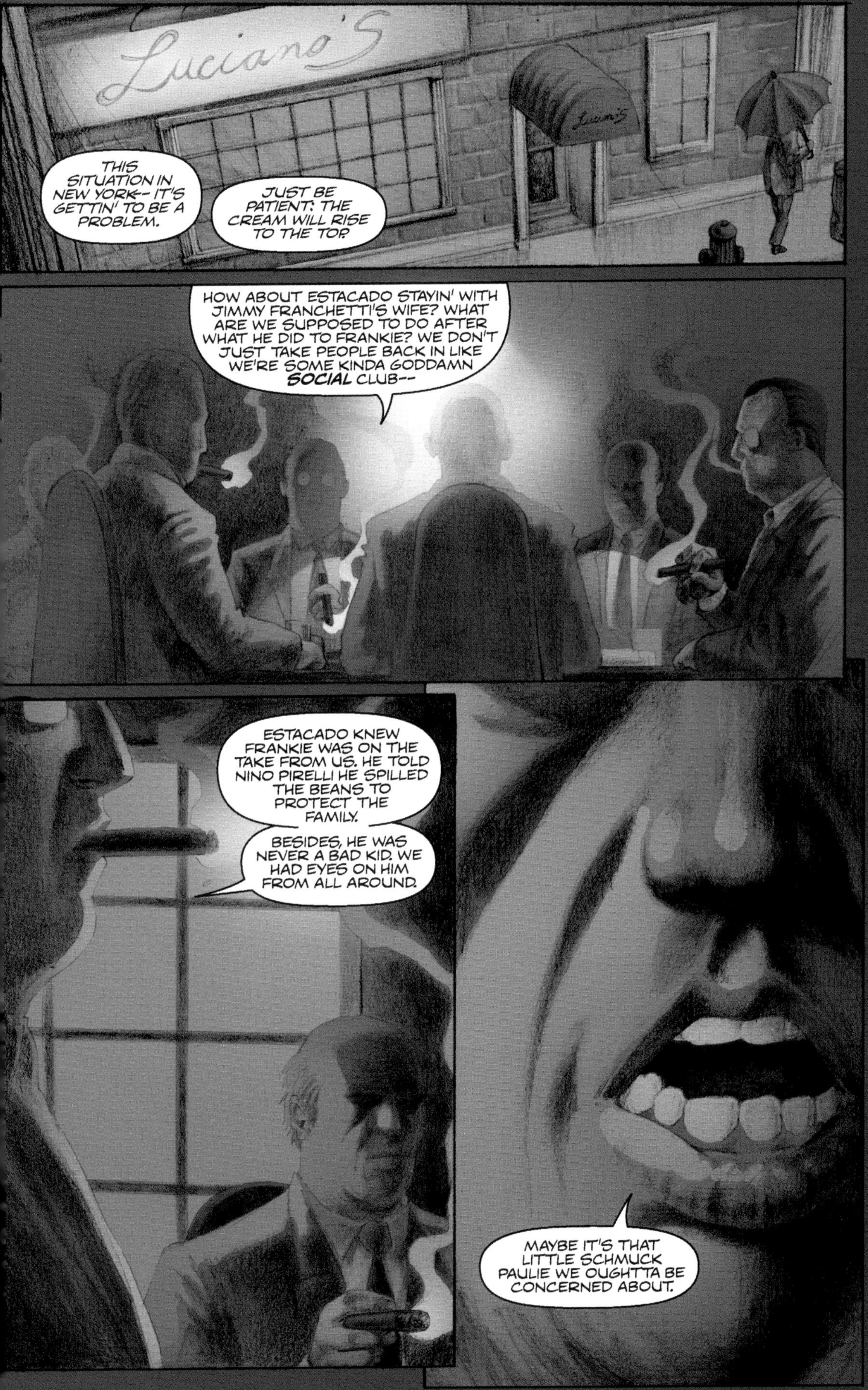
Luciano's
Luciano's
THIS SITUATION IN NEW YORK-- IT'S GETTIN' TO BE A PROBLEM.
JUST BE PATIENT: THE CREAM WILL RISE TO THE TOP.
HOW ABOUT ESTACADO STAYIN' WITH JIMMY FRANCHETTI'S WIFE? WHAT ARE WE SUPPOSED TO DO AFTER WHAT HE DID TO FRANKIE? WE DON'T JUST TAKE PEOPLE BACK IN LIKE WE'RE SOME KINDA GODDAMN SOCIAL CLUB--
ESTACADO KNEW FRANKIE WAS ON THE TAKE FROM US. HE TOLD NINO PIRELLI HE SPILLED THE BEANS TO PROTECT THE FAMILY.
BESIDES, HE WAS NEVER A BAD KID. WE HAD EYES ON HIM FROM ALL AROUND.
MAYBE IT'S THAT LITTLE SCHMUCK PAULIE WE OUGHTTA BE CONCERNED ABOUT.

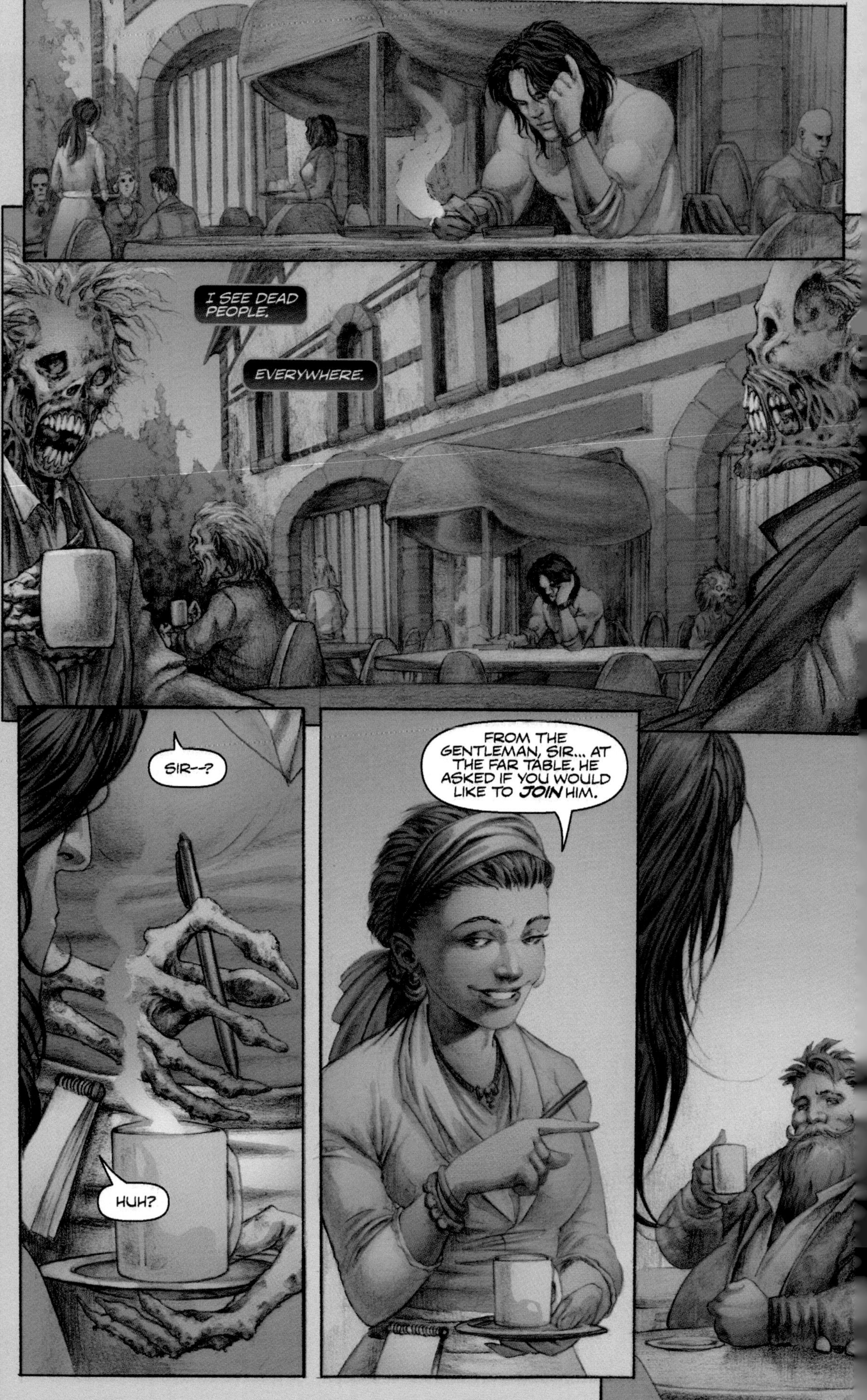
I SEE DEAD PEOPLE.
EVERYWHERE.
SIR--?
HUH?
FROM THE GENTLEMAN, SIR... AT THE FAR TABLE. HE ASKED IF YOU WOULD LIKE TO *JOIN* HIM.

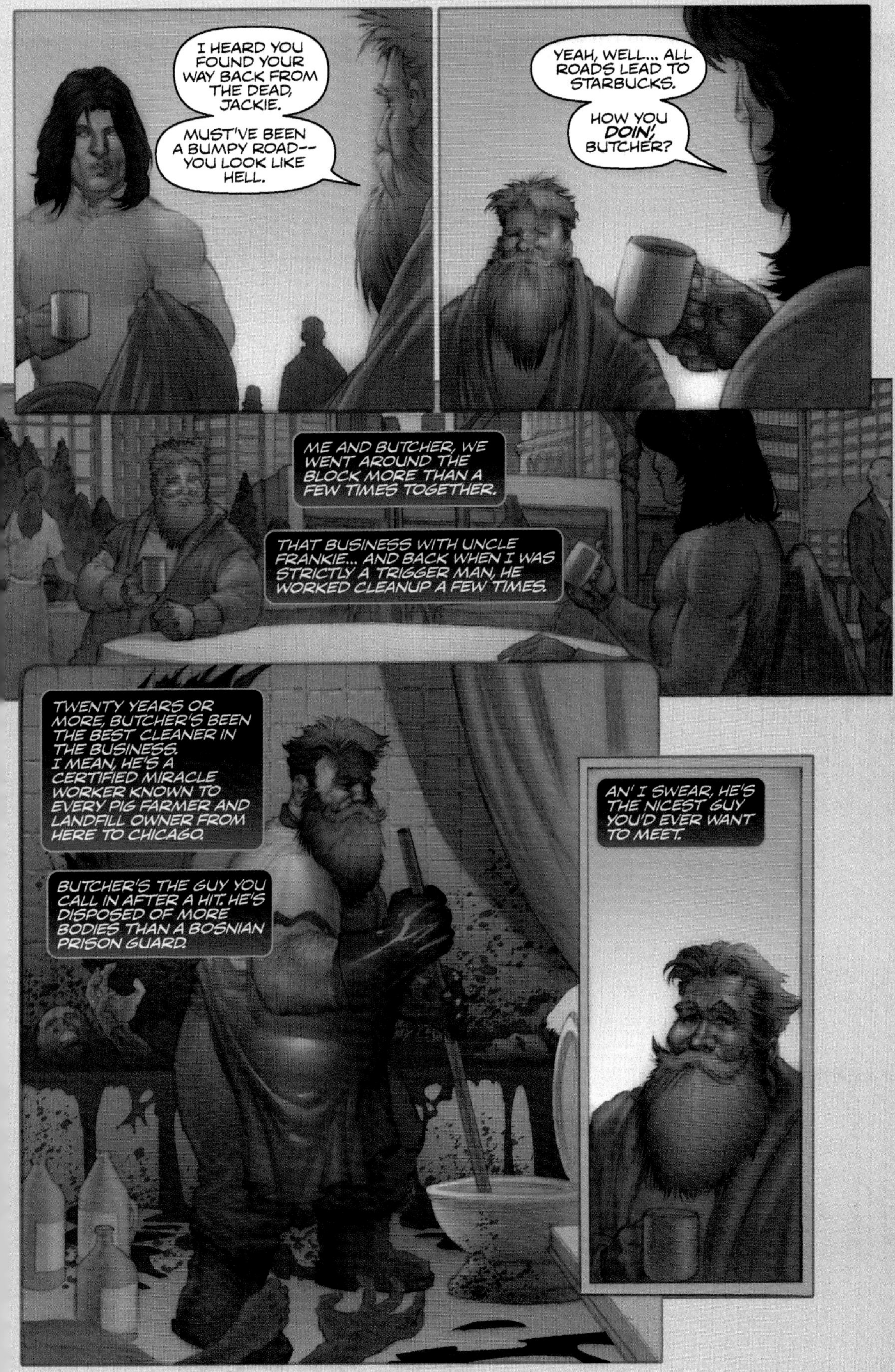
I HEARD YOU FOUND YOUR WAY BACK FROM THE DEAD, JACKIE.
MUST'VE BEEN A BUMPY ROAD-- YOU LOOK LIKE HELL.
YEAH, WELL... ALL ROADS LEAD TO STARBUCKS.
HOW YOU DOIN', BUTCHER?
ME AND BUTCHER, WE WENT AROUND THE BLOCK MORE THAN A FEW TIMES TOGETHER.
THAT BUSINESS WITH UNCLE FRANKIE... AND BACK WHEN I WAS STRICTLY A TRIGGER MAN, HE WORKED CLEANUP A FEW TIMES.
TWENTY YEARS OR MORE, BUTCHER'S BEEN THE BEST CLEANER IN THE BUSINESS. I MEAN, HE'S A CERTIFIED MIRACLE WORKER KNOWN TO EVERY PIG FARMER AND LANDFILL OWNER FROM HERE TO CHICAGO.
BUTCHER'S THE GUY YOU CALL IN AFTER A HIT. HE'S DISPOSED OF MORE BODIES THAN A BOSNIAN PRISON GUARD.
AN' I SWEAR, HE'S THE NICEST GUY YOU'D EVER WANT TO MEET.

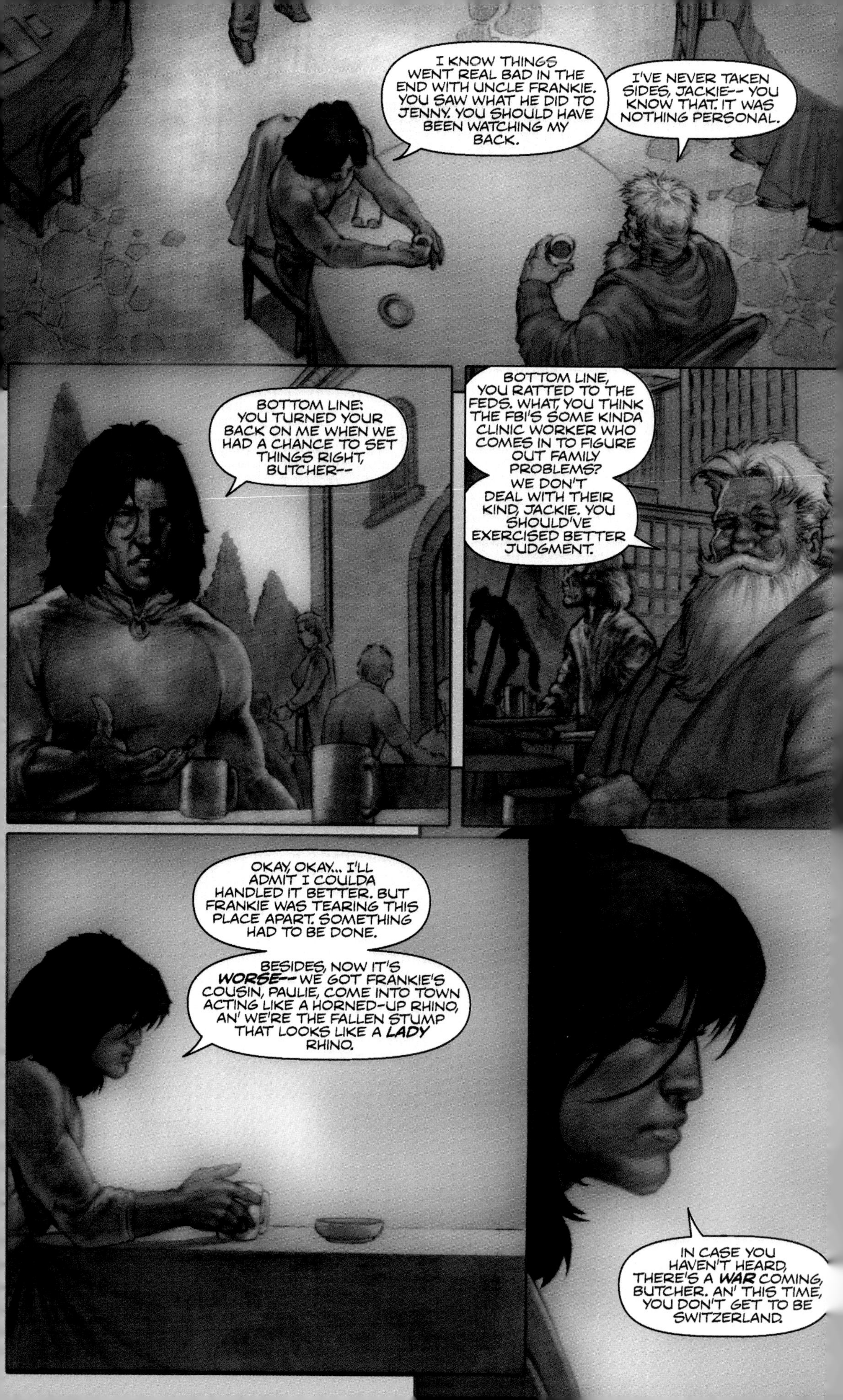
I KNOW THINGS WENT REAL BAD IN THE END WITH UNCLE FRANKIE. YOU SAW WHAT HE DID TO JENNY. YOU SHOULD HAVE BEEN WATCHING MY BACK.
I'VE NEVER TAKEN SIDES, JACKIE-- YOU KNOW THAT. IT WAS NOTHING PERSONAL.
BOTTOM LINE: YOU TURNED YOUR BACK ON ME WHEN WE HAD A CHANCE TO SET THINGS RIGHT, BUTCHER--
BOTTOM LINE, YOU RATTED TO THE FEDS. WHAT, YOU THINK THE FBI'S SOME KINDA CLINIC WORKER WHO COMES IN TO FIGURE OUT FAMILY PROBLEMS? WE DON'T DEAL WITH THEIR KIND, JACKIE. YOU SHOULD'VE EXERCISED BETTER JUDGMENT.
OKAY, OKAY... I'LL ADMIT I COULDA HANDLED IT BETTER. BUT FRANKIE WAS TEARING THIS PLACE APART. SOMETHING HAD TO BE DONE.
BESIDES, NOW IT'S WORSE-- WE GOT FRANKIE'S COUSIN, PAULIE, COME INTO TOWN ACTING LIKE A HORNED-UP RHINO, AN' WE'RE THE FALLEN STUMP THAT LOOKS LIKE A LADY RHINO.
IN CASE YOU HAVEN'T HEARD, THERE'S A WAR COMING, BUTCHER. AN' THIS TIME, YOU DON'T GET TO BE SWITZERLAND.

I DON'T *CHOOSE* SIDES, JACKIE--

BULL. WHETHER YOU LIKE IT OR NOT, YOU'RE ABOUT TO GET *DRAFTED.*

HE BLEW UP AN *ORPHANAGE,* FOR CHRISSAKES. YOU THINK THAT'S WHAT WE *DO* NOW?

EVEN *YOU* GOTTA ADMIT, IT WAS NEVER THIS WAY. YOU GOTTA HAVE SOME KINDA SENSE WHEN TO STOP, OTHERWISE IT BECOMES *CHAOS*--

SO, WHAT DO YOU WANT ME TO DO ABOUT IT?

I WANT YOU TO SET UP A MEETING-- NOTHING FANCY, JUST THE RIGHT PEOPLE FROM THE OLD OPERATION. SENSINI, MARCO... THAT OLD GUY FROM THE PIZZA HOUSE.

I WANNA GIVE 'EM MY PITCH, THAT'S ALL.

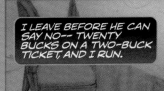

I LEAVE BEFORE HE CAN SAY NO-- TWENTY BUCKS ON A TWO-BUCK TICKET, AND I RUN.

BECAUSE SUDDENLY, I'M HAVING A HARD TIME STAYING IN THE LIGHT.

IT KEEPS PLAYING TRICKS ON MY EYES.

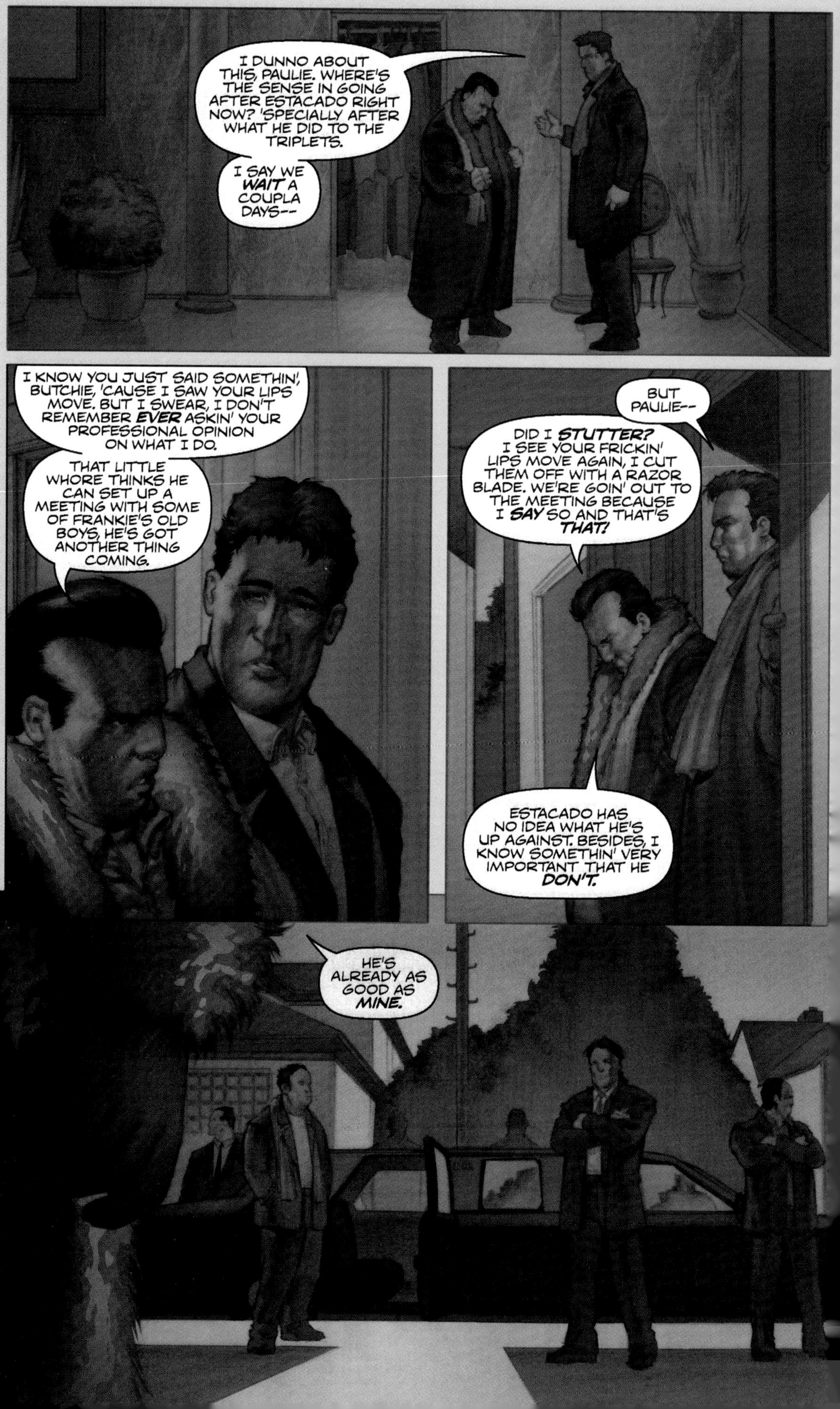
I DUNNO ABOUT THIS, PAULIE. WHERE'S THE SENSE IN GOING AFTER ESTACADO RIGHT NOW? 'SPECIALLY AFTER WHAT HE DID TO THE TRIPLETS.
I SAY WE WAIT A COUPLA DAYS--
I KNOW YOU JUST SAID SOMETHIN', BUTCHIE, 'CAUSE I SAW YOUR LIPS MOVE. BUT I SWEAR, I DON'T REMEMBER EVER ASKIN' YOUR PROFESSIONAL OPINION ON WHAT I DO.
THAT LITTLE WHORE THINKS HE CAN SET UP A MEETING WITH SOME OF FRANKIE'S OLD BOYS, HE'S GOT ANOTHER THING COMING.
BUT PAULIE--
DID I STUTTER? I SEE YOUR FRICKIN' LIPS MOVE AGAIN, I CUT THEM OFF WITH A RAZOR BLADE. WE'RE GOIN' OUT TO THE MEETING BECAUSE I SAY SO AND THAT'S THAT!
ESTACADO HAS NO IDEA WHAT HE'S UP AGAINST. BESIDES, I KNOW SOMETHIN' VERY IMPORTANT THAT HE DON'T.
HE'S ALREADY AS GOOD AS MINE.

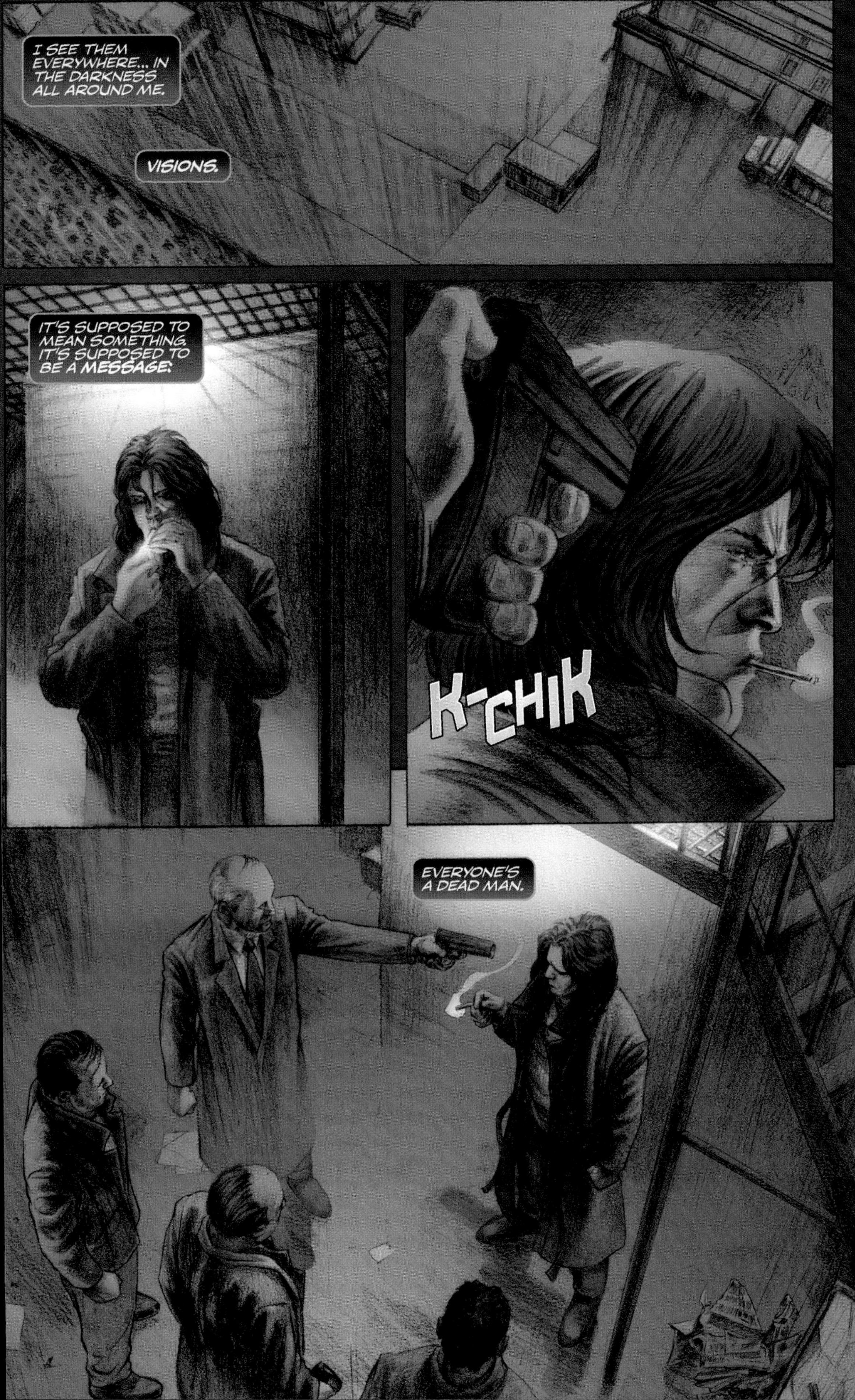
I SEE THEM EVERYWHERE... IN THE DARKNESS ALL AROUND ME.
VISIONS.
IT'S SUPPOSED TO MEAN SOMETHING. IT'S SUPPOSED TO BE A MESSAGE.
K-CHIK
EVERYONE'S A DEAD MAN.

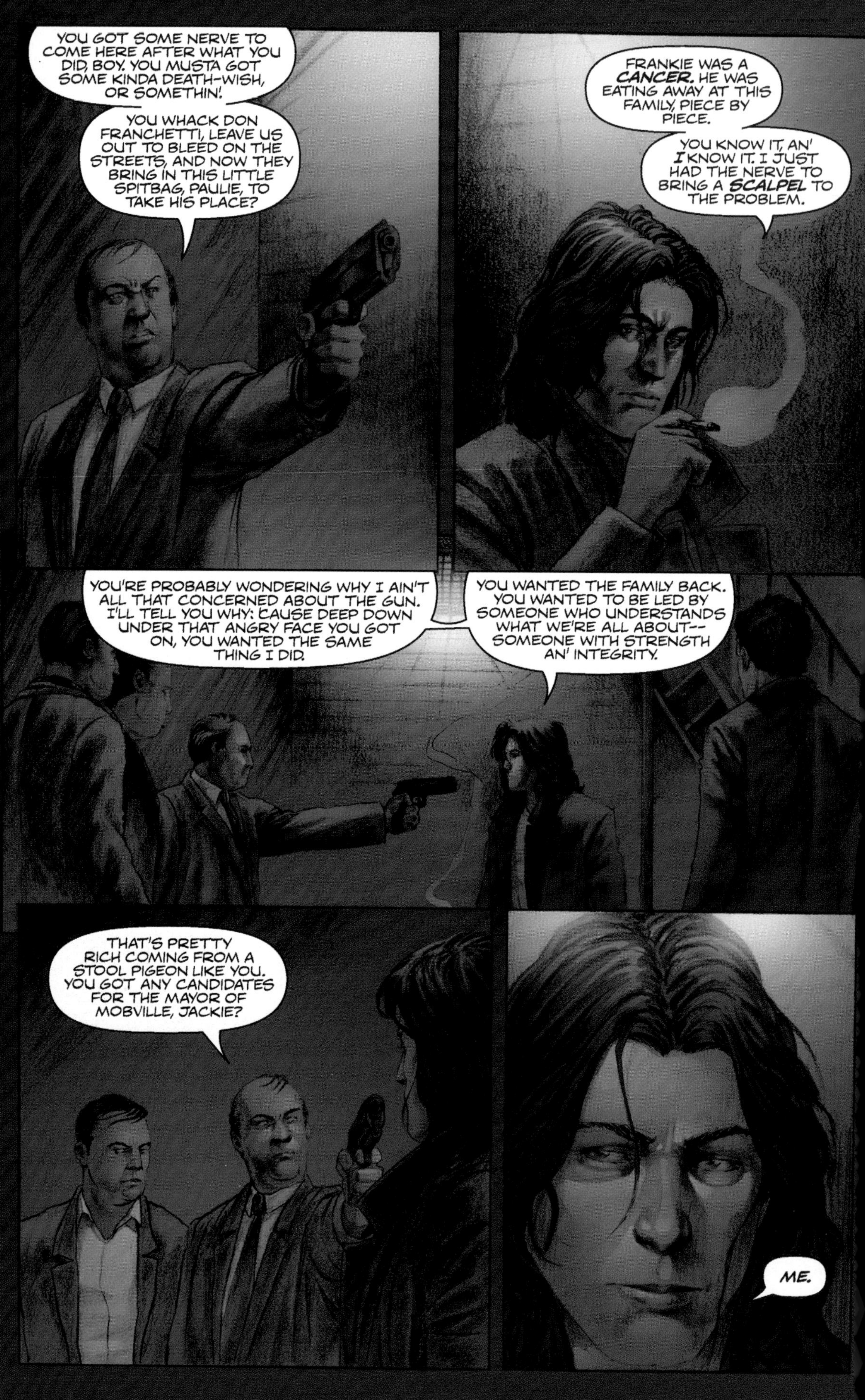

YOU GOT SOME NERVE TO COME HERE AFTER WHAT YOU DID, BOY. YOU MUSTA GOT SOME KINDA DEATH-WISH, OR SOMETHIN'.
YOU WHACK DON FRANCHETTI, LEAVE US OUT TO BLEED ON THE STREETS, AND NOW THEY BRING IN THIS LITTLE SPITBAG, PAULIE, TO TAKE HIS PLACE?
FRANKIE WAS A ***CANCER.*** HE WAS EATING AWAY AT THIS FAMILY, PIECE BY PIECE.
YOU KNOW IT, AN' ***I*** KNOW IT. I JUST HAD THE NERVE TO BRING A ***SCALPEL*** TO THE PROBLEM.
YOU'RE PROBABLY WONDERING WHY I AIN'T ALL THAT CONCERNED ABOUT THE GUN. I'LL TELL YOU WHY: 'CAUSE DEEP DOWN UNDER THAT ANGRY FACE YOU GOT ON, YOU WANTED THE SAME THING I DID.
YOU WANTED THE FAMILY BACK. YOU WANTED TO BE LED BY SOMEONE WHO UNDERSTANDS WHAT WE'RE ALL ABOUT-- SOMEONE WITH STRENGTH AN' INTEGRITY.
THAT'S PRETTY RICH COMING FROM A STOOL PIGEON LIKE YOU. YOU GOT ANY CANDIDATES FOR THE MAYOR OF MOBVILLE, JACKIE?
ME.

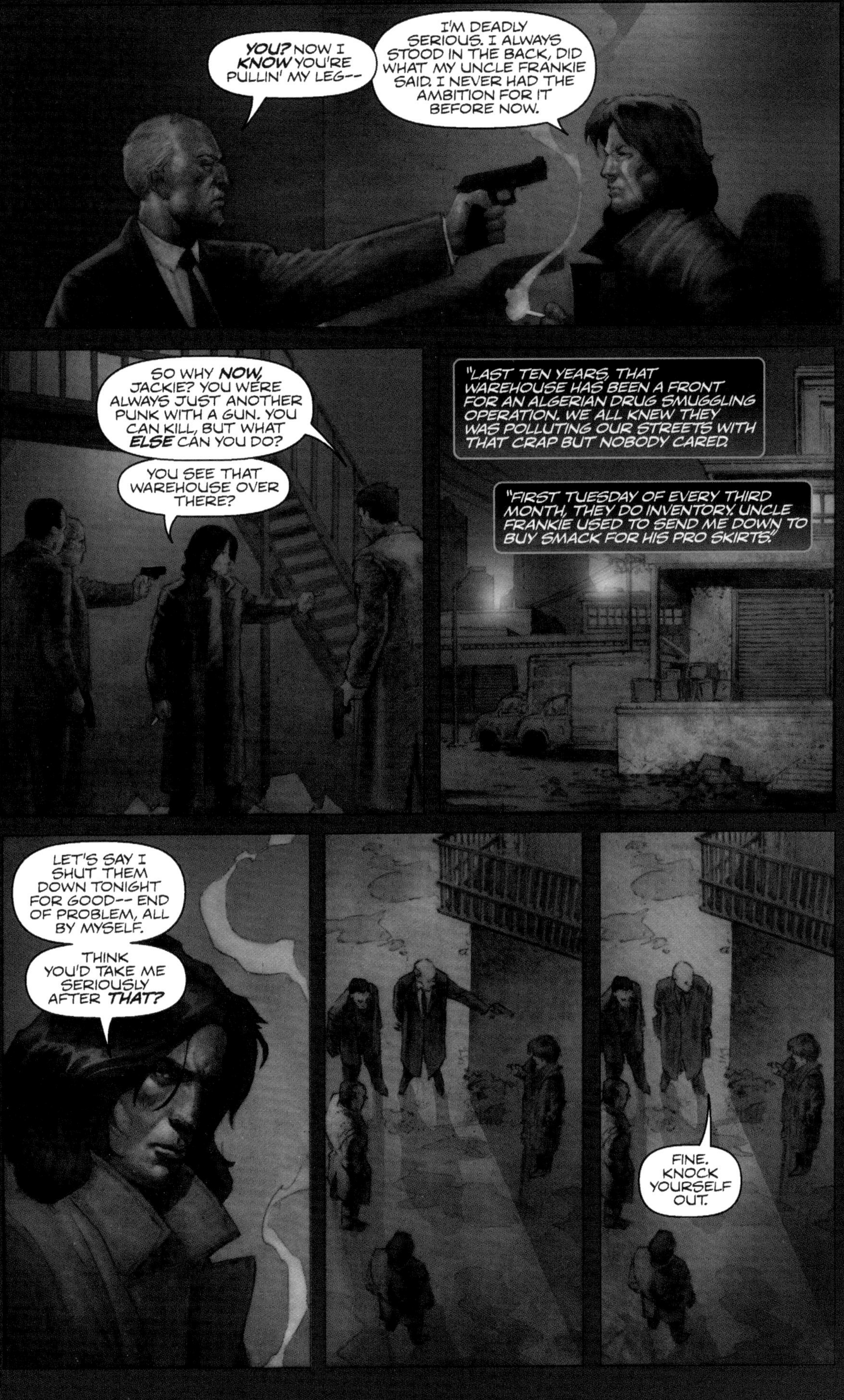
YOU? NOW I KNOW YOU'RE PULLIN' MY LEG--
I'M DEADLY SERIOUS. I ALWAYS STOOD IN THE BACK, DID WHAT MY UNCLE FRANKIE SAID. I NEVER HAD THE AMBITION FOR IT BEFORE NOW.
SO WHY NOW, JACKIE? YOU WERE ALWAYS JUST ANOTHER PUNK WITH A GUN. YOU CAN KILL, BUT WHAT ELSE CAN YOU DO?
YOU SEE THAT WAREHOUSE OVER THERE?
"LAST TEN YEARS, THAT WAREHOUSE HAS BEEN A FRONT FOR AN ALGERIAN DRUG SMUGGLING OPERATION. WE ALL KNEW THEY WAS POLLUTING OUR STREETS WITH THAT CRAP BUT NOBODY CARED.
"FIRST TUESDAY OF EVERY THIRD MONTH, THEY DO INVENTORY. UNCLE FRANKIE USED TO SEND ME DOWN TO BUY SMACK FOR HIS PRO SKIRTS."
LET'S SAY I SHUT THEM DOWN TONIGHT FOR GOOD-- END OF PROBLEM, ALL BY MYSELF.
THINK YOU'D TAKE ME SERIOUSLY AFTER THAT?
FINE. KNOCK YOURSELF OUT.

BUT I GOT A GUN IN EVERY SHADOW, JUST WAITING TO GO OFF.

SOMEONE TOLD ME ONCE, I WAS A GENERAL OF SOULS. WELL, I GOT A WAR COMING, AND I NEED AN ARMY.

I KNOW SOMETHING NOT A LOT OF PEOPLE KNOW. I'VE GOT A SECRET.

THE ALGERIANS ALWAYS INVENTORY THEIR GOODS UNDER COVER OF DARKNESS-- THAT WAY, THEY DON'T DRAW ATTENTION.

THEY MIGHT BE AN ARMY OF DEAD MEN IN MY EYES...

BUT THEY'RE FAMILY.

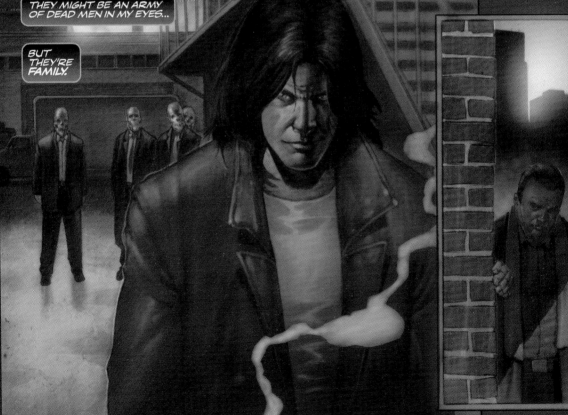

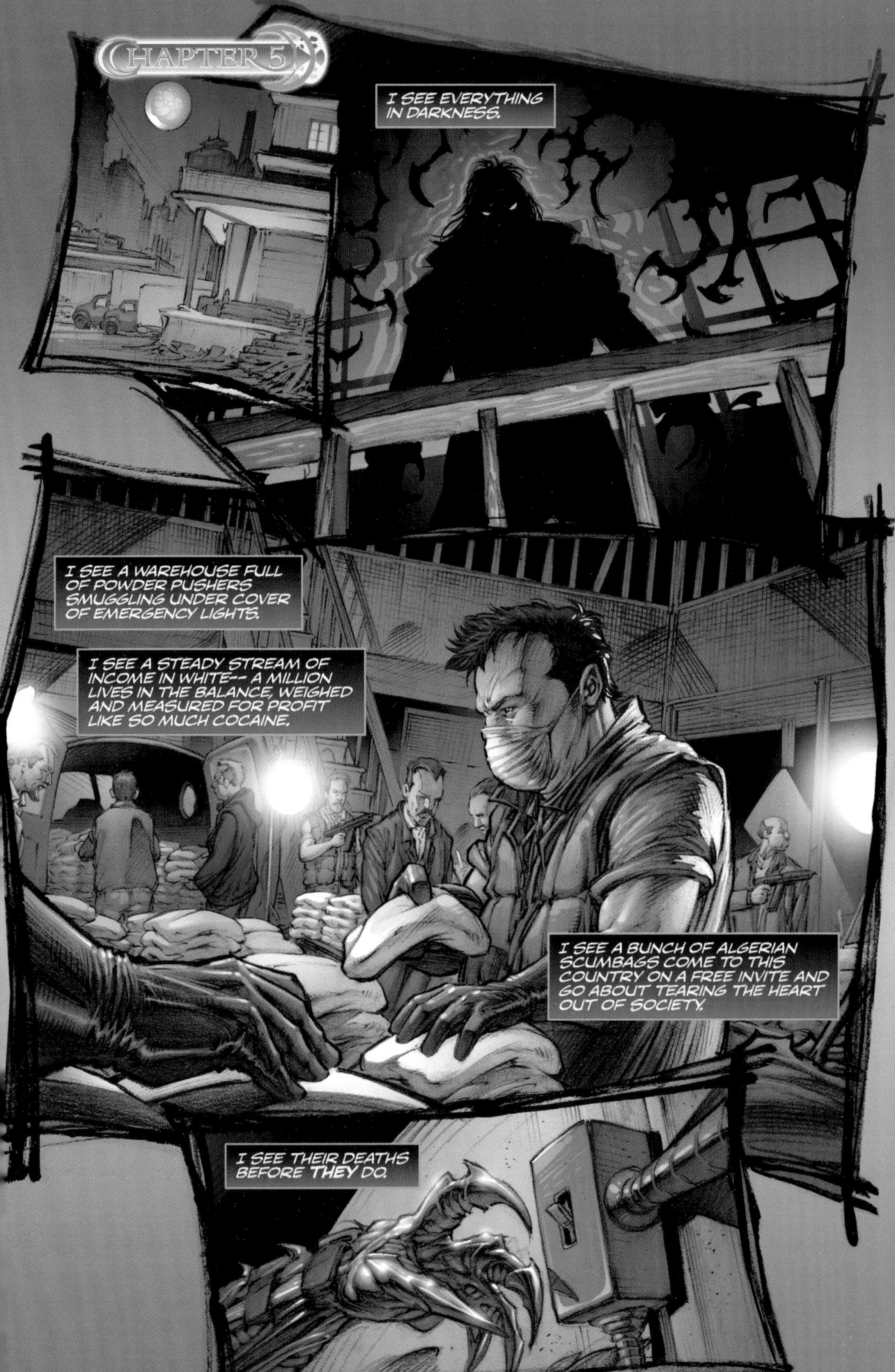
CHAPTER 5
I SEE EVERYTHING IN DARKNESS.
I SEE A WAREHOUSE FULL OF POWDER PUSHERS SMUGGLING UNDER COVER OF EMERGENCY LIGHTS.
I SEE A STEADY STREAM OF INCOME IN WHITE-- A MILLION LIVES IN THE BALANCE, WEIGHED AND MEASURED FOR PROFIT LIKE SO MUCH COCAINE.
I SEE A BUNCH OF ALGERIAN SCUMBAGS COME TO THIS COUNTRY ON A FREE INVITE AND GO ABOUT TEARING THE HEART OUT OF SOCIETY.
I SEE THEIR DEATHS BEFORE THEY DO.

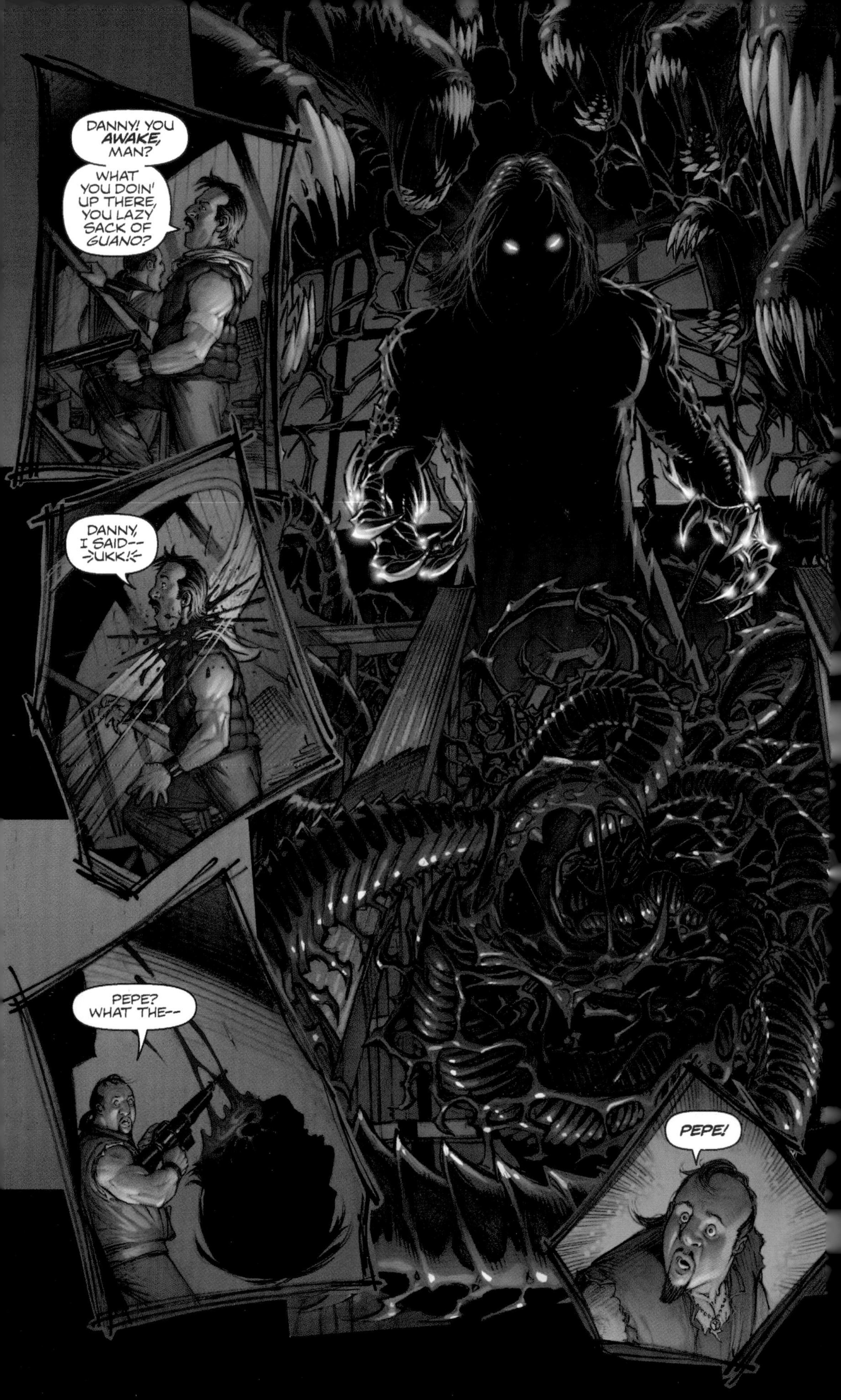
DANNY! YOU AWAKE, MAN?
WHAT YOU DOIN' UP THERE, YOU LAZY SACK OF GUANO?
DANNY, I SAID-- UKK!
PEPE? WHAT THE--
PEPE!

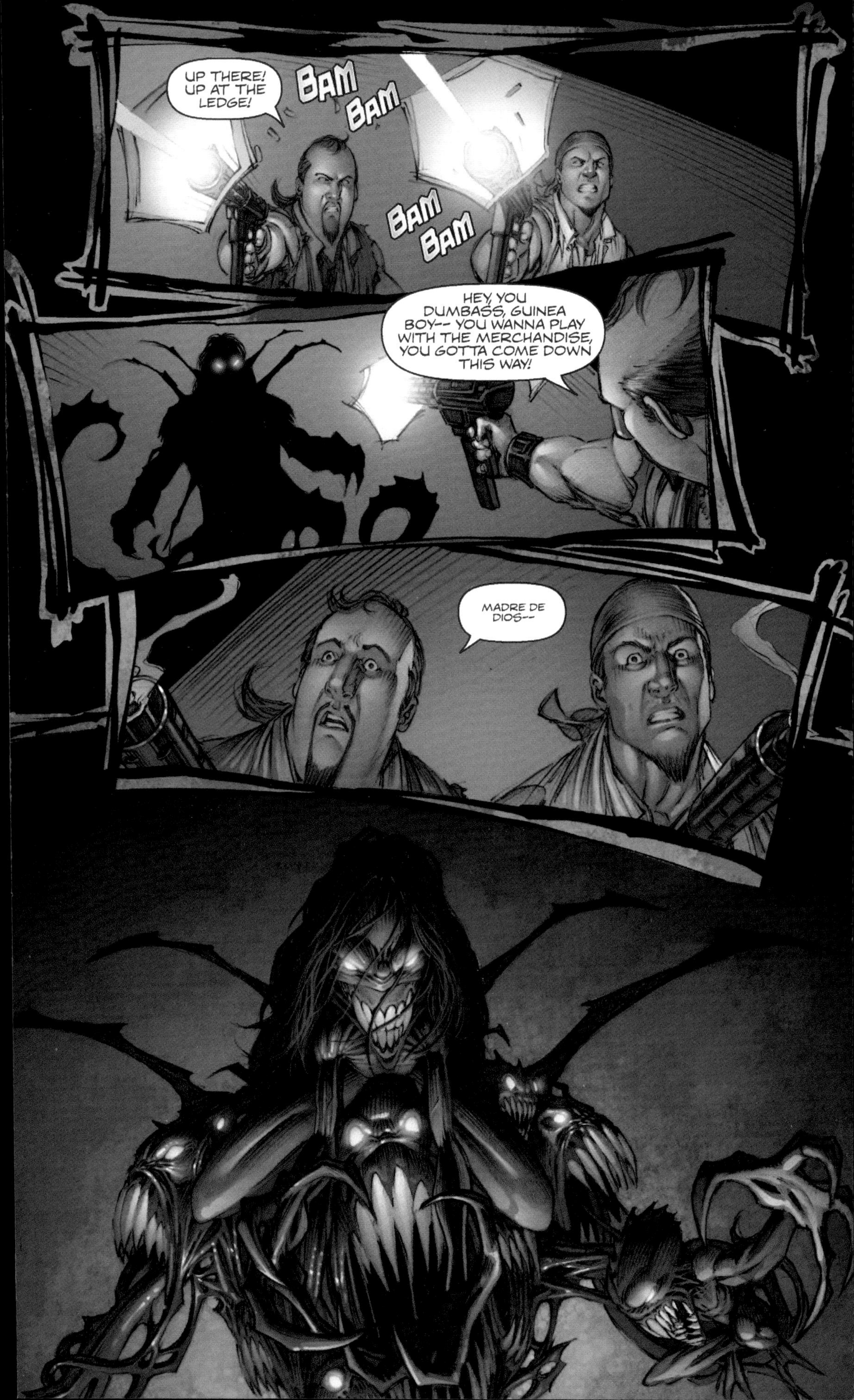
UP THERE! UP AT THE LEDGE!
BAM
BAM
BAM
BAM
HEY, YOU DUMBASS, GUINEA BOY-- YOU WANNA PLAY WITH THE MERCHANDISE, YOU GOTTA COME DOWN THIS WAY!
MADRE DE DIOS--

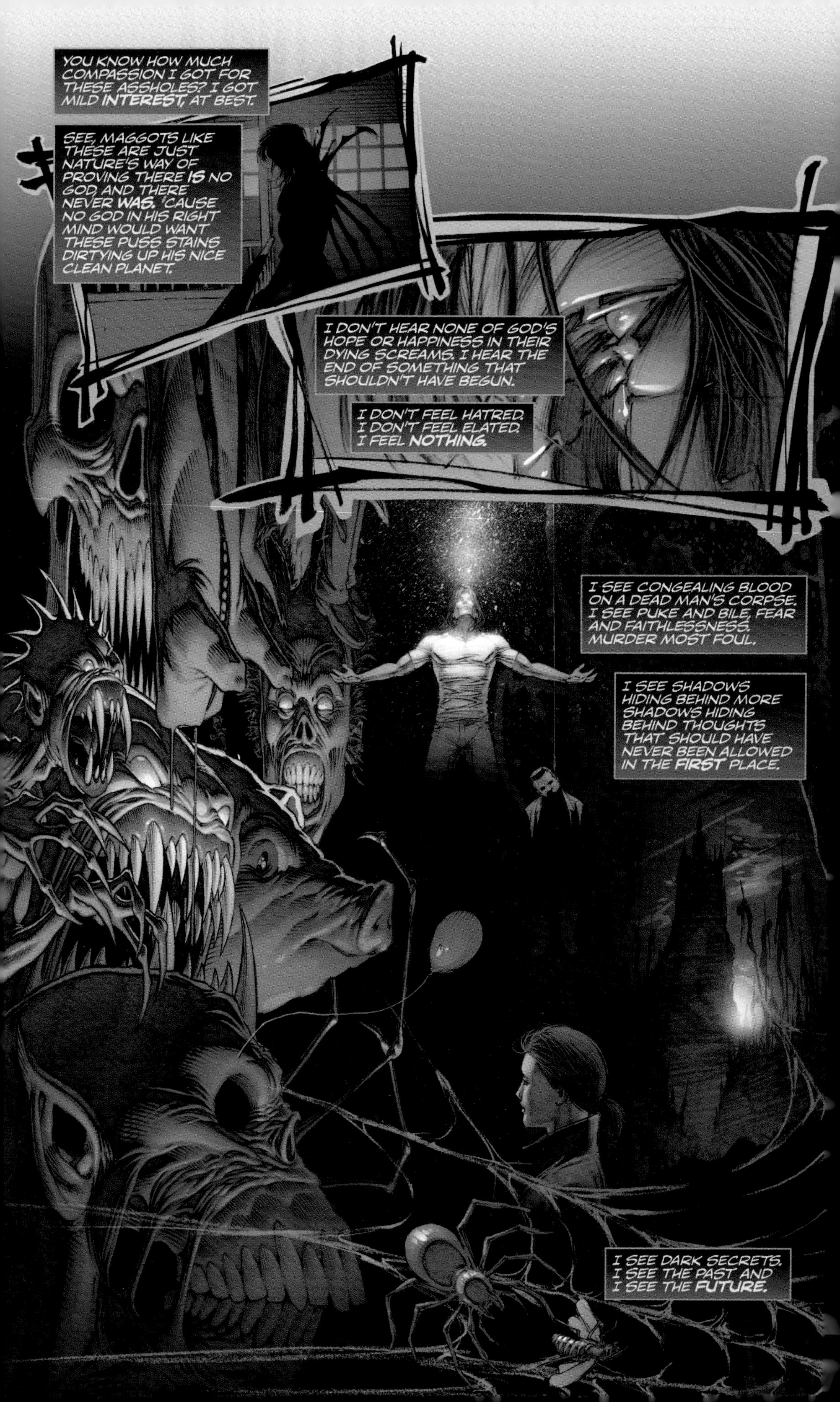
YOU KNOW HOW MUCH COMPASSION I GOT FOR THESE ASSHOLES? I GOT MILD INTEREST, AT BEST.
SEE, MAGGOTS LIKE THESE ARE JUST NATURE'S WAY OF PROVING THERE IS NO GOD, AND THERE NEVER WAS. 'CAUSE NO GOD IN HIS RIGHT MIND WOULD WANT THESE PUSS STAINS DIRTYING UP HIS NICE CLEAN PLANET.
I DON'T HEAR NONE OF GOD'S HOPE OR HAPPINESS IN THEIR DYING SCREAMS. I HEAR THE END OF SOMETHING THAT SHOULDN'T HAVE BEGUN.
I DON'T FEEL HATRED. I DON'T FEEL ELATED. I FEEL NOTHING.
I SEE CONGEALING BLOOD ON A DEAD MAN'S CORPSE. I SEE PUKE AND BILE, FEAR AND FAITHLESSNESS. MURDER MOST FOUL.
I SEE SHADOWS HIDING BEHIND MORE SHADOWS HIDING BEHIND THOUGHTS THAT SHOULD HAVE NEVER BEEN ALLOWED IN THE FIRST PLACE.
I SEE DARK SECRETS. I SEE THE PAST AND I SEE THE FUTURE.

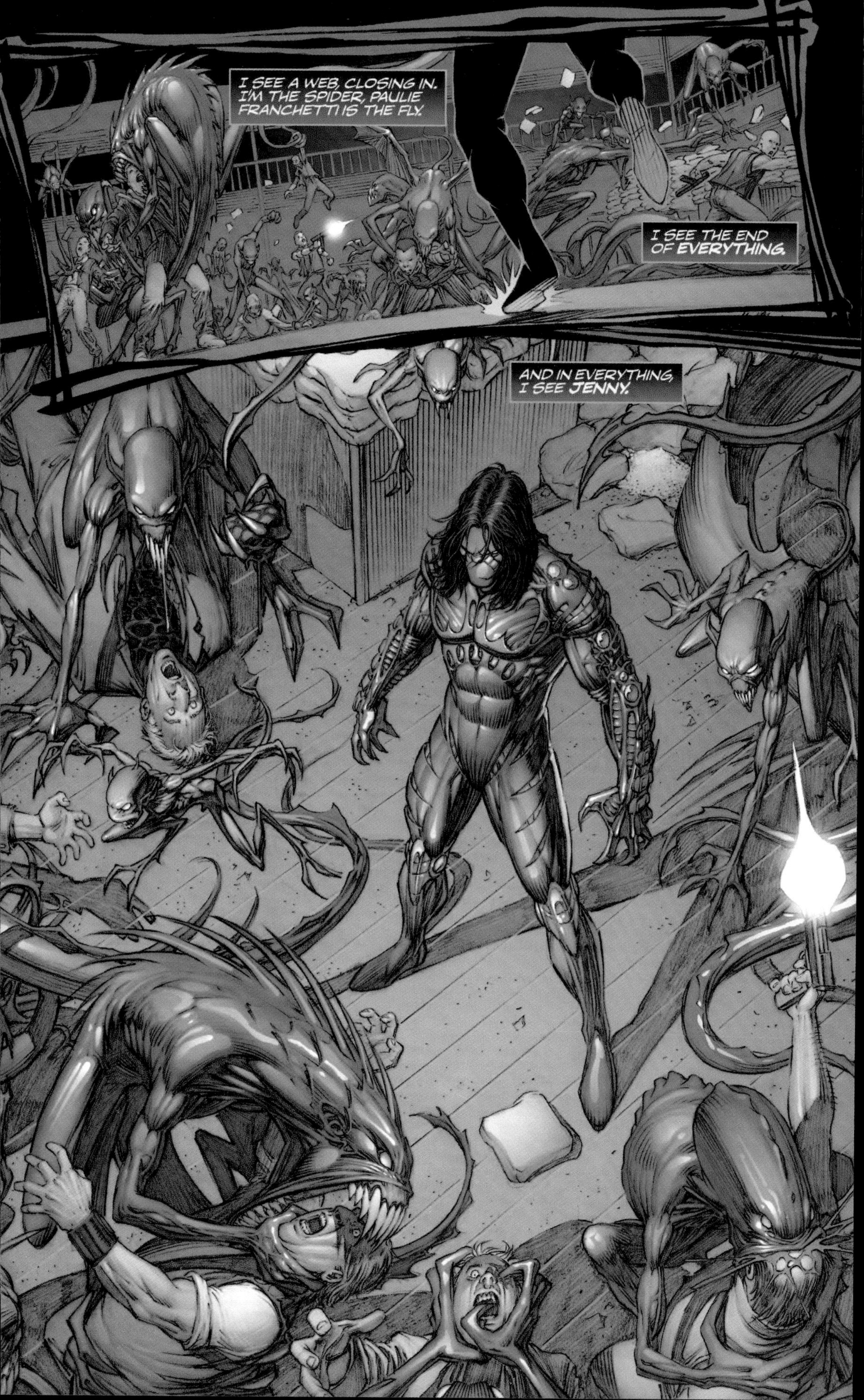
I SEE A WEB, CLOSING IN. I'M THE SPIDER, PAULIE FRANCHETTI IS THE FLY.
I SEE THE END OF EVERYTHING.
AND IN EVERYTHING, I SEE JENNY.

THIS ESTACADO KID: WHAT DO YOU MAKE OF HIM?

I HEARD A LOT OF THINGS ABOUT THE GUY FROM FRANKIE BACK WHEN HE WAS ALIVE-- HE USED T'THINK THE BOY WAS *SPECIAL*.

HEY, ANYONE WHO COULD DROP CHICO REILLY IN HIS OWN APARTMENT HAS T'BE SOMETHING. HELL, THIS GUY EVEN SENT DOWN THE TRIPLETS, SO I HEARD FROM MICKEY PIEROSKA.

YEAH, BUT THAT DON'T MEAN A THING. HE RATTED ON FRANKIE, AN' THAT MEANS HE'S *POISON*.

WE AIN'T NEVER LET SOME LITTLE PUNK CANARY BACK INTO THE ORGANIZATION BEFORE NOW. WHY'S THIS *ESTACADO* AN EXCEPTION--?

BECAUSE HE DID IT TO PROTECT THE ORGANIZATION FROM FRANKIE FRIGGIN' *FRANCHETTI*, THAT'S WHY. AN' CAN ANYONE HERE TELL ME HIS COUSIN PAULIE'S A BETTER OPTION?

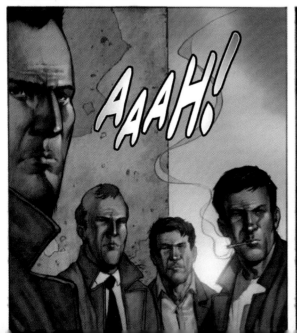

AAAH!

IT'S AGREED THEN: ESTACADO MAKES IT OUT ALIVE, HE'S OUR MAN.

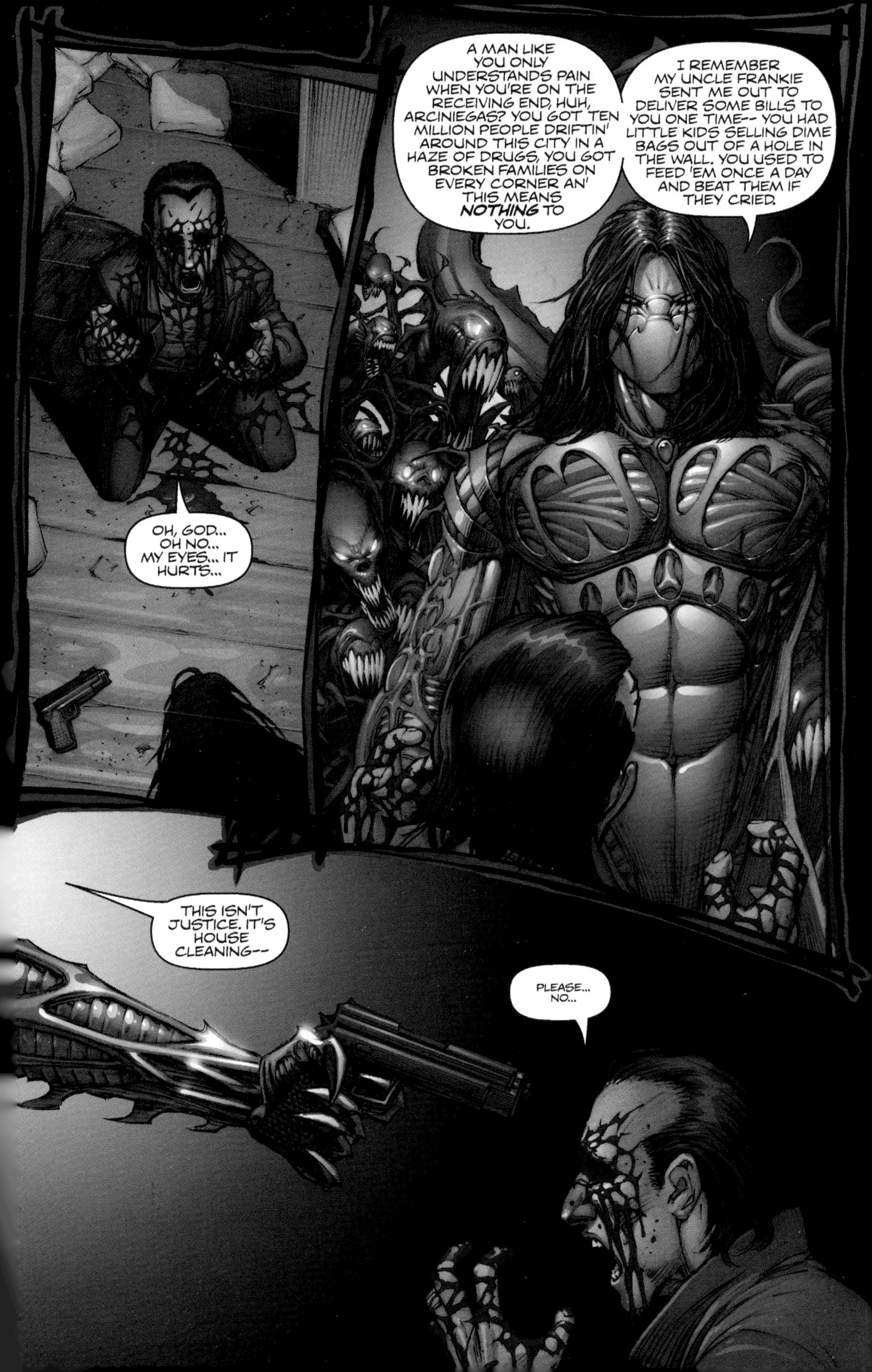
A MAN LIKE YOU ONLY UNDERSTANDS PAIN WHEN YOU'RE ON THE RECEIVING END, HUH, ARCINIEGAS? YOU GOT TEN MILLION PEOPLE DRIFTIN' AROUND THIS CITY IN A HAZE OF DRUGS, YOU GOT BROKEN FAMILIES ON EVERY CORNER AN' THIS MEANS **NOTHING** TO YOU.
I REMEMBER MY UNCLE FRANKIE SENT ME OUT TO DELIVER SOME BILLS TO YOU ONE TIME-- YOU HAD LITTLE KIDS SELLING DIME BAGS OUT OF A HOLE IN THE WALL. YOU USED TO FEED 'EM ONCE A DAY AND BEAT THEM IF THEY CRIED.
OH, GOD... OH NO... MY EYES... IT HURTS...
THIS ISN'T JUSTICE. IT'S HOUSE CLEANING--
PLEASE... NO...

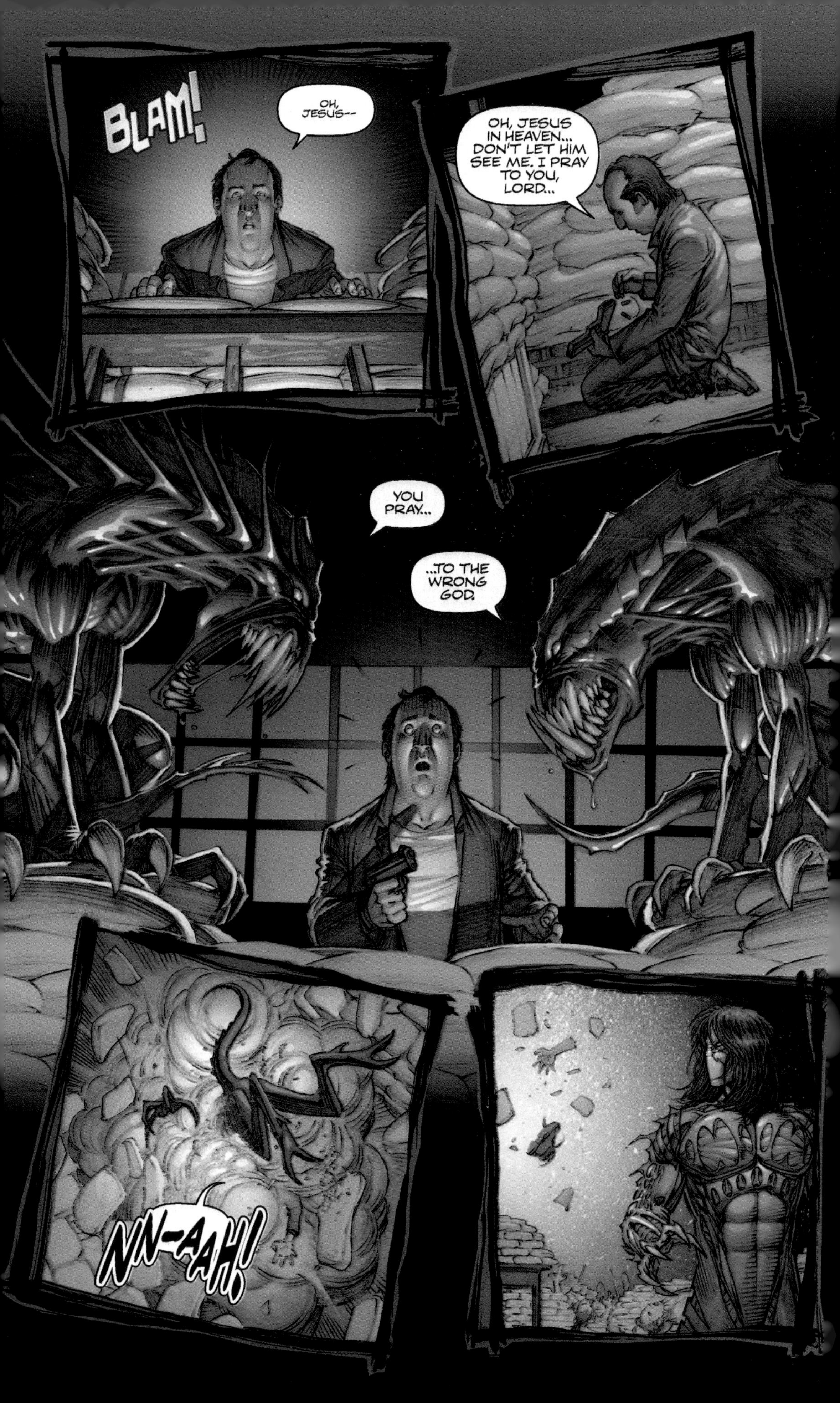
BLAM!
OH, JESUS--
OH, JESUS IN HEAVEN... DON'T LET HIM SEE ME. I PRAY TO YOU, LORD...
YOU PRAY...
...TO THE WRONG GOD.
NN-AAH!

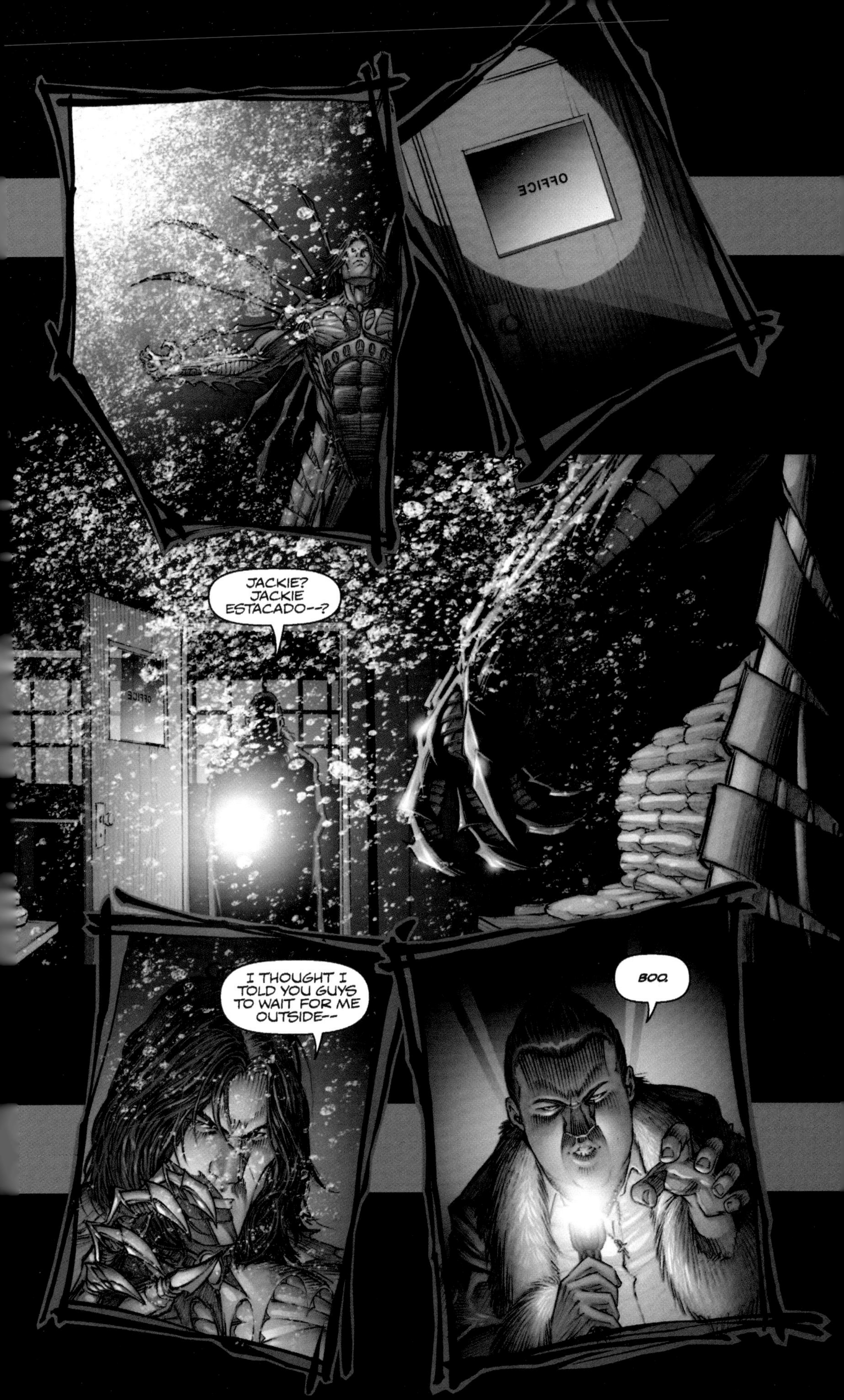
OFFICE
JACKIE? JACKIE ESTACADO--?
I THOUGHT I TOLD YOU GUYS TO WAIT FOR ME OUTSIDE--
BOO.

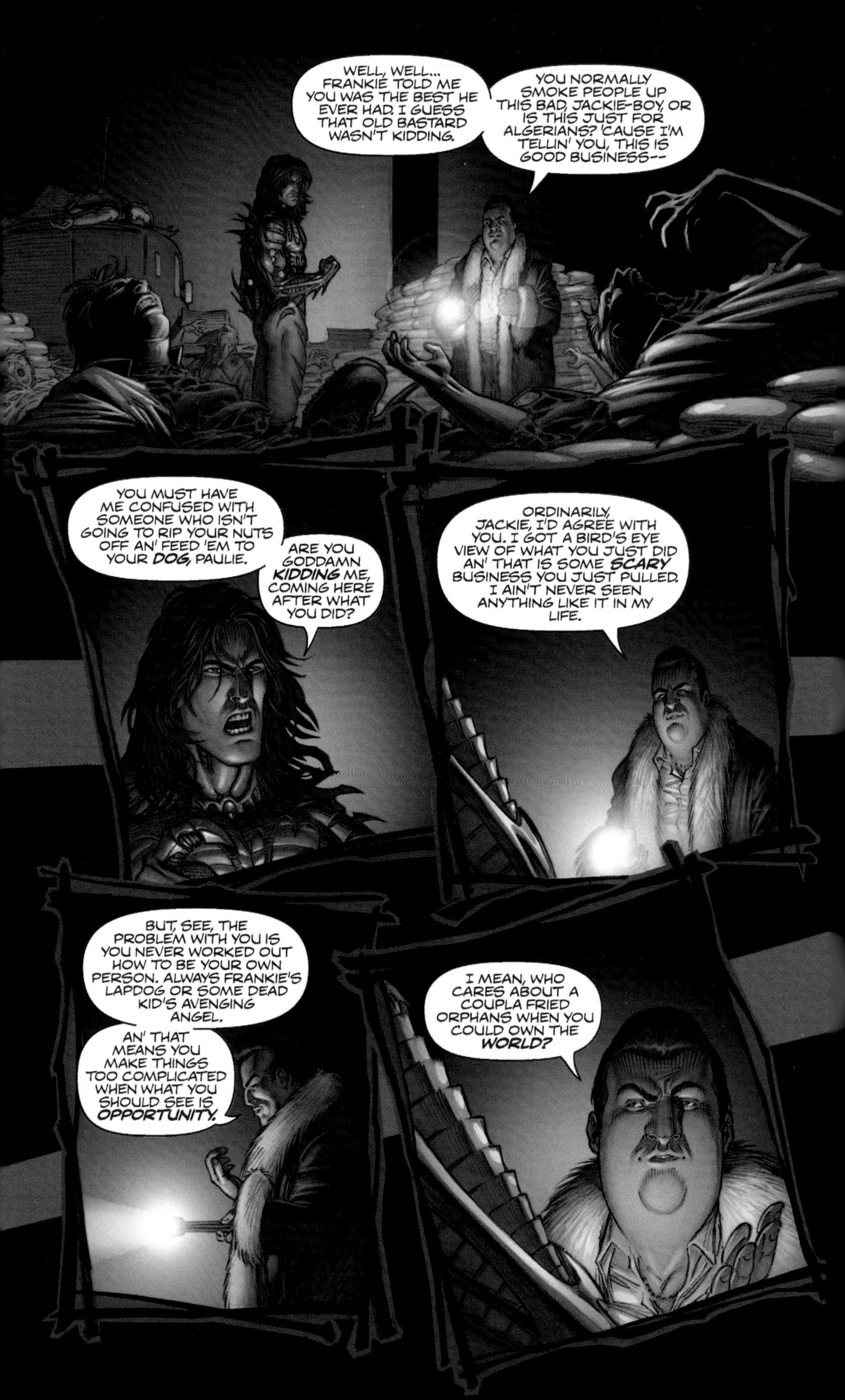
WELL, WELL... FRANKIE TOLD ME YOU WAS THE BEST HE EVER HAD. I GUESS THAT OLD BASTARD WASN'T KIDDING.
YOU NORMALLY SMOKE PEOPLE UP THIS BAD, JACKIE-BOY, OR IS THIS JUST FOR ALGERIANS? 'CAUSE I'M TELLIN' YOU, THIS IS GOOD BUSINESS--
YOU MUST HAVE ME CONFUSED WITH SOMEONE WHO ISN'T GOING TO RIP YOUR NUTS OFF AN' FEED 'EM TO YOUR DOG, PAULIE.
ARE YOU GODDAMN KIDDING ME, COMING HERE AFTER WHAT YOU DID?
ORDINARILY, JACKIE, I'D AGREE WITH YOU. I GOT A BIRD'S EYE VIEW OF WHAT YOU JUST DID AN' THAT IS SOME SCARY BUSINESS YOU JUST PULLED. I AIN'T NEVER SEEN ANYTHING LIKE IT IN MY LIFE.
BUT, SEE, THE PROBLEM WITH YOU IS YOU NEVER WORKED OUT HOW TO BE YOUR OWN PERSON. ALWAYS FRANKIE'S LAPDOG OR SOME DEAD KID'S AVENGING ANGEL.
AN' THAT MEANS YOU MAKE THINGS TOO COMPLICATED WHEN WHAT YOU SHOULD SEE IS OPPORTUNITY.
I MEAN, WHO CARES ABOUT A COUPLA FRIED ORPHANS WHEN YOU COULD OWN THE WORLD?

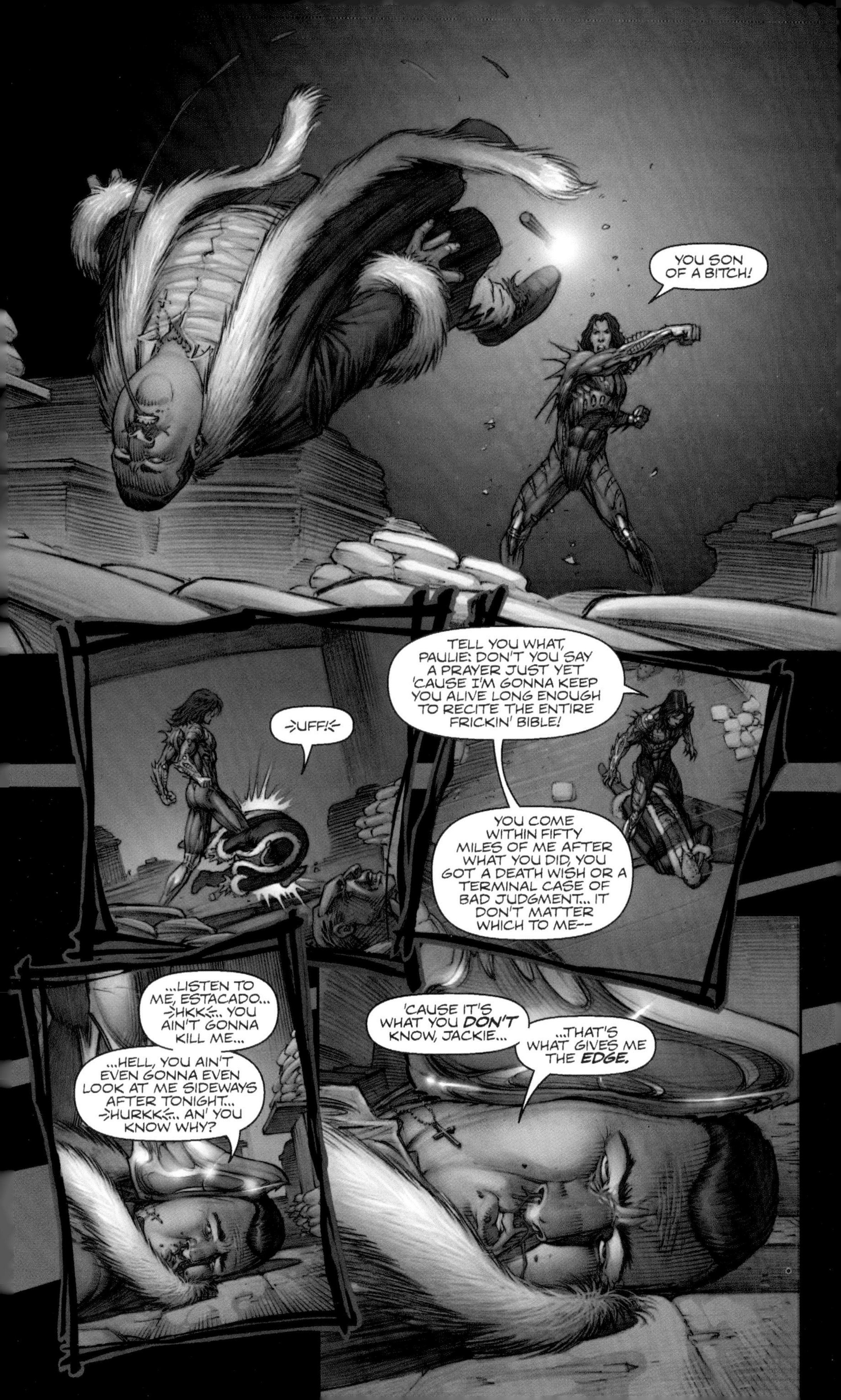

YOU SON OF A BITCH!
›UFF!‹
TELL YOU WHAT, PAULIE: DON'T YOU SAY A PRAYER JUST YET 'CAUSE I'M GONNA KEEP YOU ALIVE LONG ENOUGH TO RECITE THE ENTIRE FRICKIN' BIBLE!
YOU COME WITHIN FIFTY MILES OF ME AFTER WHAT YOU DID, YOU GOT A DEATH WISH OR A TERMINAL CASE OF BAD JUDGMENT... IT DON'T MATTER WHICH TO ME--
...LISTEN TO ME, ESTACADO... ›HKK‹.. YOU AIN'T GONNA KILL ME...
...HELL, YOU AIN'T EVEN GONNA EVEN LOOK AT ME SIDEWAYS AFTER TONIGHT... ›HURKK‹.. AN' YOU KNOW WHY?
'CAUSE IT'S WHAT YOU **DON'T** KNOW, JACKIE...
...THAT'S WHAT GIVES ME THE **EDGE.**

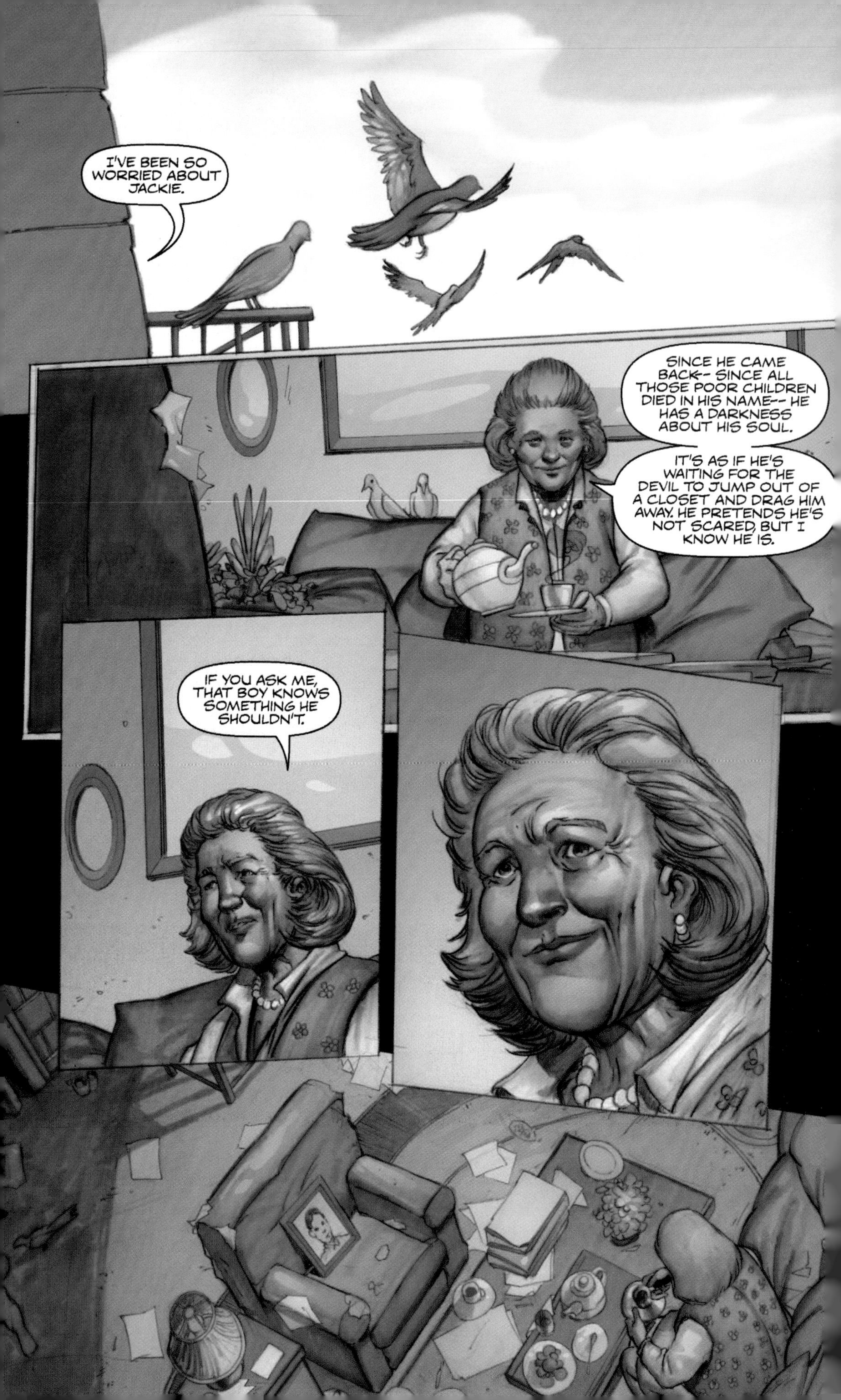
I'VE BEEN SO WORRIED ABOUT JACKIE.
SINCE HE CAME BACK-- SINCE ALL THOSE POOR CHILDREN DIED IN HIS NAME-- HE HAS A DARKNESS ABOUT HIS SOUL.
IT'S AS IF HE'S WAITING FOR THE DEVIL TO JUMP OUT OF A CLOSET AND DRAG HIM AWAY. HE PRETENDS HE'S NOT SCARED, BUT I KNOW HE IS.
IF YOU ASK ME, THAT BOY KNOWS SOMETHING HE SHOULDN'T.

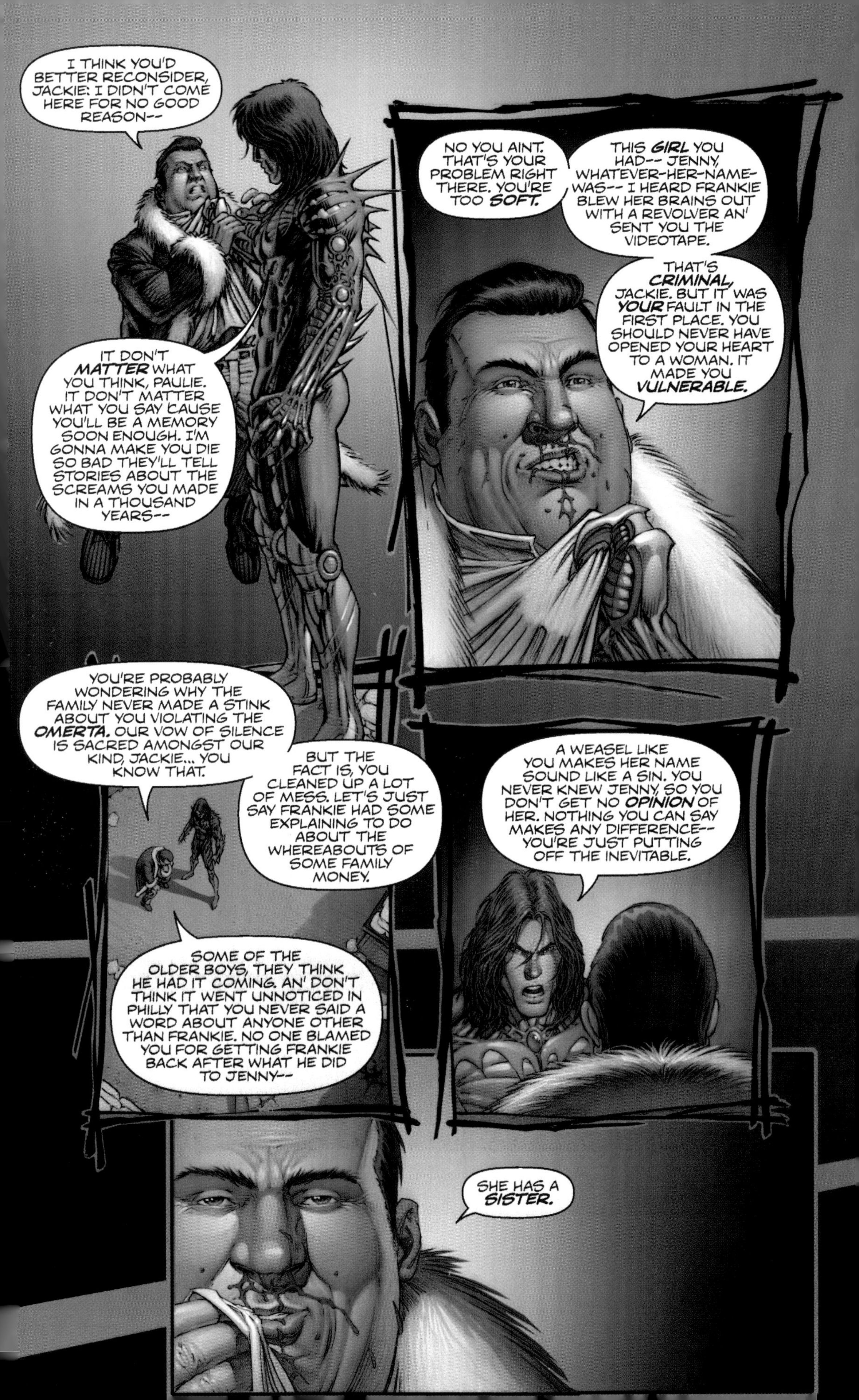
I THINK YOU'D BETTER RECONSIDER, JACKIE: I DIDN'T COME HERE FOR NO GOOD REASON--
IT DON'T MATTER WHAT YOU THINK, PAULIE. IT DON'T MATTER WHAT YOU SAY CAUSE YOU'LL BE A MEMORY SOON ENOUGH. I'M GONNA MAKE YOU DIE SO BAD THEY'LL TELL STORIES ABOUT THE SCREAMS YOU MADE IN A THOUSAND YEARS--
NO YOU AINT. THAT'S YOUR PROBLEM RIGHT THERE. YOU'RE TOO SOFT.
THIS GIRL YOU HAD-- JENNY, WHATEVER-HER-NAME-WAS-- I HEARD FRANKIE BLEW HER BRAINS OUT WITH A REVOLVER AN' SENT YOU THE VIDEOTAPE.
THAT'S CRIMINAL, JACKIE. BUT IT WAS YOUR FAULT IN THE FIRST PLACE. YOU SHOULD NEVER HAVE OPENED YOUR HEART TO A WOMAN. IT MADE YOU VULNERABLE.
YOU'RE PROBABLY WONDERING WHY THE FAMILY NEVER MADE A STINK ABOUT YOU VIOLATING THE OMERTA. OUR VOW OF SILENCE IS SACRED AMONGST OUR KIND, JACKIE... YOU KNOW THAT.
BUT THE FACT IS, YOU CLEANED UP A LOT OF MESS. LET'S JUST SAY FRANKIE HAD SOME EXPLAINING TO DO ABOUT THE WHEREABOUTS OF SOME FAMILY MONEY.
SOME OF THE OLDER BOYS, THEY THINK HE HAD IT COMING. AN' DON'T THINK IT WENT UNNOTICED IN PHILLY THAT YOU NEVER SAID A WORD ABOUT ANYONE OTHER THAN FRANKIE. NO ONE BLAMED YOU FOR GETTING FRANKIE BACK AFTER WHAT HE DID TO JENNY--
A WEASEL LIKE YOU MAKES HER NAME SOUND LIKE A SIN. YOU NEVER KNEW JENNY, SO YOU DON'T GET NO OPINION OF HER. NOTHING YOU CAN SAY MAKES ANY DIFFERENCE-- YOU'RE JUST PUTTING OFF THE INEVITABLE.
SHE HAS A SISTER.

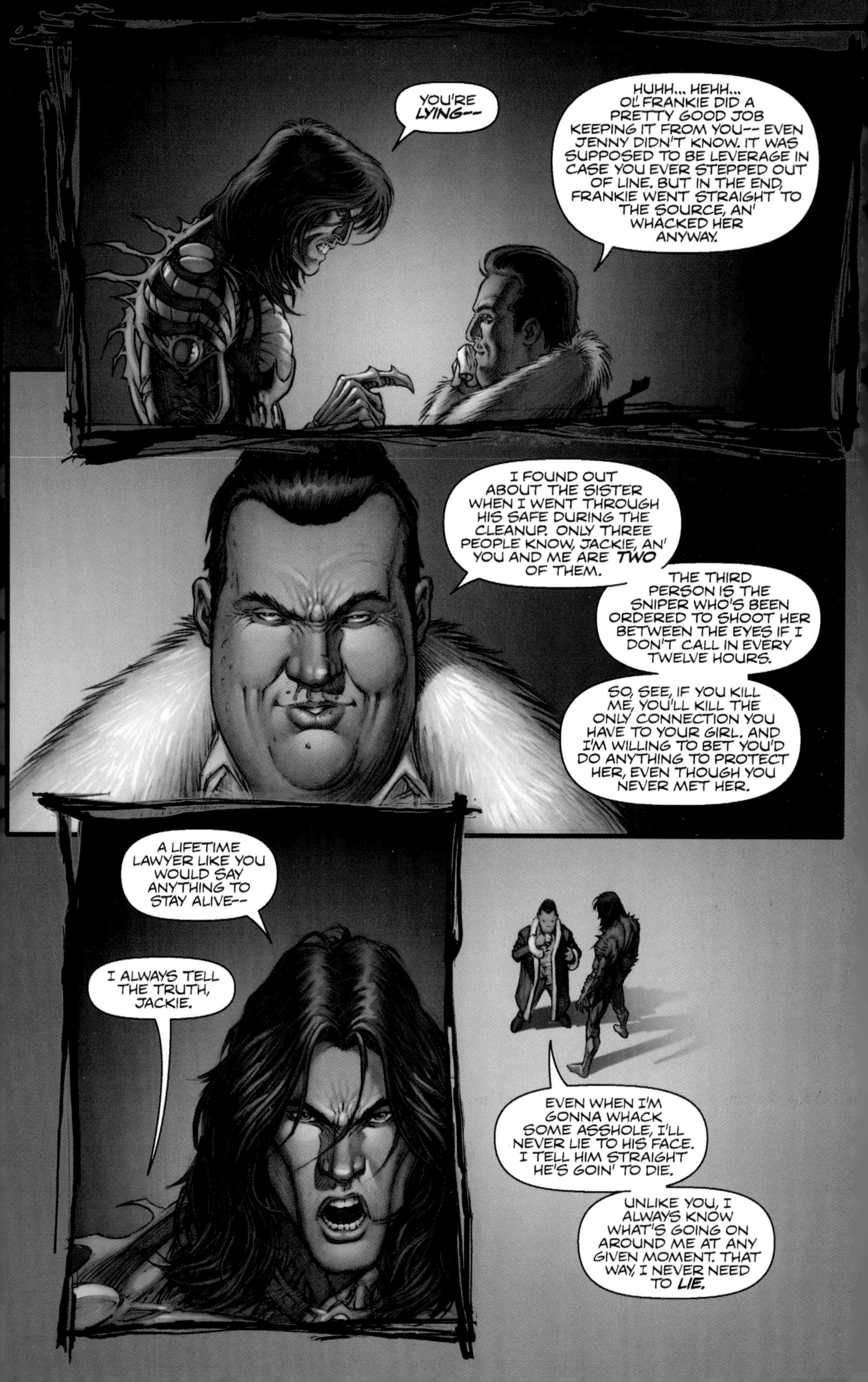

YOU'RE LYING--
HUHH... HEHH... OL' FRANKIE DID A PRETTY GOOD JOB KEEPING IT FROM YOU-- EVEN JENNY DIDN'T KNOW. IT WAS SUPPOSED TO BE LEVERAGE IN CASE YOU EVER STEPPED OUT OF LINE. BUT IN THE END, FRANKIE WENT STRAIGHT TO THE SOURCE, AN' WHACKED HER ANYWAY.
I FOUND OUT ABOUT THE SISTER WHEN I WENT THROUGH HIS SAFE DURING THE CLEANUP. ONLY THREE PEOPLE KNOW, JACKIE, AN' YOU AND ME ARE TWO OF THEM.
THE THIRD PERSON IS THE SNIPER WHO'S BEEN ORDERED TO SHOOT HER BETWEEN THE EYES IF I DON'T CALL IN EVERY TWELVE HOURS.
SO, SEE, IF YOU KILL ME, YOU'LL KILL THE ONLY CONNECTION YOU HAVE TO YOUR GIRL. AND I'M WILLING TO BET YOU'D DO ANYTHING TO PROTECT HER, EVEN THOUGH YOU NEVER MET HER.
A LIFETIME LAWYER LIKE YOU WOULD SAY ANYTHING TO STAY ALIVE--
I ALWAYS TELL THE TRUTH, JACKIE.
EVEN WHEN I'M GONNA WHACK SOME ASSHOLE, I'LL NEVER LIE TO HIS FACE. I TELL HIM STRAIGHT HE'S GOIN' TO DIE.
UNLIKE YOU, I ALWAYS KNOW WHAT'S GOING ON AROUND ME AT ANY GIVEN MOMENT. THAT WAY, I NEVER NEED TO LIE.

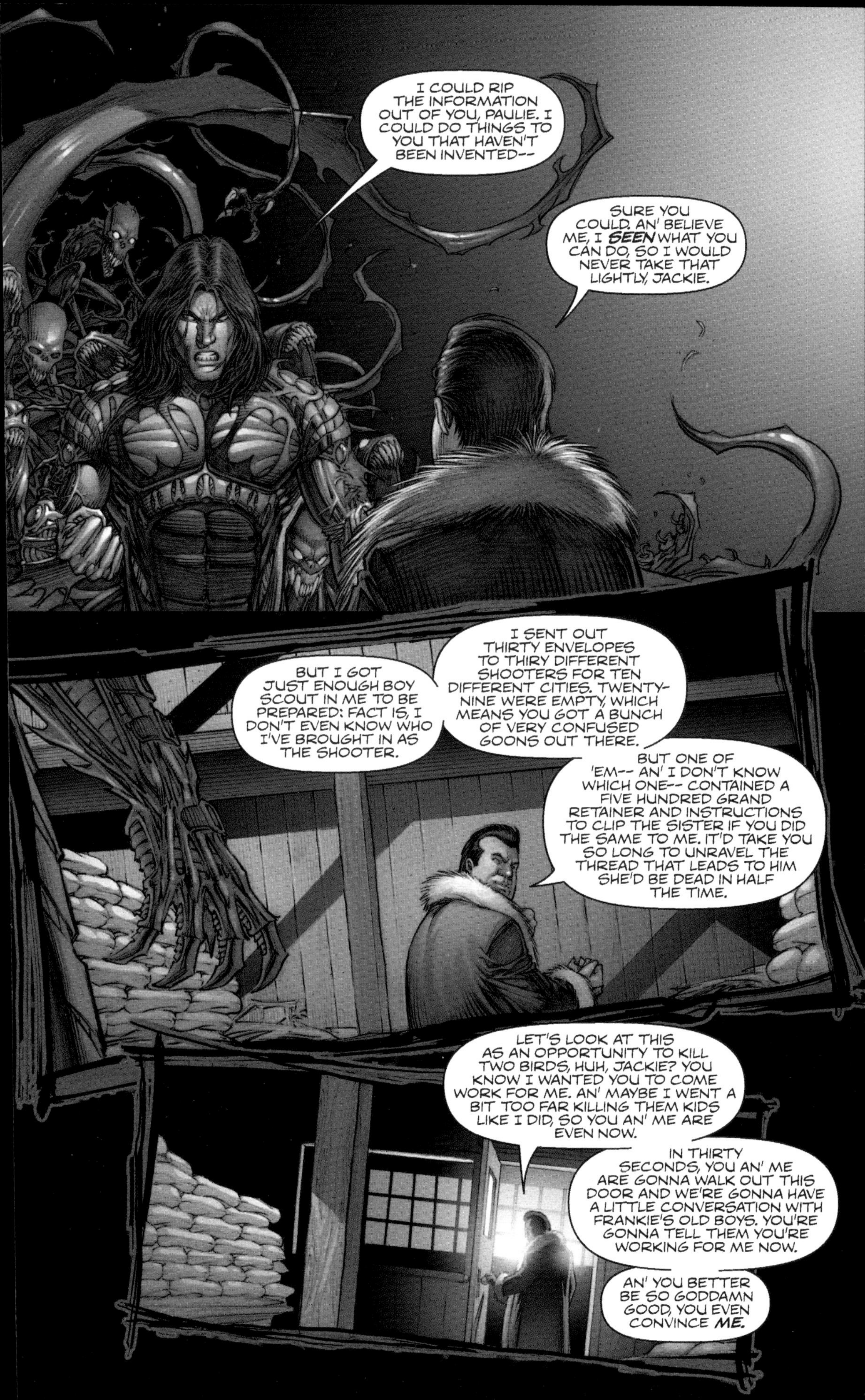
I COULD RIP THE INFORMATION OUT OF YOU, PAULIE. I COULD DO THINGS TO YOU THAT HAVEN'T BEEN INVENTED--
SURE YOU COULD. AN' BELIEVE ME, I SEEN WHAT YOU CAN DO, SO I WOULD NEVER TAKE THAT LIGHTLY, JACKIE.
BUT I GOT JUST ENOUGH BOY SCOUT IN ME TO BE PREPARED: FACT IS, I DON'T EVEN KNOW WHO I'VE BROUGHT IN AS THE SHOOTER.
I SENT OUT THIRTY ENVELOPES TO THIRY DIFFERENT SHOOTERS FOR TEN DIFFERENT CITIES. TWENTY-NINE WERE EMPTY, WHICH MEANS YOU GOT A BUNCH OF VERY CONFUSED GOONS OUT THERE.
BUT ONE OF 'EM-- AN' I DON'T KNOW WHICH ONE-- CONTAINED A FIVE HUNDRED GRAND RETAINER AND INSTRUCTIONS TO CLIP THE SISTER IF YOU DID THE SAME TO ME. IT'D TAKE YOU SO LONG TO UNRAVEL THE THREAD THAT LEADS TO HIM SHE'D BE DEAD IN HALF THE TIME.
LET'S LOOK AT THIS AS AN OPPORTUNITY TO KILL TWO BIRDS, HUH, JACKIE? YOU KNOW I WANTED YOU TO COME WORK FOR ME. AN' MAYBE I WENT A BIT TOO FAR KILLING THEM KIDS LIKE I DID, SO YOU AN' ME ARE EVEN NOW.
IN THIRTY SECONDS, YOU AN' ME ARE GONNA WALK OUT THIS DOOR AND WE'RE GONNA HAVE A LITTLE CONVERSATION WITH FRANKIE'S OLD BOYS. YOU'RE GONNA TELL THEM YOU'RE WORKING FOR ME NOW.
AN' YOU BETTER BE SO GODDAMN GOOD, YOU EVEN CONVINCE ME.

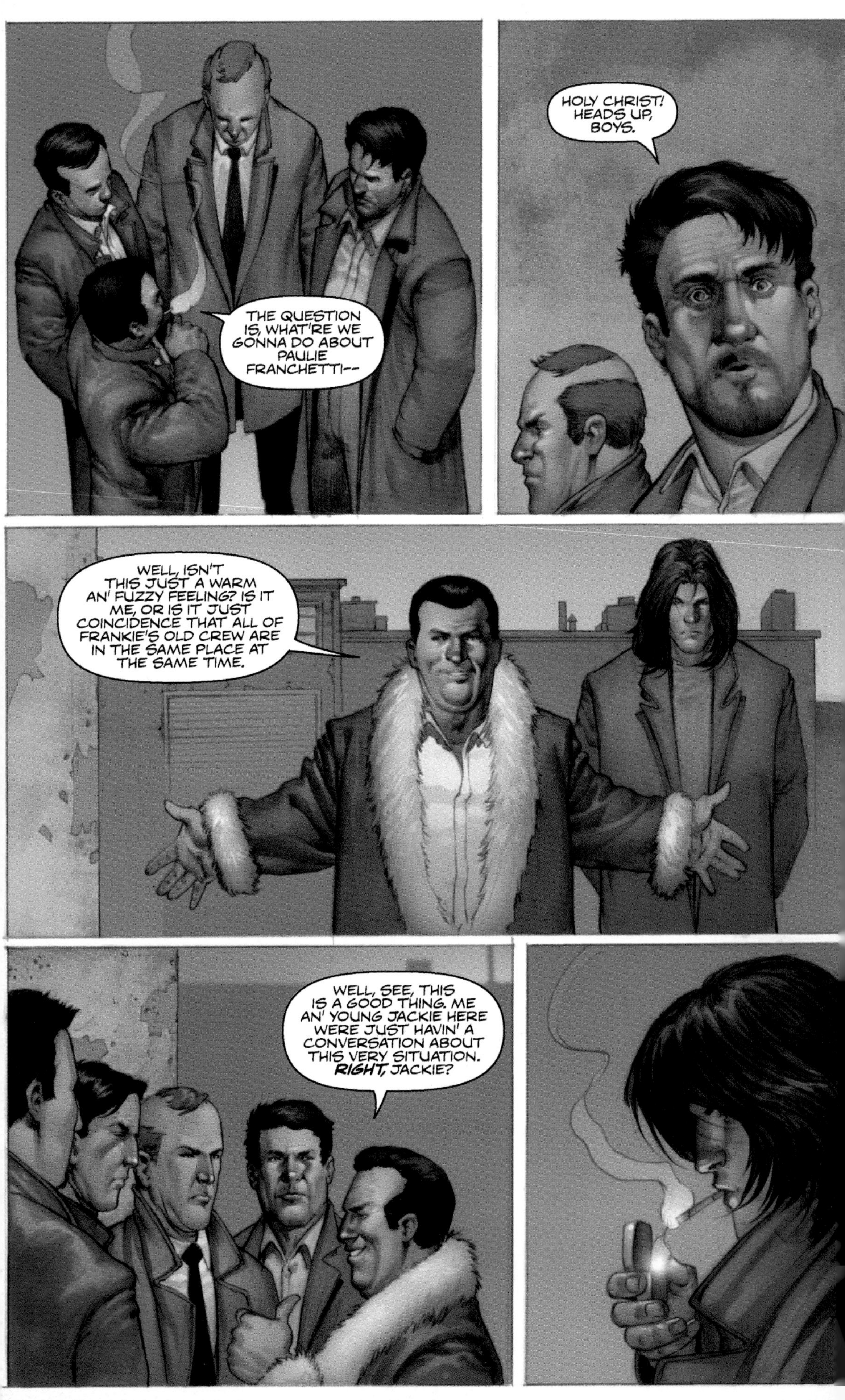
THE QUESTION IS, WHAT'RE WE GONNA DO ABOUT PAULIE FRANCHETTI--
HOLY CHRIST! HEADS UP, BOYS.
WELL, ISN'T THIS JUST A WARM AN' FUZZY FEELING? IS IT ME, OR IS IT JUST COINCIDENCE THAT ALL OF FRANKIE'S OLD CREW ARE IN THE SAME PLACE AT THE SAME TIME.
WELL, SEE, THIS IS A GOOD THING. ME AN' YOUNG JACKIE HERE WERE JUST HAVIN' A CONVERSATION ABOUT THIS VERY SITUATION. ***RIGHT,*** JACKIE?

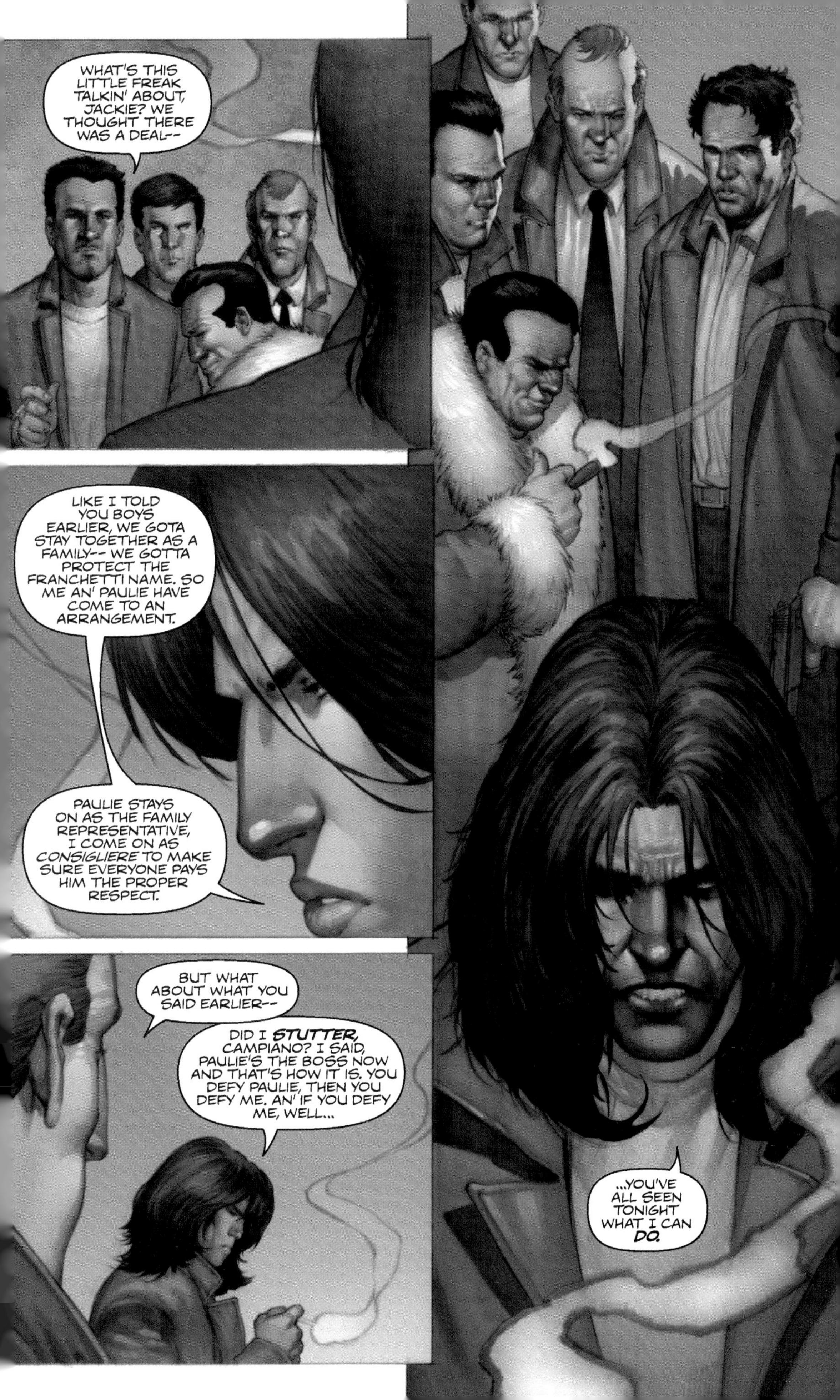
WHAT'S THIS LITTLE FREAK TALKIN' ABOUT, JACKIE? WE THOUGHT THERE WAS A DEAL--
LIKE I TOLD YOU BOYS EARLIER, WE GOTA STAY TOGETHER AS A FAMILY-- WE GOTTA PROTECT THE FRANCHETTI NAME. SO ME AN' PAULIE HAVE COME TO AN ARRANGEMENT.
PAULIE STAYS ON AS THE FAMILY REPRESENTATIVE, I COME ON AS CONSIGLIERE TO MAKE SURE EVERYONE PAYS HIM THE PROPER RESPECT.
BUT WHAT ABOUT WHAT YOU SAID EARLIER--
DID I STUTTER, CAMPIANO? I SAID, PAULIE'S THE BOSS NOW AND THAT'S HOW IT IS. YOU DEFY PAULIE, THEN YOU DEFY ME. AN' IF YOU DEFY ME, WELL...
...YOU'VE ALL SEEN TONIGHT WHAT I CAN DO.

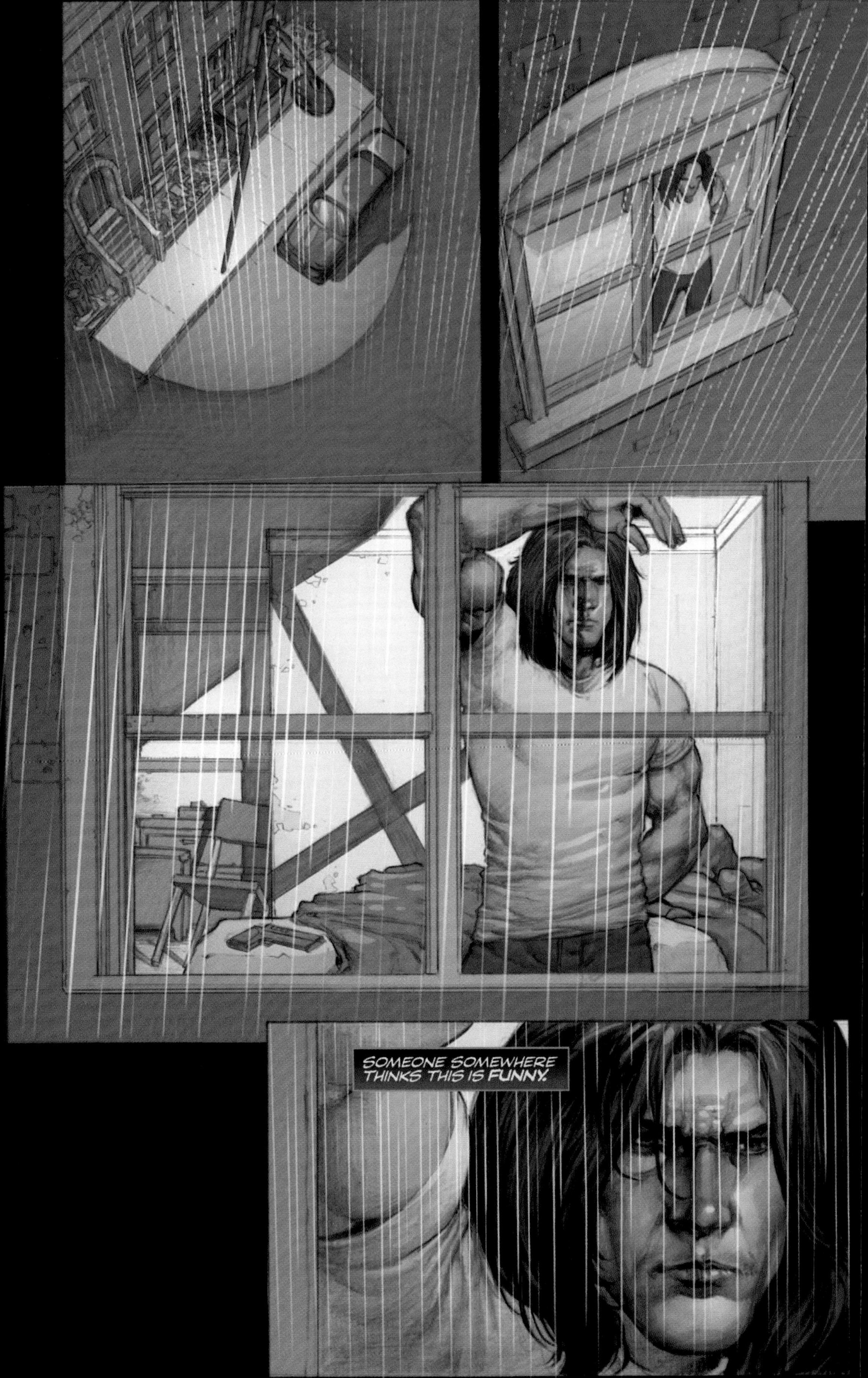
SOMEONE SOMEWHERE THINKS THIS IS FUNNY.

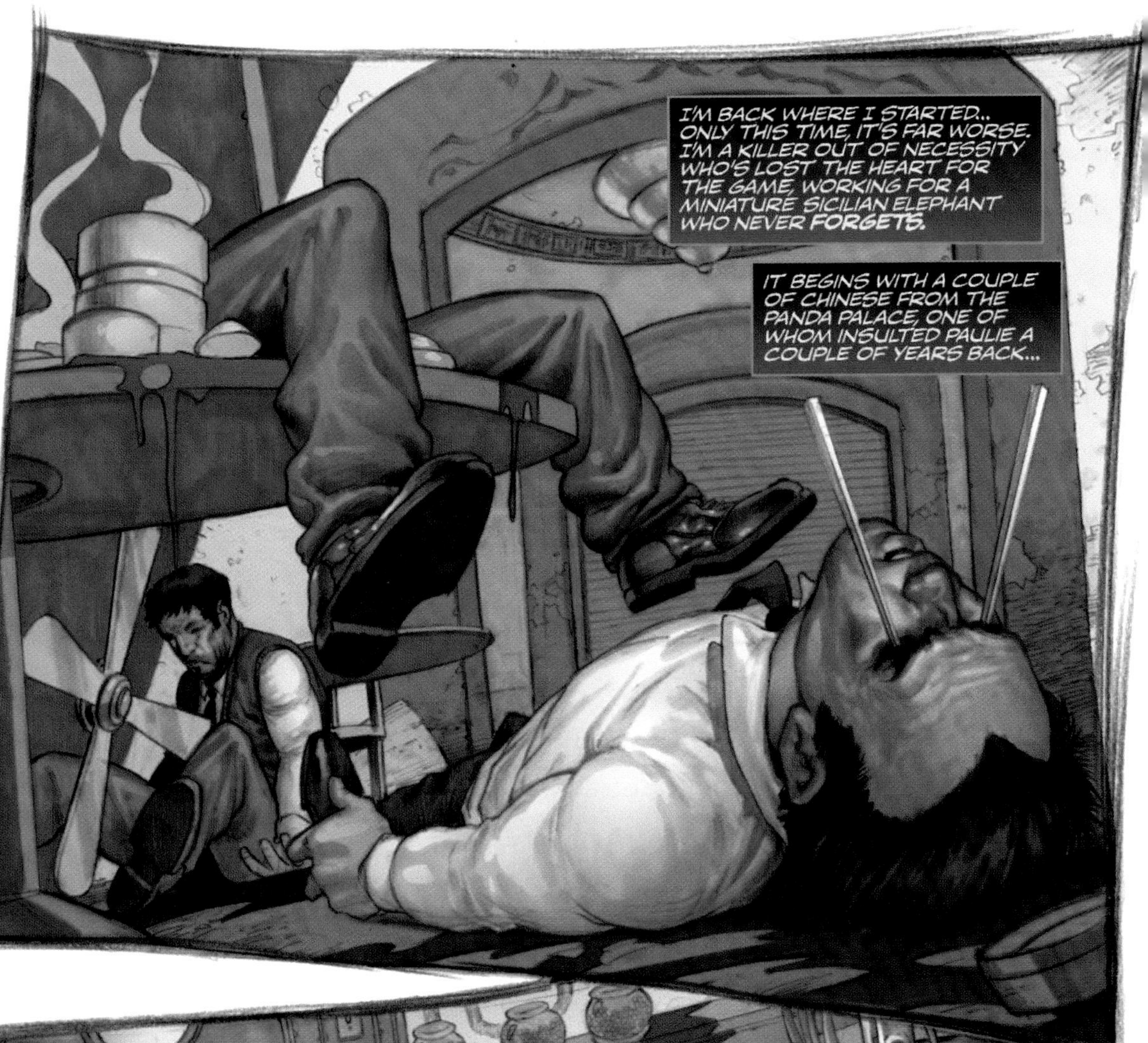
I'M BACK WHERE I STARTED... ONLY THIS TIME, IT'S FAR WORSE. I'M A KILLER OUT OF NECESSITY WHO'S LOST THE HEART FOR THE GAME, WORKING FOR A MINIATURE SICILIAN ELEPHANT WHO NEVER FORGETS.
IT BEGINS WITH A COUPLE OF CHINESE FROM THE PANDA PALACE, ONE OF WHOM INSULTED PAULIE A COUPLE OF YEARS BACK...

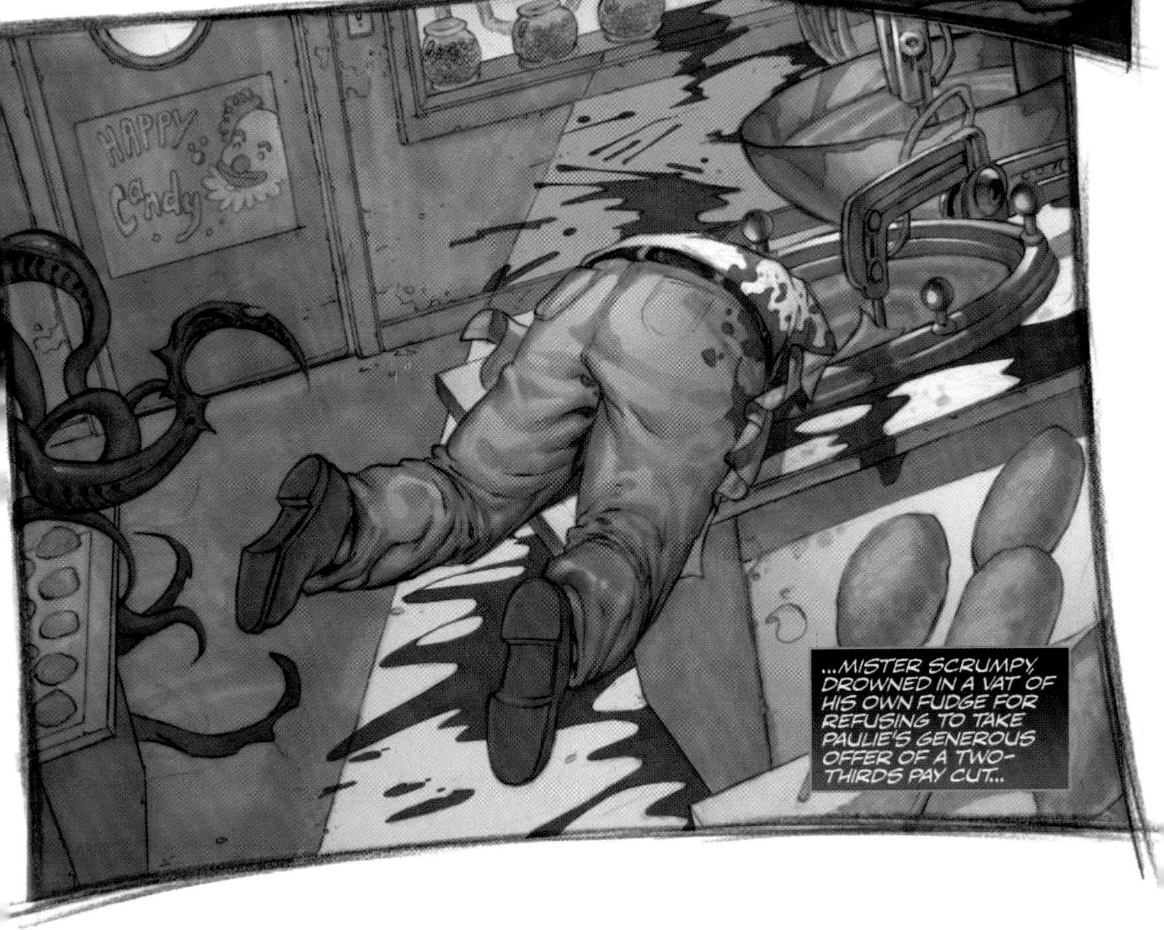
HAPPY Candy
...MISTER SCRUMPY, DROWNED IN A VAT OF HIS OWN FUDGE FOR REFUSING TO TAKE PAULIE'S GENEROUS OFFER OF A TWO-THIRDS PAY CUT...

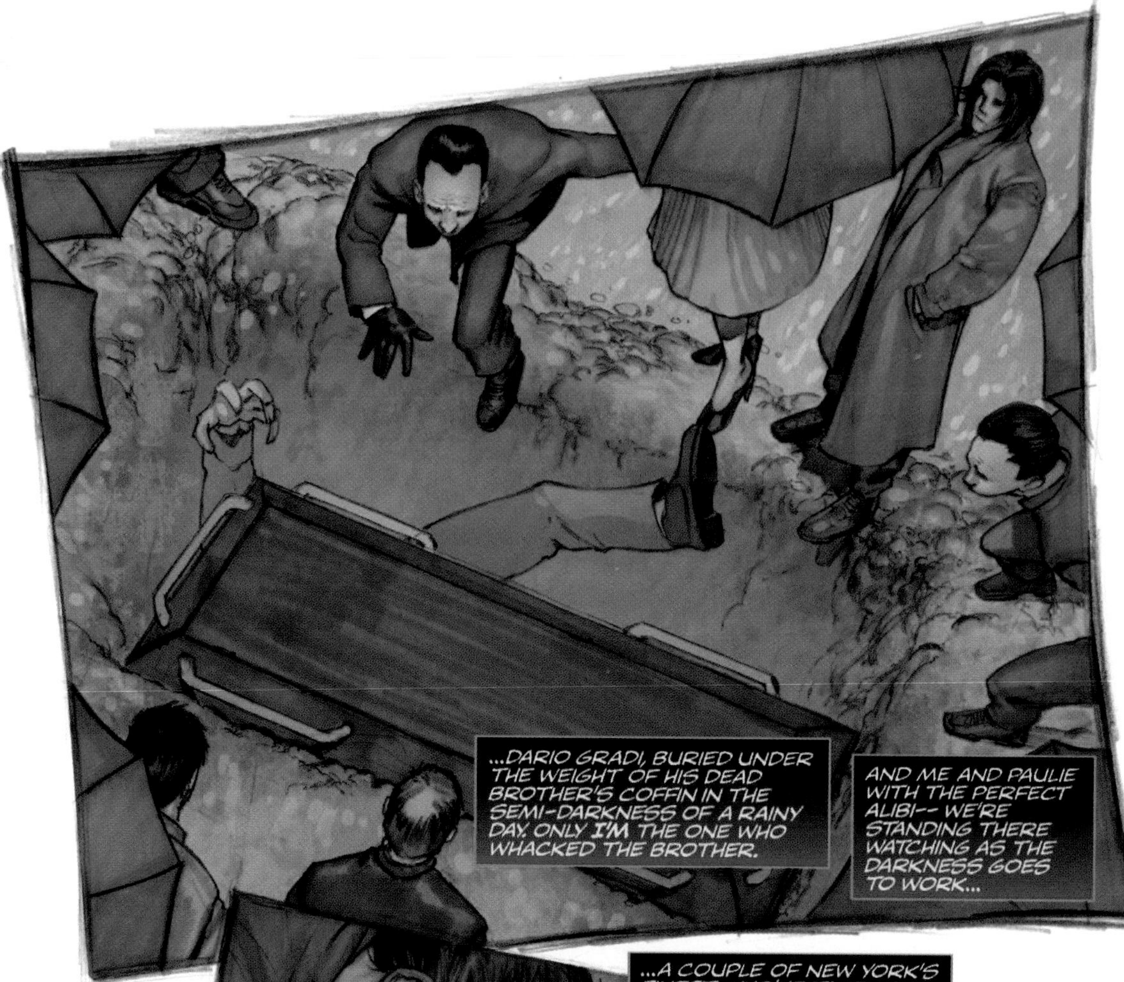
...DARIO GRADI, BURIED UNDER THE WEIGHT OF HIS DEAD BROTHER'S COFFIN IN THE SEMI-DARKNESS OF A RAINY DAY. ONLY I'M THE ONE WHO WHACKED THE BROTHER.
AND ME AND PAULIE WITH THE PERFECT ALIBI-- WE'RE STANDING THERE WATCHING AS THE DARKNESS GOES TO WORK...

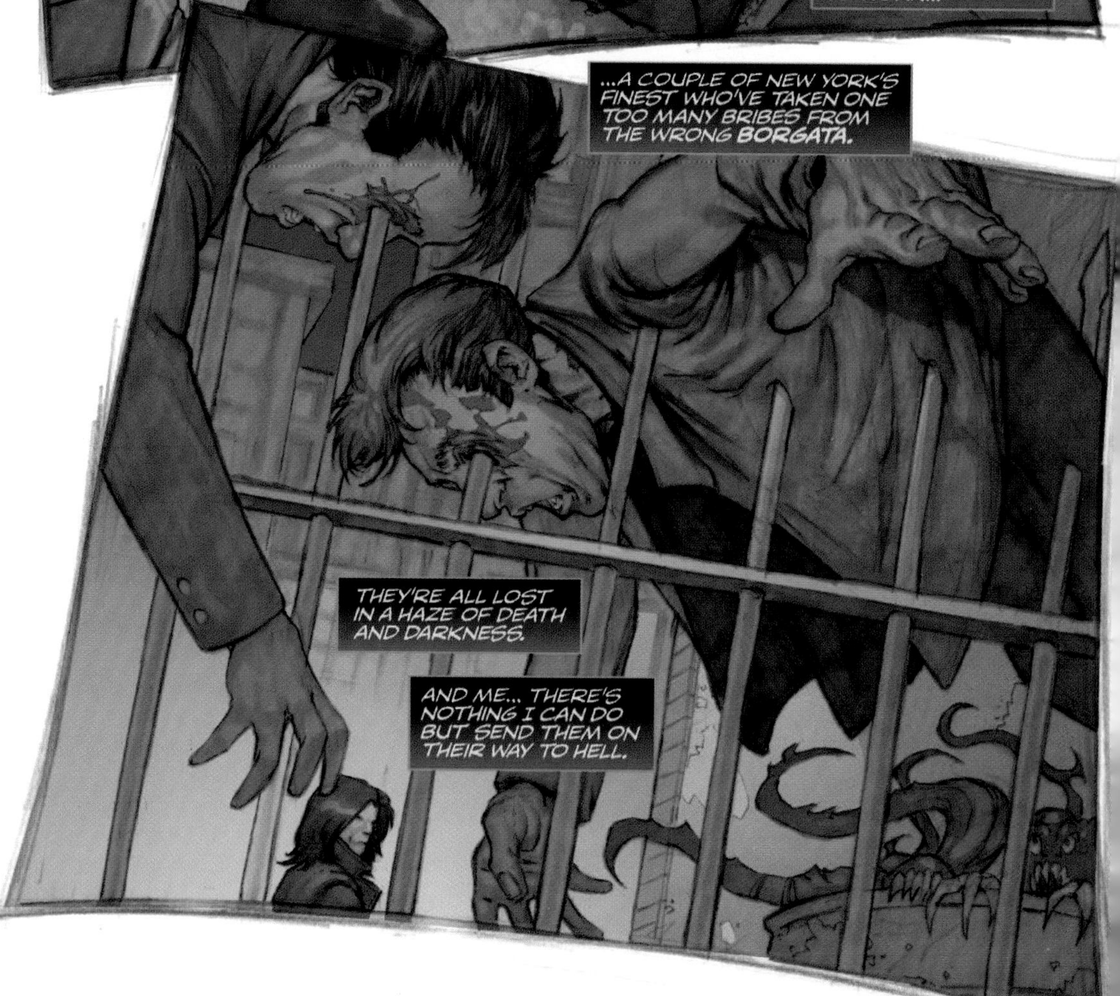
...A COUPLE OF NEW YORK'S FINEST WHO'VE TAKEN ONE TOO MANY BRIBES FROM THE WRONG BORGATA.
THEY'RE ALL LOST IN A HAZE OF DEATH AND DARKNESS.
AND ME... THERE'S NOTHING I CAN DO BUT SEND THEM ON THEIR WAY TO HELL.

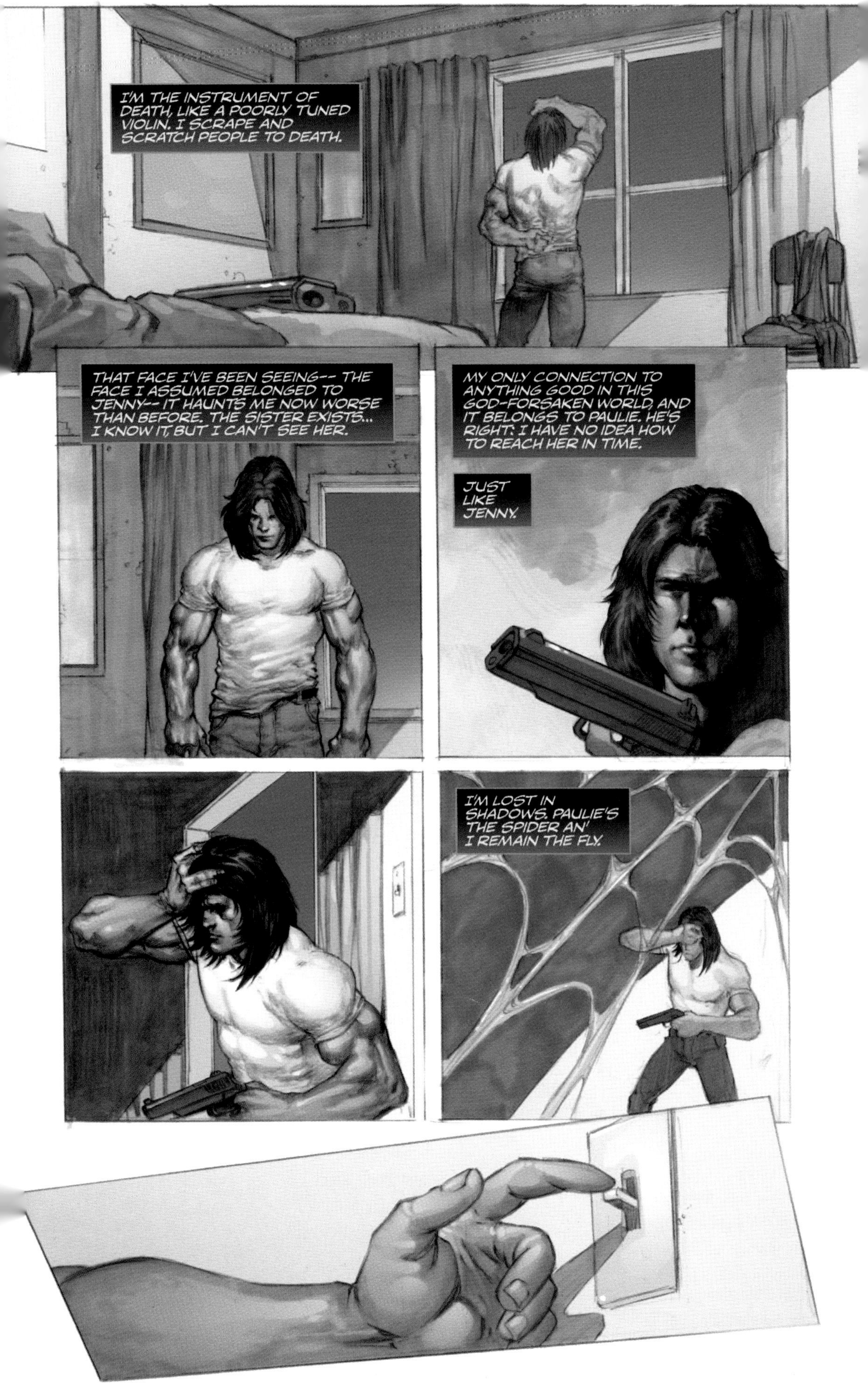
I'M THE INSTRUMENT OF DEATH, LIKE A POORLY TUNED VIOLIN. I SCRAPE AND SCRATCH PEOPLE TO DEATH.
THAT FACE I'VE BEEN SEEING-- THE FACE I ASSUMED BELONGED TO JENNY-- IT HAUNTS ME NOW WORSE THAN BEFORE. THE SISTER EXISTS... I KNOW IT, BUT I CAN'T SEE HER.
MY ONLY CONNECTION TO ANYTHING GOOD IN THIS GOD-FORSAKEN WORLD, AND IT BELONGS TO PAULIE. HE'S RIGHT: I HAVE NO IDEA HOW TO REACH HER IN TIME.
JUST LIKE JENNY.
I'M LOST IN SHADOWS. PAULIE'S THE SPIDER AN' I REMAIN THE FLY.

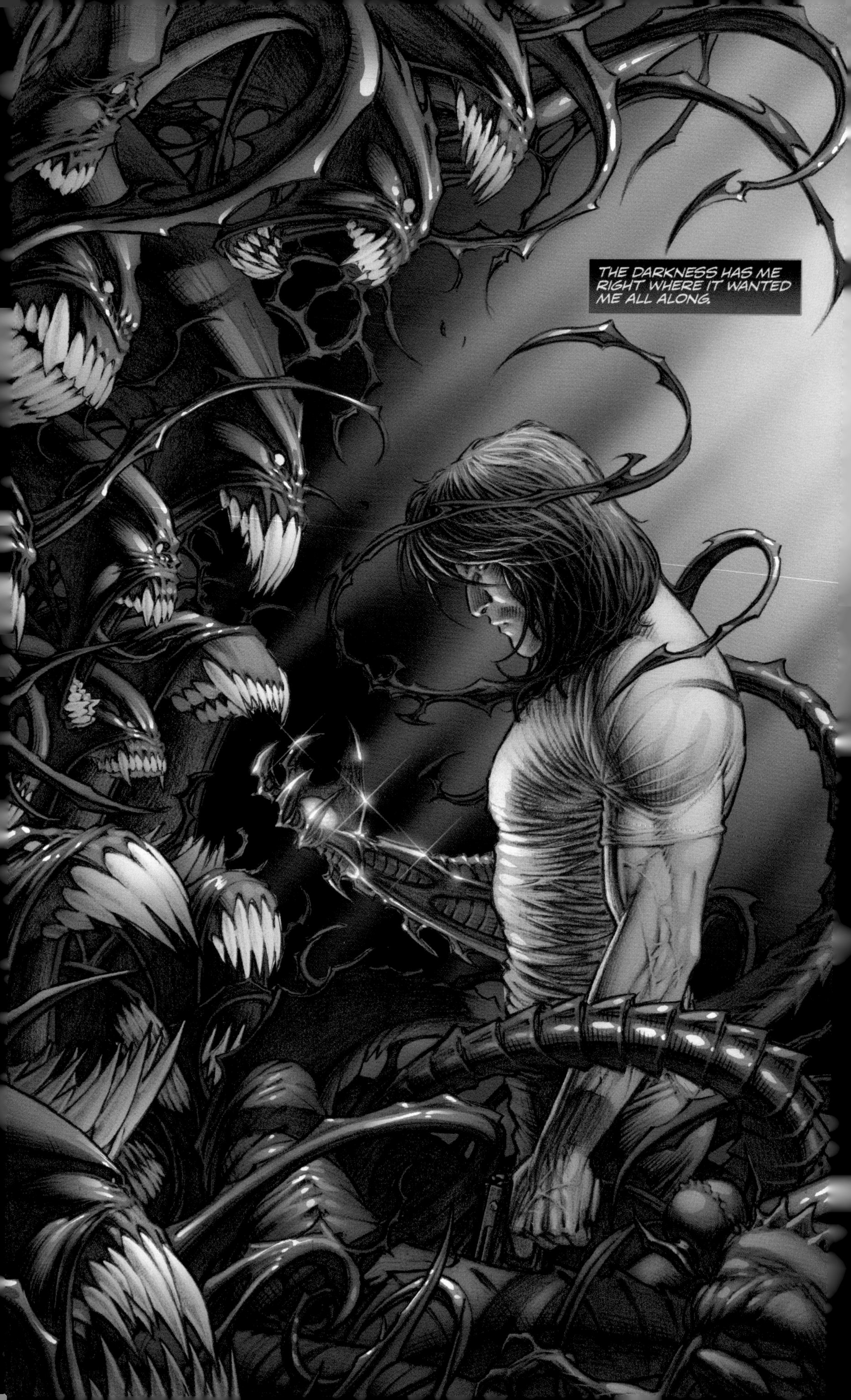
THE DARKNESS HAS ME RIGHT WHERE IT WANTED ME ALL ALONG.

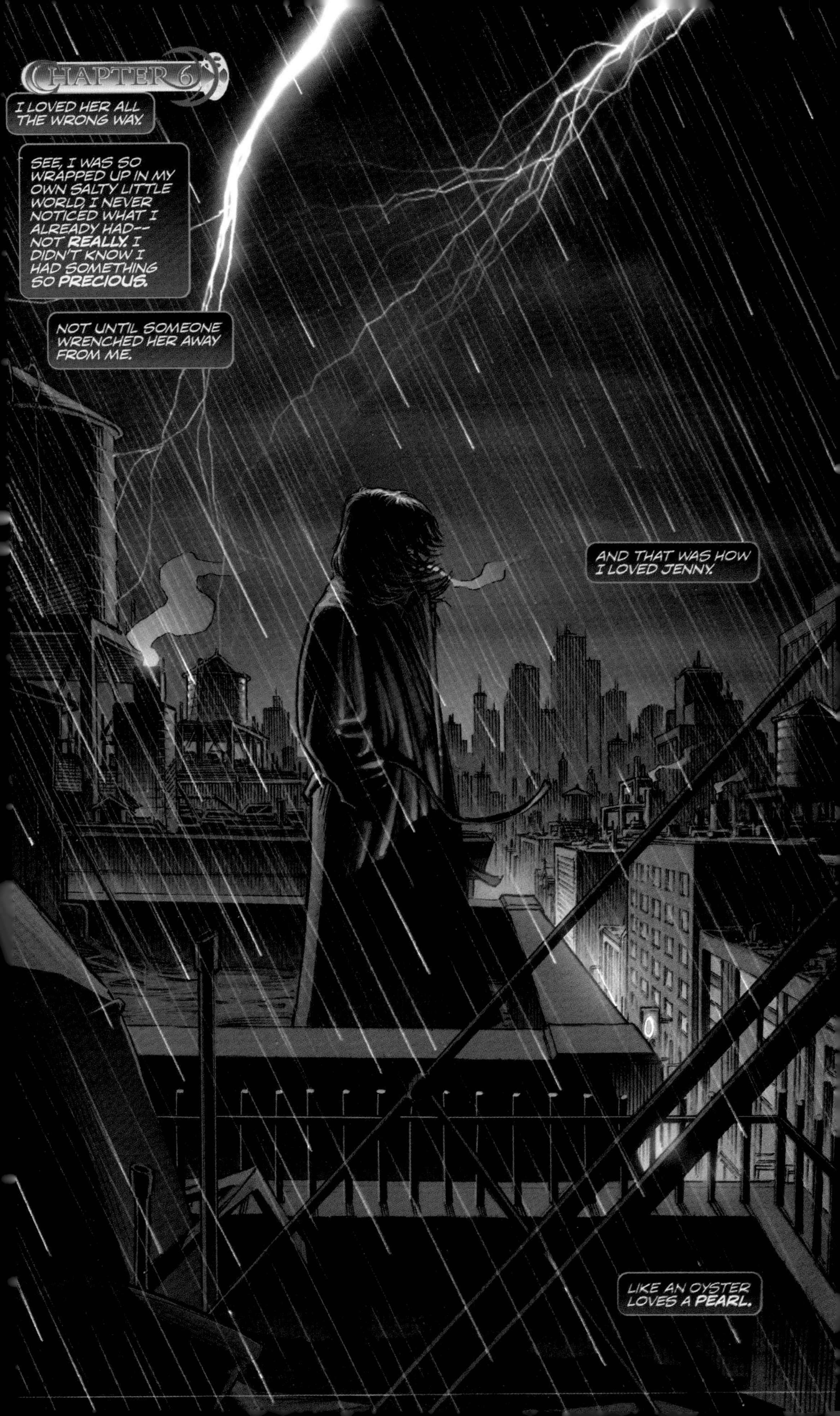
CHAPTER 6
I LOVED HER ALL THE WRONG WAY.
SEE, I WAS SO WRAPPED UP IN MY OWN SALTY LITTLE WORLD, I NEVER NOTICED WHAT I ALREADY HAD-- NOT **REALLY.** I DIDN'T KNOW I HAD SOMETHING SO **PRECIOUS.**
NOT UNTIL SOMEONE WRENCHED HER AWAY FROM ME.
AND THAT WAS HOW I LOVED JENNY.
LIKE AN OYSTER LOVES A **PEARL.**

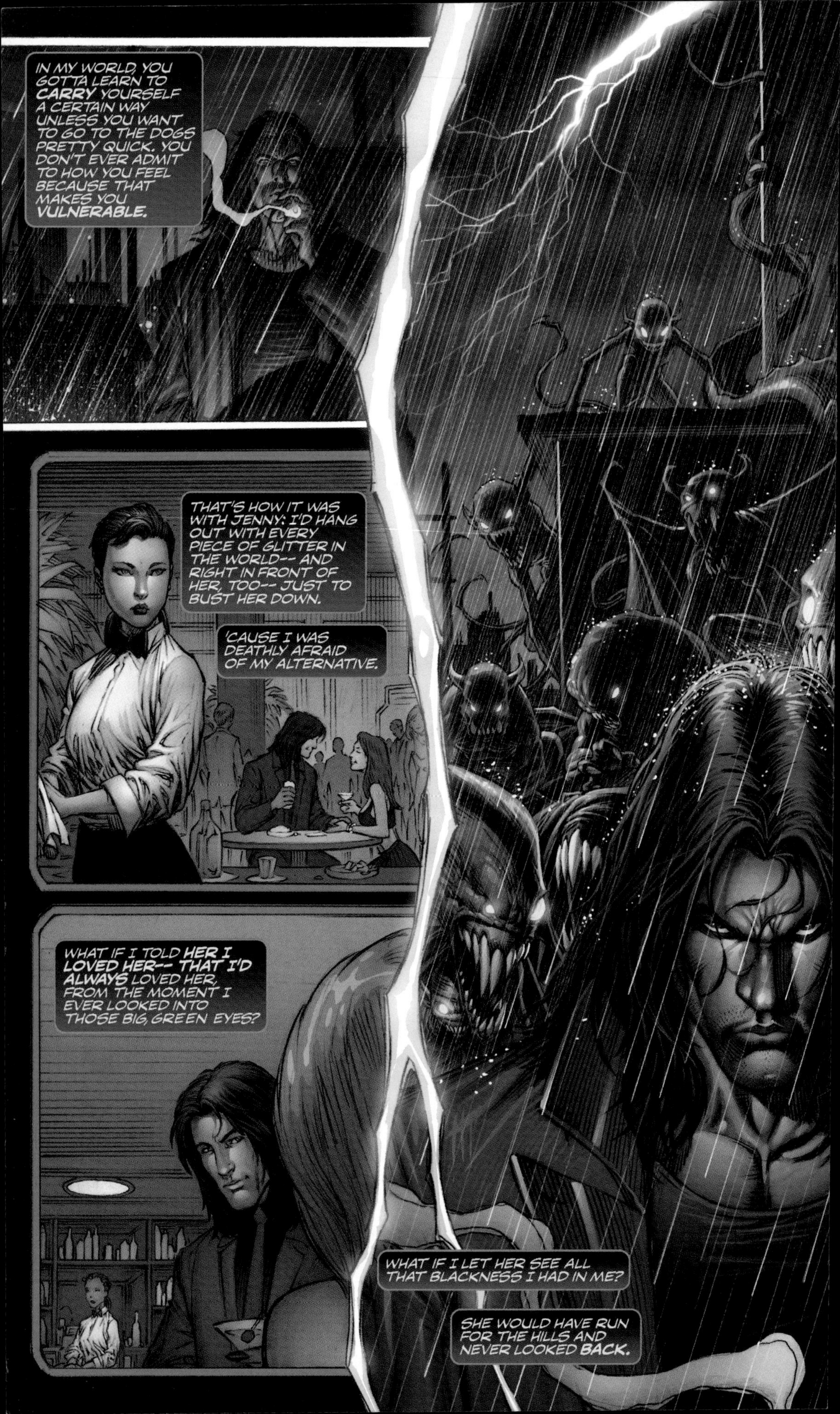
IN MY WORLD, YOU GOTTA LEARN TO CARRY YOURSELF A CERTAIN WAY UNLESS YOU WANT TO GO TO THE DOGS PRETTY QUICK. YOU DON'T EVER ADMIT TO HOW YOU FEEL BECAUSE THAT MAKES YOU VULNERABLE.
THAT'S HOW IT WAS WITH JENNY: I'D HANG OUT WITH EVERY PIECE OF GLITTER IN THE WORLD-- AND RIGHT IN FRONT OF HER, TOO-- JUST TO BUST HER DOWN.
'CAUSE I WAS DEATHLY AFRAID OF MY ALTERNATIVE.
WHAT IF I TOLD HER I LOVED HER-- THAT I'D ALWAYS LOVED HER, FROM THE MOMENT I EVER LOOKED INTO THOSE BIG, GREEN EYES?
WHAT IF I LET HER SEE ALL THAT BLACKNESS I HAD IN ME?
SHE WOULD HAVE RUN FOR THE HILLS AND NEVER LOOKED BACK.

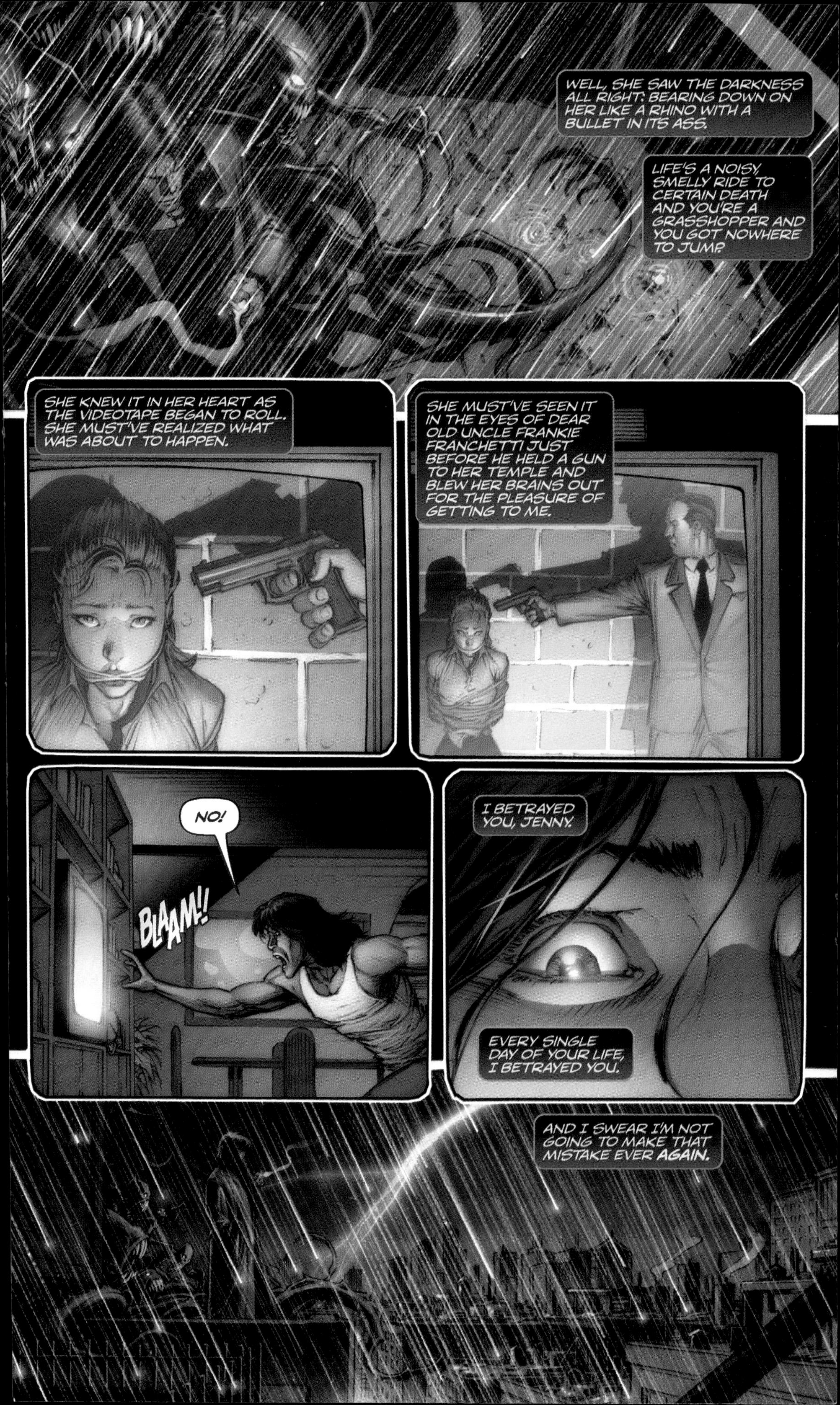
WELL, SHE SAW THE DARKNESS ALL RIGHT: BEARING DOWN ON HER LIKE A RHINO WITH A BULLET IN ITS ASS.
LIFE'S A NOISY, SMELLY RIDE TO CERTAIN DEATH AND YOU'RE A GRASSHOPPER AND YOU GOT NOWHERE TO JUMP?
SHE KNEW IT IN HER HEART AS THE VIDEOTAPE BEGAN TO ROLL. SHE MUST'VE REALIZED WHAT WAS ABOUT TO HAPPEN.
SHE MUST'VE SEEN IT IN THE EYES OF DEAR OLD UNCLE FRANKIE FRANCHETTI JUST BEFORE HE HELD A GUN TO HER TEMPLE AND BLEW HER BRAINS OUT FOR THE PLEASURE OF GETTING TO ME.
NO!
BLAAM!!
I BETRAYED YOU, JENNY.
EVERY SINGLE DAY OF YOUR LIFE, I BETRAYED YOU.
AND I SWEAR I'M NOT GOING TO MAKE THAT MISTAKE EVER **AGAIN.**

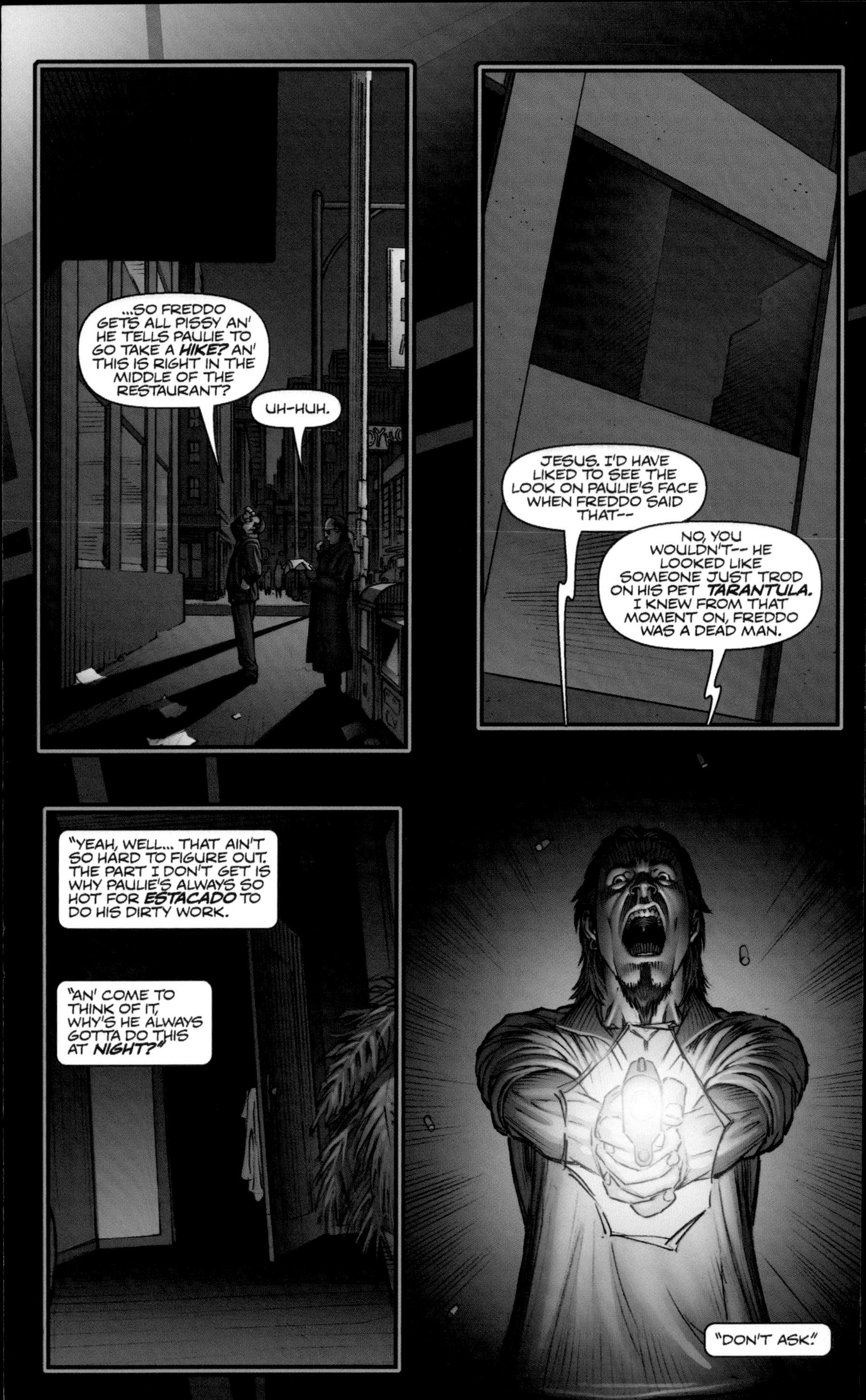
...SO FREDDO GETS ALL PISSY AN' HE TELLS PAULIE TO GO TAKE A ***HIKE?*** AN' THIS IS RIGHT IN THE MIDDLE OF THE RESTAURANT?
UH-HUH.
JESUS. I'D HAVE LIKED TO SEE THE LOOK ON PAULIE'S FACE WHEN FREDDO SAID THAT--
NO, YOU WOULDN'T-- HE LOOKED LIKE SOMEONE JUST TROD ON HIS PET ***TARANTULA.*** I KNEW FROM THAT MOMENT ON, FREDDO WAS A DEAD MAN.
"YEAH, WELL... THAT AIN'T SO HARD TO FIGURE OUT. THE PART I DON'T GET IS WHY PAULIE'S ALWAYS SO HOT FOR ***ESTACADO*** TO DO HIS DIRTY WORK.
"AN' COME TO THINK OF IT, WHY'S HE ALWAYS GOTTA DO THIS AT ***NIGHT?"***
"DON'T ASK."

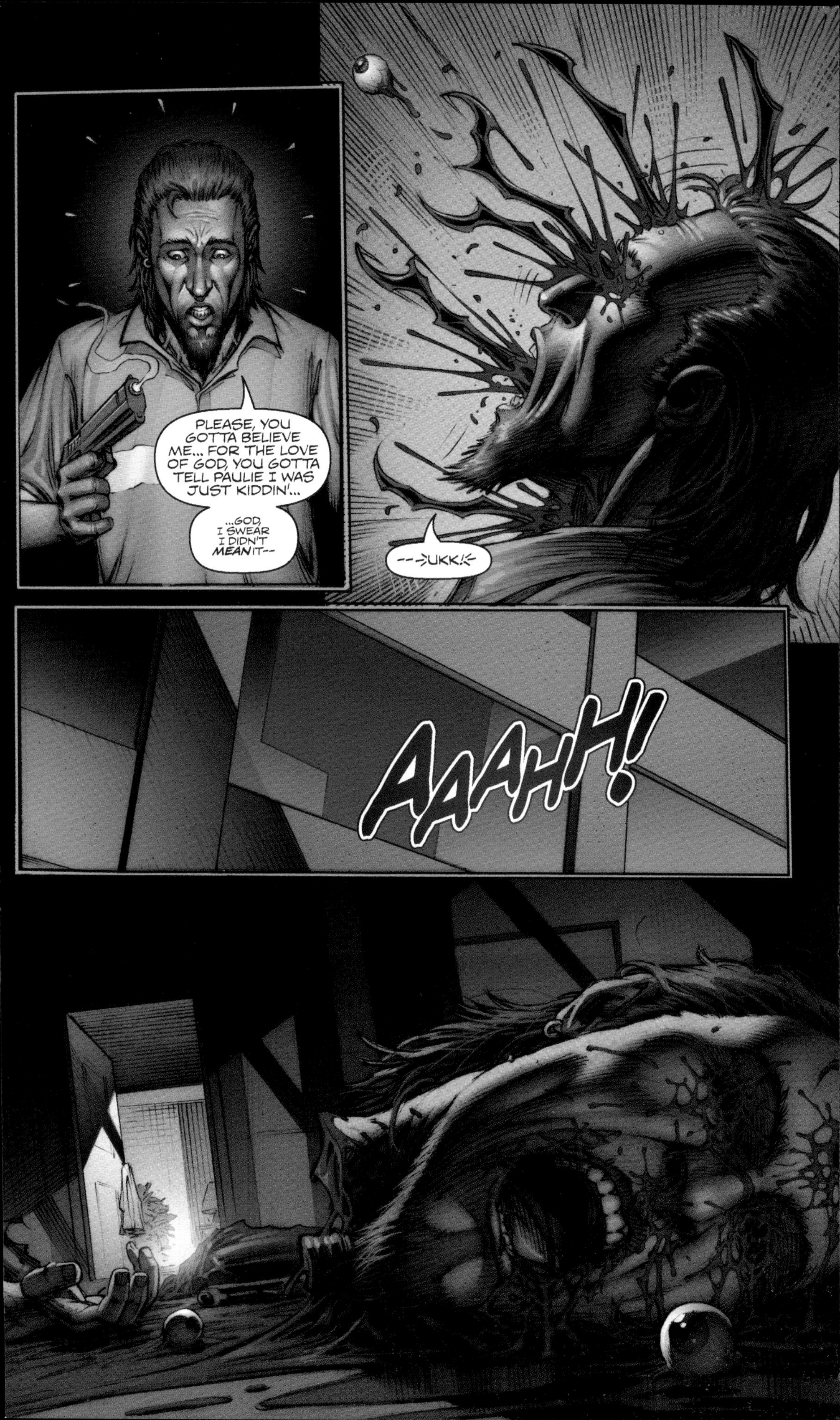
PLEASE, YOU GOTTA BELIEVE ME... FOR THE LOVE OF GOD, YOU GOTTA TELL PAULIE I WAS JUST KIDDIN'...
...GOD, I SWEAR I DIDN'T MEAN IT--
--UKK!--
AAAHH!

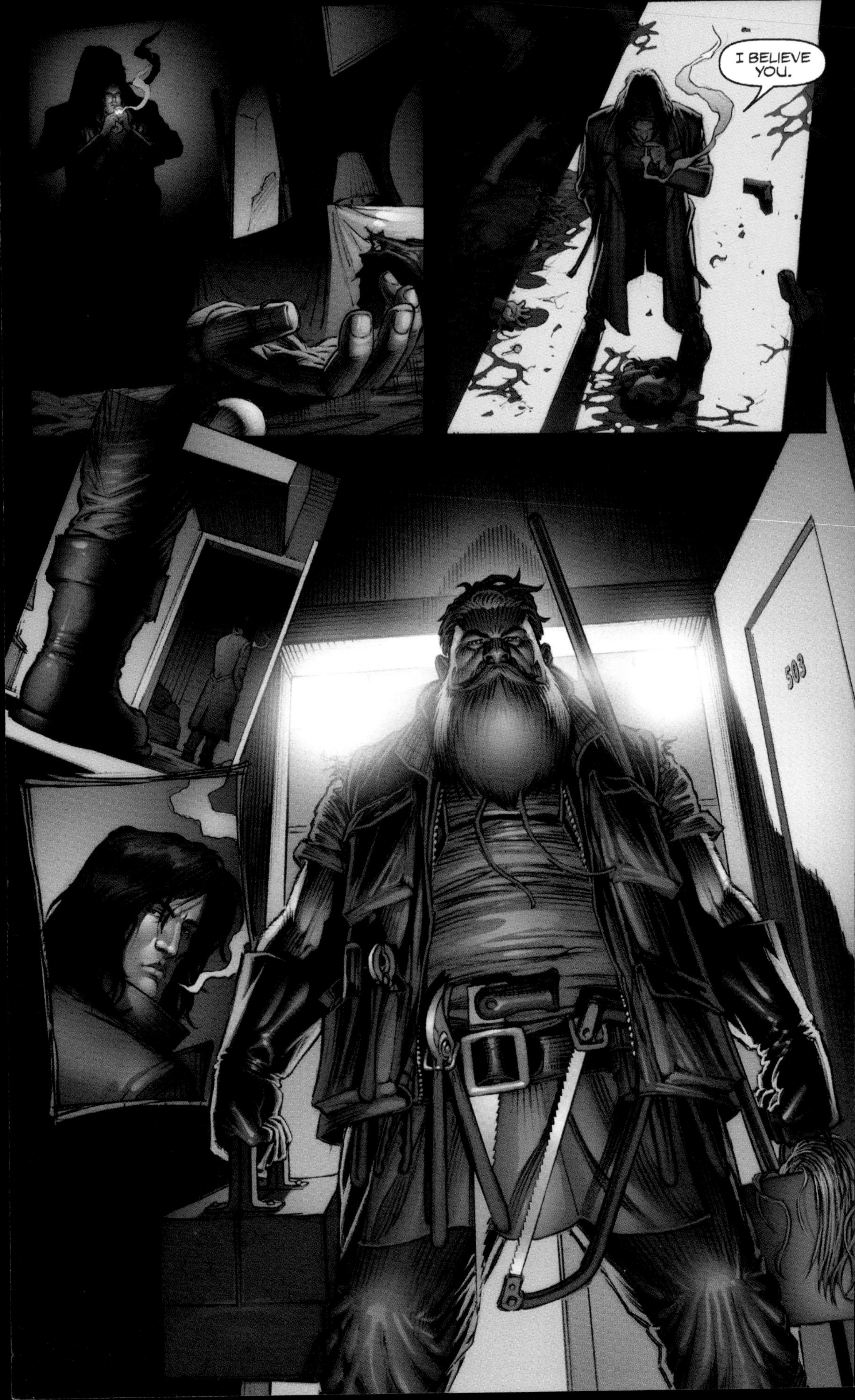
I BELIEVE YOU.
503

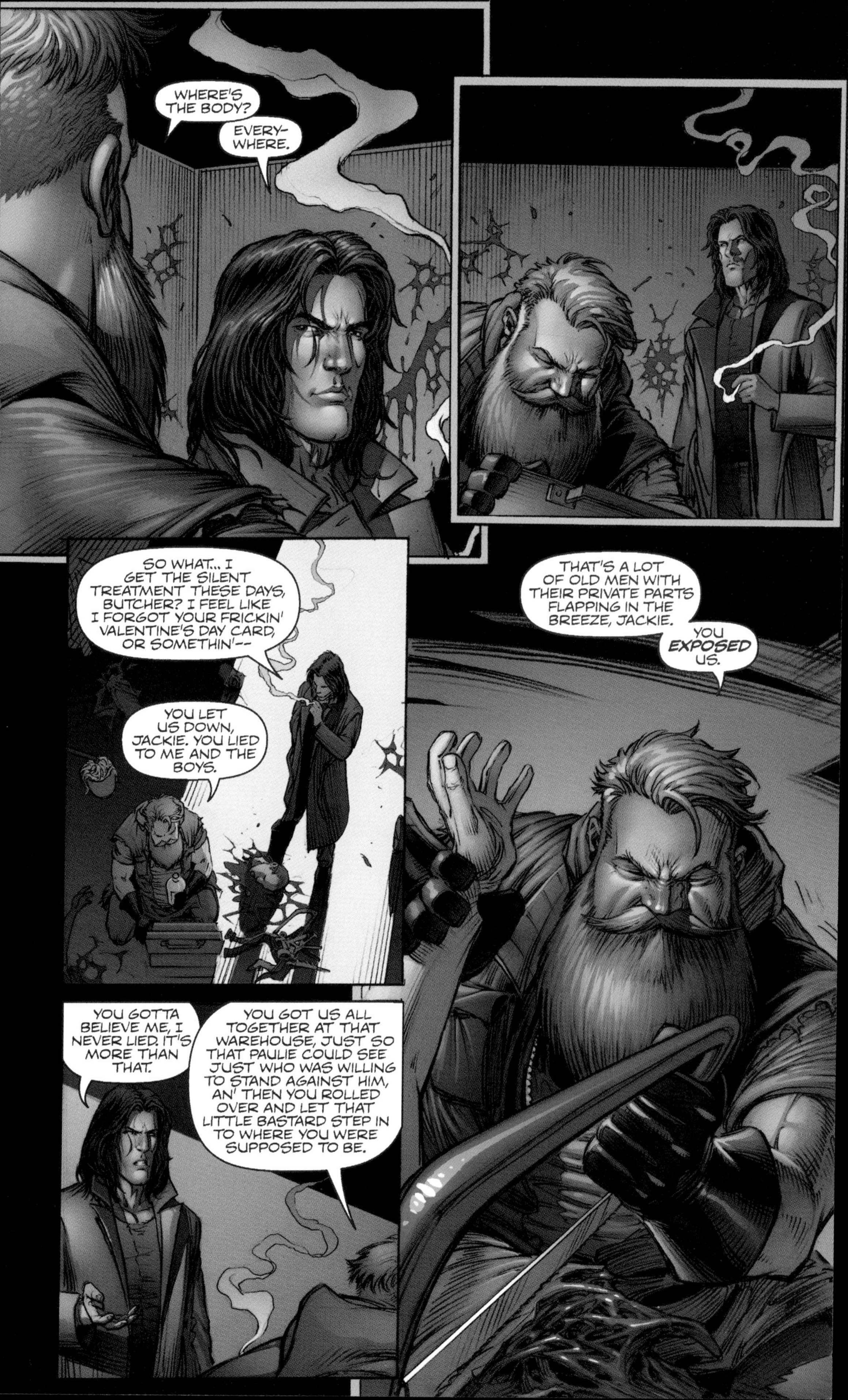
WHERE'S THE BODY?
EVERY-WHERE.
SO WHAT... I GET THE SILENT TREATMENT THESE DAYS, BUTCHER? I FEEL LIKE I FORGOT YOUR FRICKIN' VALENTINE'S DAY CARD, OR SOMETHIN'--
YOU LET US DOWN, JACKIE. YOU LIED TO ME AND THE BOYS.
THAT'S A LOT OF OLD MEN WITH THEIR PRIVATE PARTS FLAPPING IN THE BREEZE, JACKIE.
YOU *EXPOSED* US.
YOU GOTTA BELIEVE ME, I NEVER LIED. IT'S MORE THAN THAT.
YOU GOT US ALL TOGETHER AT THAT WAREHOUSE, JUST SO THAT PAULIE COULD SEE JUST WHO WAS WILLING TO STAND AGAINST HIM, AN' THEN YOU ROLLED OVER AND LET THAT LITTLE BASTARD STEP IN TO WHERE YOU WERE SUPPOSED TO BE.

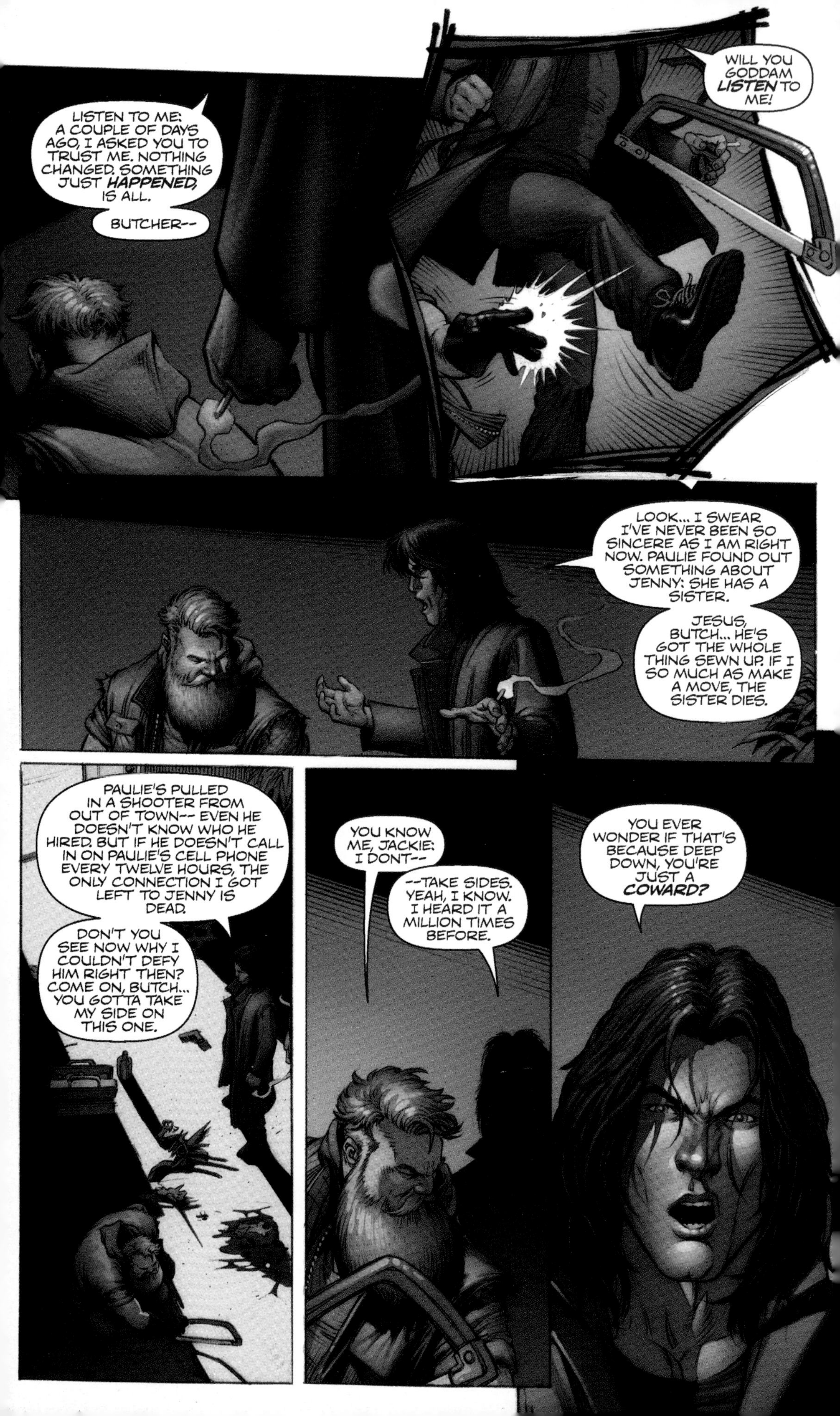
LISTEN TO ME: A COUPLE OF DAYS AGO, I ASKED YOU TO TRUST ME. NOTHING CHANGED. SOMETHING JUST *HAPPENED,* IS ALL.
BUTCHER--
WILL YOU GODDAM *LISTEN* TO ME!
LOOK... I SWEAR I'VE NEVER BEEN SO SINCERE AS I AM RIGHT NOW. PAULIE FOUND OUT SOMETHING ABOUT JENNY: SHE HAS A SISTER.
JESUS, BUTCH... HE'S GOT THE WHOLE THING SEWN UP. IF I SO MUCH AS MAKE A MOVE, THE SISTER DIES.
PAULIE'S PULLED IN A SHOOTER FROM OUT OF TOWN-- EVEN HE DOESN'T KNOW WHO HE HIRED. BUT IF HE DOESN'T CALL IN ON PAULIE'S CELL PHONE EVERY TWELVE HOURS, THE ONLY CONNECTION I GOT LEFT TO JENNY IS DEAD.
DON'T YOU SEE NOW WHY I COULDN'T DEFY HIM RIGHT THEN? COME ON, BUTCH... YOU GOTTA TAKE MY SIDE ON THIS ONE.
YOU KNOW ME, JACKIE: I DONT--
--TAKE SIDES. YEAH, I KNOW. I HEARD IT A MILLION TIMES BEFORE.
YOU EVER WONDER IF THAT'S BECAUSE DEEP DOWN, YOU'RE JUST A *COWARD?*

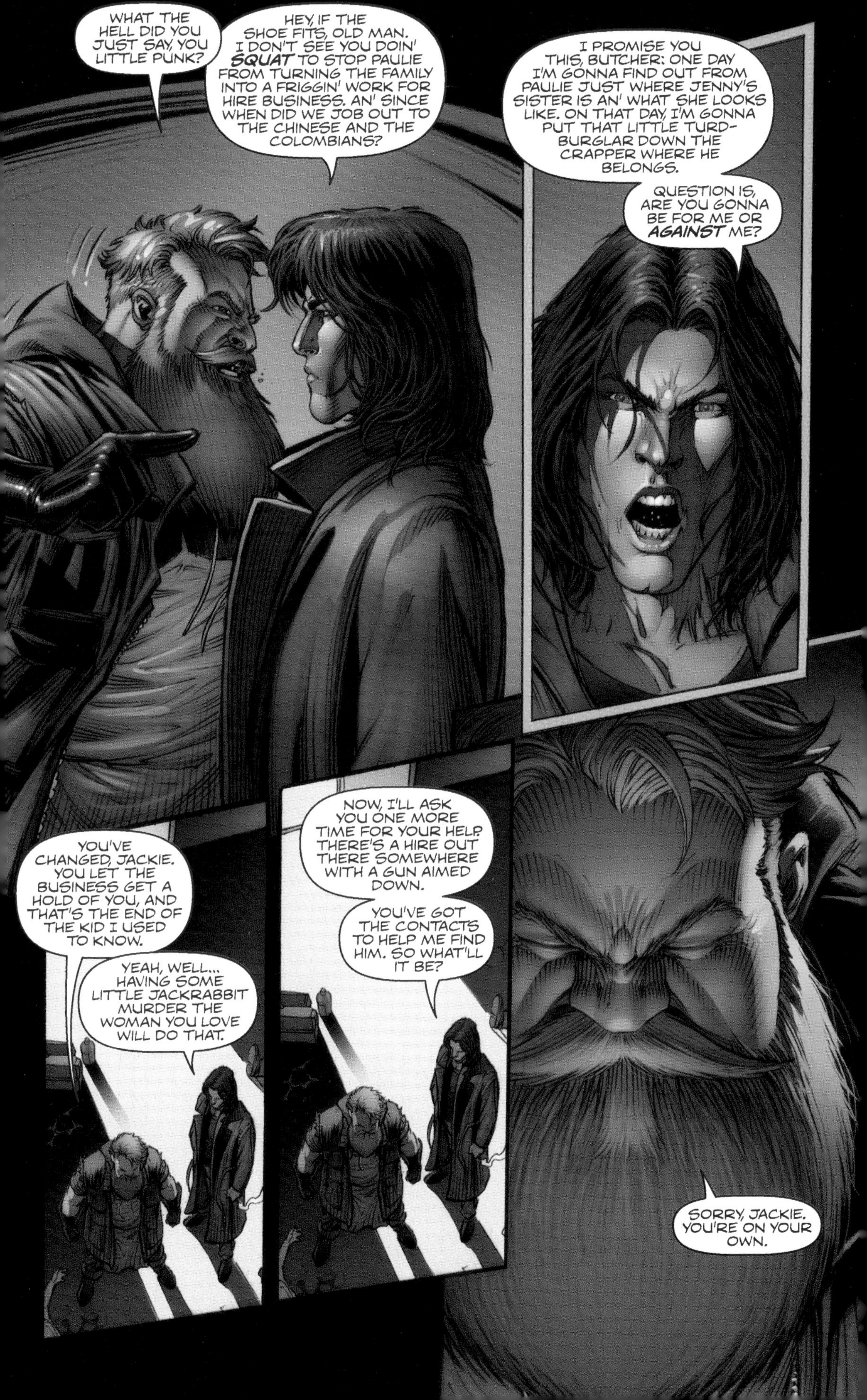
WHAT THE HELL DID YOU JUST SAY, YOU LITTLE PUNK?
HEY, IF THE SHOE FITS, OLD MAN. I DON'T SEE YOU DOIN' SQUAT TO STOP PAULIE FROM TURNING THE FAMILY INTO A FRIGGIN' WORK FOR HIRE BUSINESS. AN' SINCE WHEN DID WE JOB OUT TO THE CHINESE AND THE COLOMBIANS?
I PROMISE YOU THIS, BUTCHER: ONE DAY I'M GONNA FIND OUT FROM PAULIE JUST WHERE JENNY'S SISTER IS AN' WHAT SHE LOOKS LIKE. ON THAT DAY, I'M GONNA PUT THAT LITTLE TURD-BURGLAR DOWN THE CRAPPER WHERE HE BELONGS.
QUESTION IS, ARE YOU GONNA BE FOR ME OR AGAINST ME?
YOU'VE CHANGED, JACKIE. YOU LET THE BUSINESS GET A HOLD OF YOU, AND THAT'S THE END OF THE KID I USED TO KNOW.
YEAH, WELL... HAVING SOME LITTLE JACKRABBIT MURDER THE WOMAN YOU LOVE WILL DO THAT.
NOW, I'LL ASK YOU ONE MORE TIME FOR YOUR HELP. THERE'S A HIRE OUT THERE SOMEWHERE WITH A GUN AIMED DOWN.
YOU'VE GOT THE CONTACTS TO HELP ME FIND HIM. SO WHAT'LL IT BE?
SORRY, JACKIE. YOU'RE ON YOUR OWN.

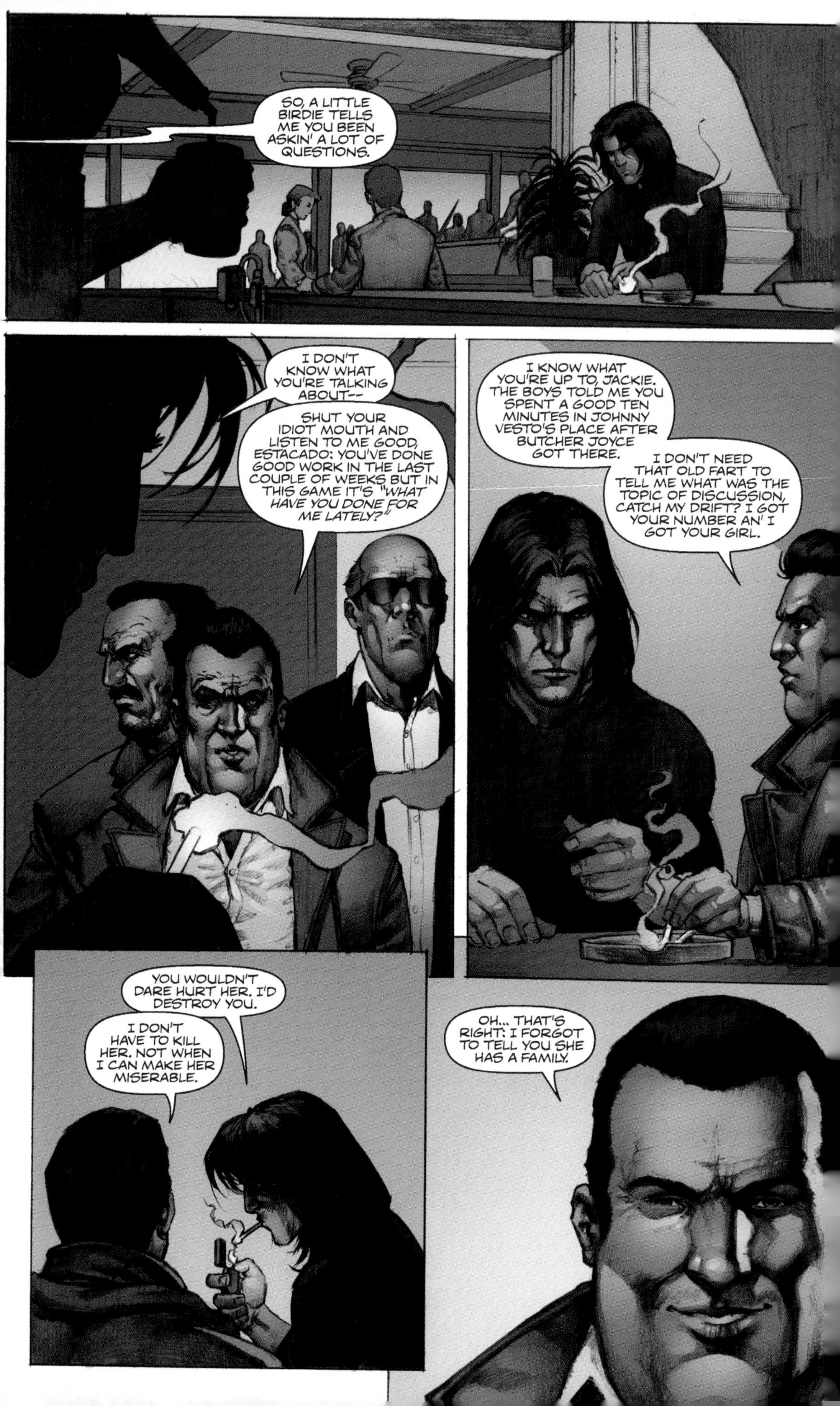
SO, A LITTLE BIRDIE TELLS ME YOU BEEN ASKIN' A LOT OF QUESTIONS.
I DON'T KNOW WHAT YOU'RE TALKING ABOUT--
SHUT YOUR IDIOT MOUTH AND LISTEN TO ME GOOD, ESTACADO: YOU'VE DONE GOOD WORK IN THE LAST COUPLE OF WEEKS BUT IN THIS GAME IT'S "WHAT HAVE YOU DONE FOR ME LATELY?"
I KNOW WHAT YOU'RE UP TO, JACKIE. THE BOYS TOLD ME YOU SPENT A GOOD TEN MINUTES IN JOHNNY VESTO'S PLACE AFTER BUTCHER JOYCE GOT THERE.
I DON'T NEED THAT OLD FART TO TELL ME WHAT WAS THE TOPIC OF DISCUSSION, CATCH MY DRIFT? I GOT YOUR NUMBER AN' I GOT YOUR GIRL.
YOU WOULDN'T DARE HURT HER. I'D DESTROY YOU.
I DON'T HAVE TO KILL HER. NOT WHEN I CAN MAKE HER MISERABLE.
OH... THAT'S RIGHT: I FORGOT TO TELL YOU SHE HAS A FAMILY.

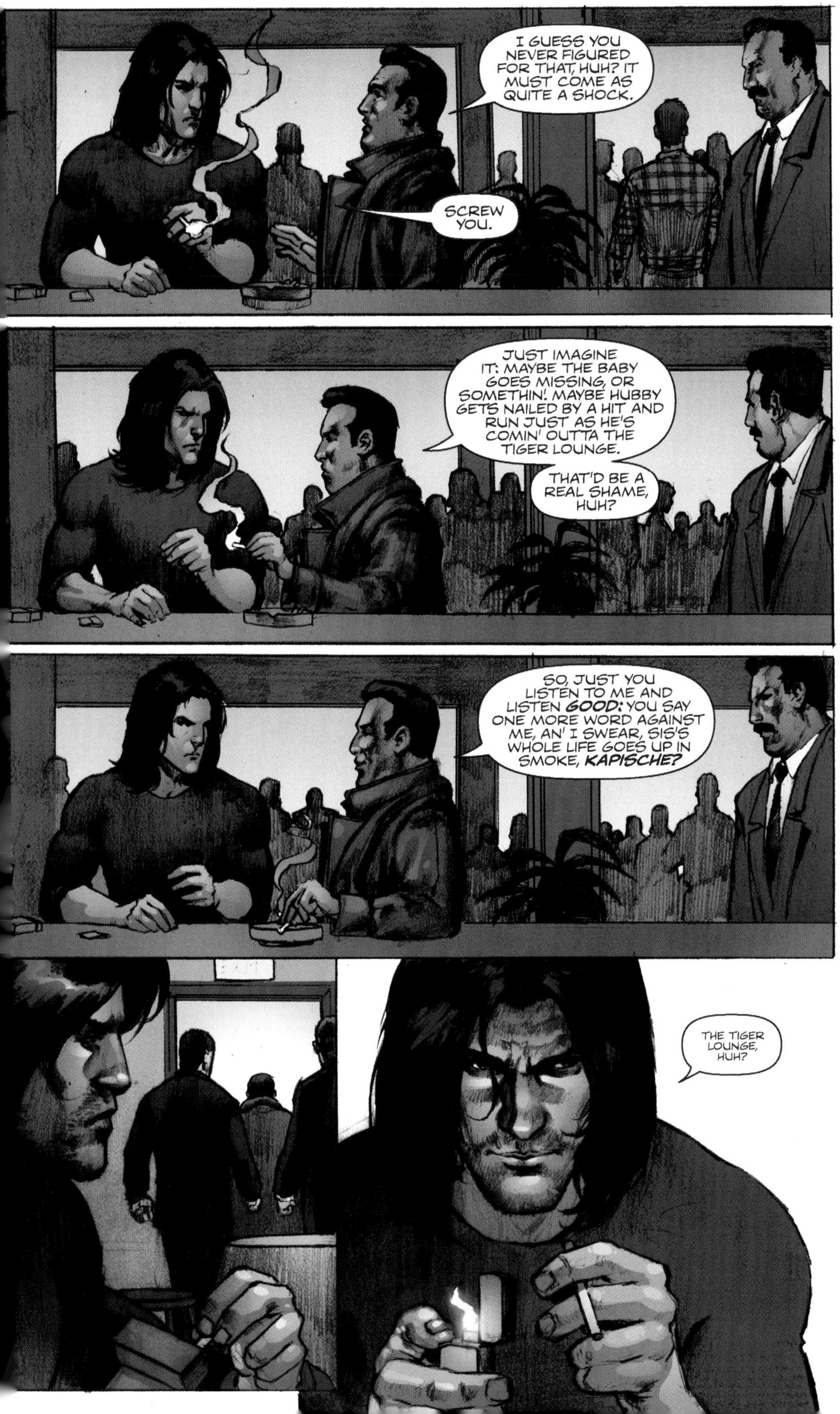
I GUESS YOU NEVER FIGURED FOR THAT, HUH? IT MUST COME AS QUITE A SHOCK.
SCREW YOU.
JUST IMAGINE IT: MAYBE THE BABY GOES MISSING, OR SOMETHIN'. MAYBE HUBBY GETS NAILED BY A HIT AND RUN JUST AS HE'S COMIN' OUTTA THE TIGER LOUNGE.
THAT'D BE A REAL SHAME, HUH?
SO, JUST YOU LISTEN TO ME AND LISTEN GOOD: YOU SAY ONE MORE WORD AGAINST ME, AN' I SWEAR, SIS'S WHOLE LIFE GOES UP IN SMOKE, KAPISCHE?
THE TIGER LOUNGE, HUH?

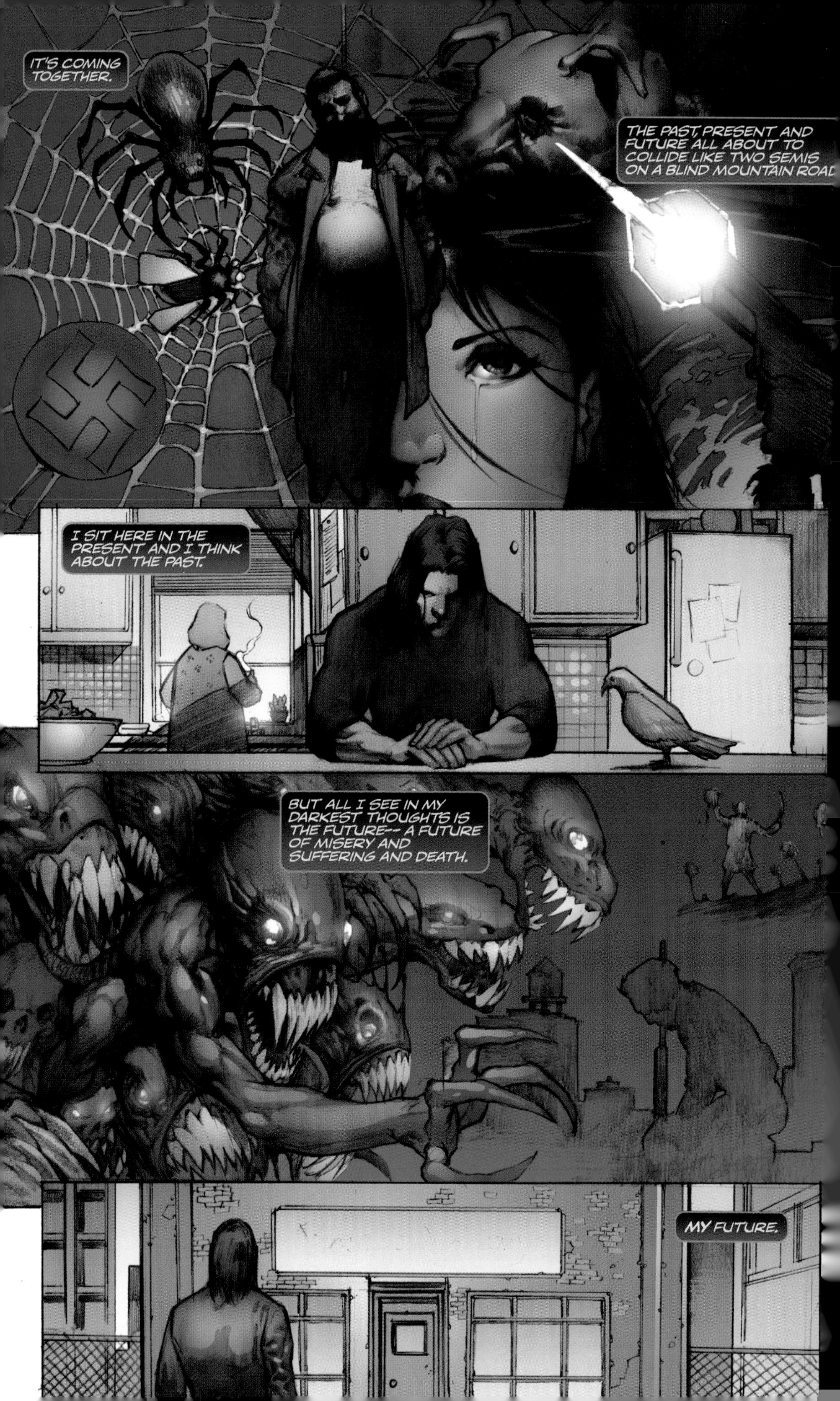
IT'S COMING TOGETHER.
THE PAST, PRESENT AND FUTURE ALL ABOUT TO COLLIDE LIKE TWO SEMIS ON A BLIND MOUNTAIN ROAD.
I SIT HERE IN THE PRESENT AND I THINK ABOUT THE PAST.
BUT ALL I SEE IN MY DARKEST THOUGHTS IS THE FUTURE-- A FUTURE OF MISERY AND SUFFERING AND DEATH.
MY FUTURE.

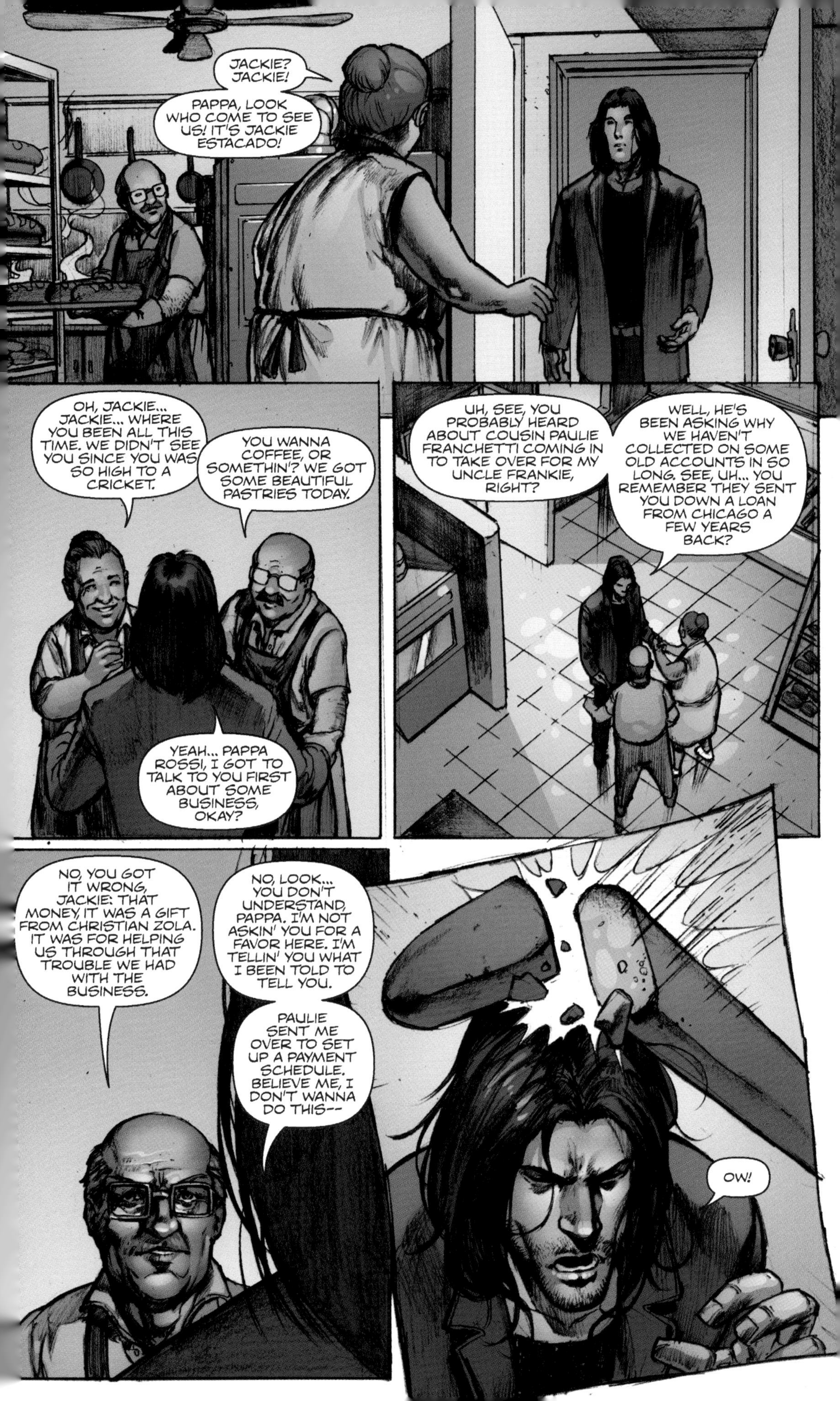
JACKIE? JACKIE!
PAPPA, LOOK WHO COME TO SEE US! IT'S JACKIE ESTACADO!
OH, JACKIE... JACKIE... WHERE YOU BEEN ALL THIS TIME. WE DIDN'T SEE YOU SINCE YOU WAS SO HIGH TO A CRICKET.
YOU WANNA COFFEE, OR SOMETHIN'? WE GOT SOME BEAUTIFUL PASTRIES TODAY.
YEAH... PAPPA ROSSI, I GOT TO TALK TO YOU FIRST ABOUT SOME BUSINESS, OKAY?
UH, SEE, YOU PROBABLY HEARD ABOUT COUSIN PAULIE FRANCHETTI COMING IN TO TAKE OVER FOR MY UNCLE FRANKIE, RIGHT?
WELL, HE'S BEEN ASKING WHY WE HAVEN'T COLLECTED ON SOME OLD ACCOUNTS IN SO LONG. SEE, UH... YOU REMEMBER THEY SENT YOU DOWN A LOAN FROM CHICAGO A FEW YEARS BACK?
NO, YOU GOT IT WRONG, JACKIE: THAT MONEY, IT WAS A GIFT FROM CHRISTIAN ZOLA. IT WAS FOR HELPING US THROUGH THAT TROUBLE WE HAD WITH THE BUSINESS.
NO, LOOK... YOU DON'T UNDERSTAND, PAPPA. I'M NOT ASKIN' YOU FOR A FAVOR HERE. I'M TELLIN' YOU WHAT I BEEN TOLD TO TELL YOU.
PAULIE SENT ME OVER TO SET UP A PAYMENT SCHEDULE. BELIEVE ME, I DON'T WANNA DO THIS--
OW!

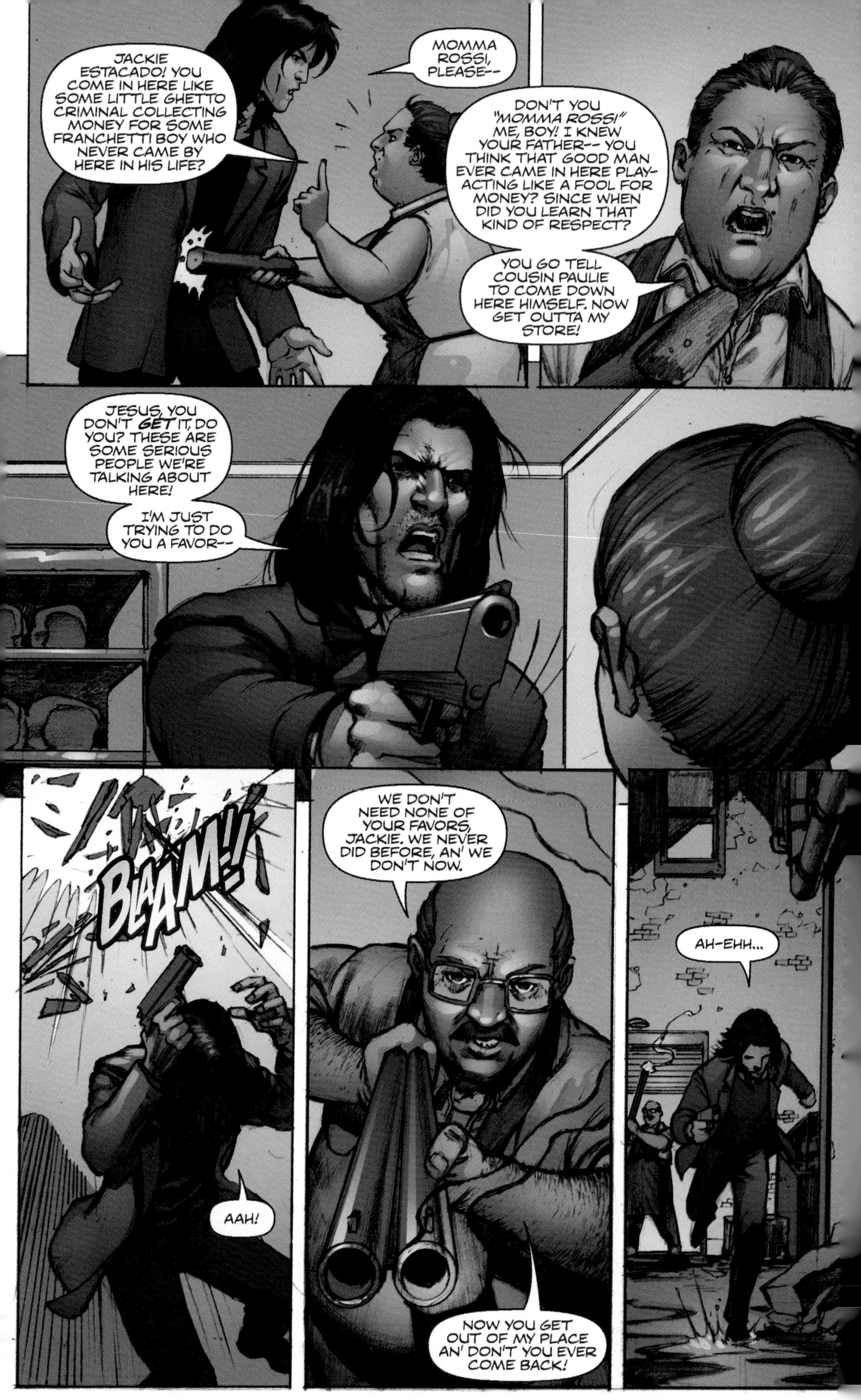
JACKIE ESTACADO! YOU COME IN HERE LIKE SOME LITTLE GHETTO CRIMINAL COLLECTING MONEY FOR SOME FRANCHETTI BOY WHO NEVER CAME BY HERE IN HIS LIFE?
MOMMA ROSSI, PLEASE--
DON'T YOU "MOMMA ROSSI" ME, BOY! I KNEW YOUR FATHER-- YOU THINK THAT GOOD MAN EVER CAME IN HERE PLAY-ACTING LIKE A FOOL FOR MONEY? SINCE WHEN DID YOU LEARN THAT KIND OF RESPECT?
YOU GO TELL COUSIN PAULIE TO COME DOWN HERE HIMSELF. NOW GET OUTTA MY STORE!
JESUS, YOU DON'T GET IT, DO YOU? THESE ARE SOME SERIOUS PEOPLE WE'RE TALKING ABOUT HERE!
I'M JUST TRYING TO DO YOU A FAVOR--
BLAAM!!
AAH!
WE DON'T NEED NONE OF YOUR FAVORS, JACKIE. WE NEVER DID BEFORE, AN' WE DON'T NOW.
NOW YOU GET OUT OF MY PLACE AN' DON'T YOU EVER COME BACK!
AH-EHH...

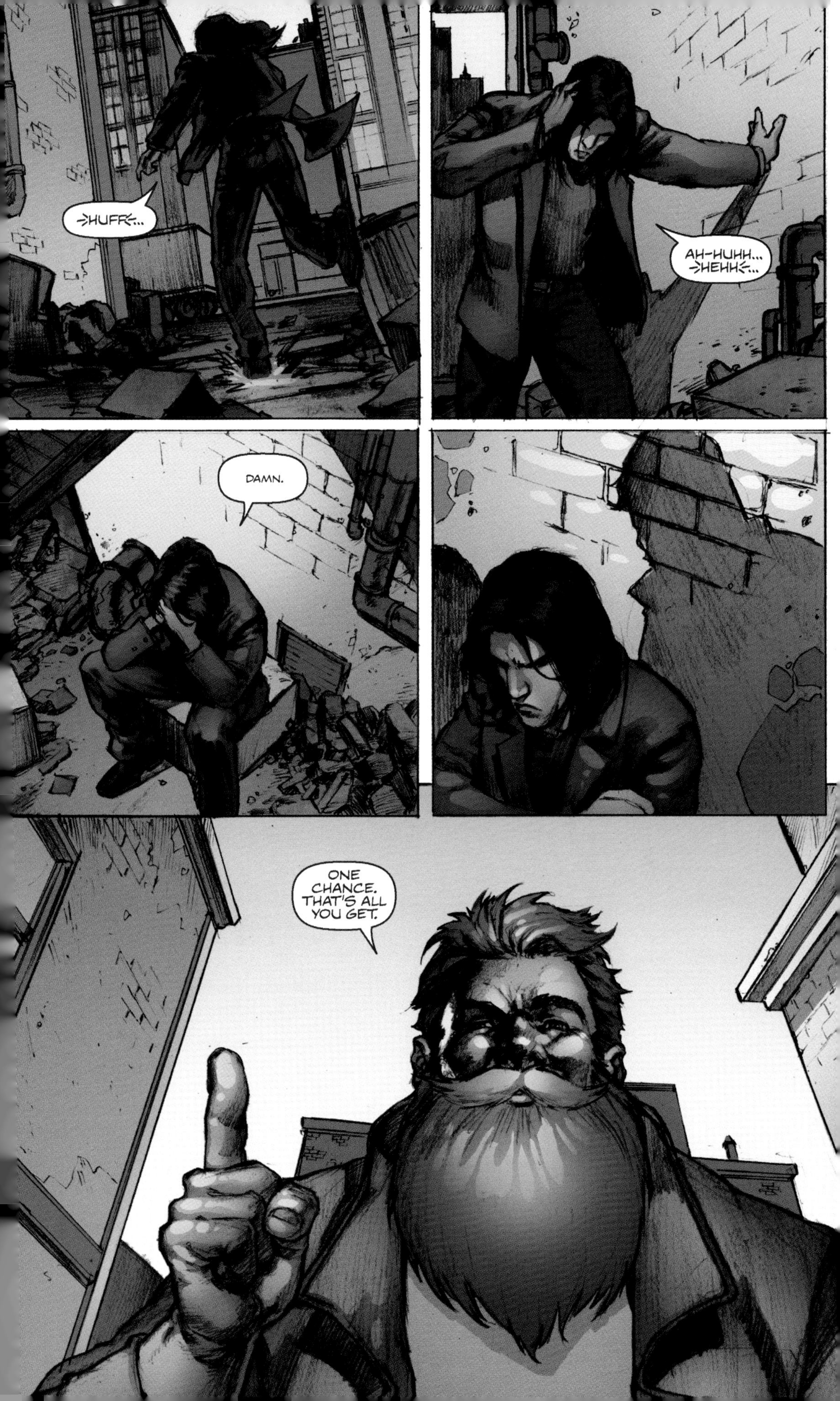

HUFF...
AH-HUHH... HEHH...
DAMN.
ONE CHANCE. THAT'S ALL YOU GET.

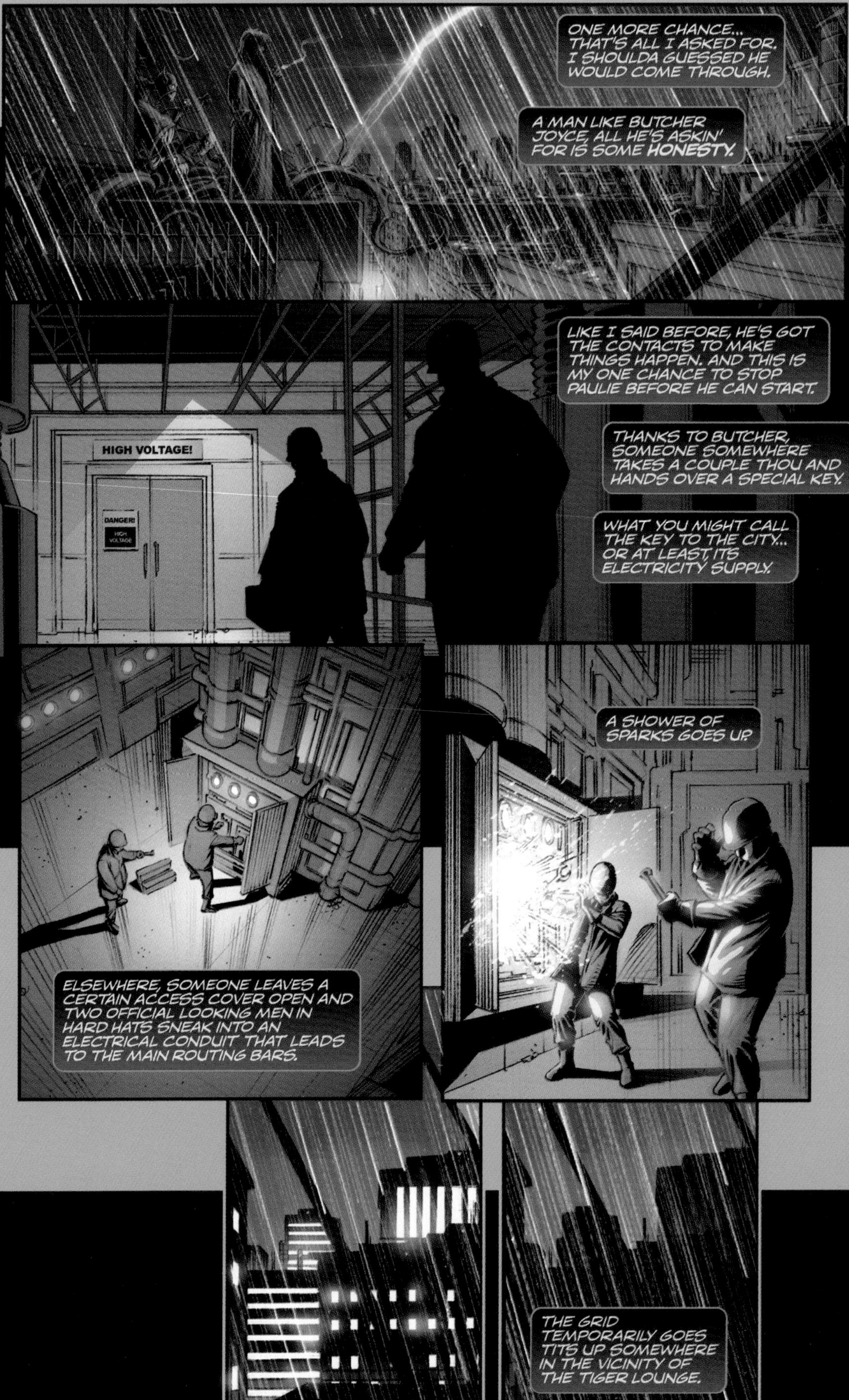
ONE MORE CHANCE... THAT'S ALL I ASKED FOR. I SHOULDA GUESSED HE WOULD COME THROUGH.
A MAN LIKE BUTCHER JOYCE, ALL HE'S ASKIN' FOR IS SOME HONESTY.
LIKE I SAID BEFORE, HE'S GOT THE CONTACTS TO MAKE THINGS HAPPEN. AND THIS IS MY ONE CHANCE TO STOP PAULIE BEFORE HE CAN START.
THANKS TO BUTCHER, SOMEONE SOMEWHERE TAKES A COUPLE THOU AND HANDS OVER A SPECIAL KEY.
WHAT YOU MIGHT CALL THE KEY TO THE CITY... OR AT LEAST, ITS ELECTRICITY SUPPLY.
HIGH VOLTAGE!
DANGER! HIGH VOLTAGE
ELSEWHERE, SOMEONE LEAVES A CERTAIN ACCESS COVER OPEN AND TWO OFFICIAL LOOKING MEN IN HARD HATS SNEAK INTO AN ELECTRICAL CONDUIT THAT LEADS TO THE MAIN ROUTING BARS.
A SHOWER OF SPARKS GOES UP.
THE GRID TEMPORARILY GOES TITS UP SOMEWHERE IN THE VICINITY OF THE TIGER LOUNGE.

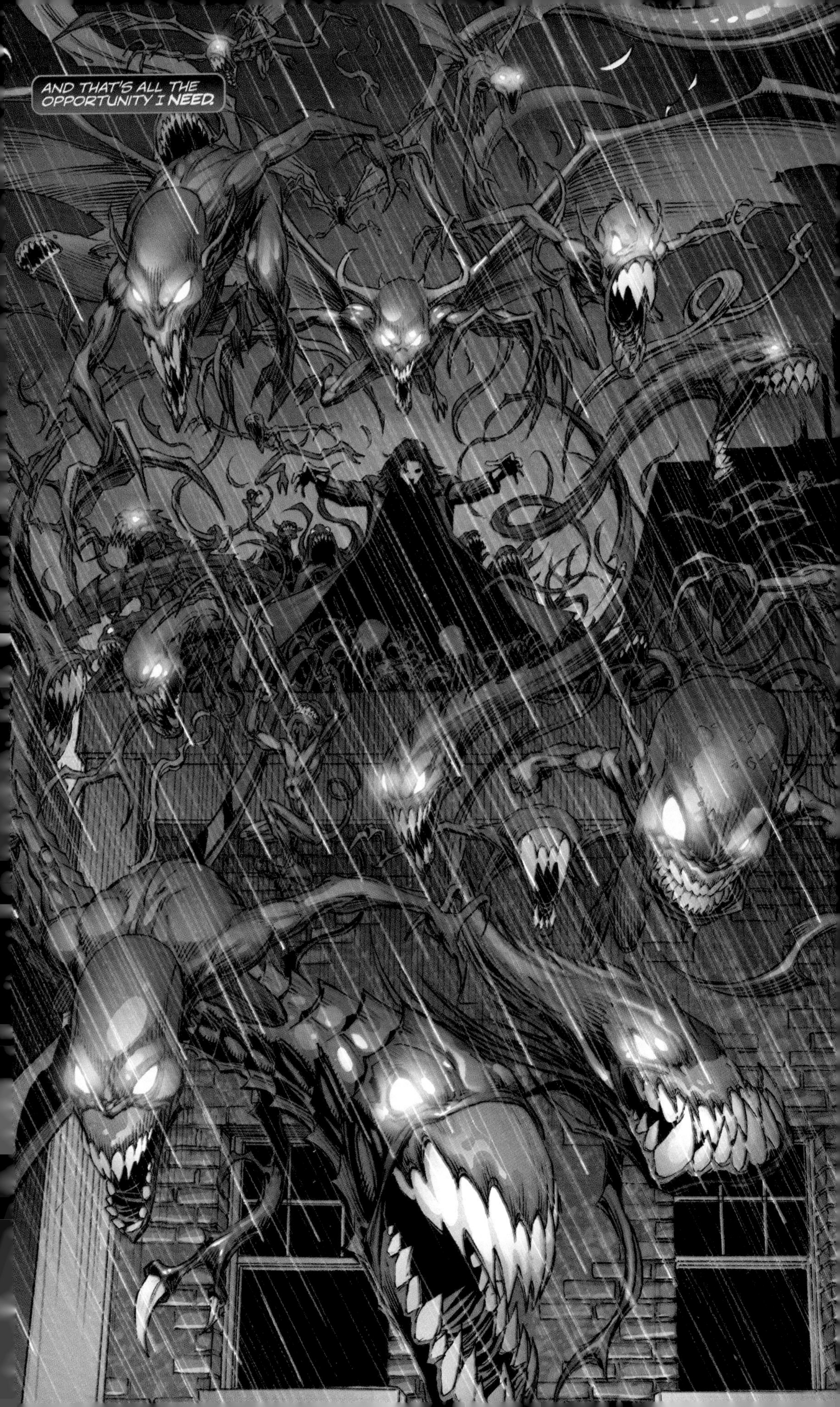
AND THAT'S ALL THE OPPORTUNITY I NEED.

I GO INTO THE SHADOWS WITH THE DARKNESS. TOGETHER, WE SEARCH THROUGH EVERY DARK CREVICE OF THE HEART THAT EXISTS WITHIN THREE OR FOUR BLOCKS FROM HERE:

THERE'S AN OLD DRUNK WHO CAN'T REMEMBER HIS NAME. HE DOESN'T CARE ABOUT THE RAIN FILLING HIS BOTTLE OF GREEN DEATH-- THAT'S BECAUSE HE HAS FIVE MINUTES BEFORE HE SUCCUMBS TO EXPOSURE.

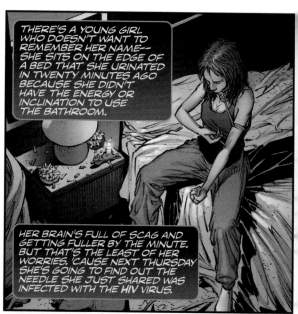

THERE'S A YOUNG GIRL WHO DOESN'T WANT TO REMEMBER HER NAME-- SHE SITS ON THE EDGE OF A BED THAT SHE URINATED IN TWENTY MINUTES AGO BECAUSE SHE DIDN'T HAVE THE ENERGY OR INCLINATION TO USE THE BATHROOM.

HER BRAIN'S FULL OF SCAG AND GETTING FULLER BY THE MINUTE. BUT THAT'S THE LEAST OF HER WORRIES. 'CAUSE NEXT THURSDAY SHE'S GOING TO FIND OUT THE NEEDLE SHE JUST SHARED WAS INFECTED WITH THE *HIV* VIRUS.

THERE'S A GUY WHO WISHES TO REMAIN NAMELESS-- THAT'S BECAUSE HE GETS OFF ON STARING THROUGH THE WINDOW OF THE WORKING GIRL ACROSS THE STREET FROM HIM.

NOT THAT SUCH A DESPERATE, SAD SACK OF BONES INTERESTS HIM IN THE SLIGHTEST. HER THIRTEEN YEAR-OLD DAUGHTER ON THE OTHER HAND...

BUT ME, I DON'T CARE ABOUT ANY OF THEM. IT'S ONLY THE DARKNESS WHO THRIVES ON THEIR MISERY.

THIS IS THE ONE I WANT.

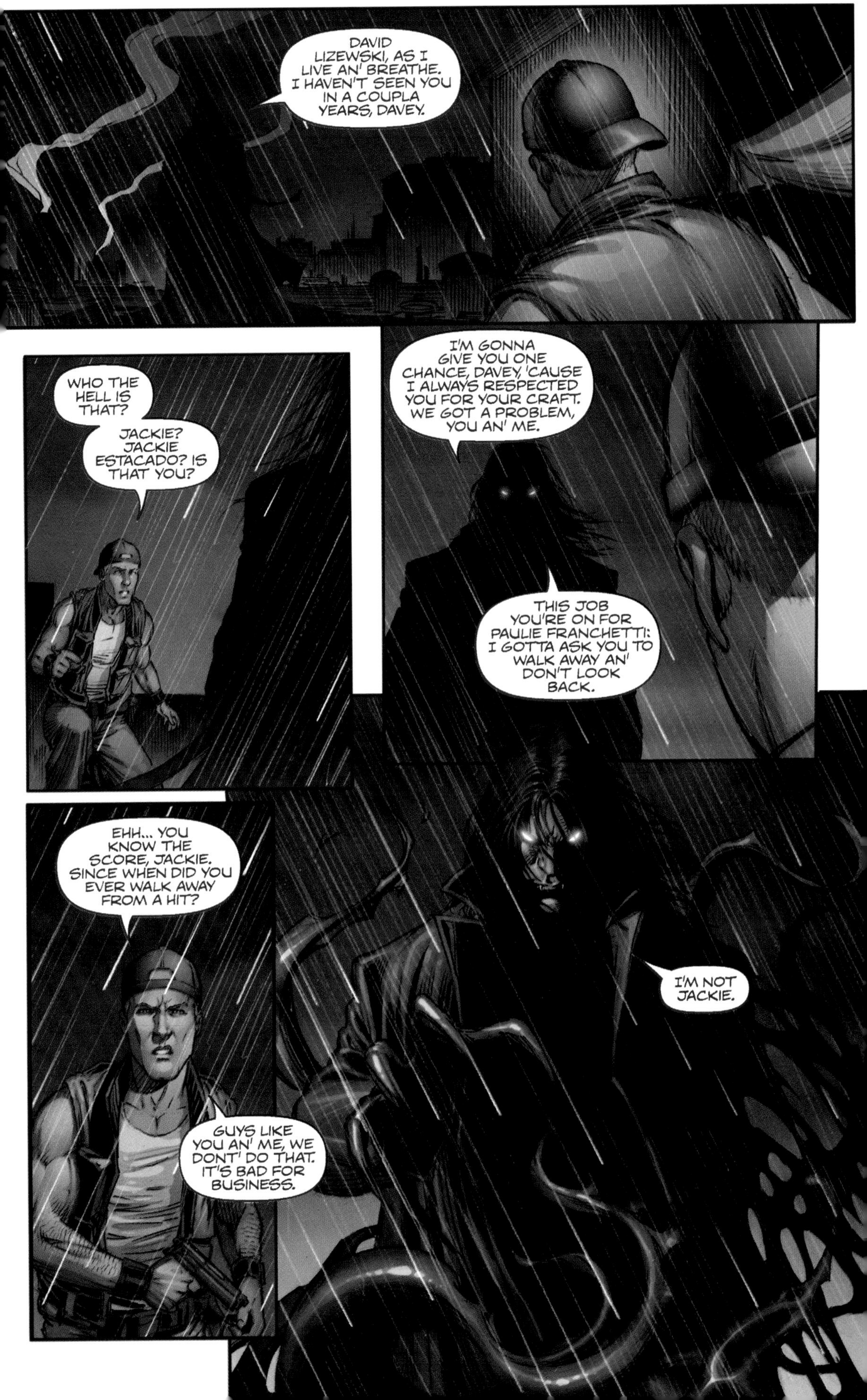
DAVID LIZEWSKI, AS I LIVE AN' BREATHE. I HAVEN'T SEEN YOU IN A COUPLA YEARS, DAVEY.
WHO THE HELL IS THAT?
JACKIE? JACKIE ESTACADO? IS THAT YOU?
I'M GONNA GIVE YOU ONE CHANCE, DAVEY, 'CAUSE I ALWAYS RESPECTED YOU FOR YOUR CRAFT. WE GOT A PROBLEM, YOU AN' ME.
THIS JOB YOU'RE ON FOR PAULIE FRANCHETTI: I GOTTA ASK YOU TO WALK AWAY AN' DON'T LOOK BACK.
EHH... YOU KNOW THE SCORE, JACKIE. SINCE WHEN DID YOU EVER WALK AWAY FROM A HIT?
GUYS LIKE YOU AN' ME, WE DONT' DO THAT. IT'S BAD FOR BUSINESS.
I'M NOT JACKIE.

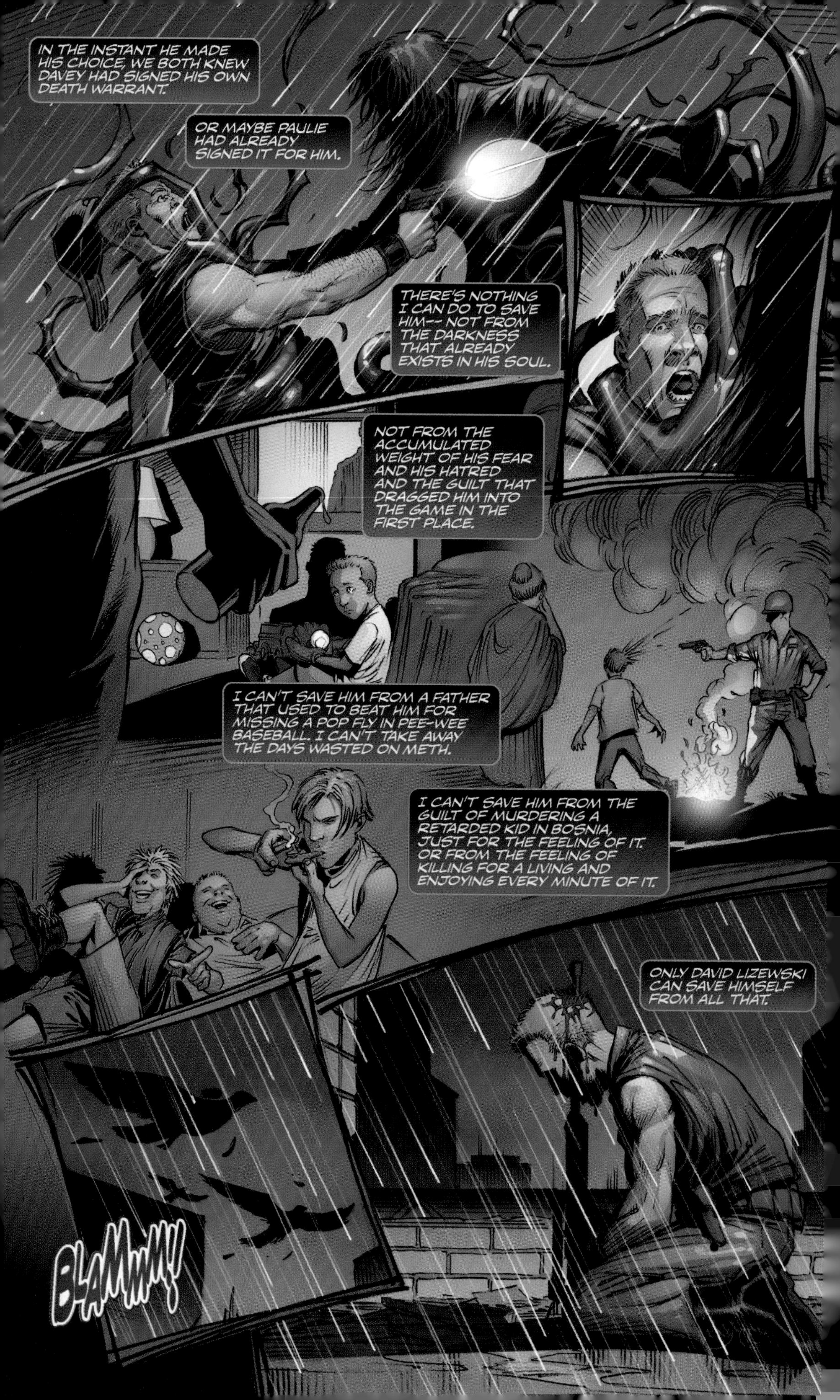
IN THE INSTANT HE MADE HIS CHOICE, WE BOTH KNEW DAVEY HAD SIGNED HIS OWN DEATH WARRANT.
OR MAYBE PAULIE HAD ALREADY SIGNED IT FOR HIM.
THERE'S NOTHING I CAN DO TO SAVE HIM-- NOT FROM THE DARKNESS THAT ALREADY EXISTS IN HIS SOUL.
NOT FROM THE ACCUMULATED WEIGHT OF HIS FEAR AND HIS HATRED AND THE GUILT THAT DRAGGED HIM INTO THE GAME IN THE FIRST PLACE.
I CAN'T SAVE HIM FROM A FATHER THAT USED TO BEAT HIM FOR MISSING A POP FLY IN PEE-WEE BASEBALL. I CAN'T TAKE AWAY THE DAYS WASTED ON METH.
I CAN'T SAVE HIM FROM THE GUILT OF MURDERING A RETARDED KID IN BOSNIA, JUST FOR THE FEELING OF IT. OR FROM THE FEELING OF KILLING FOR A LIVING AND ENJOYING EVERY MINUTE OF IT.
ONLY DAVID LIZEWSKI CAN SAVE HIMSELF FROM ALL THAT.
BLAMMM!

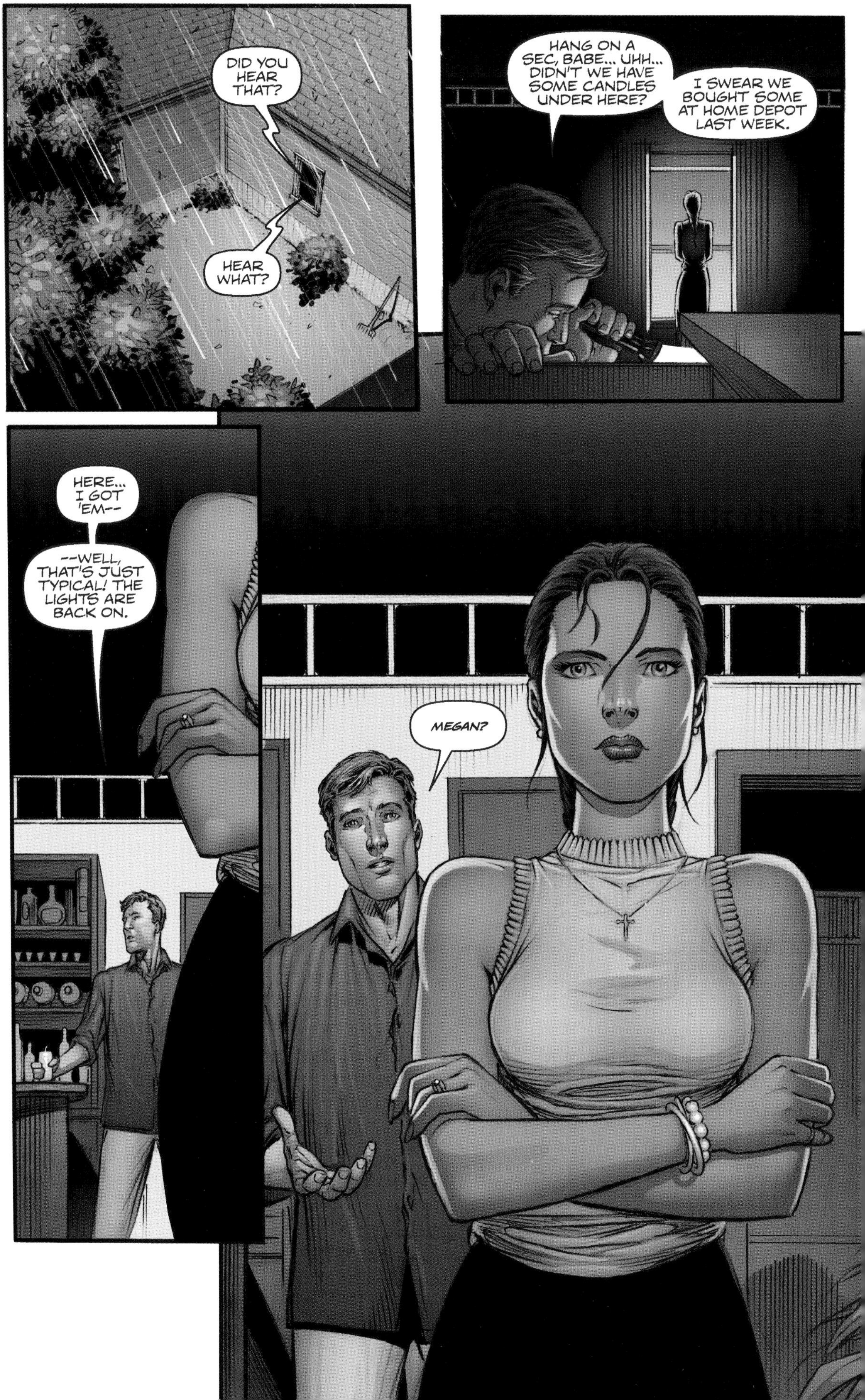
DID YOU HEAR THAT?
HEAR WHAT?
HANG ON A SEC, BABE... UHH... DIDN'T WE HAVE SOME CANDLES UNDER HERE?
I SWEAR WE BOUGHT SOME AT HOME DEPOT LAST WEEK.
HERE... I GOT 'EM--
--WELL, THAT'S JUST TYPICAL! THE LIGHTS ARE BACK ON.
MEGAN?

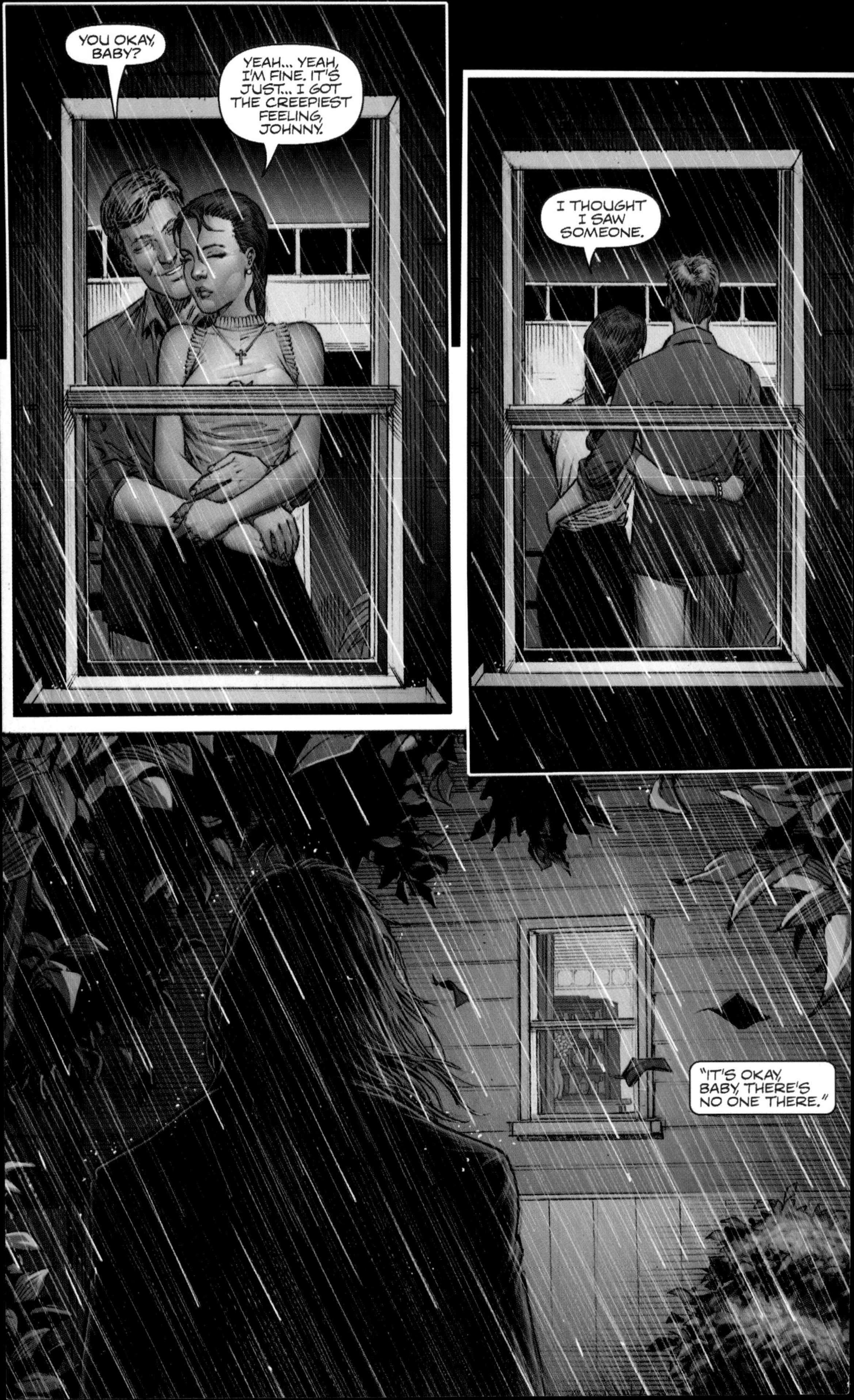

YOU OKAY, BABY?
YEAH... YEAH, I'M FINE. IT'S JUST... I GOT THE CREEPIEST FEELING, JOHNNY.
I THOUGHT I SAW SOMEONE.
"IT'S OKAY, BABY, THERE'S NO ONE THERE."

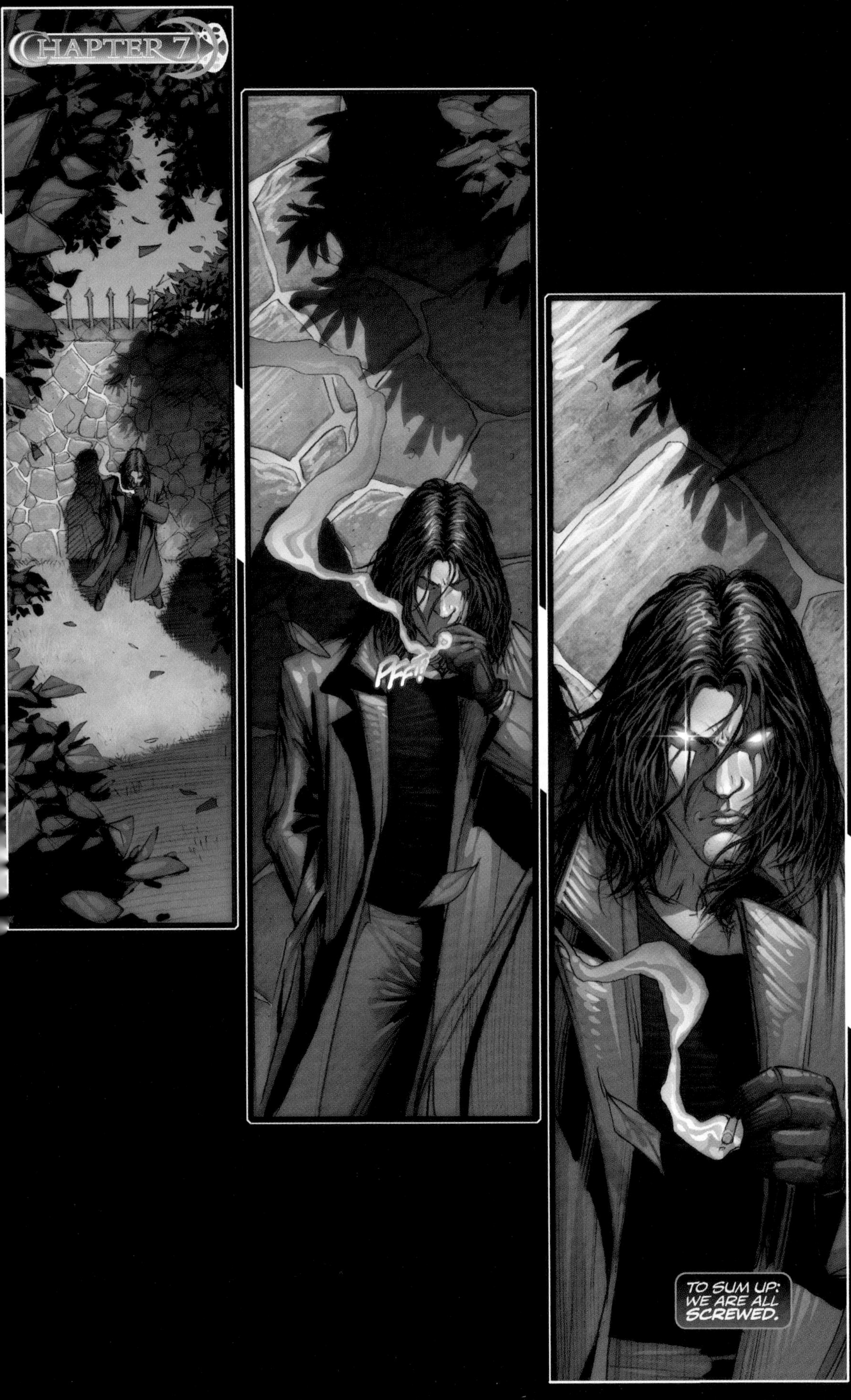
CHAPTER 7
PFFT!
TO SUM UP: WE ARE ALL SCREWED.

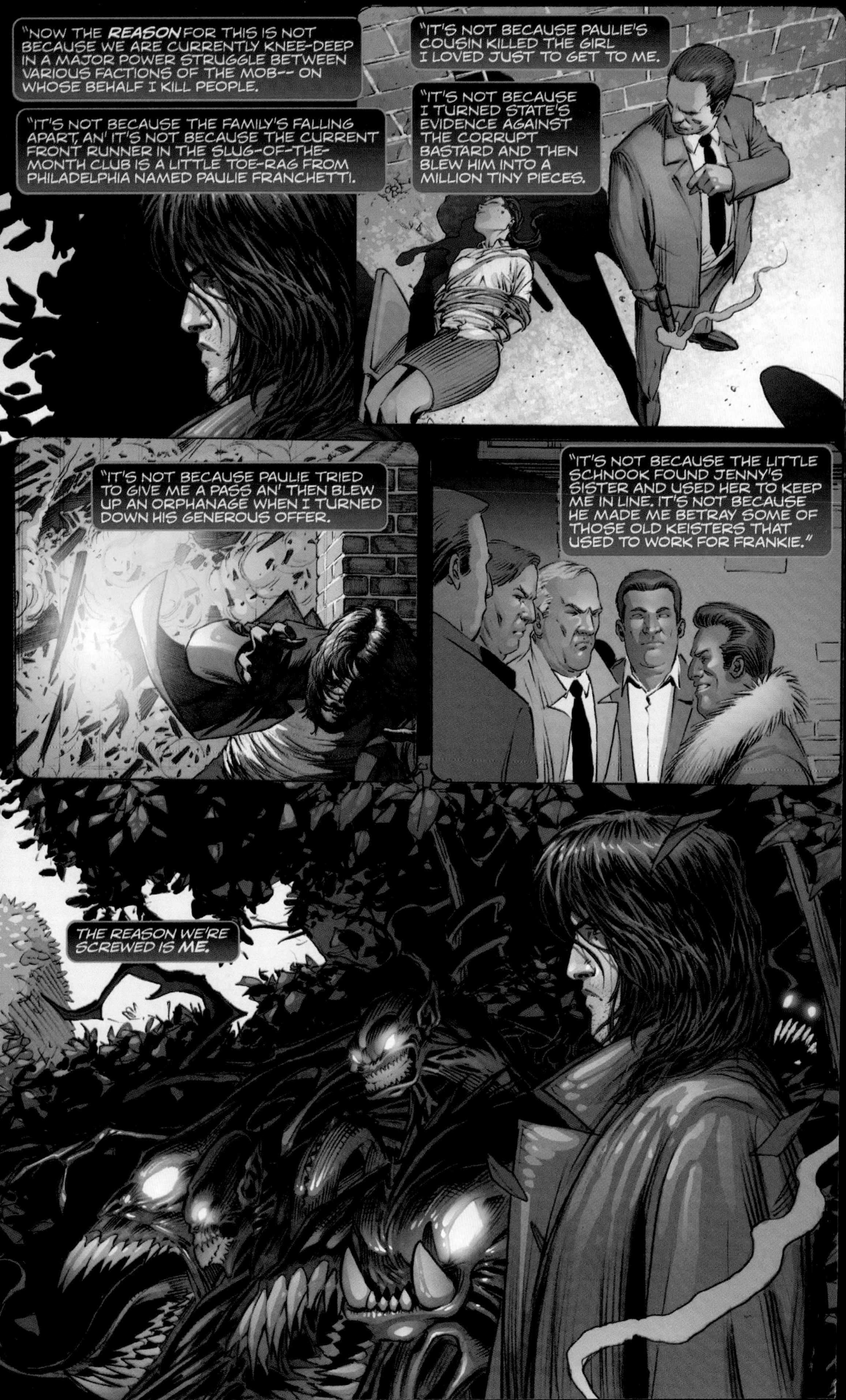
"NOW THE **REASON** FOR THIS IS NOT BECAUSE WE ARE CURRENTLY KNEE-DEEP IN A MAJOR POWER STRUGGLE BETWEEN VARIOUS FACTIONS OF THE MOB-- ON WHOSE BEHALF I KILL PEOPLE.
"IT'S NOT BECAUSE THE FAMILY'S FALLING APART, AN' IT'S NOT BECAUSE THE CURRENT FRONT RUNNER IN THE SLUG-OF-THE-MONTH CLUB IS A LITTLE TOE-RAG FROM PHILADELPHIA NAMED PAULIE FRANCHETTI.
"IT'S NOT BECAUSE PAULIE'S COUSIN KILLED THE GIRL I LOVED JUST TO GET TO ME.
"IT'S NOT BECAUSE I TURNED STATE'S EVIDENCE AGAINST THE CORRUPT BASTARD AND THEN BLEW HIM INTO A MILLION TINY PIECES.
"IT'S NOT BECAUSE PAULIE TRIED TO GIVE ME A PASS AN' THEN BLEW UP AN ORPHANAGE WHEN I TURNED DOWN HIS GENEROUS OFFER.
"IT'S NOT BECAUSE THE LITTLE SCHNOOK FOUND JENNY'S SISTER AND USED HER TO KEEP ME IN LINE. IT'S NOT BECAUSE HE MADE ME BETRAY SOME OF THOSE OLD KEISTERS THAT USED TO WORK FOR FRANKIE."
*THE REASON WE'RE SCREWED IS **ME**.*

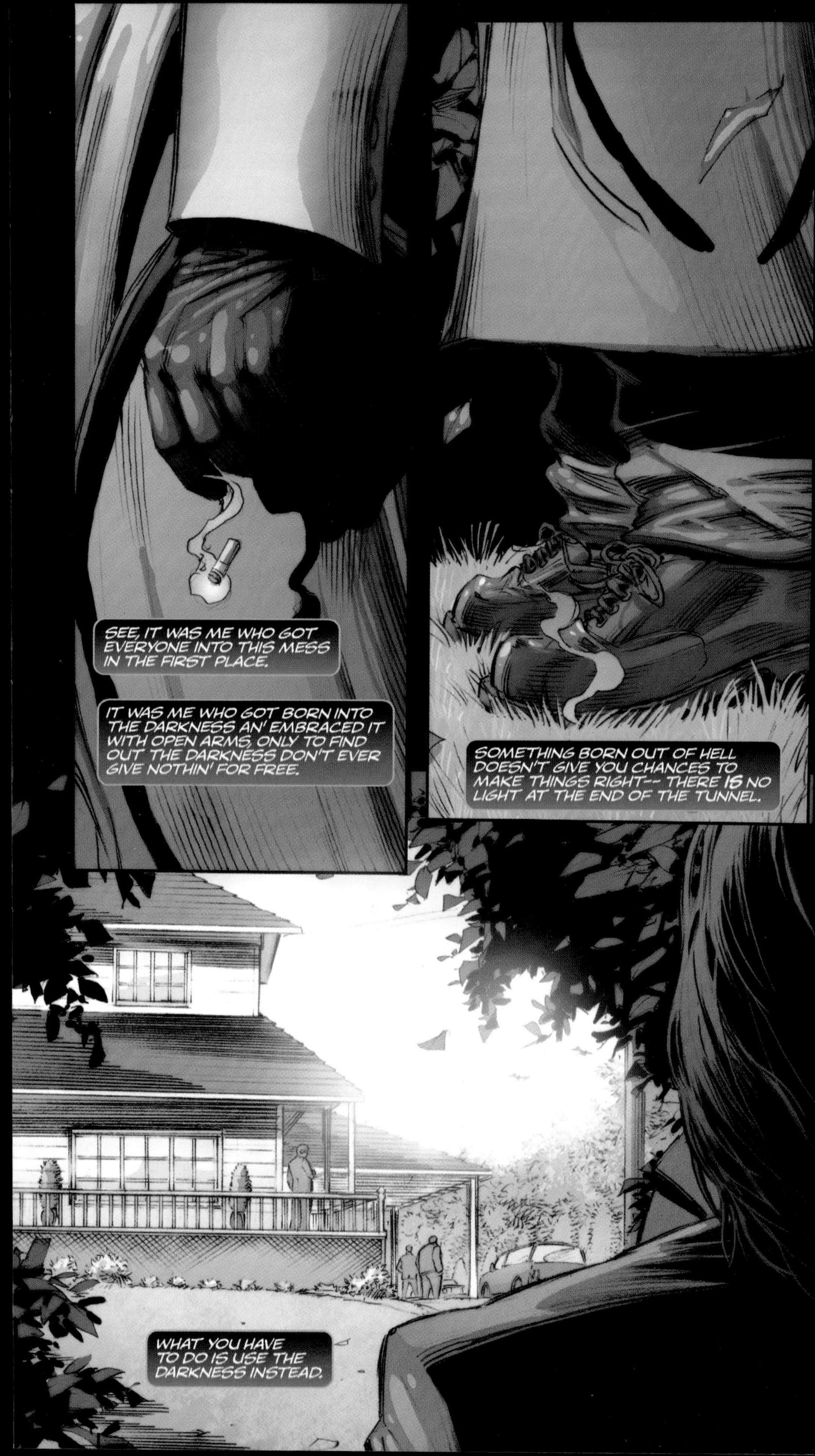
SEE, IT WAS ME WHO GOT EVERYONE INTO THIS MESS IN THE FIRST PLACE.
IT WAS ME WHO GOT BORN INTO THE DARKNESS AN' EMBRACED IT WITH OPEN ARMS, ONLY TO FIND OUT THE DARKNESS DON'T EVER GIVE NOTHIN' FOR FREE.
SOMETHING BORN OUT OF HELL DOESN'T GIVE YOU CHANCES TO MAKE THINGS RIGHT-- THERE IS NO LIGHT AT THE END OF THE TUNNEL.
WHAT YOU HAVE TO DO IS USE THE DARKNESS INSTEAD.

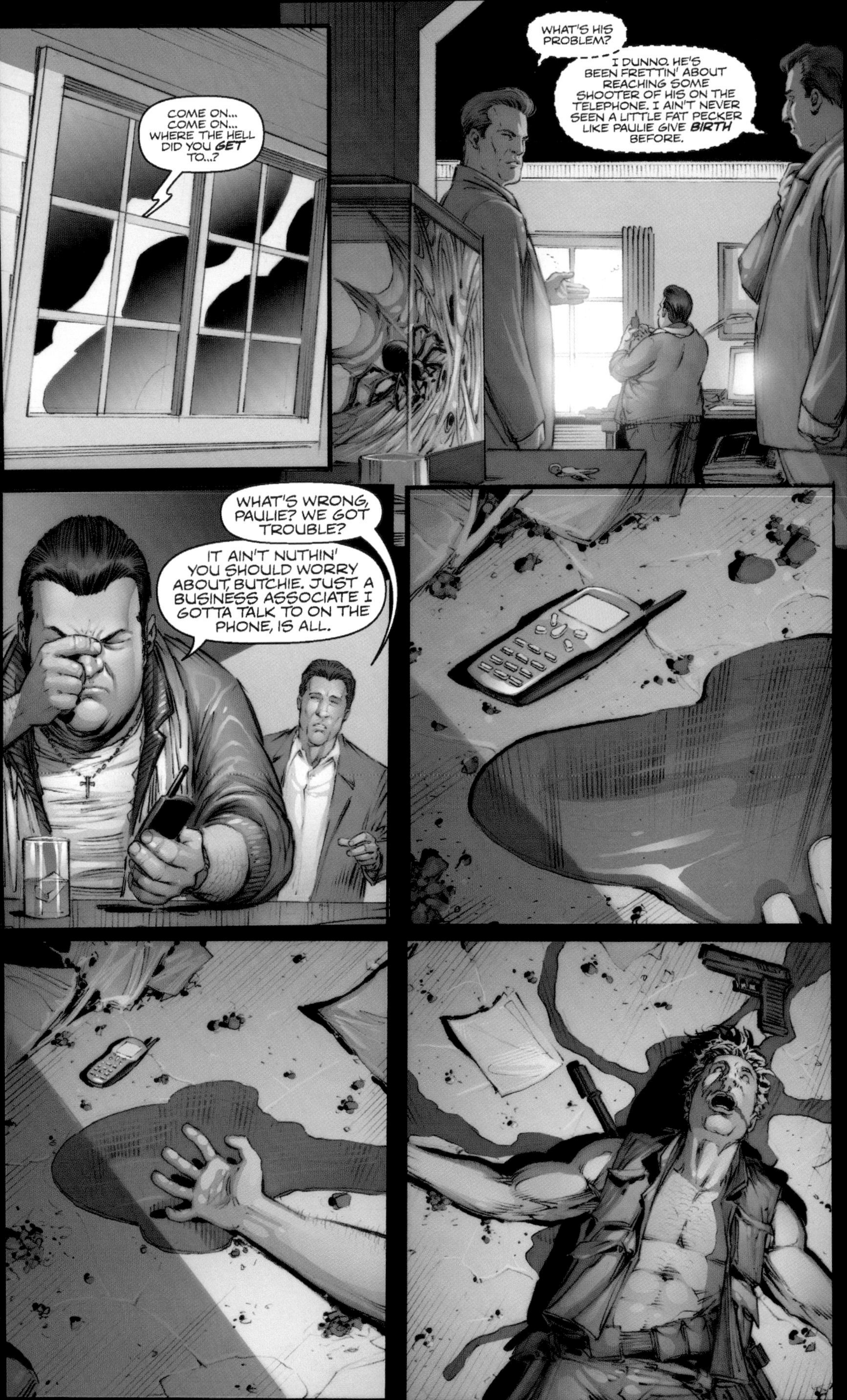
COME ON... COME ON... WHERE THE HELL DID YOU GET TO...?
WHAT'S HIS PROBLEM?
I DUNNO. HE'S BEEN FRETTIN' ABOUT REACHING SOME SHOOTER OF HIS ON THE TELEPHONE. I AIN'T NEVER SEEN A LITTLE FAT PECKER LIKE PAULIE GIVE BIRTH BEFORE.
WHAT'S WRONG, PAULIE? WE GOT TROUBLE?
IT AIN'T NUTHIN' YOU SHOULD WORRY ABOUT, BUTCHIE. JUST A BUSINESS ASSOCIATE I GOTTA TALK TO ON THE PHONE, IS ALL.

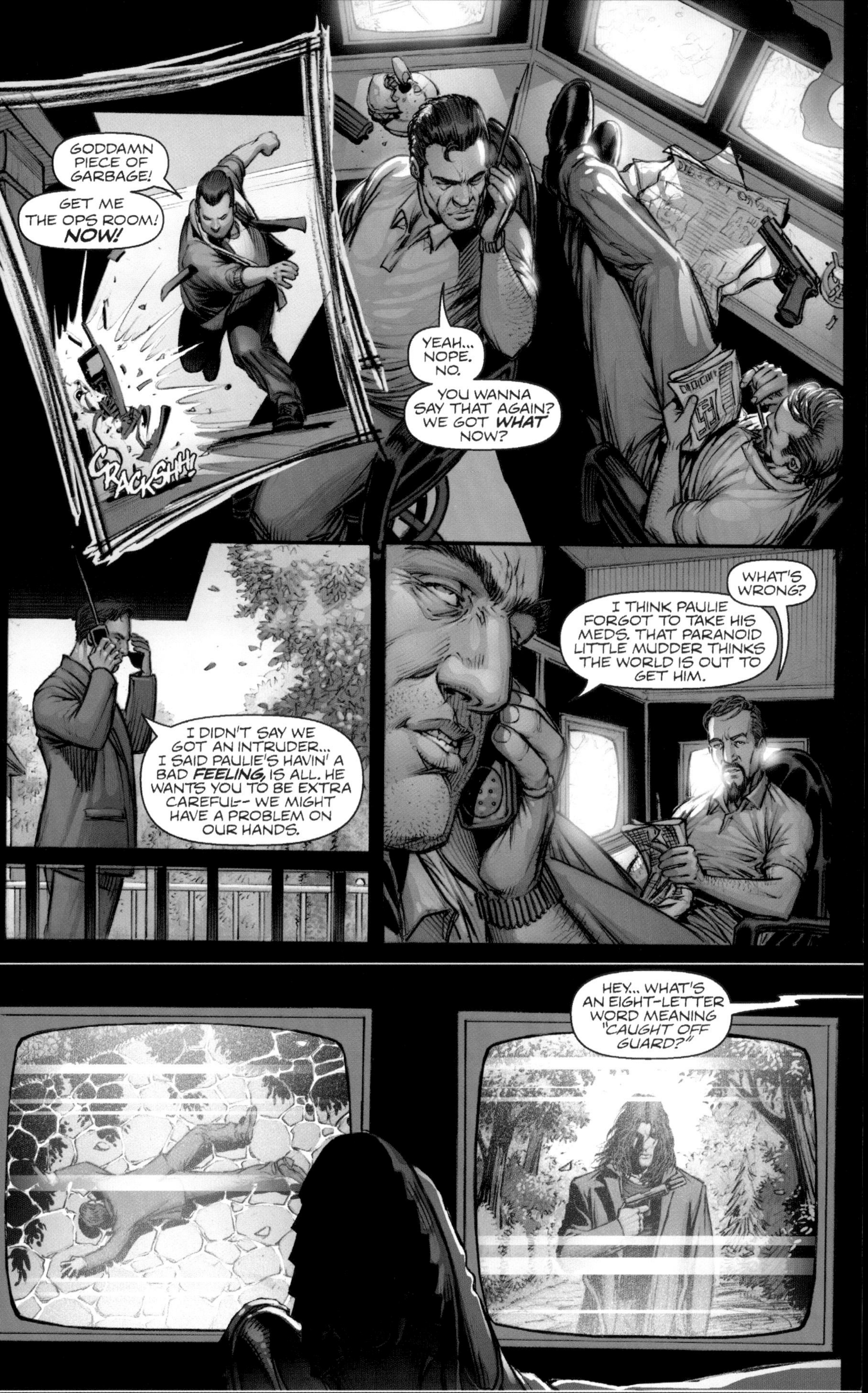

GODDAMN PIECE OF GARBAGE!
GET ME THE OPS ROOM! NOW!
CRACKSHH!
YEAH... NOPE. NO.
YOU WANNA SAY THAT AGAIN? WE GOT WHAT NOW?
I DIDN'T SAY WE GOT AN INTRUDER... I SAID PAULIE'S HAVIN' A BAD FEELING, IS ALL. HE WANTS YOU TO BE EXTRA CAREFUL-- WE MIGHT HAVE A PROBLEM ON OUR HANDS.
WHAT'S WRONG?
I THINK PAULIE FORGOT TO TAKE HIS MEDS. THAT PARANOID LITTLE MUDDER THINKS THE WORLD IS OUT TO GET HIM.
HEY... WHAT'S AN EIGHT-LETTER WORD MEANING "CAUGHT OFF GUARD?"

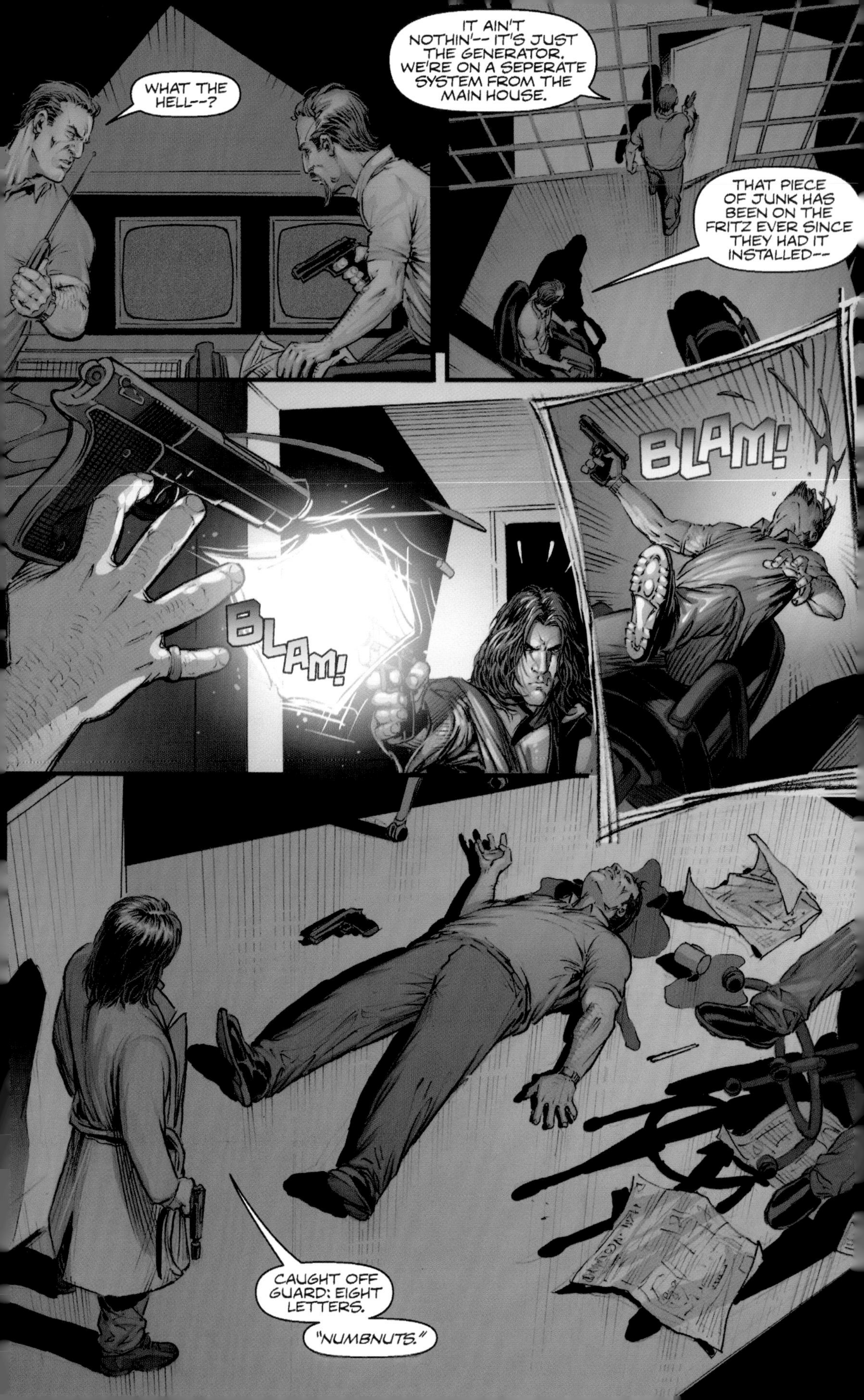

WHAT THE HELL--?
IT AIN'T NOTHIN'-- IT'S JUST THE GENERATOR. WE'RE ON A SEPERATE SYSTEM FROM THE MAIN HOUSE.
THAT PIECE OF JUNK HAS BEEN ON THE FRITZ EVER SINCE THEY HAD IT INSTALLED--
BLAM!
BLAM!
CAUGHT OFF GUARD: EIGHT LETTERS.
"NUMBNUTS."

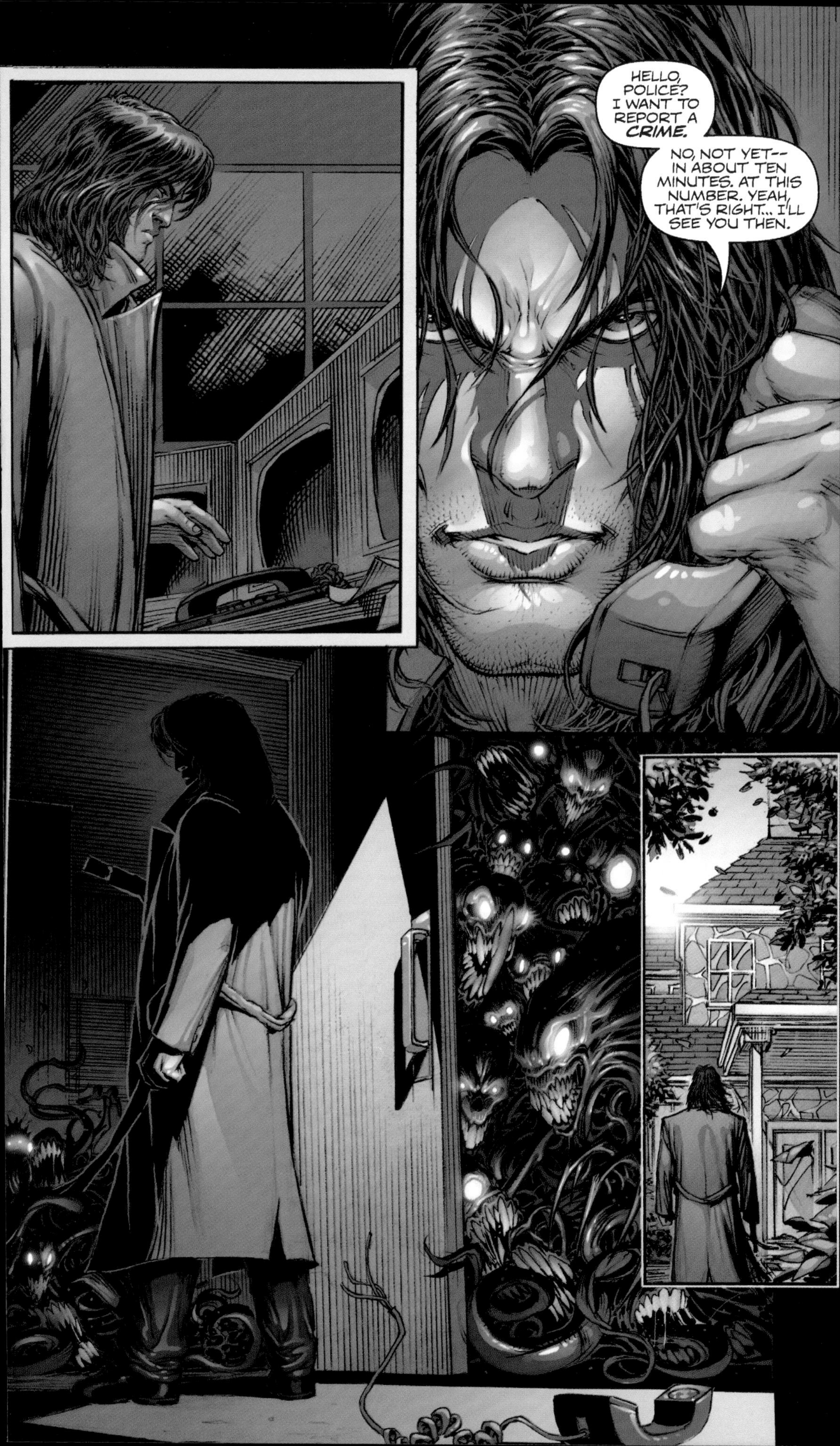
HELLO, POLICE? I WANT TO REPORT A *CRIME.*
NO, NOT YET-- IN ABOUT TEN MINUTES. AT THIS NUMBER. YEAH, THAT'S RIGHT... I'LL SEE YOU THEN.

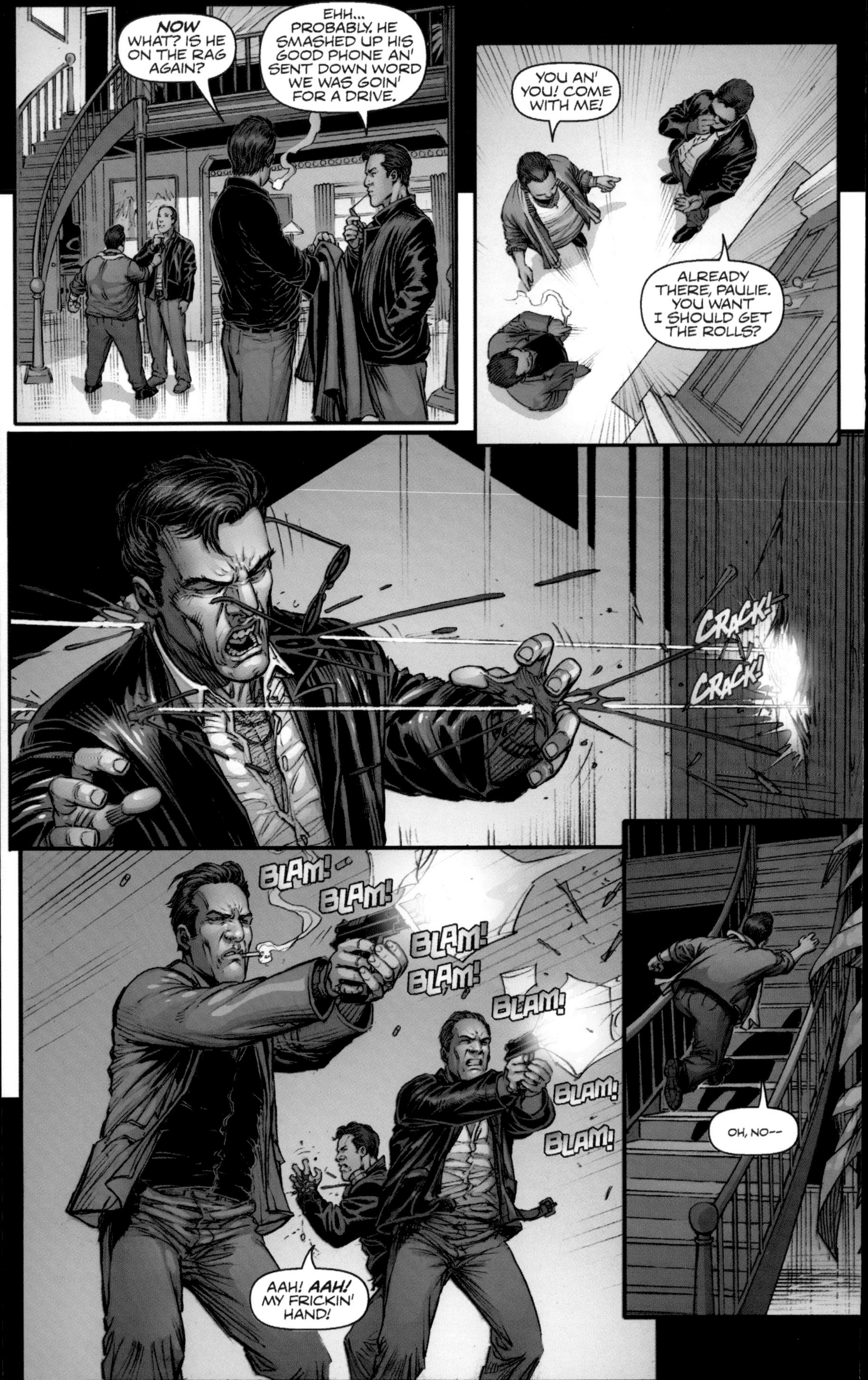
NOW WHAT? IS HE ON THE RAG AGAIN?
EHH... PROBABLY. HE SMASHED UP HIS GOOD PHONE AN' SENT DOWN WORD WE WAS GOIN' FOR A DRIVE.
YOU AN' YOU! COME WITH ME!
ALREADY THERE, PAULIE. YOU WANT I SHOULD GET THE ROLLS?
CRACK!
CRACK!
BLAM!
BLAM!
BLAM!
BLAM!
BLAM!
BLAM!
BLAM!
AAH! AAH! MY FRICKIN' HAND!
OH, NO--

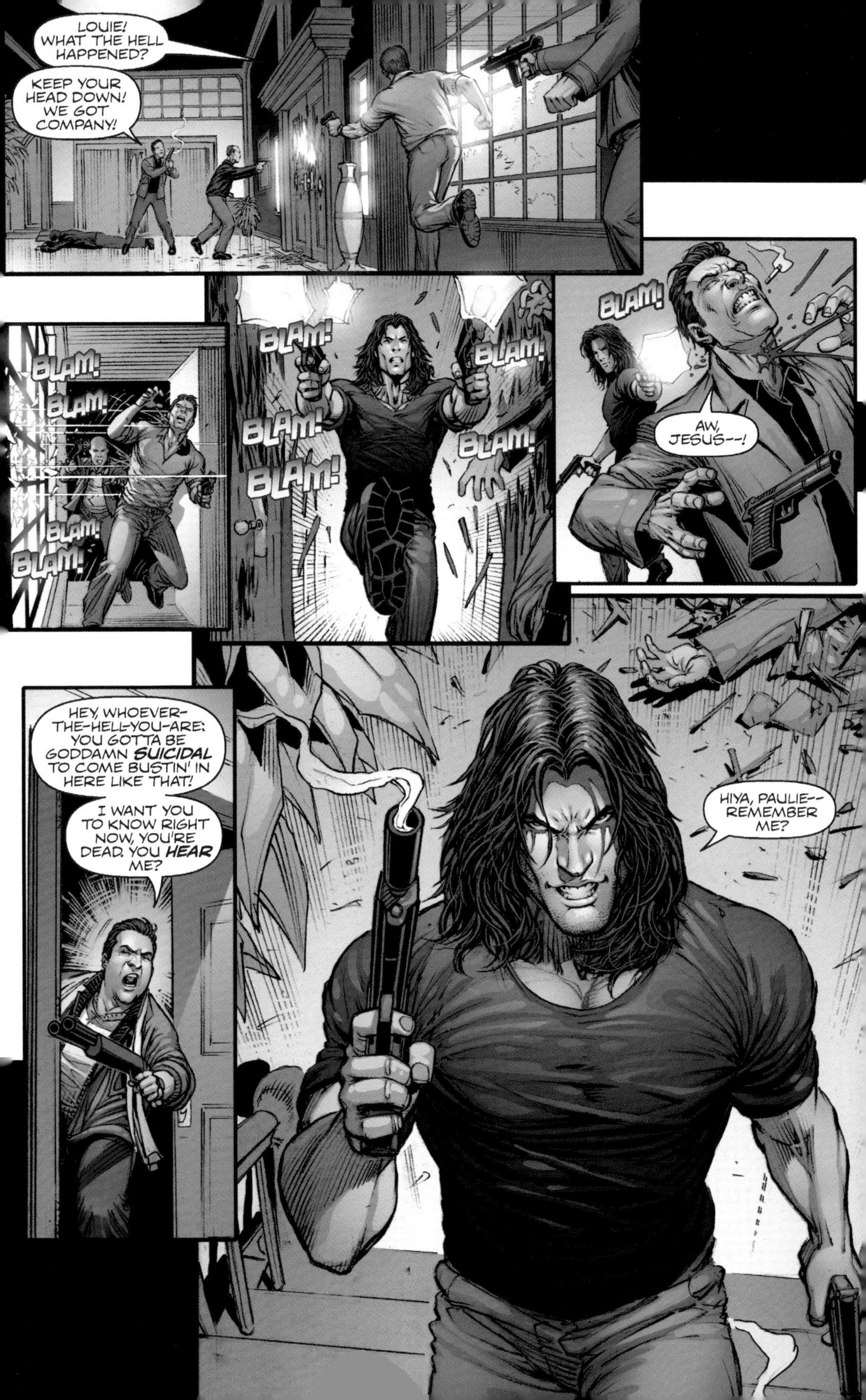
LOUIE! WHAT THE HELL HAPPENED?
KEEP YOUR HEAD DOWN! WE GOT COMPANY!
BLAM!
BLAM!
BLAM!
BLAM!
BLAM!
BLAM!
BLAM!
BLAM!
BLAM!
BLAM!
AW, JESUS--!
HEY, WHOEVER-THE-HELL-YOU-ARE: YOU GOTTA BE GODDAMN SUICIDAL TO COME BUSTIN' IN HERE LIKE THAT!
I WANT YOU TO KNOW RIGHT NOW, YOU'RE DEAD. YOU HEAR ME?
HIYA, PAULIE-- REMEMBER ME?

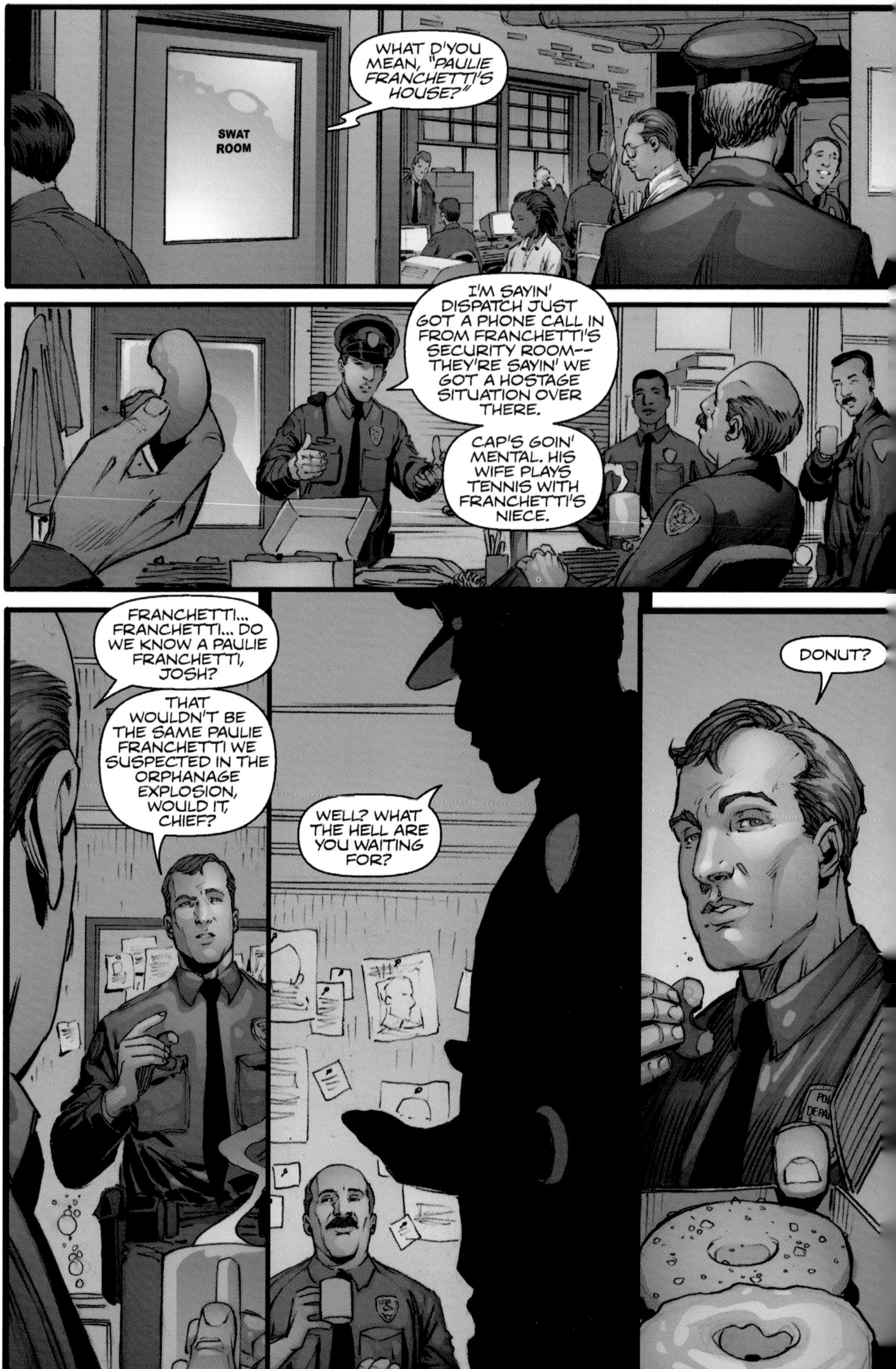
SWAT ROOM
WHAT D'YOU MEAN, "PAULIE FRANCHETTI'S HOUSE?"
I'M SAYIN' DISPATCH JUST GOT A PHONE CALL IN FROM FRANCHETTI'S SECURITY ROOM-- THEY'RE SAYIN' WE GOT A HOSTAGE SITUATION OVER THERE.
CAP'S GOIN' MENTAL. HIS WIFE PLAYS TENNIS WITH FRANCHETTI'S NIECE.
FRANCHETTI... FRANCHETTI... DO WE KNOW A PAULIE FRANCHETTI, JOSH?
THAT WOULDN'T BE THE SAME PAULIE FRANCHETTI WE SUSPECTED IN THE ORPHANAGE EXPLOSION, WOULD IT, CHIEF?
WELL? WHAT THE HELL ARE YOU WAITING FOR?
DONUT?

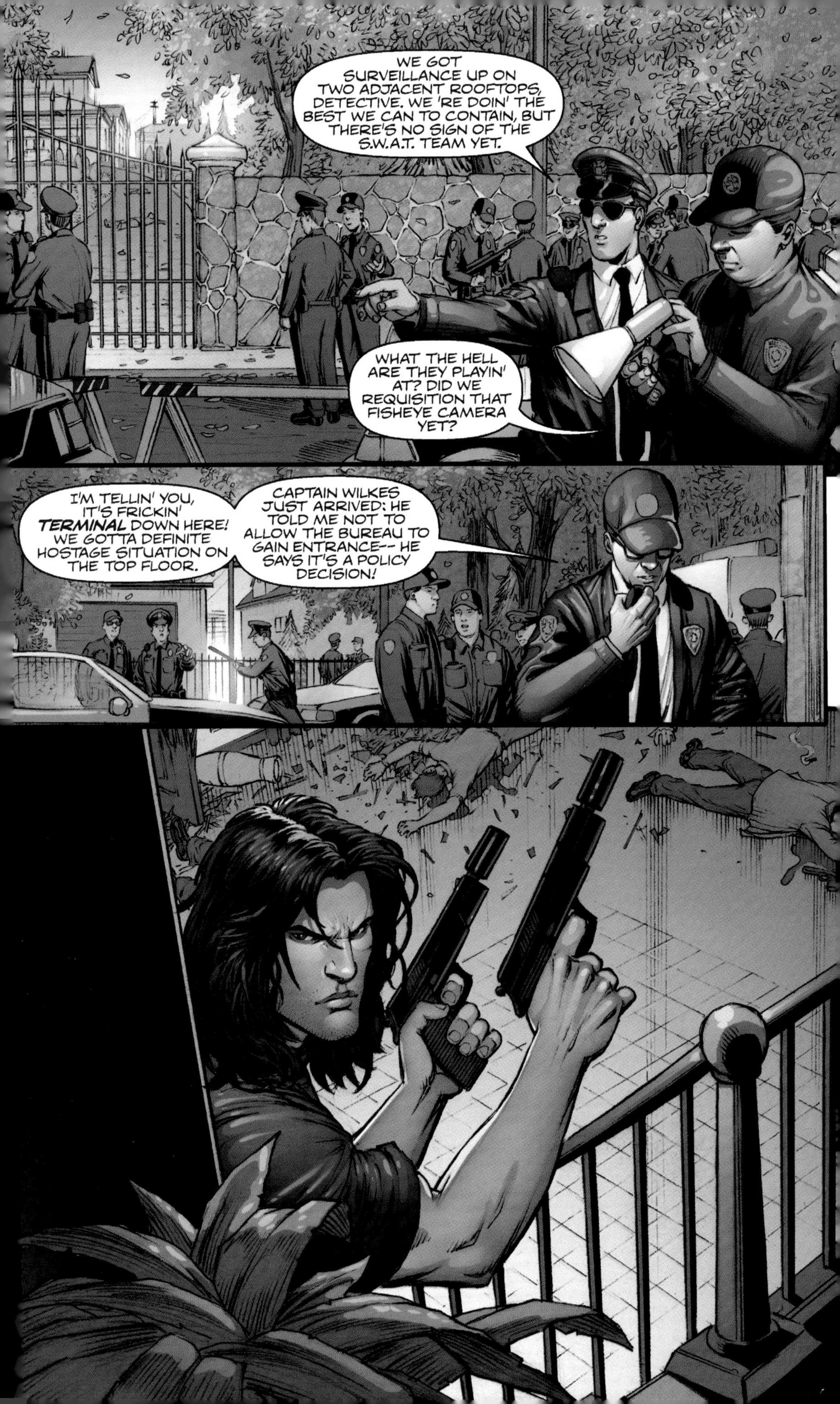
WE GOT SURVEILLANCE UP ON TWO ADJACENT ROOFTOPS, DETECTIVE. WE 'RE DOIN' THE BEST WE CAN TO CONTAIN, BUT THERE'S NO SIGN OF THE S.W.A.T. TEAM YET.
WHAT THE HELL ARE THEY PLAYIN' AT? DID WE REQUISITION THAT FISHEYE CAMERA YET?
I'M TELLIN' YOU, IT'S FRICKIN' *TERMINAL* DOWN HERE! WE GOTTA DEFINITE HOSTAGE SITUATION ON THE TOP FLOOR.
CAPTAIN WILKES JUST ARRIVED: HE TOLD ME NOT TO ALLOW THE BUREAU TO GAIN ENTRANCE-- HE SAYS IT'S A POLICY DECISION!

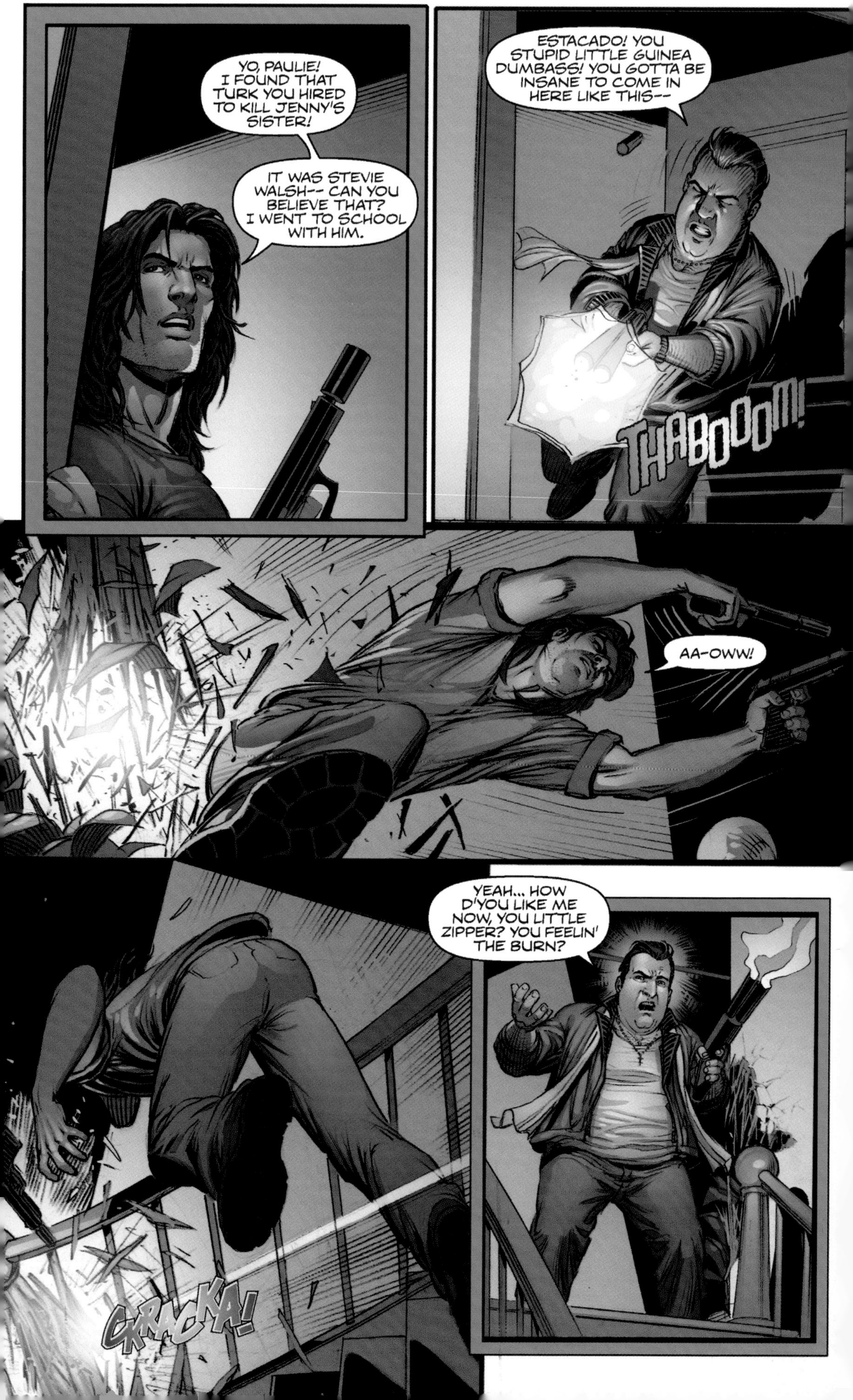
YO, PAULIE! I FOUND THAT TURK YOU HIRED TO KILL JENNY'S SISTER!
IT WAS STEVIE WALSH-- CAN YOU BELIEVE THAT? I WENT TO SCHOOL WITH HIM.
ESTACADO! YOU STUPID LITTLE GUINEA DUMBASS! YOU GOTTA BE INSANE TO COME IN HERE LIKE THIS--
THABOOOM!
AA-OWW!
CKRACKA!
YEAH... HOW D'YOU LIKE ME NOW, YOU LITTLE ZIPPER? YOU FEELIN' THE BURN?

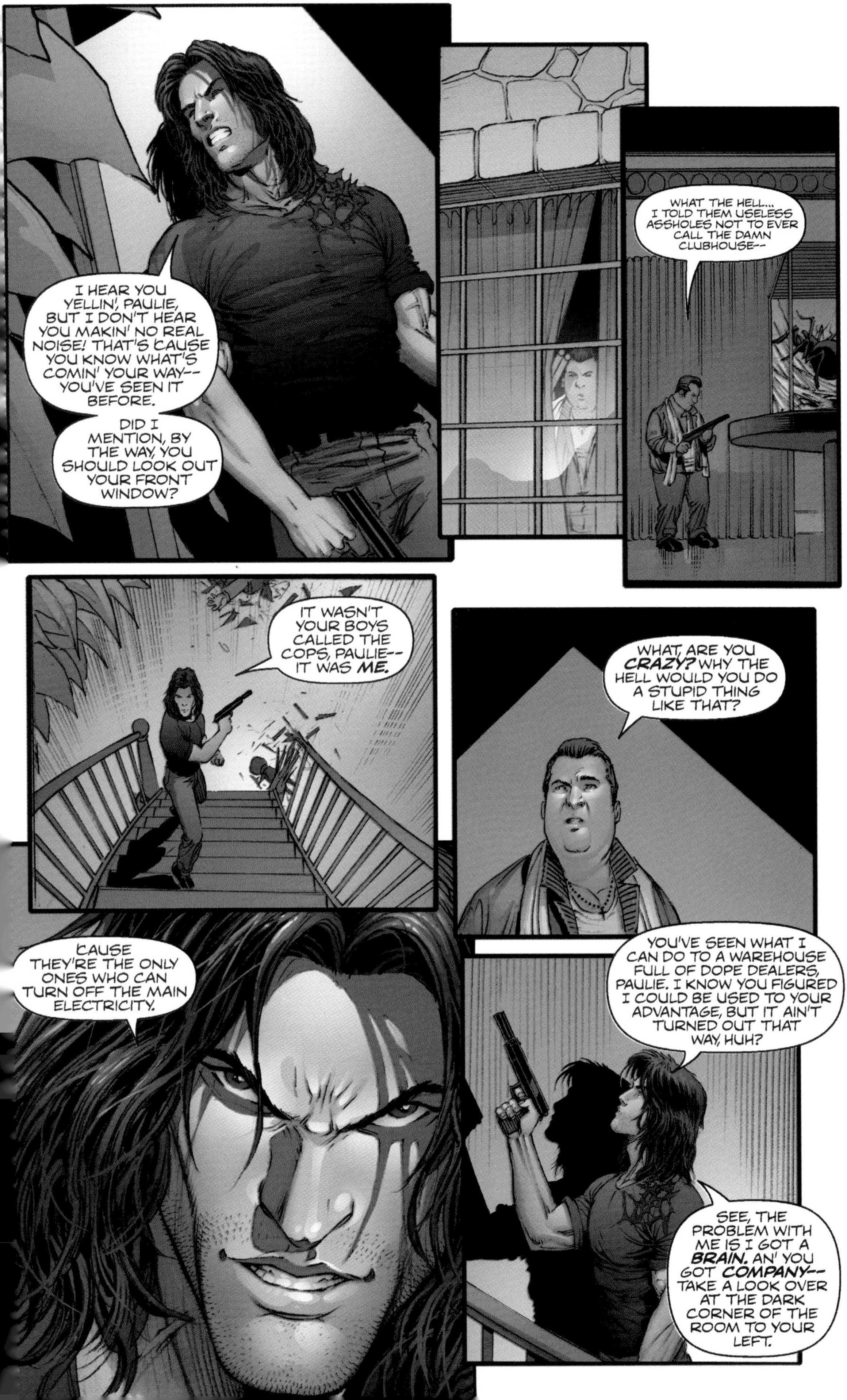
I HEAR YOU YELLIN', PAULIE, BUT I DON'T HEAR YOU MAKIN' NO REAL NOISE! THAT'S 'CAUSE YOU KNOW WHAT'S COMIN' YOUR WAY-- YOU'VE SEEN IT BEFORE.
DID I MENTION, BY THE WAY, YOU SHOULD LOOK OUT YOUR FRONT WINDOW?
WHAT THE HELL... I TOLD THEM USELESS ASSHOLES NOT TO EVER CALL THE DAMN CLUBHOUSE--
IT WASN'T YOUR BOYS CALLED THE COPS, PAULIE-- IT WAS ME.
WHAT, ARE YOU CRAZY? WHY THE HELL WOULD YOU DO A STUPID THING LIKE THAT?
'CAUSE THEY'RE THE ONLY ONES WHO CAN TURN OFF THE MAIN ELECTRICITY.
YOU'VE SEEN WHAT I CAN DO TO A WAREHOUSE FULL OF DOPE DEALERS, PAULIE. I KNOW YOU FIGURED I COULD BE USED TO YOUR ADVANTAGE, BUT IT AIN'T TURNED OUT THAT WAY, HUH?
SEE, THE PROBLEM WITH ME IS I GOT A BRAIN. AN' YOU GOT COMPANY-- TAKE A LOOK OVER AT THE DARK CORNER OF THE ROOM TO YOUR LEFT.

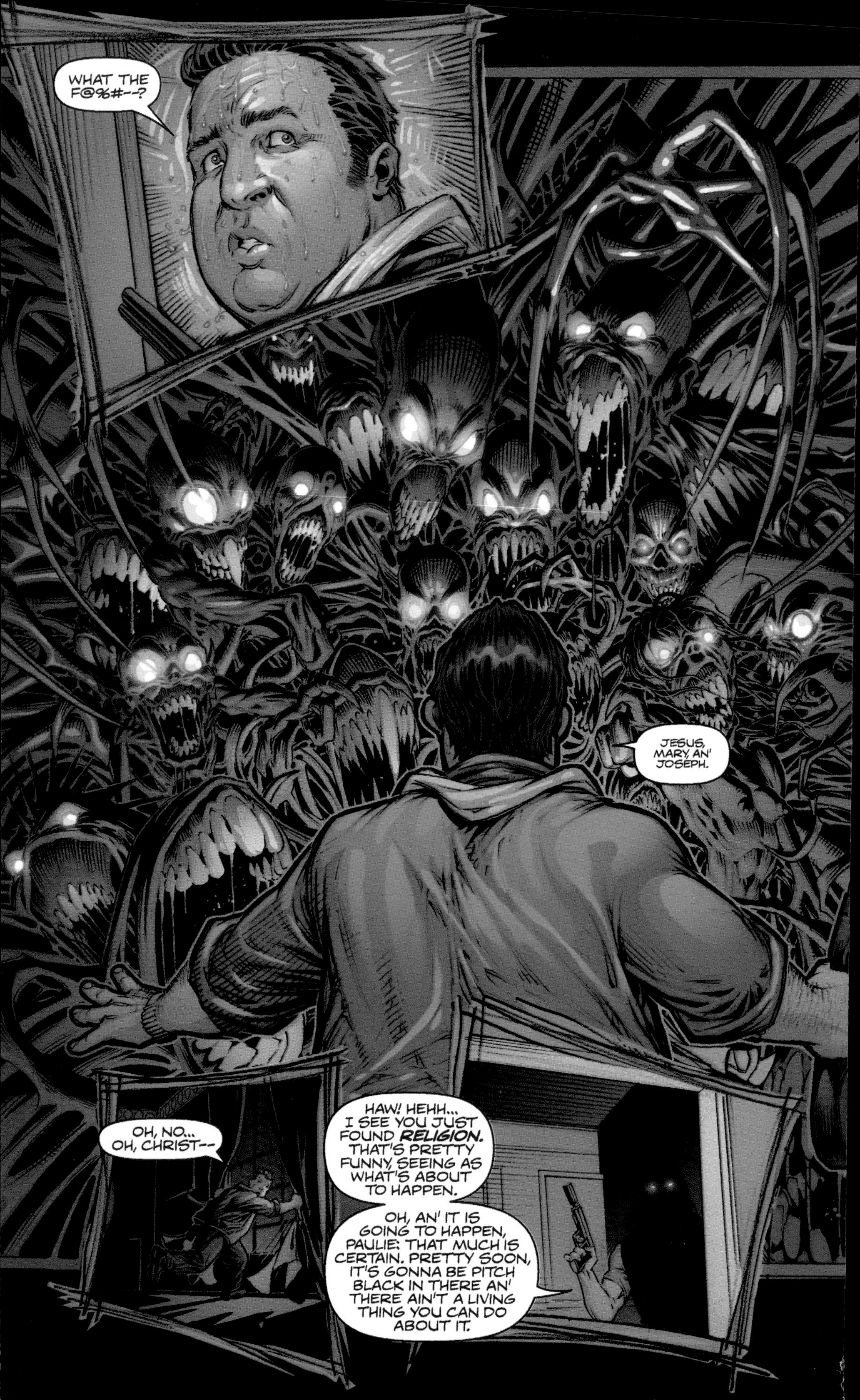
WHAT THE F@%#--?
JESUS, MARY, AN' JOSEPH.
OH, NO... OH, CHRIST--
HAW! HEHH... I SEE YOU JUST FOUND RELIGION. THAT'S PRETTY FUNNY, SEEING AS WHAT'S ABOUT TO HAPPEN.
OH, AN' IT IS GOING TO HAPPEN, PAULIE: THAT MUCH IS CERTAIN. PRETTY SOON, IT'S GONNA BE PITCH BLACK IN THERE AN' THERE AIN'T A LIVING THING YOU CAN DO ABOUT IT.

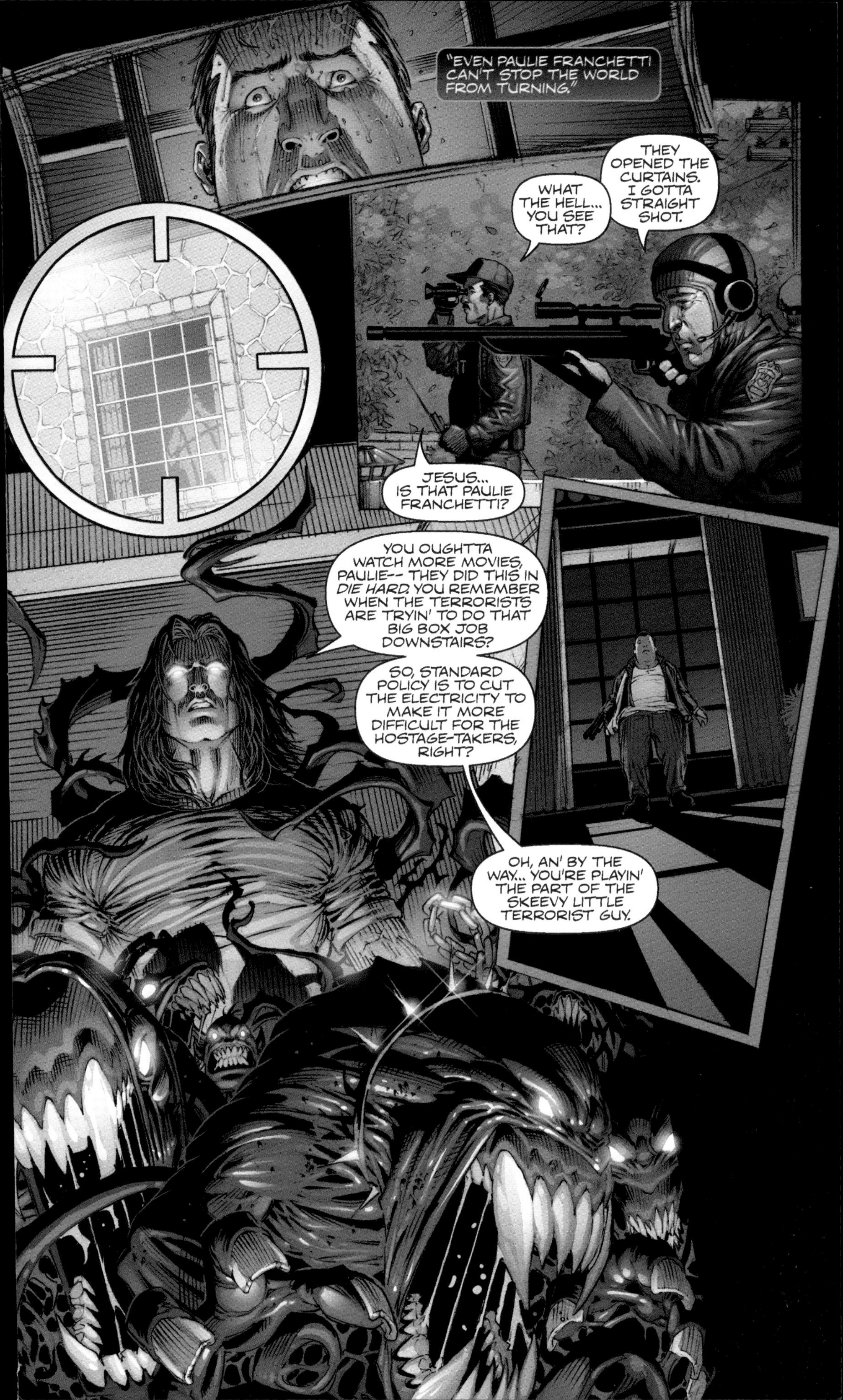
"EVEN PAULIE FRANCHETTI CAN'T STOP THE WORLD FROM TURNING."
WHAT THE HELL... YOU SEE THAT?
THEY OPENED THE CURTAINS. I GOTTA STRAIGHT SHOT.
JESUS... IS THAT PAULIE FRANCHETTI?
YOU OUGHTTA WATCH MORE MOVIES, PAULIE-- THEY DID THIS IN *DIE HARD.* YOU REMEMBER WHEN THE TERRORISTS ARE TRYIN' TO DO THAT BIG BOX JOB DOWNSTAIRS?
SO, STANDARD POLICY IS TO CUT THE ELECTRICITY TO MAKE IT MORE DIFFICULT FOR THE HOSTAGE-TAKERS, RIGHT?
OH, AN' BY THE WAY... YOU'RE PLAYIN' THE PART OF THE SKEEVY LITTLE TERRORIST GUY.

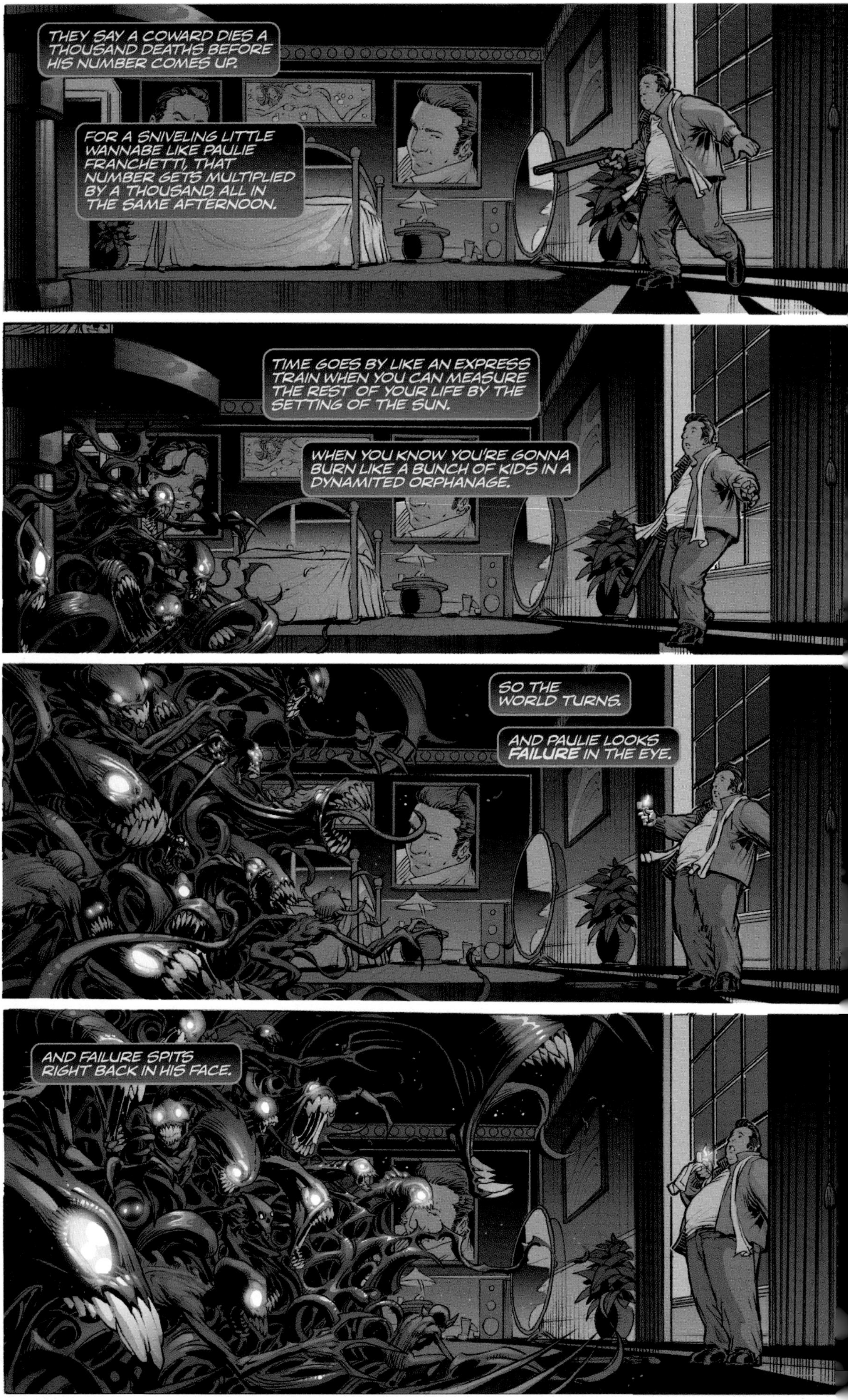
THEY SAY A COWARD DIES A THOUSAND DEATHS BEFORE HIS NUMBER COMES UP.
FOR A SNIVELING LITTLE WANNABE LIKE PAULIE FRANCHETTI, THAT NUMBER GETS MULTIPLIED BY A THOUSAND, ALL IN THE SAME AFTERNOON.
TIME GOES BY LIKE AN EXPRESS TRAIN WHEN YOU CAN MEASURE THE REST OF YOUR LIFE BY THE SETTING OF THE SUN.
WHEN YOU KNOW YOU'RE GONNA BURN LIKE A BUNCH OF KIDS IN A DYNAMITED ORPHANAGE.
SO THE WORLD TURNS.
AND PAULIE LOOKS FAILURE IN THE EYE.
AND FAILURE SPITS RIGHT BACK IN HIS FACE.

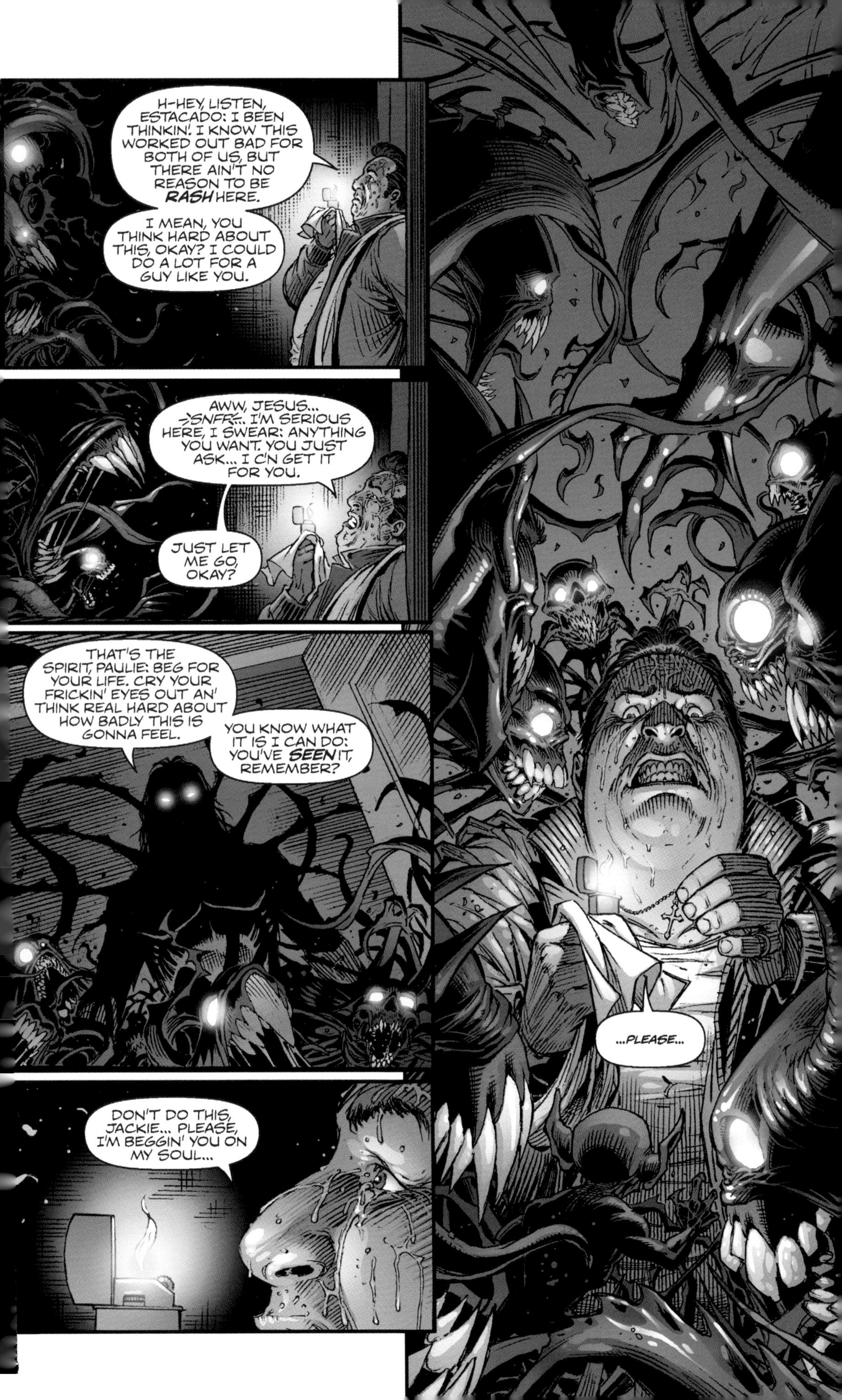
H-HEY, LISTEN, ESTACADO: I BEEN THINKIN'. I KNOW THIS WORKED OUT BAD FOR BOTH OF US, BUT THERE AIN'T NO REASON TO BE RASH HERE.
I MEAN, YOU THINK HARD ABOUT THIS, OKAY? I COULD DO A LOT FOR A GUY LIKE YOU.
AWW, JESUS... >SNFF<... I'M SERIOUS HERE, I SWEAR: ANYTHING YOU WANT. YOU JUST ASK... I C'N GET IT FOR YOU.
JUST LET ME GO, OKAY?
THAT'S THE SPIRIT, PAULIE: BEG FOR YOUR LIFE. CRY YOUR FRICKIN' EYES OUT AN' THINK REAL HARD ABOUT HOW BADLY THIS IS GONNA FEEL.
YOU KNOW WHAT IT IS I CAN DO: YOU'VE SEEN IT, REMEMBER?
DON'T DO THIS, JACKIE... PLEASE, I'M BEGGIN' YOU ON MY SOUL...
...PLEASE...

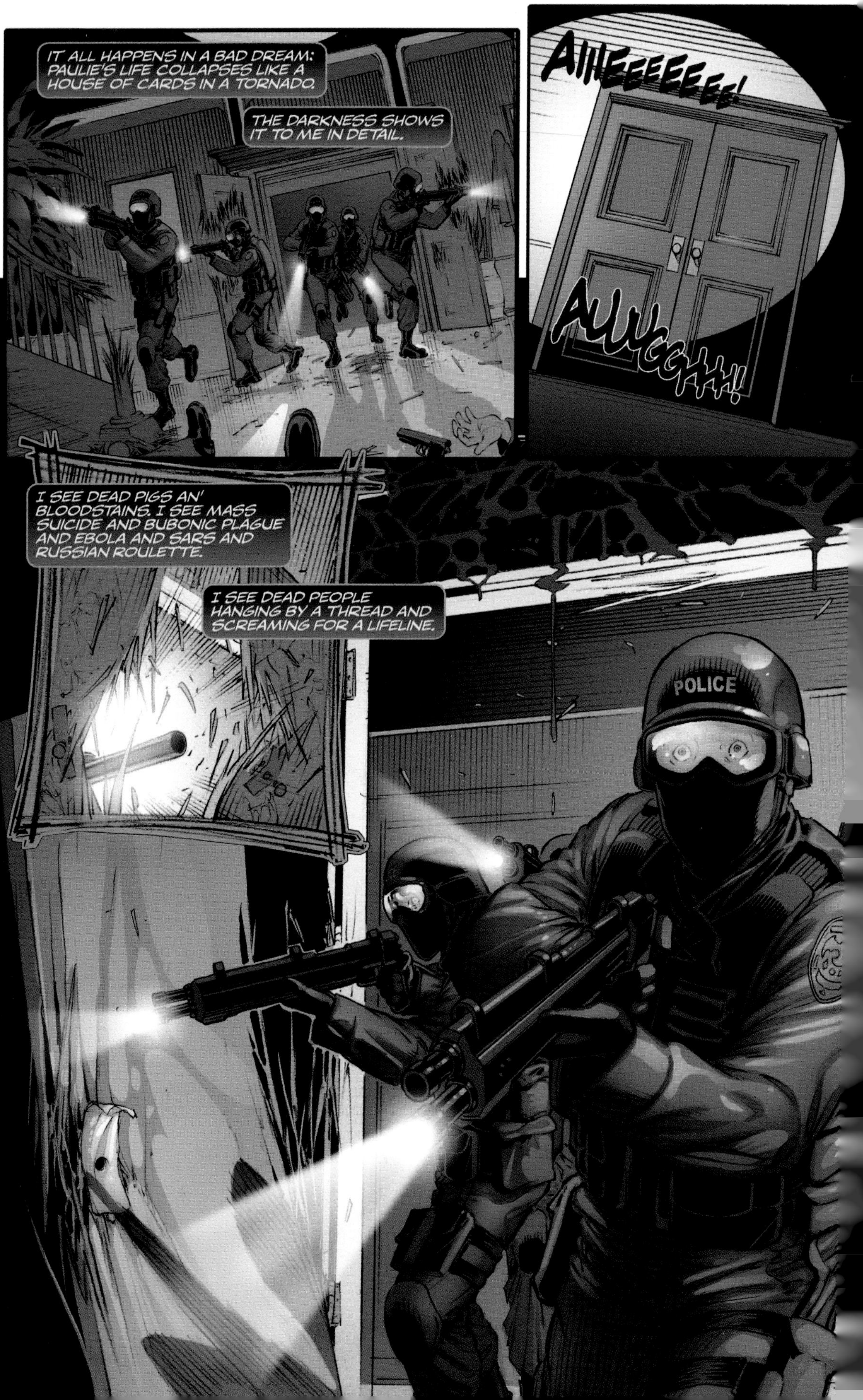
IT ALL HAPPENS IN A BAD DREAM: PAULIE'S LIFE COLLAPSES LIKE A HOUSE OF CARDS IN A TORNADO.
THE DARKNESS SHOWS IT TO ME IN DETAIL.
AIIEEEEEEEEE!
AUUGGHHH!!
I SEE DEAD PIGS AN' BLOODSTAINS. I SEE MASS SUICIDE AND BUBONIC PLAGUE AND EBOLA AND SARS AND RUSSIAN ROULETTE.
I SEE DEAD PEOPLE HANGING BY A THREAD AND SCREAMING FOR A LIFELINE.
POLICE

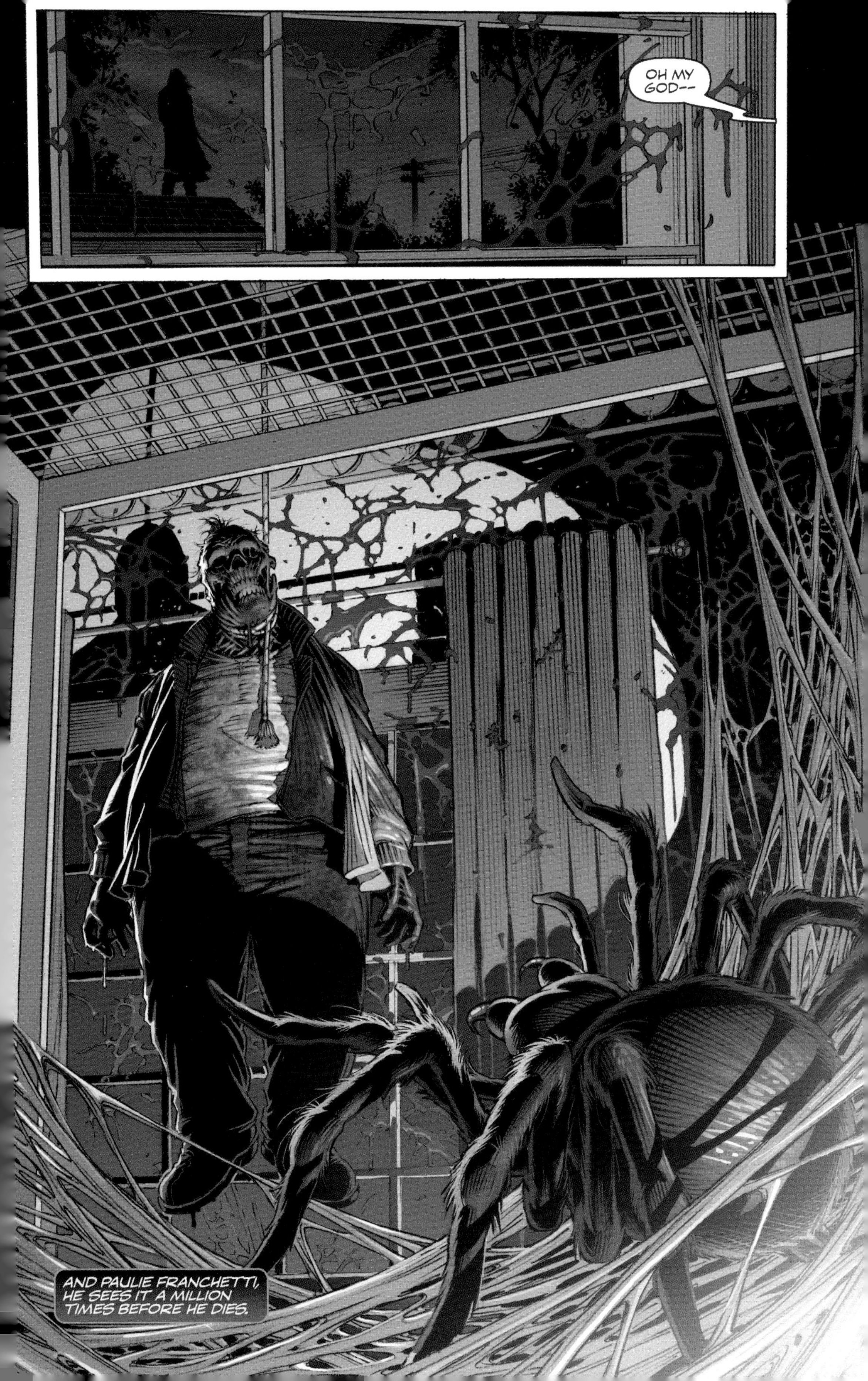
OH MY GOD--
AND PAULIE FRANCHETTI, HE SEES IT A MILLION TIMES BEFORE HE DIES.

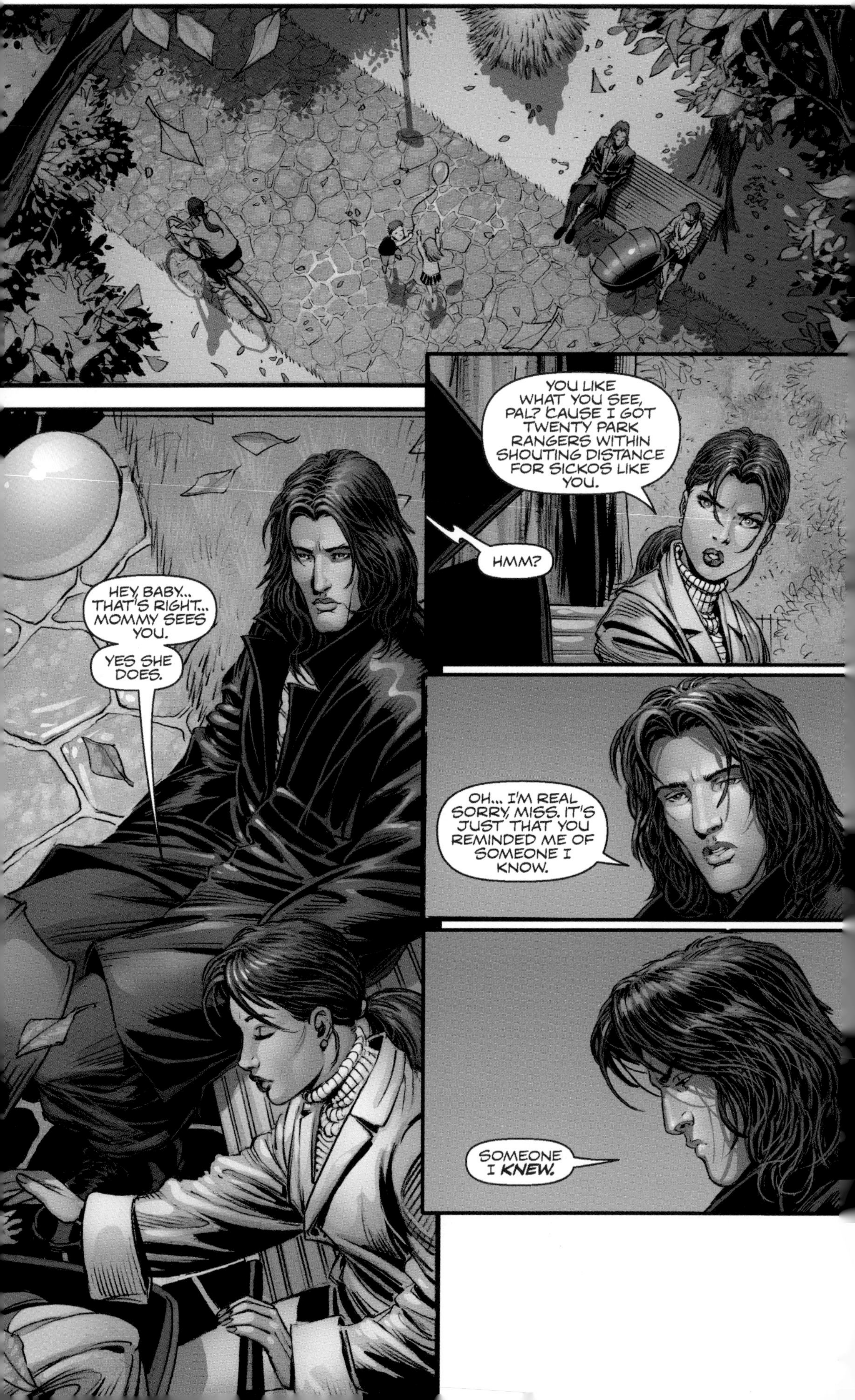
YOU LIKE WHAT YOU SEE, PAL? CAUSE I GOT TWENTY PARK RANGERS WITHIN SHOUTING DISTANCE FOR SICKOS LIKE YOU.
HMM?
HEY, BABY... THAT'S RIGHT... MOMMY SEES YOU.
YES SHE DOES.
OH... I'M REAL SORRY, MISS. IT'S JUST THAT YOU REMINDED ME OF SOMEONE I KNOW.
SOMEONE I KNEW.

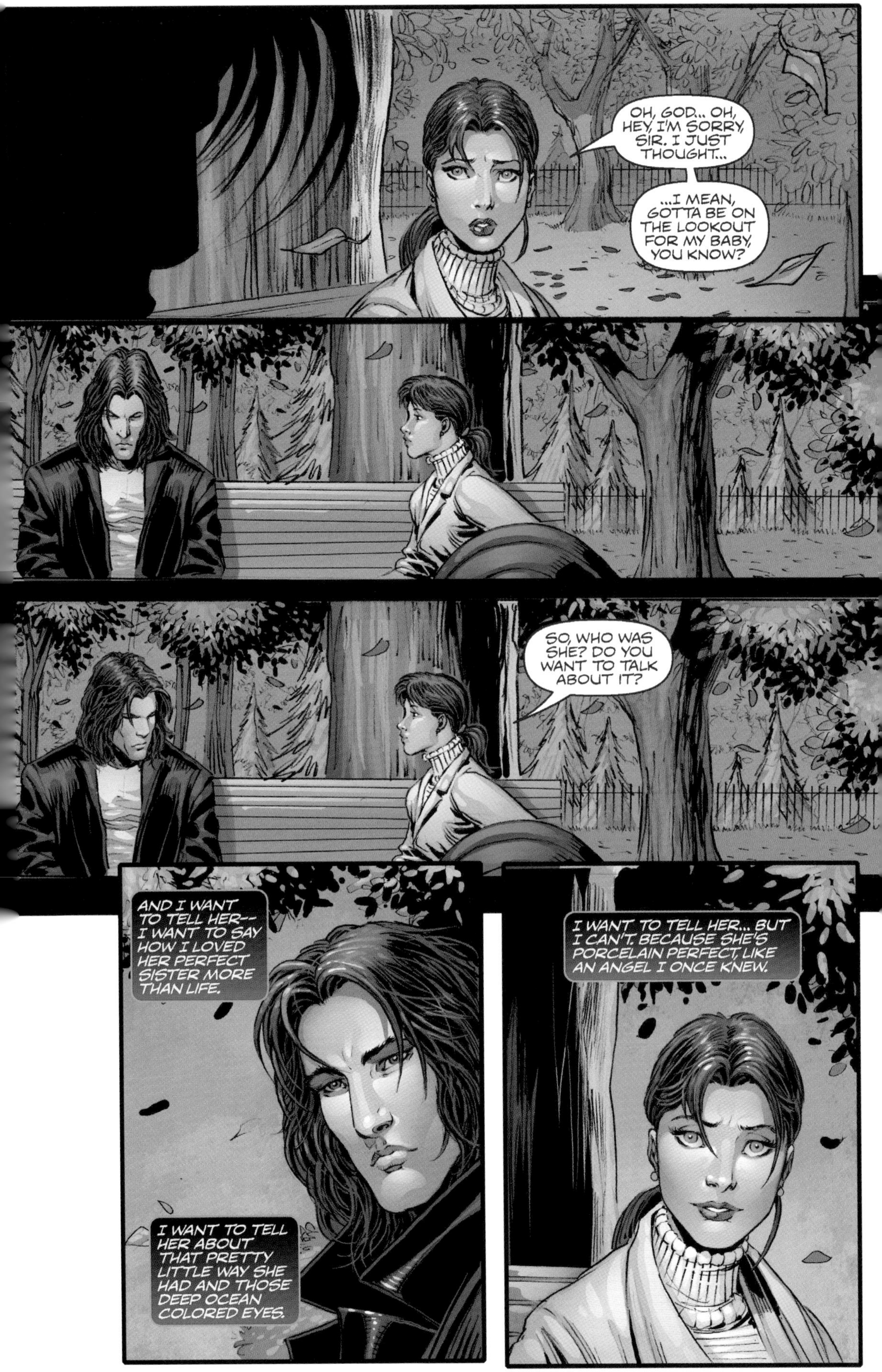
OH, GOD... OH, HEY, I'M SORRY, SIR. I JUST THOUGHT...
...I MEAN, GOTTA BE ON THE LOOKOUT FOR MY BABY, YOU KNOW?
SO, WHO WAS SHE? DO YOU WANT TO TALK ABOUT IT?
AND I WANT TO TELL HER-- I WANT TO SAY HOW I LOVED HER PERFECT SISTER MORE THAN LIFE.
I WANT TO TELL HER ABOUT THAT PRETTY LITTLE WAY SHE HAD AND THOSE DEEP OCEAN COLORED EYES.
I WANT TO TELL HER... BUT I CAN'T. BECAUSE SHE'S PORCELAIN PERFECT, LIKE AN ANGEL I ONCE KNEW.

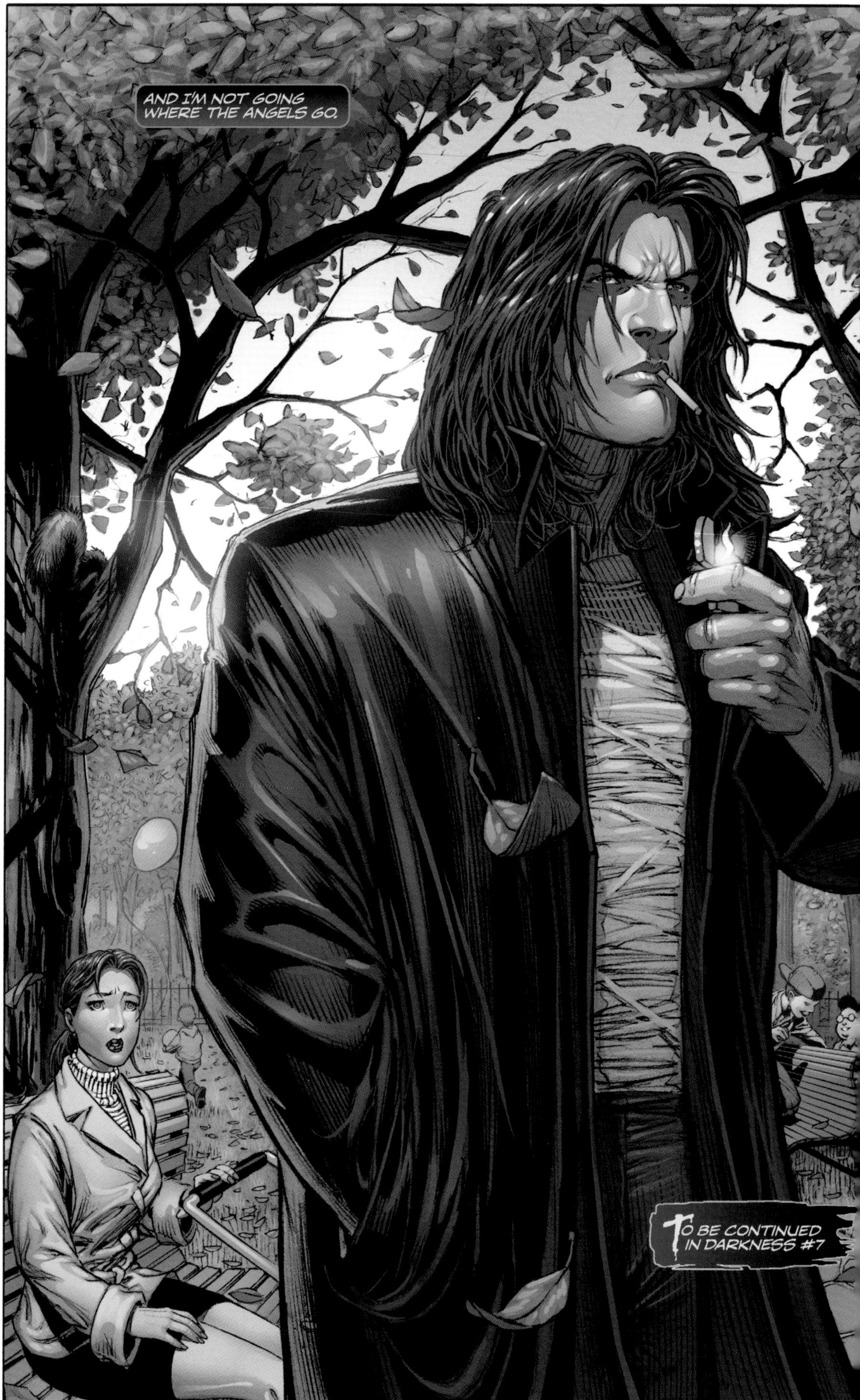
AND I'M NOT GOING WHERE THE ANGELS GO.
TO BE CONTINUED IN DARKNESS #7

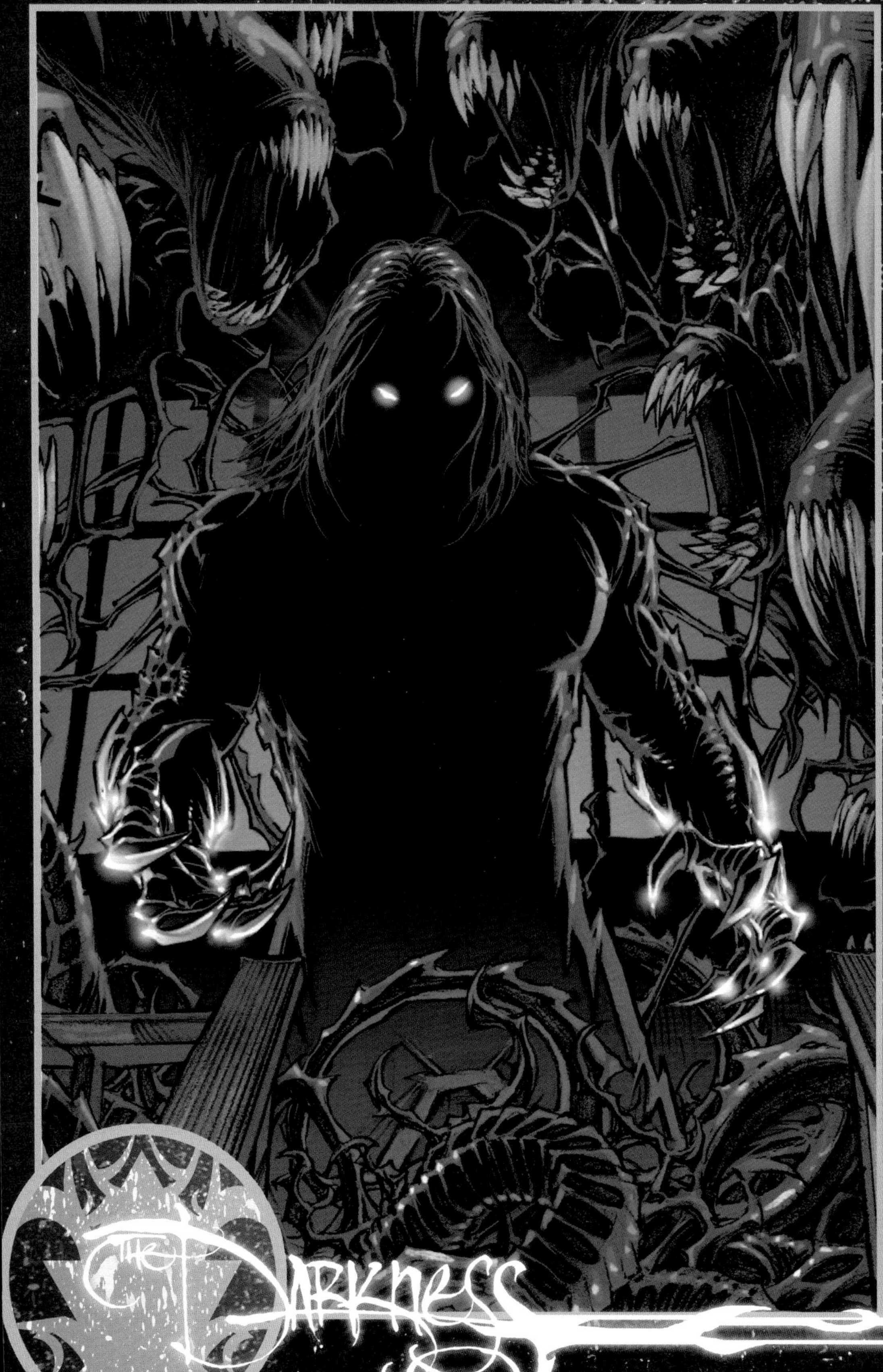

The Darkness
Cover Gallery

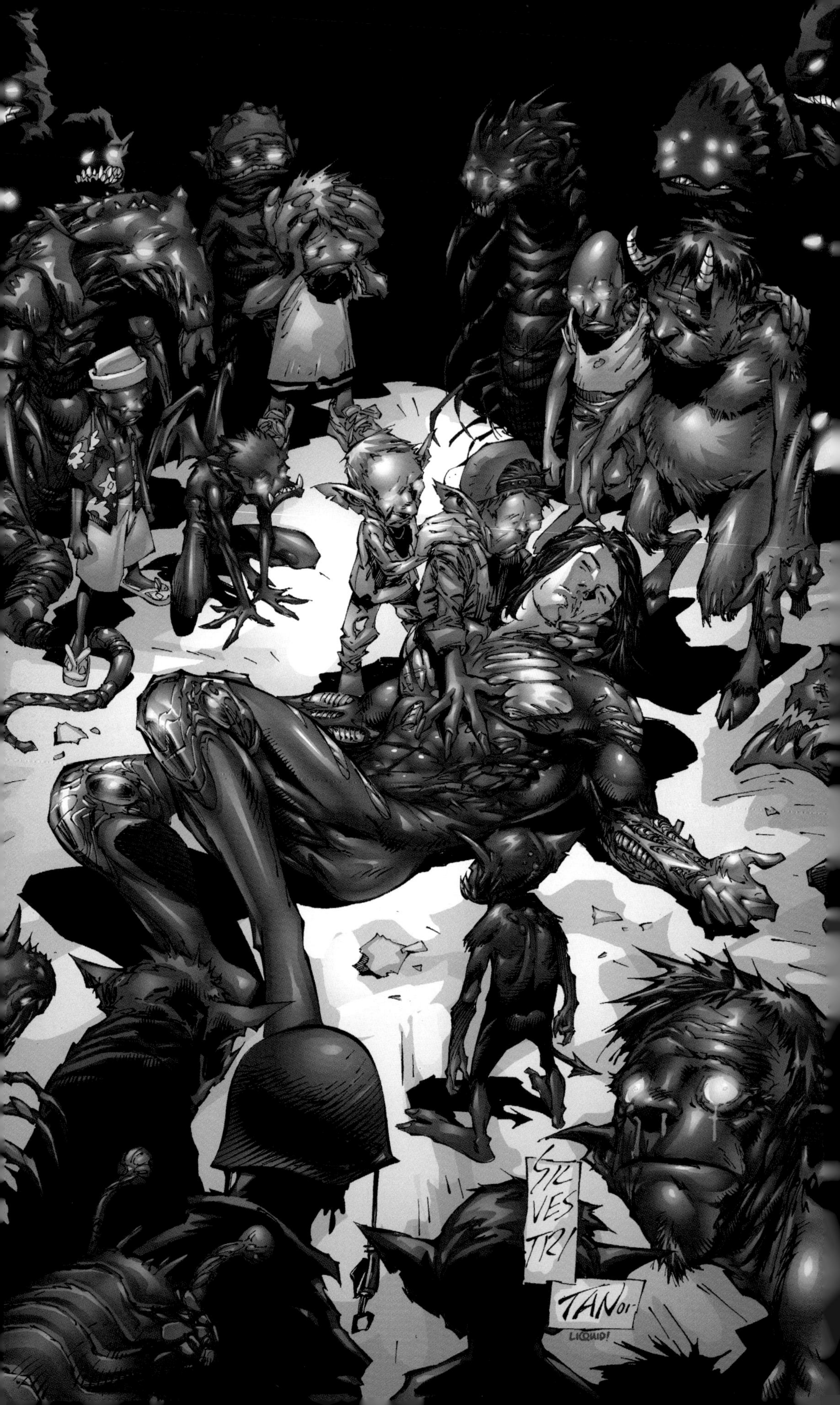
SILVESTRI
TAN 01
LIQUID!

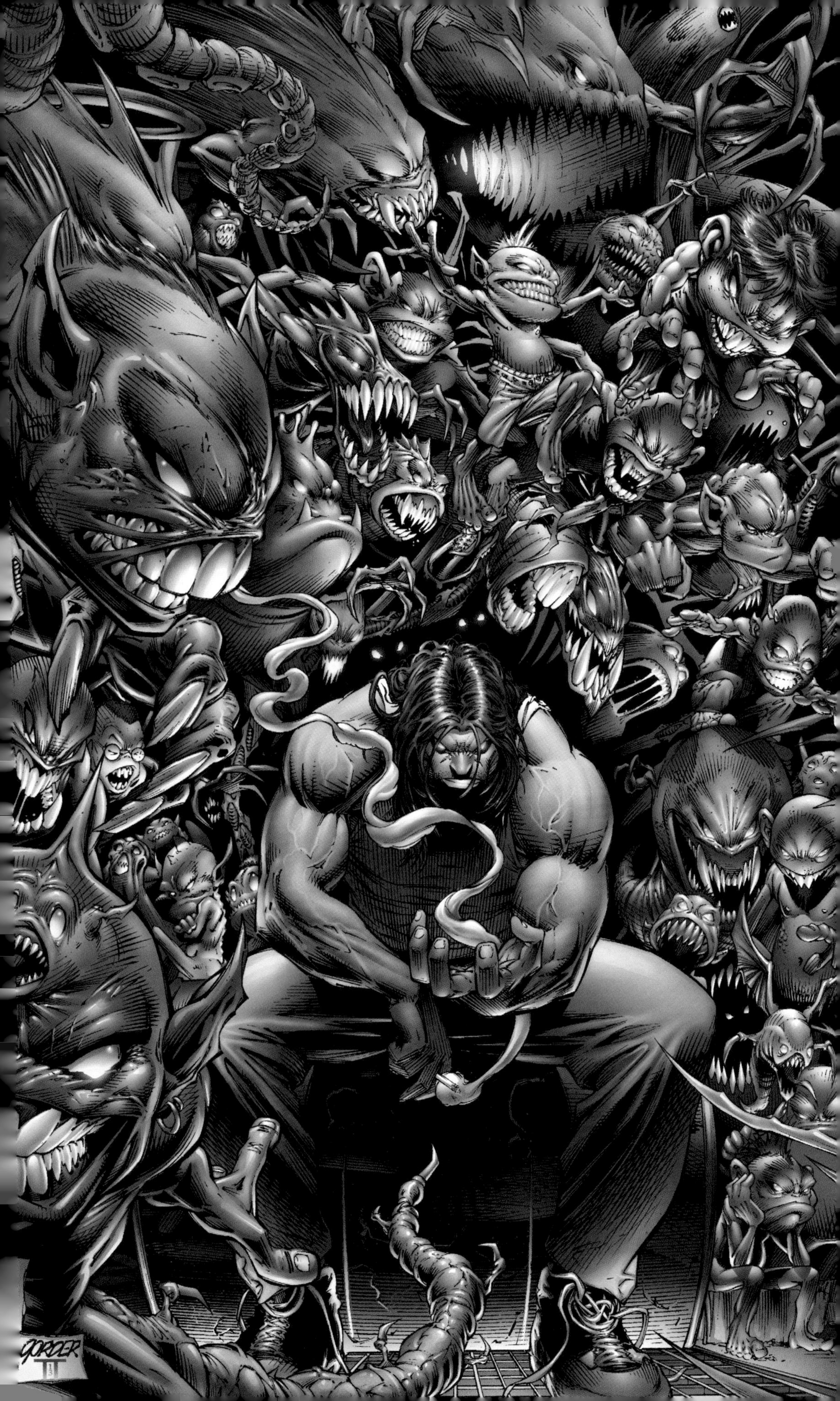
GORDER

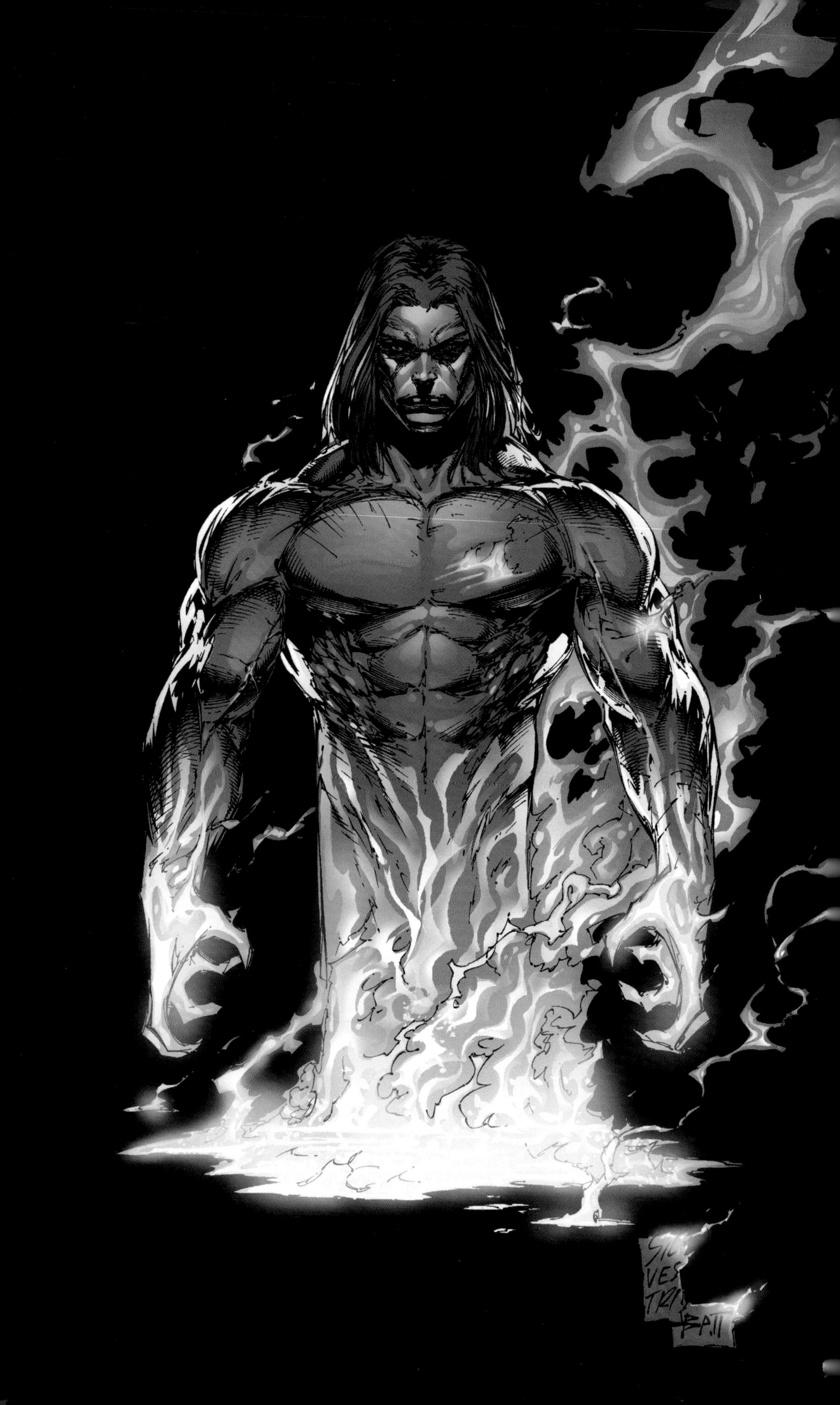

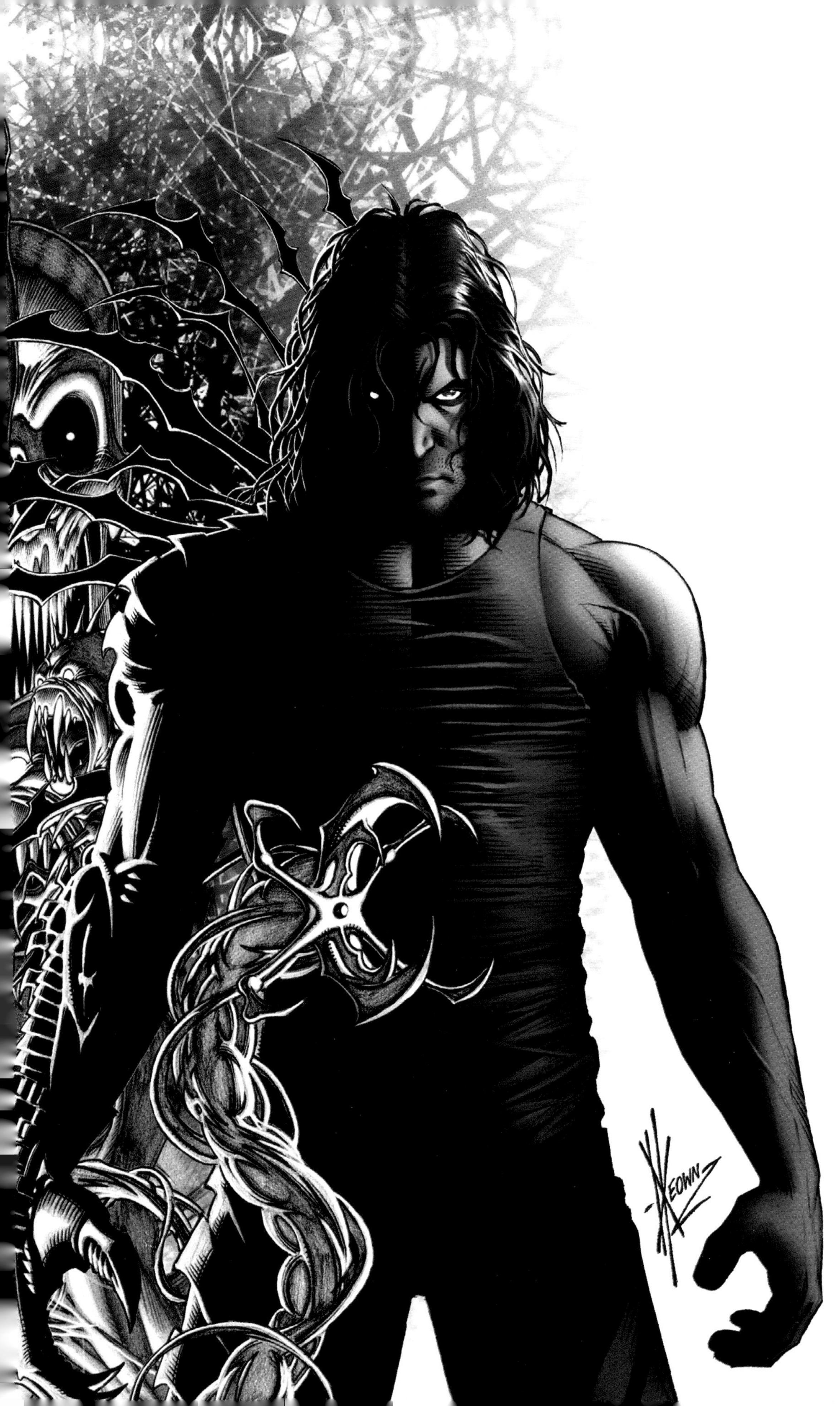
KEOWN

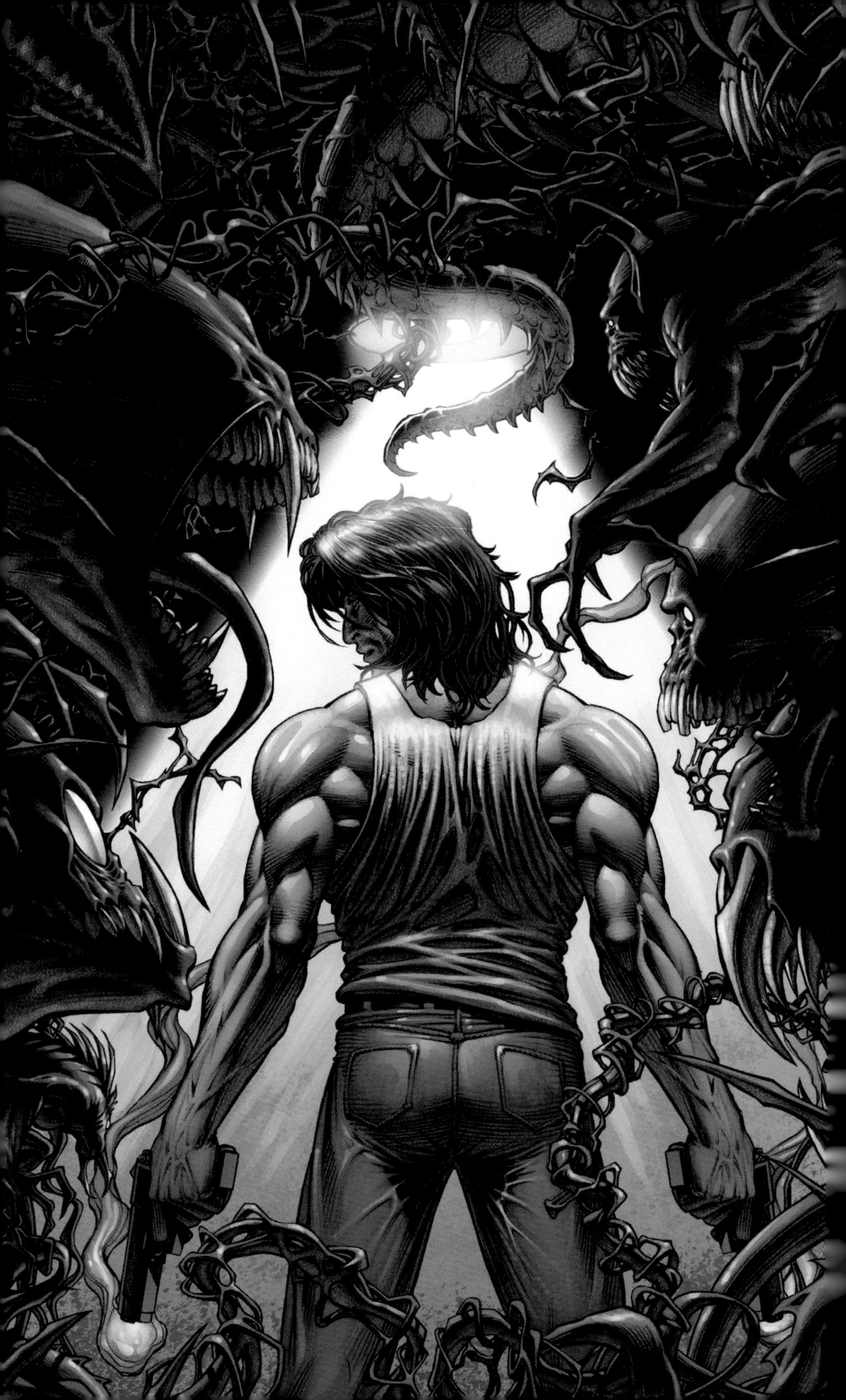

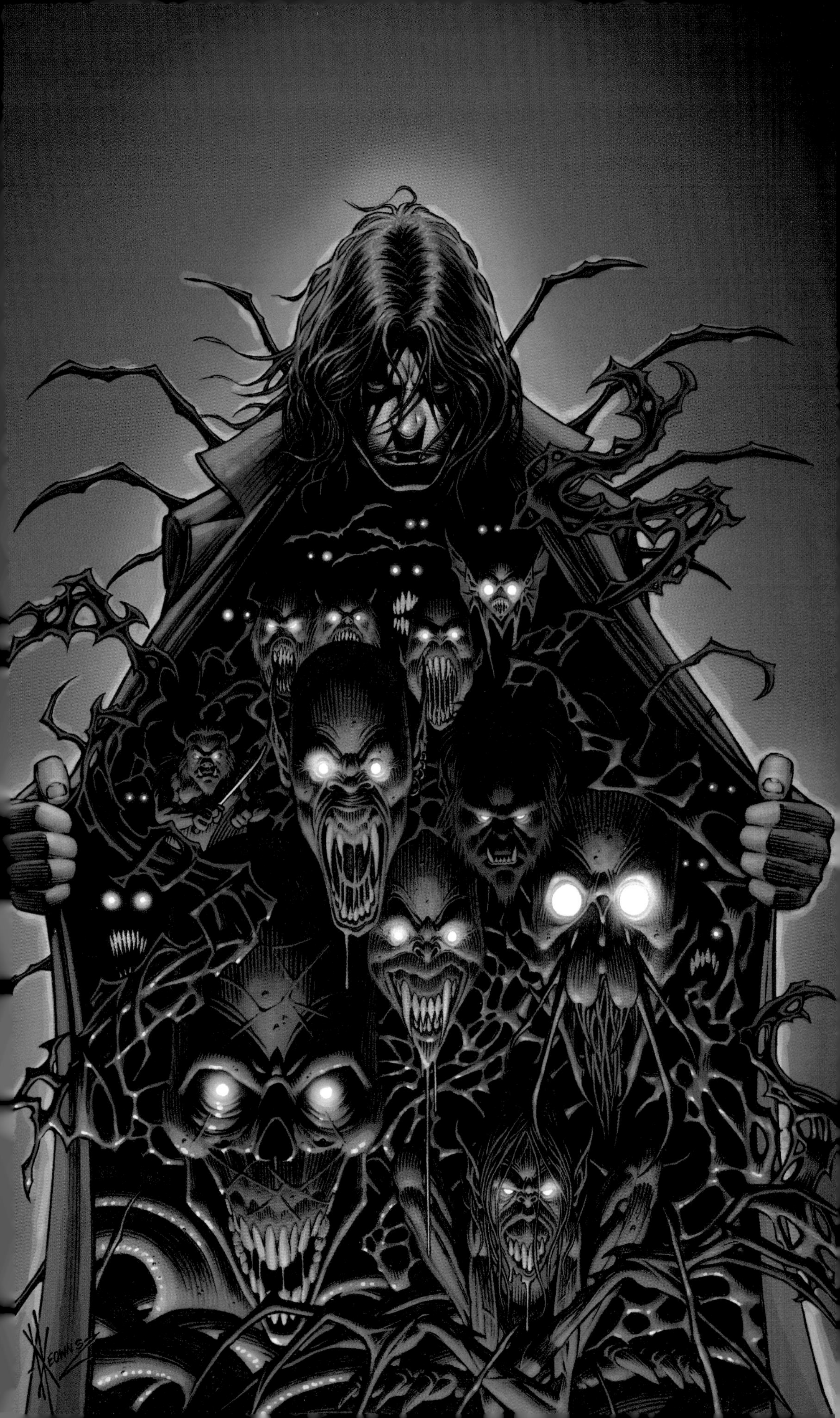

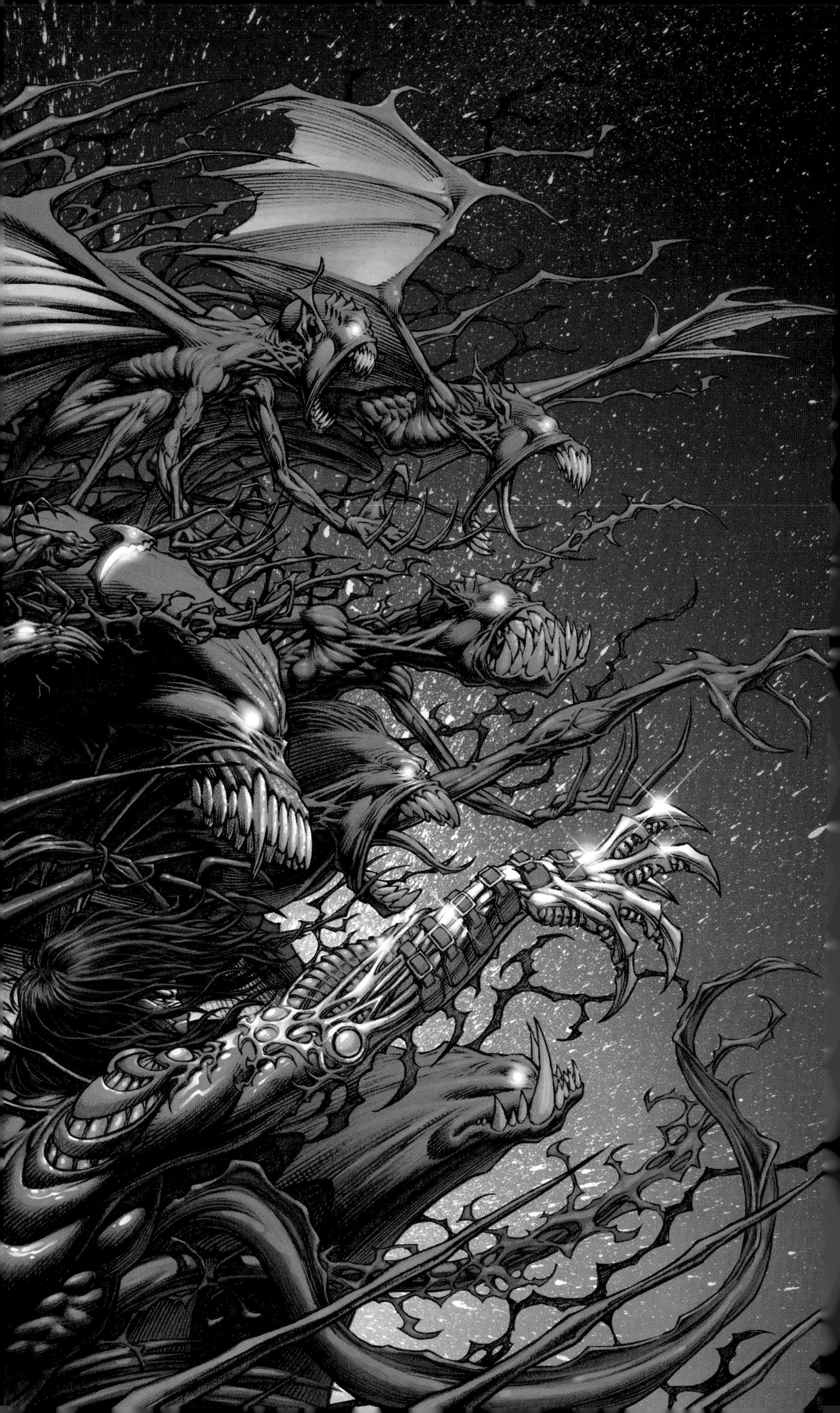

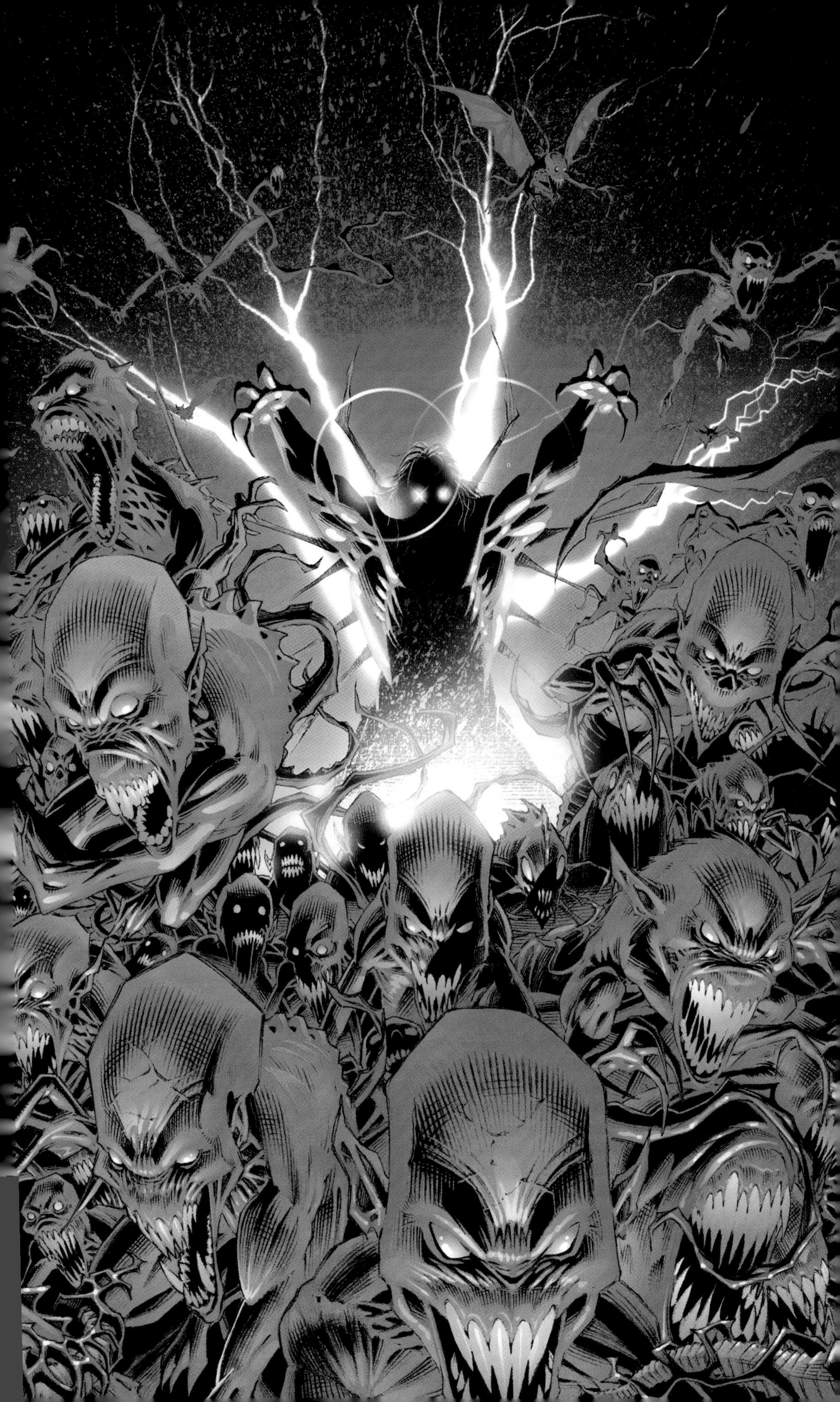

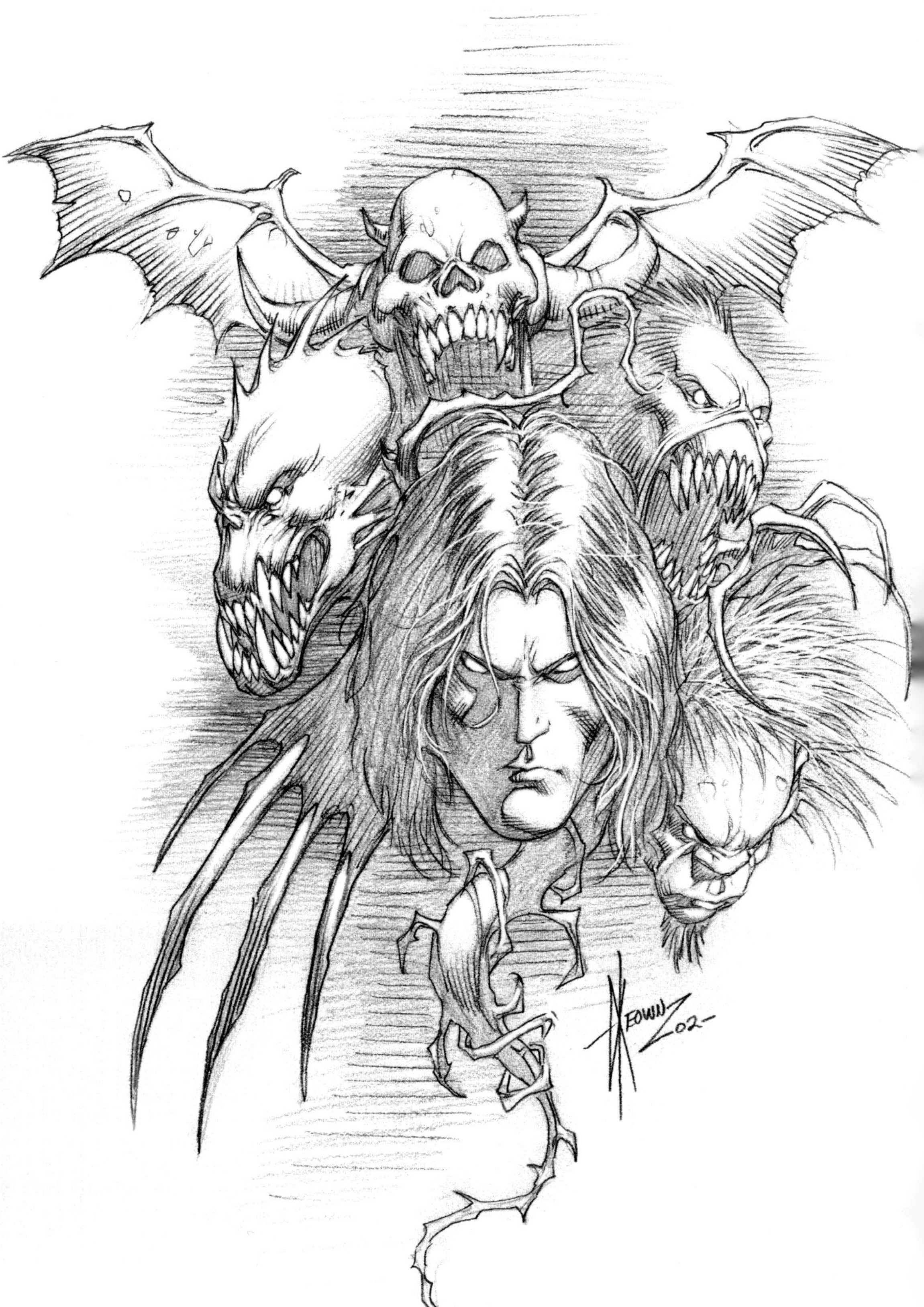
KEOWN
02

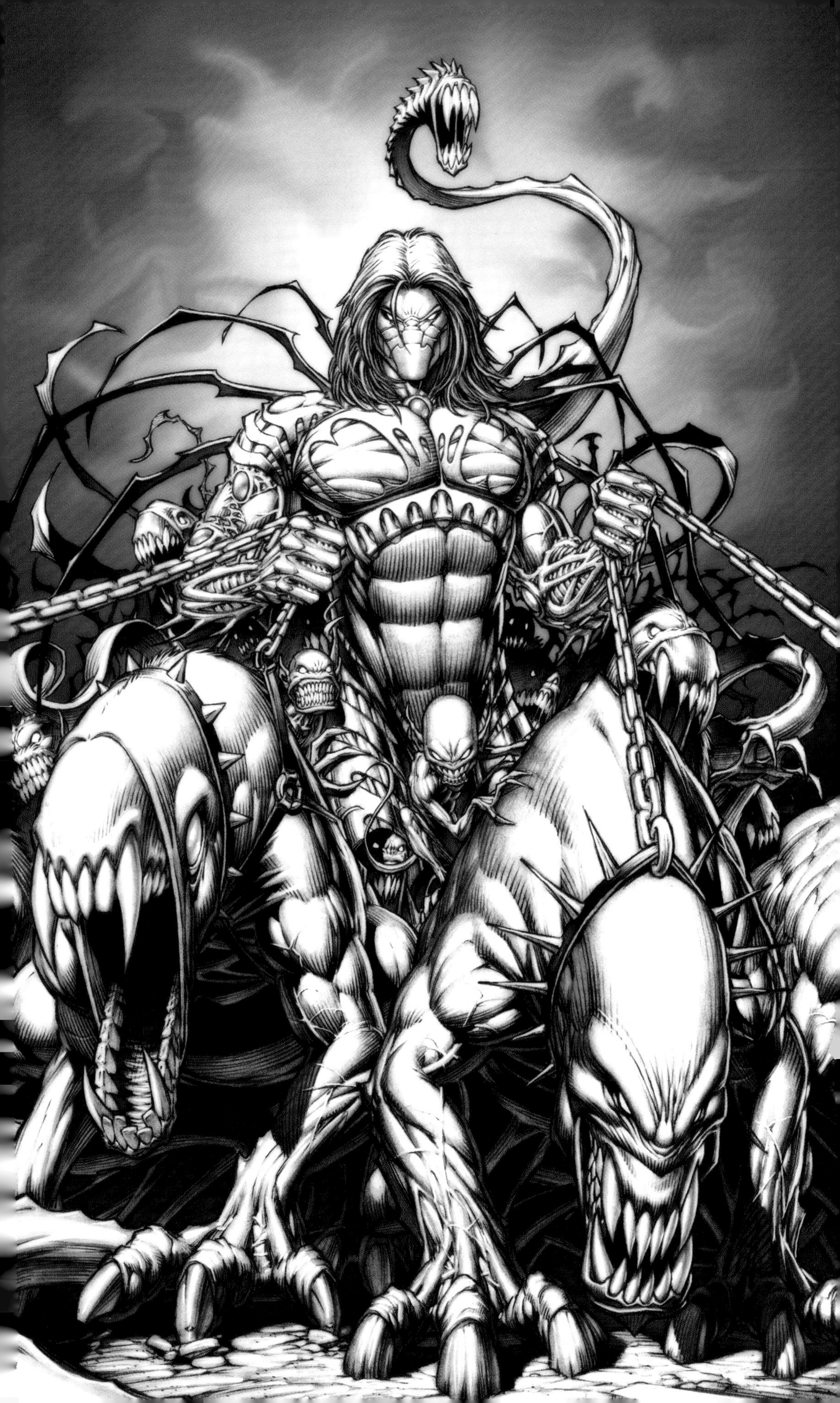

Also available from Top Cow Productions & Image Comics:

Battle of the Planets: Trial By Fire (ISBN: 1-58240-289-2)

Battle of the Planets: Blood Red Sky (ISBN: 1-58240-323-6)

Cyberforce: Assault with a Deadly Woman (ISBN: 1-887279-04-0)

Cyberforce: Tin Men of War (ISBN: 1-58240-190-x)

The Darkness: Coming of Age (ISBN: 1-58240-032-6)

The Darkness: Spear of Destiny (ISBN: 1-58240-147-0)

The Darkness: Heart of Darkness (ISBN: 1-58240-205-1)

Delicate Creatures (ISBN: 1-58240-225-6)

J. Michael Straczynski's Midnight Nation (ISBN: 1-58240-272-8)

Kin: Descent of Man (ISBN: 1-58240-224-8)

Magdalena: Blood Divine (ISBN: 1-58240-215-9)

Medieval Spawn/Witchblade (ISBN: 1-887279-44-x)

Michael Turner's Fathom Hard Cover (ISBN: 1-58240-158-6)

Michael Turner's Fathom Hard Cover Limited Edition (ISBN: 1-58240-159-4)

Michael Turner's Fathom: Paperback (ISBN: 1-58240-210-8)

No Honor (ISBN: 1-58240-321-x)

Rising Stars: Born in Fire (ISBN: 1-58240-172-1)

Rising Stars: Power (ISBN: 1-58240-226-4)

Rising Stars: Visitations (ISBN: 1-58240-268-x)

Tomb Raider: Saga of the Medusa Mask (ISBN: 1-58240-164-0)

Tomb Raider: Mystic Artifacts (ISBN: 1-58240-202-7)

Tomb Raider: Chasing Shangri-La (ISBN: 1-58240-267-1)

Tomb Raider/Witchblade: Trouble Seekers (ISBN: 1-58240-279-5)

Witchblade: Origins (ISBN: 1-887279-65-2)

Witchblade: Revelations (ISBN: 1-58240-161-6)

Witchblade: Prevailing (ISBN: 1-58240-175-6)

Witchblade: Distinctions (ISBN: 1-58240-199-3)

Witchblade: Obakemono (ISBN: 1-58240-259-0)

Witchblade/Darkness: Family Ties (ISBN: 1-58240-030-x)

Witchblade: Blood Relations (ISBN: 1-58240-315-5)